the complete book of

Fitness

the complete book of

Fitness

MIND · BODY · SPIRIT

Editors of *Fitness* Magazine
with Karen Andes

Three Rivers Press
New York

Author's Note: This book proposes a program of physical exercise and dietary recommendations for the reader to follow. However, before starting this or any other exercise program or diet regimen, you should consult your physician.

Published by Three Rivers Press, a division of Crown Publishers, Inc., 201 East 50th Street, New York, New York 10022. Member of the Crown Publishing Group.

Random House, Inc. New York, Toronto, London, Sydney, Auckland
www.randomhouse.com

THREE RIVERS PRESS and colophon are trademarks of Crown Publishers, Inc.

Printed in the United States of America

For Roundtable Press
Directors: Julie Merberg, Marsha Melnick, Susan E. Meyer
Contributors: Karen Andes, Diane A. Welland, M.S., R.D.
Illustrator: Pam Bergman
Assistant Editor: John Glenn

For Fitness Magazine
Editor-in-chief: Sally Lee
Fitness Director: Nicole Dorsey
Creative Director: Jeffrey Saks
Diet and Nutrition Editor: Kate Lawler

For G+J USA Publishing
President and Chief Executive Officer: John Heins
Licensing Manager: Tammy Palazzo

ISBN 0-7394-0289-7

acknowledgments

We'd like to thank the following individuals and organizations for their time and expertise:

American Botanical Society, American College of Sports Medicine, American Council on Exercise, American Diabetic Association, American Dietetic Association, American Heart Association, American Institute of Cancer Research, Brigham and Women's Hospital in Boston, California Almond Board Association, Calorie Control Council, Cancer Research Foundation of America, Center for Science in the Public Interest/*Nutrition Action Healthletter,* Nancy Clark, Dairy Council of Wisconsin, Clarkson Potter/Publishers—Katie Workman, Erica Youngren, John Son, Andrea Peabbles, Wendy Schuman, Kate Reid, and Lauren Shakely—Duckling Council, Susan Male Smith and Denise Webb at Environmental Nutrition, Food and Drug Administration, *FDA Consumer Magazine,* Gatorade Company, Idaho Bean Commission, International Food and Information Council, Intertech Corporation, Johns Hopkins University, Kushi Institute, Mayo Clinic, Monell Chemical Senses Center, National Academy of Sciences, National Broiler Council, National Cancer Institute, National Cattlemen's Association, National Center for Health Statistics, National Cholesterol Education Program, National Dairy Council, National Fisheries Institute, National Institute of Alcohol Abuse and Alcoholism, National Organic Trade Association, National Pasta Association, National Pork Producers Council, National Strength and Conditioning Association, National Turkey Federation, The Peanut Institute, *Runner's World,* The Salt Institute, The Steel Packaging Association, The Sugar Association, *Tufts University Health and Nutrition Letter,* United Fresh Fruit and Vegetable Association, USA Dry Pea and Lentil Council, Clare Hasler and Barbara Klein at the University of Illinois, U.S. Department of Agriculture, *University of California Berkley Wellness Letter,* Walnut Marketing Board, Wheat Foods Council, and Wisconsin Milk Marketing Board.

contents

Cardiovascular training 149

Diet and nutrition 254

Wellness — 391

foreword

As editor-in-chief of *Fitness* magazine, I often hear readers say that they want to make changes in their eating and exercise habits, but don't know where to start. Now I've got the answer. The *Complete Book of Fitness* is the first and only comprehensive guide to getting and staying healthy in mind, body, and spirit. Think of it as your total-body answer book, whether you want to know which vitamins are best for you, the most effective ways to build muscle, or how to do easy, stress-relieving moves. You'll find the tools you need to custom-design your own personal wellness plan. With step-by-step sections on diet and nutrition, cardiovascular exercise, strength training, and health and wellness, this will become your personal health and fitness reference, the only one you'll ever need, and one you'll refer back to again and again. There are no gimmicky diets or impossible exercise routines—just sane, simple strategies that work.

Here's to your health.

Sally Lee,
editor-in-chief,
Fitness magazine

strength
training

In textbook definitions,

strength can be measured. It is the maximum amount of weight you can lift in one repetition and the amount of force generated by the musculoskeletal system.

How strong you might become is also largely determined by things that can be measured. First there are the things you *can't* control: gender, age, length of limbs, muscles, and tendons, and the distribution of muscle fiber types—whether you have more fast-twitch (strength) fibers or slow (endurance) fibers (see **Endurance,** page 175). Then there are the things you *can* control: levels of activity, rest, and energy from food.

But there are other, more elusive, subjective things that influence strength that can't be so easily measured. Your moods, stress and hormone levels, and whether you're fighting an illness contribute to natural fluctuations in strength. Everyone deals with a different set of circumstances. Therefore, there's no point comparing your level of strength to anyone else's. Only compare yourself to you. When training with weights, use a weight that causes muscle fatigue after 8 to 12 (or 13) reps for the upper body and 8 to 15 (or 20) for legs and buttocks.

The genetic component

Very few people have the genetic cards stacked in their favor when it comes to building a champion physique. But if all you want to do is to simply improve your body's function and appearance, genetics are not a factor. Your best course of action is to positively affect those things you can control and to do the best with what you've got.

Gender

Men have about 20 percent more muscle mass than women. They also have more testosterone (a male hormone), which makes muscles grow bigger and stronger in response to training. On average, women are about 50 percent weaker in the upper body, but in the legs they are, pound for pound, just as strong, if not stronger. If you compare strength to percentages of lean body mass, men's and women's strength ratios are about equal.

Length of limbs

A person with short arms, legs, and torso has an easier time lifting the same weight as a person with long limbs. Shorter people have shorter levers, which give them a big advantage in the gym. Tall people need to lift lighter weights.

Length of muscles and tendons

Most people have short muscles and long tendons. The ideal (in muscle sports) is the opposite. How do you know what you have? Flex your biceps. Place your other hand between the crook of your flexed elbow and the beginning of your biceps. How many fingers fit there?

One finger means you have long muscles and short tendons. (Congratulations, you're genetically gifted for strength.) Two fingers means medium muscles and tendons. (This is still pretty good, genetically speaking.) Three or more fingers indicates short muscles and long tendons. (It's not going to be easy to build those biceps. But take heart, you're in the majority.)

Muscle fiber types

Without a biopsy it's hard to know what kind of muscle fiber you've got. But if endurance sports feel natural, you probably have more slow-twitch fibers. If building strength is more your style, you probably have more fast-twitch fibers. Scientists still don't know if this is due to nature or nurture, or if we can change our distribution of fibers based on the activities we do.

Age

It's believed that males reach maximum muscle strength capacity between ages twenty and thirty and that females reach it at twenty. Older people hear this and think, "Well, it's too late for me." But muscle never stops responding to resistance, no matter what your age.

Numerous studies have shown that strength can improve by 50, 60, 100, even 150 percent in a few months of training, two or three days a week, in people up to *ninety-six years old.* Older people who choose not to strength train lose about ½ pound of muscle a year—and with it they also lose: bone strength, posture, balance, a faster metabolism, and confidence.

Strength and menstruation

Little has been written about menstruation and its effect on women's strength. Yet almost every woman who exercises regularly knows that energy levels and strength can fall by as much as 10 to 20 percent in the two weeks before a period. Of course, this doesn't happen to every woman, every month. But with most women, this is the cycle:

On the first day of the period (commonly counted as day one), estrogen levels begin a gradual two-week ascent, peaking at ovulation. During this time (called the follicular phase), the body is prepping an egg for possible fertilization. Most women feel best during this part of the cycle and are energized and optimistic. They also sleep better and strength levels peak.

Whether that egg has been fertilized or not, once it's in position, estrogen levels drop and progesterone (a female hormone) levels increase (to protect the egg), which in turn makes women more inclined to slow down. Progesterone peaks between days twenty and twenty-two, about three weeks after the first day of the period, and women respond very differently. Some feel crazed with PMS, some feel depressed, some enjoy the sedative effects. Other responses include fatigue, reduced concentration, reduced desire for activity or sex, and a slower, sluggish digestion (a throwback to our cave days—this holds nourishment for a fertilized egg during times of famine).

All of this adds up to a noticeable drop in strength, which women may feel immediately after ovulation, at days twenty to twenty-two, or just before or on the first day of bleeding.

You don't have to stop training during the "reign of progesterone." But it's a good time to lighten weights, increase reps, and *maintain* rather than try to gain strength.

Once menstruation begins, estrogen begins to climb again and metabolism goes up by 10 to 15 percent.

Illness and strength

During times of illness, more energy goes into fighting off infection and healing. So strength decreases, sometimes drastically.

If you have a minor head cold (only sinus congestion and no hacking cough) you can do a light workout. But if you're sick—coughing, running a fever, have stomach cramps or diarrhea—don't exercise. You'll only prolong the sickness because you'll use up the energy you need to heal.

abdominals

Abdominal muscles, or abs, are put together in an impressively supportive design. There are three layers of ab muscles, woven together with the grain or muscle fibers, crisscrossing each other like the magic fingers on an old-fashioned girdle. Since there's no bone to offer support in the front of the abdominal cavity, these muscles need to be strong enough to hold the body upright. But as many of us know, this doesn't necessarily happen naturally. Usually, this strength needs to be built. Like other muscles in the body, abs respond best when the muscles are addressed from different angles. And traditional crunches alone don't adequately do the job.

Transverse abs

These, the deepest of the ab muscles, are horizontal fibers that run, like tree rings, around the torso. They don't have a specific movement function other than to supply intra-abdominal pressure, as when you cough. They also get stretched out during pregnancy. These can be strengthened with regular abdominal curls (see **Pregnancy and Exercise,** page 217). Hissing as you lift into your curls will also help strengthen the transverse abs.

Internal obliques

The internal obliques are the next layer closer to the skin. If you look at both sets of internal obliques, together their fiber patterns form an *A* shape. Crunches with a twist to the *same* knee (i.e., move right shoulder to right knee) work these.

External obliques

The external obliques are the next layer. (Looked at as a pair, their fiber patterns form a *V.*) Crunches with a twist toward the *opposite* knee (i.e., twist right shoulder to left knee) work these.

Rectus abdominis

This is the most visible and obvious ab muscle on the front of the abdominal wall. This is the one we try to "chisel" with exercises. Although it's one muscle, it's really made up of two parallel bands of muscle that run from rib cage to pubic bone. Little tendons separate the rectus into eight separate sections. On a very lean, muscularly developed person, the separate chunks are visible. This is what we call washboard abs or a six-pack. These get worked in regular and reverse crunches (pelvic tilts) and also when stabilizing the torso (see **Stabilization,** page 133).

Can you burn fat with ab work?

Despite the claims made in infomercials selling ab contraptions, crunches (and all other "spot toning" exercises) will not burn fat around the waist. You can have the strongest abs in the world, but if they're surrounded by fat, you'll never see them no matter how many ab exercises you do. Ab work helps you build torso strength. But only sweating off the excess fat with cardiovascular exercise will burn fat and help you achieve more defined abs.

crunches

Targets rectus abdominis

The basic crunch is still the most effective and simplest way to work the abs. Lie on your back with your feet resting on a bench or on the floor. (If your feet are on the floor or elevated on a chair, press your *heels* down and lift your toes to improve torso stability.) Rest your head in your hands, keep the back of the neck long, look at the ceiling, and slowly raise your shoulders off the floor. If you find this position too difficult, cross your hands over your chest as you lift your shoulders off the floor. To challenge yourself, slow down and keep the muscle contracted longer. You can also hold a small 5- or 10-pound weight behind your head.

Caveats: Lift your shoulders off the floor about 30 degrees, but no higher. Full sit-ups were banned from the exercise world years ago as unsafe at any speed. They not only strain the back but fail to work abdominals after the first third of the motion.

Better lifting tips: If you want to work the upper and lower abs simultaneously, lift your tailbone one inch as you lift your shoulders.

crunches with a twist

Targets external obliques

Lie on your back, as for crunches. Rest your right ankle on your left knee and, with your left hand behind your head, raise your left *shoulder* (not the elbow) to the right knee. Both your chest and supporting elbow should be *open* as you lift your torso. The right arm can rest on the floor. Switch sides.

Targets internal obliques

Still lying on your back, with your right ankle on your left knee, reach your left hand toward your left ankle, keeping your shoulders off the floor. Repeat on the other side.

Caveats: Be careful not to jerk your whole body as you lift the shoulders—focus the movement on your abdominal muscles.

Better lifting tips: Keep your head in line with your spine as you lift.

pelvic tilts

Targets rectus abdominis

This is a very subtle motion that barely looks like motion at all. But if you're doing it right, you'll know. Lie on the floor and place your feet on a bench or bend your knees, keeping your feet on the floor. Your hands can rest by your sides. Tighten your abdominals as if bracing to receive a punch in the stomach. With your abs contracted, pull your tailbone one inch off the floor, curling your pelvis toward your nose. If your feet are resting on a bench, make sure you're not putting weight on them as you lift the tailbone.

Caveats: Don't be overly ambitious and try to lift your tailbone higher in the hopes of working harder. You'll just shift the work out of your abs.

Better lifting tips: If your neck gets tense, roll up a towel or sweatshirt and place it under your head.

anabolic and catabolic

Anabolic

Anabolic describes an internal state that promotes an increase in muscle strength and size. Everybody possesses the organic ability to be anabolic, or "muscle building"; "catabolic," on the other hand, is muscle "eating" itself for fuel. With dedication, sufficient rest, and proper nutrition, anyone can make slow, steady anabolic progress. Unfortunately, people who are eager for fast results have sought out external anabolic substances that can be hazardous.

What does it take to be naturally anabolic?

First, subject your muscles to *sufficient stress*—say, a weight workout with each set at a relatively high intensity. This creates microtraumas in the muscle that will ultimately build strength. If you do a very light workout with little weight, chances are you won't work hard enough to stimulate the anabolic cycle of recovery and growth. To be anabolic, you have to find the intensity level that works your muscles without overexertion.

Next, let your body heal. Over the course of the next forty-eight to seventy-two hours, the body will adapt by: growing bigger muscle fibers, increasing the muscles' ability to contract, and growing stronger bones.

To build and repair muscle and bone, you must provide your body with foods that it can convert to fuel, such as a protein-packed chicken breast, which will be broken down into amino acids, the building blocks for making stronger, bigger tissue, or white rice, a starch, which will be converted into slow-burning glucose so you will continue to have energy while your muscles are under repair.

If you go back to those muscles you've just traumatized and work them hard again before they've recovered, you'll interrupt the anabolic recovery process and impede your progress. Wait until your muscles are no longer sore before working them again.

Catabolic

Catabolic is the opposite of anabolic. Muscles in a catabolic state get weak and shrink, not from lack of use but from overuse. When the anabolic recovery process is interrupted often enough, the muscle tissue gets broken down to such an extent that the body can no longer regenerate muscle tissue.

You are in danger of entering a catabolic state when you train muscles more than three times a week or train before your muscles have had a chance to recover from the last workout. Avoid overtraining and beware of the following warning signs: chronic fatigue, poor appetite, elevated resting heart rate, insomnia, depression, and overall poor coordination and athletic performance.

The best ways out of the catabolic state, and to ensure full muscle recovery, are to rest or reduce the intensity of your workout.

Hypertrophy—Atrophy

You may have read somewhere that 8 to 12 reps at relatively high intensity cause muscle hypertrophy. Hypertrophy is what happens after you follow the anabolic recipe—your muscles grow. You get a "hyper" (big) "trophy" (growth) you can show off to your friends.

On a microscopic level, hypertrophy means there's an increase in both the size and numbers of myofibrils—little fibers responsible for muscle size, strength, and sensation. Men's muscles hypertrophy faster than women's because the male hormone testosterone inspires a greater production of the little proteins responsible for contraction in these fibers.

The opposite of hypertrophy is atrophy, the wasting away of a muscle or organ from lack of use. If you are prone to inactivity, here are some statistics that might make you sprint out of your chair to prevent muscle atrophy:

- Without activity, you lose about ½ to 1 pound of lean muscle mass each year.
- One pound of muscle uses about 50 calories a day just to function, so by the end of the decade, your inactive body would use 250 to 500 fewer calories a day. If

you were to eat as much as before, the food you don't use would be stored as fat.
- Muscles begin to lose strength and size after only four days of lack of use.
- Even one day of bed rest can result in some degree of muscle atrophy. (Your body needs to receive gravity in a vertical position in order to maintain both muscular function and aerobic capacity.)
- Just as your little myofibrils get big with training, so do they shrink with neglect.

The good news is that, at any age, muscles can switch from atrophy to hypertrophy. All it takes is work and the anabolic recipe.

- You can double, triple, or quadruple your strength after one year of training for 30 to 45 minutes, two or three times a week.
- This return to hypertrophy can boost your metabolism by 250 to 500 more calories per day.
- Even after six to ten weeks of strength training at a relatively high intensity (lifting the maximum amount of weight possible with good form for 8 to 12 repetitions), you can regenerate those little myofibrils and restore them to full size and greater sensation!

Anabolic steroids

It's estimated that between 1 and 3 million Americans have taken anabolic steroids to build muscle and enhance athletic performance—many of them women and teenagers of both sexes. Steroids are chemical derivatives of testosterone, a key ingredient in creating hypertrophy.

Steroids first came into existence when a French scientist in the late 1880s injected himself with an extract of the liquid found in the testicles of a dog and guinea pig. In the fifties, East German and Bulgarian athletes on steroids outlifted, outdistanced, and outperformed other athletes in the Olympics. From that moment on, athletes from around the world began a dance with the devil that continues today, as compulsive competitors look to "magic pills" for an "edge." The saddest part is that steroids haven't just polluted the ranks of professional sports. Amateurs with no ambitions beyond improving their appearance can find a steroid connection in just about any "grunt" gym (a no-frills gym with a generally burly clientele).

Many of the side effects of steroids are irreversible. So someone who took steroids when he was young may have grown older and wiser, but he'll still have to live with the consequences of his steroid use for the rest of his life. Steroids not only promote out-of-control growth of all sorts of tissues (including tumors), but they tamper with sexual identity. In other words, steroids have both anabolic and androgenic side effects.

Here Are Some of the Anabolic Side Effects of Steroids:

- Liver damage: causes jaundice (yellow skin), cysts, tumors, possible liver cancer, or liver failure
- Kidney damage: kidney stones, tumors, kidney failure
- Increased risk of coronary heart disease by increasing blood pressure and raising the level of low density lipoproteins, LDL—bad cholesterol
- Irregular heartbeats and elevated resting heart rates
- Decreased functioning of the immune system
- Extreme mood swings from " 'road rage" to depression
- Stunted bone growth in teenagers
- Weakened tendons and ligaments, creating a high risk for injury
- Puffiness in the face
- Acne, especially on the back
- Hair loss
- Nosebleeds
- Possible blood poisoning and exposure to HIV from contaminated needles

Androgenic Side Effects of Steroids

IN WOMEN
A deeper voice
Hair growth on the face
An enlarged clitoris
Decreased breast size
Irregular periods or no periods at all
Increased risk of breast cancer
Atrophy of the uterus
Thinning or balding hair

IN MEN
A high-pitched voice
An enlarged prostate
Testicle shrinkage
Gynecomastia, or little breasts
Lowered sperm count or sterility
Impotence

Steroid alternatives

Despite the simple anabolic recipe, the search for a magic pill continues. Go into any health food store and you will see supplements that claim to be "naturally anabolic" and also, not coincidentally, "fat burning." Yet even many of the so-called organic anabolics have dangerous side effects and do little to produce any noticeable changes in muscle size or body-fat content. Do not take anything without your doctor's approval. Do your homework and read up about any substance (and not just on the label) before you put it into your body. The following are just some of the dubious substances.

Glenbuterol. Originally used for building animal muscle, this illegal drug was quickly adopted by compulsive bodybuilders.

Human growth hormone. This is already produced in the body. Worse, HGH supplementation is created from the pituitary glands of dead people. Side effects include excessive growth of the brow and jaw and an increased risk of diabetes and coronary heart disease.

GHB. Otherwise known as gamma hydroxybutyric acid, this was formerly sold in health food stores and became popular with both bodybuilders and people looking for a relaxing drug. It also sent several people to the emergency room.

Chromium picolinate. Claims to build muscle, burn fat, and inspire the body's release of human growth hormone (HGH).

Ma Huang. This Chinese herb is an upper that contains ephedrine. It can cause nervousness, irregular heartbeats, and hypertension.

Yohimbe. Like Ma Huang, this is an upper (it comes from tree bark) and shares similar side effects.

anaerobic

By now you probably know that aerobic means "with oxygen," and therefore anaerobic means "without oxygen." But you may be wondering: What does that really mean?

Whenever you sprint half a block to catch a bus, push your way through a bench press, or whack a tennis ball with all you've got, you're doing anaerobic exercise.

Anaerobic exercise is typically made up of short, intense bursts of activity, sometimes strung together with intervals of rest. The body responds to this activity burst by sending out the signal "I need energy *now.*" The easiest form of energy the body can pull out of storage comes from glucose (carbs stored in the liver as ready energy—also called glycogen). But this lasts only about 45 to 90 seconds. Another even more readily available form of energy comes from creatine phosphate, a compound that is stored in muscles but fizzles after 10 seconds.

Aerobic work also uses glucose for fuel. You may be wondering what the difference is between these two things if they essentially use the same fuel. There's a *big* difference.

Aerobic work is sustained and steady, burns fat along with glucose and oxygen, and creates sweat and carbon dioxide. It also builds endurance in the heart, lungs, and muscles.

Anaerobic work is short and intense, burns glucose (not fat or oxygen), and generates the release of lactic acid, creating the sensation we know as "the burn." It builds strength and some endurance in muscles. While anaerobic work does not directly attack fat, the resulting lean muscle mass it creates speeds up the metabolism, which helps the body burn fat.

The anaerobic threshold

You're in a step class and suddenly the instructor wants you to "do propulsions," bounding up and over the step. Or you're out for an easy run and suddenly get inspired to charge up a hill. Chances are good you'll cross over the anaerobic threshold if you switch into a high intensity workout.

The body takes it cue from your heart rate. Go beyond the high number on your target heart zone and you'll become anaerobic. The less fit you are, the sooner you cross over—your threshold can be as low as 50 percent of your maximum heart rate. The more fit you are, the higher your threshold.

Intermingled bouts of aerobic and anaerobic work are called intervals. Crossing back and forth over your anaerobic threshold is not recommended for beginners. More advanced exercisers, however, can increase aerobic capacity, delay the beginning anaerobic threshold, and prolong the release of lactic acid with intense anaerobic intervals lasting from 30 seconds to 4 minutes, at 85 percent of the max. heart rate—or higher if fitness allows.

What exercise is anaerobic?

Almost any form of activity can be either aerobic or anaerobic, depending on how you do it and on how fit you are. The following numbers are only averages.

- Sprinting a 50-yard dash is about 100 percent anaerobic.
- Doing 1 to 6 heavy reps of a squat or bench press is about 100 percent anaerobic.
- Doing 8 to 12 slow, moderately heavy reps to failure of any strength exercise is about 100 percent anaerobic.
- Stringing 10 sets together without resting between sets and sprinting from exercise to exercise (but not speeding through each set) turns your workout into 60 to 70 percent anaerobic, 40 to 30 percent aerobic.
- Doing several sets of 15 to 25 reps with light weights but not to muscle failure is 40 to 20 percent anaerobic and 60 to 80 percent aerobic.
- Playing singles tennis is 60 to 70 percent anaerobic, 40 to 30 percent aerobic. (The numbers are about the same for doubles, but less overall energy is expended.)
- Playing offense in a soccer game is 60 to 80 percent anaerobic, 40 to 20 percent aerobic. It's more anaerobic on defense.
- In-line skating is about 20 percent anaerobic, 80 percent aerobic. It switches to about 60 to 80 percent anaerobic, 40 to 20 percent aerobic if you play aggressive roller hockey.
- Swimming freestyle for advanced swimmers is 40 to 30 percent anaerobic, 60 to 70 percent aerobic. Swimming freestyle for a beginner is about 100 percent anaerobic.

arms

Biceps

Ask to see someone's muscle and typically they'll flex you their biceps, not a quad or a glute. The biceps muscles are the biceps brachii (the big one) and the brachialis (the smaller one that lies under the biceps brachii). (Biceps means "two heads.") These muscles are in the front of the upper arm and both bend (flex) and rotate (supinate) the wrist.

Triceps

Triceps are to biceps what hamstrings are to quads. They're the bigger opposing muscle group. The three triceps muscles are the long head (the one that hangs down if you lift your arm parallel to the floor), the lateral head (the other visible muscle in the center of the arm), and the medial head (which lies under the long head). These all function to extend the elbow and can be worked in a number of ways.

Basic exercises for arms

Whether you're using free weights, machines, cables, or resistance bands, the form is essentially the same for each of the following exercises. Remember to

- maintain a steady torso (see **Neutral Spine,** page 95)
- focus on the muscle you want to work (consciously squeeze and flex it)
- eliminate other extraneous motions (like wobbling or using momentum)
- work the muscle group hard enough so you truly fatigue it after 8 to 15 repetitions
- work slowly and deliberately

Stop or finish the set with a lighter weight when your form falls apart.

Note: Various routines appear later in this section. See also **Sets and Reps,** page 119, for more detailed information on weights, numbers of repetitions, and sets.

standing bar curls

Targets biceps

Hold the bar in a palm-up grip, arms down at your sides. Before you lift the bar, check that your grip is balanced and your posture is correct. Keep your knees soft, shoulders back, spine in neutral. As you curl the bar, lift from a 6 to a 10 o'clock position, then return to starting position. These are good for building basic biceps strength.

Caveats: Lifting elbows forward or back works the shoulders unnecessarily and robs the biceps of work. Don't arch your back to "cheat" up the bar.

Better lifting tips: Squeeze your upper arms into your torso and keep your chest up. Keep wrists straight and try holding the bar without using your thumbs.

dumbbell curls

Targets biceps

Dumbbells are good for balancing uneven arm strength. Stand or sit with arms straight at your side. Curl the dumbbells from a 6 to a 10 o'clock position as above. To make this move easier, start with palms facing in. To make this harder, start with palms facing up. Finish both versions with palms up.

Caveats: Be careful not to "pump" the weights too fast if you alternate sides.

Better lifting tips: Alternating curls gives you more time to rest. Try doing this exercise one arm at a time.

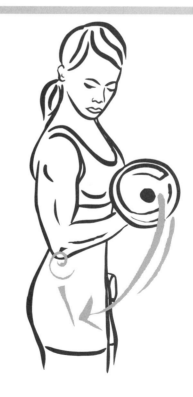

one-arm triceps extension

Targets triceps

Hold a weight over your head in one hand. Bend your arm so the elbow points straight to the ceiling. Be sure to take the weight *behind* your head and lower from a 12 to an 8 o'clock position. As you lift the arm, be sure not to lock the elbow. To keep upper arm stable, spot yourself with your other hand.

Caveats: Beware of clunking yourself on the head with the weight, but don't rest your forearm on your head. This muscle fails quickly. To rescue yourself when it fails, simply lower elbow. Keep your torso stable, as well. Any time you lift a weight overhead, your torso tends to wobble.

Better lifting tips: Keep a little space between your working arm and your ear (don't shrug). Keep wrists straight.

triceps press-down

Targets triceps

Stand facing an overhead cable that has an attached bar, rope, or single handle. (If you use a bar, incline your torso slightly forward to allow a greater range of motion in the arms.) Lower hands from a 10 to a 6 o'clock position, so arms straighten.

Caveats: Avoid lifting elbows as bar rises. This brings shoulders in and minimizes triceps work.

Better lifting tips: Keep upper arms squeezed into your torso to better isolate the triceps. Keep wrists straight to give triceps an extra, final squeeze.

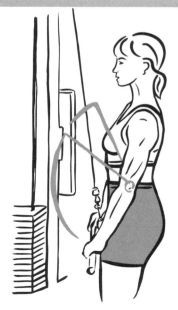

back

Latissimus dorsi (lats)

The latissimus, or lats, is a big fan-shaped muscle in the back that gives the torso a *V* shape. This muscle essentially runs from under the shoulder joint to the points of origin in the lower four ribs, the vertebrae in the mid- and lower back, and down to the top of the pelvic bone (the sacrum). All pulling or rowing moves work the lats.

Rhomboids

These upper back muscles can prevent slumped posture. The rhomboids are under the trapezius (see right) and run from the upper portion of the spine into the shoulder joint.

Trapezius

The trapezius, or traps, is a big trapezoid-shaped muscle that runs from the top of the spine, fans out to the shoulders, and then runs down into the middle back. Its primary function is to raise and lower the shoulders.

Erectors

The erectors spinae muscles, or erectors, are three muscles that run the length of the spine from the tailbone to the upper back. They're involved in all sorts of moves—squats, dead lifts, hyperextensions—and contribute to torso stability and good standing posture.

pull-downs to the chest

Targets latissimus dorsi (lats)
Sit under a pull-down cable. Use a slightly wider than shoulder-width grip on a straight or angled bar (or use a *V* handle or wider bar with handles that enable palms to rotate toward each other). Pull the bar to your chest. As you do this, lift your chest up to meet the bar and hold abdominals and lower back strong and steady.

Caveats: Avoid arching the lower back as you pull the bar down. Also avoid collapsing your chest and rounding your lower back, another common mistake.

Better lifting tips: Initiate the pull from your back first, *then* add your arms. If you only use your arms and round your lower back you won't be able to contract the lats.

seated cable row

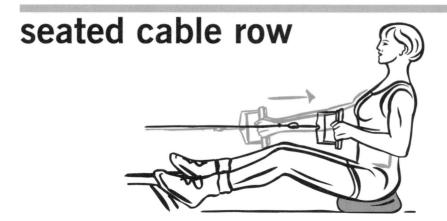

Targets

Sometimes called a low row. Be careful as you reach forward to grab the handle (use your legs to get yourself into position). Before you begin, sit upright with your knees slightly bent. Squeeze your shoulders back before you bend your arms, then pull the handle to your belly. As you release the handle and straighten arms, remain seated upright.

Caveats: Don't round your back as you reach forward. This can injure both the lower back and shoulder rotators. You can, however, incline your torso slightly forward and keep shoulders down to stretch lats.

Better lifting tips: As you pull toward your chest, lift the chest forward, contract the abdominals, and keep your elbows close to your torso, as if you wanted to touch them together behind your back.

high rows

Targets rhomboids

If you don't have a specific machine for this, you can use the same seated row machine as above to strengthen the rhomboids. Simply pull the bar higher, in line with your shoulders (some machines let you set pulley height) and use a wider bar and shoulder-width grip.

Caveats: Be careful not to round the lower back or use excessive forward and back swing in the torso. Some machines have a chest pad to hold you in place.

Better lifting tips: Initiate the movement from your back before bending your arms. When palms face each other, biceps make this easier. For an extra challenge, use an overhand grip.

shoulder shrug

Targets trapezius

Stand holding a dumbbell in each hand. Lift the shoulder blades straight up toward your ears. Lower with a controlled, slow motion.

Caveats: Be sure you lift the shoulders up in a vertical line. Rotating the shoulders forward or backward could irritate delicate shoulder joints. The "traps" can handle a lot of weight. Be careful not to get so ambitious with your shrugs that your shoulders get impossibly sore for days. Overdeveloped traps also aren't the most attractive on a woman (they create the linebacker look).

Better lifting tips: Keep your torso steady as you elevate your shoulders. Don't throw your back into it.

hyperextensions

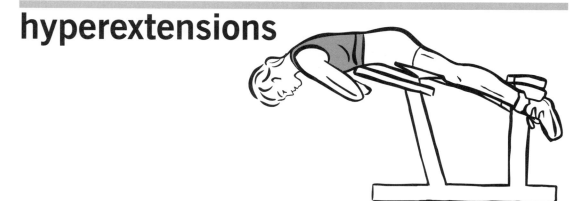

Targets erectors

If you have access to a hyperextension bench, secure ankles under the pad and lower torso to a 45-degree angle (hanging straight down puts excessive pressure on the discs in the lower spine). Lift spine to straight or slightly beyond straight (without arching your back) for a mild hyperextension. Think of this as an abdominal crunch in reverse. Some benches work you at a higher angle, but the range of motion is about the same.

You can also do this exercise on the floor. Lie face down, lift opposite arm and leg, hold for a second or two, and lower. Keep neck straight.

Caveats: Beware of bouncing up into a dangerously arched position.

Better lifting tips: Work this slowly and carefully. If you're doing this on a bench and want to add more resistance, hug a 5- or 10-pound plate to your chest.

balance

One of the best ways to stay strong, fit, active, and to prevent injury as we age is to maintain muscle balance. Although the concept of balance may seem elusive in other areas of our lives, in the body it's very concrete. Muscle balance is a matter of having equal strength (proportional to muscle size) and flexibility in opposing muscle groups. When muscle strength and flexibility are in balance:

- posture stays upright
- joints stay supple
- activity levels are maintained (so body fat is controlled and bones stay strong)
- little aches and pains aren't as frequent

When muscles *aren't* in balance:

- joints and muscles are more vulnerable to injury
- posture gets worse
- fitness is lost (and depression sets in)
- falls (and later in life, fractures) become more likely
- nagging pains like lower-back aches and other joint problems become more chronic
- moving becomes a chore

Most muscle imbalances that are due to weak or stiff muscles, joints, and connective tissue are temporary and can be fixed with a good strengthening and stretching program. Most lower-back problems, for instance, could be alleviated by strengthening and stretching the lower back and abs. Imbalances due to skeletal deformities, like scoliosis (a lateral *S* curvature of the spine) are permanent. But even some imbalances caused by problems like scoliosis can be improved with strengthening and stretching. (For more details on scoliosis and imbalances caused by other postural problems, see **Posture,** page 100.)

Slumped positions, bad habits (for instance, always carrying a heavy bag on one side), and an incomplete fitness program will, over time, etch themselves silently on your posture. You don't even realize you're out of balance because you adapt to these changes. It's easy to mask the resultant pain by taking acetaminophen. Unfortunately, these imbalances eventually work their way to the bones, changing the shape of the skeleton. Once that happens, it's too late to make significant changes. The best way to avoid this is through a regular exercise program that strengthens and stretches all the major muscles.

Opposing muscle groups

Every muscle group has a twin, a mirror opposite. Technically these are called agonists (the main movers) and antagonists (the muscles on the other side that respond by tightening, stretching, or standing still). More commonly, they're called opposing muscle groups, although they don't really compete against each other. If you pay a lot of attention to one muscle group, you have to give equal time to the other. Most of the ignored muscles are on the back of the body. (They're easier to ignore since we don't see them in the mirror.)

Here are the main opposing muscle groups:

- Upper back and chest
- Hamstrings and quads
- Lower back and abs
- Inner and outer thigh (adductors and abductors)
- Rear and front delts
- Delts and lats
- Triceps and biceps
- Calves and shins

Work opposing muscle groups either in the same workout or in separate, consecutive workouts within a few days (see **Routines for All Levels,** page 113).

Training your balance muscles

Every year more than 1.5 million elderly people fall and fracture bones. Osteoporosis causes bone fragility (see "Osteoporosis," page 34). But balance plays a key role in preventing falls. Weak, tight muscles make for poor balance and coordination.

The muscles most responsible for maintaining balance are the torso stabilizers (the abs and lower back) and the pelvic stabilizers (the inner and outer thigh muscles, the adductors and abductors).

All people who do not already have osteoporosis should keep these muscles strong by doing regularly the Basic Exercises for these muscles at the beginning of this section and other forms of exercise. Patients with osteoporosis should be on doctor-monitored programs and should not attempt to do things like ab crunches (which could cause a fractured vertebra).

Balance and strength go hand in hand. The stronger you are, the better your balance. The better your balance, the stronger you'll be.

body types

Genetics determine your body type—from the shape of your hips to the length of your limbs, to where you store body fat, to the types of muscle fibers you possess in greater numbers, which, in turn, determine if you'll be quick and strong like a weight lifter or slow but steady like a marathon runner. You can't change your body type, but you can enhance it and take advantage of its gifts.

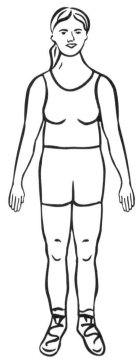

Endomorph

Endomorphs tend to have a high percentage of body fat and gain weight easily. They are also strong and have no trouble building muscle.

Exercise priority: Burning calories to control body fat and strength training to increase lean body mass.

Aerobic exercise

The best activity for endomorphs is power walking. It's easy on the joints, and you can do it anywhere. Begin with a 40-minute walk and build up to 60 minutes. Shoot for 60 percent of your maximum heart rate—you're exercising at the right intensity if you can hold a conversation while you're working out. Do this three to five times a week to keep your weight in check. **Avoid** stair climbing or step classes, which can bulk up your lower body.

Strength training

Focus on building the upper body to balance and draw attention away from a heavier lower body. Don't spend too much time on your hips and thighs; they're probably strong enough already. Good exercises for endomorphs include:

- Dumbbell bench press for the chest, front of shoulders, and triceps (see page 48)
- Rear delt row to work the back (see page 18)
- Lat pull-down to work the mid- and upper back and shoulders (see page 17)

Flexibility workouts

Stretch for five minutes after every workout and/or add one yoga or stretch-only workout per week to lengthen muscles.

Mesomorph

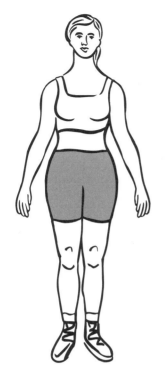

Mesomorphs tend to have plenty of muscle and low body fat. Mesomorphs adapt to many activities, thus you can perform feats requiring both strength and speed. If overweight, you've probably got shapely muscles hiding under body fat. You can build muscle quite easily—in fact, you could probably become a competitive bodybuilder if you so desire.

Exercise priority: Concentrate on flexibility exercises because you have tighter joints and are more prone to exercise-related injuries.

Aerobic exercise

Try in-line skating to work the legs and increase your heart rate. Running, step classes, and stair climbing will also provide a good heart and lung workout. You should exercise at 70 to 85 percent of your maximum heart rate for about 30 minutes, three to four days a week.

Strength training

Since you have naturally powerful chest, biceps, and calf muscles, you should focus on the complementary muscle groups, particularly the upper back, triceps, and shins to balance your build. Stick to lighter loads with increased reps and work out with weights three to four days a week for half an hour. The following are particularly good for mesomorphs:

- Seated lat row to work the mid- and upper back (see page 18)
- Triceps extension to work the back of your arms (see page 16)

Avoid presses and pulls with heavy weight if you don't want to get too bulky.

Flexibility workouts

Stretch for 15 to 20 minutes five days a week, including after each workout. This will lengthen the muscles.

Ectomorph

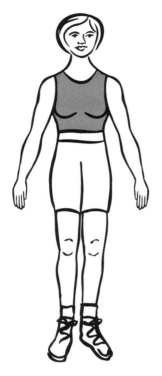

Ectomorphs are long-limbed, wiry, and narrow, and have a hard time gaining weight (though weight gains are distributed evenly when they do occur). This body type takes the longest to develop muscle.

Exercise priority: Since you have such a fast metabolism and weight gain is never a problem, focus more on building muscles.

Aerobic exercise

You're a natural runner. Go for a 20-minute jog three to four days a week, keeping your heart rate between 60 and 85 percent of maximum. In-line skating, cycling, and stair climbing are also good for ectomorphs.

Strength training

You should focus on compound exercises to work several muscle groups at once. Begin by building strength in your torso. Focus on chest, back, abdominals, and legs (leg strength enhances torso stability). As your torso gets strong enough to hold you steady as you lift, add heavier weights that cause muscles to fail (or almost fail) after 8 to 12 reps. Do the following exercises for 35 to 40 minutes a day, three or four days a week:

- Back hyperextension to work the lower back (see page 19)
- Barbell squats for the glutes, hamstrings, and quadriceps (see page 40)
- Weighted crunches for the abdominals (see page 6)

Avoid high reps of low weights. This will do nothing to stimulate muscle growth.

Flexibility workouts

Make sure you stretch for five minutes after your weight workouts to stave off muscle soreness and/or add at least one full-body stretch workout to maintain flexibility.

Meso-endomorph

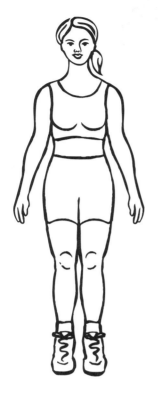

This body type combines the natural strength of a mesomorph with the curves of an endomorph, particularly in the hips and thighs.

Exercise priority: Burn fat and increase lean muscle mass with long, less intense cardio workouts and upper-body focused strength training.

Aerobic exercise

Swimming is perfect for your strong, naturally buoyant body. Other low stress activities like biking are also good. Exercise for 40 minutes a day, four to six days a week, at 60 to 70 percent of your maximum heart rate.

Avoid high-impact exercises such as running, which can be hard on the knees.

Strength training

Focus more on the upper body and less on the legs and hips, which are strengthened during daily activities. You should train with weights for 20 minutes, three or four days a week. Good exercises for the chest, biceps, and back:

- Bench press for the chest, triceps, and front of shoulders (see page 48)
- Dumbbell curls to work the biceps (see page 15)

Flexibility workouts

Stretch for 10 minutes after every workout.

What type are you?

Few people are pure examples of the four so-called somatypes. Most of us are combinations of two or three. However, one body type tends to dominate. (If you don't know which body type dominates, combine the two approaches—basing your choice on results and how you're feeling.)

body image

Although women have felt uncomfortable about their bodies for a number of reasons—small breasts, skinny legs, wrinkled faces, thinning hair—the number-one reason women dislike their bodies is fat.

Caucasian American women are most at risk for suffering from a poor body image because there are more rigorously buffed, cut, svelte, and emaciated examples of white female beauty in the media. Black and Latina women, who are more likely to carry more body fat, are much less likely to describe themselves as "fat," although the media influence is catching up there, so suffering related to body image is becoming more cross-cultural. Yet black, Latina, Middle Eastern, and Samoan women are still more likely to be called beautiful for being large.

But a woman's race and messages from the media are not the only factors that affect body image. Women who felt clumsy, awkward, and ugly as young girls, who felt they weren't valued as highly as their thin, popular sisters, classmates, and friends, tend to look in the mirror and feel shame. Even pretty women—models, celebrities, women who receive praise and money for their looks—have body image issues. Any woman who feels that her looks determine her self-worth is vulnerable to self-attack.

Women's Bodies: The Ideal, the Real, and the Emerging Female

In reality, 60 percent of all women in the United States wear a size 12 or larger. Despite the $30 to $50 billion per year spent on diet and fitness-related goods and services, at least 33 percent of Americans are considered "dangerously overweight." Clearly, something isn't working.

Two things need to change here:

1. Our ideals need to reflect what is real so we can achieve more sensible expectations about ourselves as beautiful mature women of all shapes and sizes.

2. We need to shift our focus away from external solutions (fad diets and strange exercise contraptions) and focus on answers that come from within—a steady lifestyle of activity, enjoying healthy and even nonhealthy foods in sensible amounts, a positive outlook, and acceptance of ourselves.

Pointers for Boosting Body-Esteem

There are always things you can do to feel better about yourself. Here are a few suggestions:

- Think of all the things you've promised yourself you'll do when you have a more "acceptable" body. Pick one and do it today.

- Identify the kind of movement or activity you love to do most and do it today. (If it's downhill skiing and it's summer, pick another one.)

- Wear an outfit that compliments how you feel when you're doing your chosen activity. (Streamlined, flowy, towering, and proud enough to take up space?)

- Focus on the details of your movement, such as how your feet touch lightly on the pavement or floor. Focus on the subtle motions of your hands, your face, your hips, rather than big motions of arms and legs. Do it *your* way. Don't copy a role model that makes you feel clumsy. Be graceful. Be joyful.

- Treat yourself with care and respect. Give yourself moderate exercise, healthy foods, sensual pleasures, and relaxation every day.

- Tell yourself: "I don't need a perfect body to be happy."

- Remind yourself: "I am whole, happy, and perfect just as I am."

- Detoxify yourself of anger, resentment, unhappiness. Leave any blame behind and take pleasure in yourself.

- Dress up your best features—your eyes, your smile, your hair.

- Throw out all clothes that don't fit or flatter you. The first things to go should be whatever requires you to lose weight and any outfits that make you feel uncomfortable.

- Take stock of your magnificent intellect, spirit, and creative abilities.

bodybuilding

Of the millions of people who train with weights to stay lean and fit, few actually call themselves bodybuilders, although most are building strength with weights. Bodybuilding techniques are at the core of many strength training practices. Only the names, numbers of reps, and amounts of weight have been changed to appeal to different audiences.

Also known as strength training, bodybuilding is for people who want to build muscle strength, shape, size, definition, and a symmetrically shaped body. Although most people bodybuild for health reasons, to improve their appearance, and for personal satisfaction, some also do it to win competitions and to get modeling and acting jobs. Serious bodybuilders, competitive or not, often embrace the whole bodybuilding lifestyle, which includes a highly disciplined cross-training and eating regimen. At the extreme end of the bodybuilding scale, this lifestyle can be obsessive and unhealthy. A balanced lifestyle of bodybuilding, cross training, and conscious eating habits, however, can produce profound improvements in health, function, appearance, and longevity.

Many bodybuilders use a variety of methods and equipment to get results. Most favor a steady dose of moderately heavy weights that bring on muscle failure after 8 to 12 repetitions, believed to be the ideal number for building muscle size. Those who compete or perform tend to use heavy weights and low reps in the off-season to build muscle mass, and higher reps and lighter weight at contest time to bring out the definition (or cuts). The theory that low reps build size and high reps build definition has never been proven.

Women who fear that bodybuilding with moderately heavy weights will produce "big, manly muscles" are sadly misinformed (see **Women and Muscle,** page 147).

Body sculpting

Body sculpting, or toning, is bodybuilding's little sister. The term *body sculpting* was probably coined to make the weight-lifting atmosphere less intimidating, especially to women. Many of the exercises used in body sculpting classes come straight from bodybuilding: squats, lunges, presses, pulls, flyes, and so on. But body sculpting typically employs light weights, elastic resistance (tubing or bands, etc.), or body weight alone combined with higher repetitions of between 12 and 24, or more. Body sculptors usually seek muscle definition, not muscle mass, and because they use lighter weights and high reps, they tend to achieve muscle endurance rather than strength. What many body sculptors don't understand, however, is that definition doesn't come from light weights and more reps. It comes from many factors: from doing fewer reps of moderately heavy weight with good form (bodybuilding), possibly combined with some higher reps for muscular endurance; from frequent cardio workouts; from a low-fat diet; even from a person's genetic predisposition (see **Women and Muscle,** page 147).

Olympic-style lifting

Olympic-style lifting combines lifting heavy weight with momentum in three fairly complex lifts. The lifts, called the overhead press, the snatch, and the clean and jerk are heavy and explosive moves that require a tremendous amount of practice—and even then are potentially dangerous and provide few health benefits. After the initial part of the lift, which overcomes inertia, very little resistance is placed on the muscle (once you set the weight in motion it almost continues to lift itself). Yet the muscles, skeleton, and connective tissue receive a tremendous amount of stress.

Power lifting

This is a show of brute strength—usually the heaviest amount of weight that can be lifted in a single repetition. Power lifts are the squat, bench press, and dead lift. Although power lifts can be impressive to watch, like Olympic lifts, they also require a lot of practice and provide few health benefits. Subjecting the body to such heavy amounts of weight for one repetition puts the body under extreme orthopedic risk and can raise the blood pressure to dangerously high levels.

In Brief

Bodybuilding: 8 to 12 reps, moderate weight—for muscle strength, shape, size, definition, proportion

Body sculpting and toning: 12 to 15 or more reps, light weight—for muscle endurance, some definition

Power lifting and Olympic-style lifting: 1 to 6 reps, heavy weight, explosive movements—for pure strength; high-risk moves with few fitness benefits

What stronger muscles can do . . .

- Improve body composition by creating more muscle, less fat (This raises the metabolism, the best edge against fat gain.)
- Increase the amount of calories used *after* exercise and during rest
- Improve posture
- Give muscles a more pleasing shape
- Improve and maintain functional strength, thus enhancing longevity
- Promote lower levels of total cholesterol, thereby reducing the risk of heart disease
- Improve the strength of tendons and bones even in peri- and postmenopausal women.

. . . And how training can strengthen the mind

- Improve focusing skills
- Improve self-image, raise self-esteem
- Relieve stress, and possibly strengthen the immune system
- Balance extreme moods
- Increase energy
- Heighten sensitivity between body and mind

How the body gets stronger

It takes two to three weeks for the body to develop coordination to perform basic strength training moves. After that it takes six to eight weeks for the body to experience its first phase of muscle growth. During that time

- skin tightens
- metabolism speeds up
- energy increases

The point at which results begin to appear depends on the level of body fat and staying on a program that combines weight training with cardiovascular fitness and a low-fat eating regimen.

In the beginning of a new program, strength typically improves by 50 to 75 percent or more in the first three months. Gains tend to slow down after that and plateau.

If body fat is . . .	Results may appear in . . .
15–20%	3–6 weeks
20–30%	6–12 weeks
above 30%	2–3 months

To keep improving, do one of five things

1. Increase weight—when you can do 15 repetitions with ease, increase weight by 5 percent or less.

2. Increase reps—if you can do 8 reps with good form, but the weight is challenging, try adding 1 or 2 more reps.

3. Add "negatives" at the end of a set—get some assistance on the lift (with a spotter, trainer, or partner) and slowly lower the weight, or go to failure with one weight, then complete the set with progressively lighter weights, also to failure.

4. Change the order of your exercises.

5. Make sure you get adequate rest between workouts; avoid overtraining.

Good Lifting Form Defined

Good form combines many factors:

- A steady torso (see **Posture,** page 100)
- Going slowly enough to maximize the time muscles are in contraction and minimize momentum
- Holding each contraction (when muscles shorten, get harder) for a split second. (Most people are weakest in this part of the lift. It also smoothes the transition between the lift and the lower.)
- Consciously stretching muscles as they lengthen, but not so far that joints feel pain

bones

Bones aren't simply the hard substance that holds us upright. They're versatile, vital *organs* that serve many functions. They

- provide a cage to protect our organs
- store calcium and other minerals
- produce red blood cells deep in the spongy marrow within
- provide a leverage system so we can move our muscles

Contrary to what some people think, bones are alive! Like other organs, they've got nerves and blood vessels. They consist mostly of calcium but also contain magnesium, phosphorus, collagen (a protein), water, and mineral salts. Although they're hard, they're also flexible and blessed with the ability to reshape and regenerate themselves on a daily basis.

Whenever we walk, run, dance, play a sport, or lift weights, we subject our muscles to the stressful forces of gravity and momentum. This causes the muscles to tug on the bones, and if that tugging is strong enough, it sends a message to the bones to get stronger so they'll be prepared for heavier workloads in the future. They then store more calcium and grow thicker collagen fibers.

When there isn't sufficient stress, the bones don't thicken. In fact, it's the skeleton's intention to stay as light as it needs to be so small, weak muscles don't have to lug around big, heavy bones. As muscles get stronger, so do bones (although it takes longer to build bone strength). Although exercise provides the best stimulus for bone growth, gravity alone is a powerful force. Astronauts in space and people who are bedridden or have a leg in a cast lose bone density at an alarmingly fast rate. Just being vertical and walking is good for bones.

When there's *too much* stress on a bone, without sufficient muscle strength to protect it, fractures develop. (The terms *too much* and *not enough* are relative to each person.) Athletes often experience stress fractures from overuse. Older women with stooped-over postures (dowager's humps) also get this way from fractured spinal vertebrae.

Bones have the capacity to stay strong throughout a lifetime. Animal bones usually do. Human bones, however, deteriorate, mostly from disuse. When this deterioration gets severe, osteoporosis results (see **Osteoporosis,** page 34). This condition is reaching epidemic proportions, especially in modern industrialized nations (the United States, for instance, has the highest spinal fracture rate in the world). Clearly, our sedentary lifestyles and calcium deficient diets are silently eating away at our structures like termites. But bone loss can be prevented.

What bones are made of

Bones have their own delicately balanced eco-system, complete with specific cells assigned to different tasks.

Osteoclasts chew up old bone tissue. They get rid of old bone so new bone can be built in its place. As osteoclasts deconstruct the old bone, they take calcium, magnesium, and phosphorus with it and dump them into the blood.

Osteoblasts lay down new bone tissue. As osteoblasts build new bone, they pull a fresh supply of calcium, magnesium, and phosphorus out of the blood and into the bones.

When this system works optimally and stresses are strong enough to inspire new bone growth, bones can get stronger. But typically, with age, the rate of bone deterioration outpaces bone repair, creating the conditions for bone loss and osteoporosis. Whether or not this is purely physiological or simply a lifestyle choice (deciding to move much less) is a subject of debate. And not all women and men experience bone loss.

How exercise affects bones

Weight-bearing exercise subjects the body either to its own body weight (as in walking and running) or additional weight (as in weight lifting). Weight-bearing exercise inspires bone growth by strengthening the repair portion of the bone-building cycle (osteoblasts) and increasing the bones' uptake of calcium. Exercise is one of the best preventions against bone loss. Although many older people who regularly exercise may still experience some bone loss, exercise can prevent fractures, because it maintains the bones' ability for self-repair.

Calcium and bones

Though bones are partly made of calcium, the body doesn't produce calcium. It has to get it from food. Every day some calcium gets lost in sweat, excretion, and in the production of hair and nails. When there isn't enough calcium coming in from food, the body takes it out of the bones. (Add menopause, smoking, certain medications, and excessive alcohol, caffeine, carbonated beverages, and protein and even more calcium gets lost.)

Simply taking the RDA (Recommended Daily Allowance) for calcium doesn't do enough to prevent bone loss. Neither does exercise alone. The best way to ensure healthy bones is to do both.

How age and hormones affect bone health

The sex hormones estrogen and progesterone play an important role in bone health, but doctors and researchers don't fully know to what extent.

Before menopause, women maintain bone mass because estrogen helps slow the destruction of old bone tissue. (Estrogen prevents the osteoclasts from destroying too much bone.) However, estrogen doesn't do anything to inspire new bone growth. Only progesterone and exercise do that by stimulating the osteoblasts.

After menopause, lower levels of estrogen mean that bone loss can occur at a faster rate. This is one reason why estrogen-replacement therapy and other medications slow bone loss.

Both pre- and postmenopausal women are being prescribed weight training as a way to stimulate bone growth. A study at Tufts University showed that two weight-lifting workouts a week, for forty-five minutes each, were enough to help women gain 1 percent bone density in just one year.

Eating for healthy bones

Many people know that dairy products contain calcium and protein, which are good for bones. But they may not know that eating too much protein can actually leach calcium from bones and, therefore, weaken them. So, if you drink a lot of milk and eat yogurt for bone health and then consume large amounts of protein in one day, you may actually be doing more harm than good. This is one reason why high-protein diets can be especially dangerous for women, whose aging bones are already at risk. Too much protein can also weaken the immune system. With excess protein, the immune system can't determine what's "self" and what's "foreign" and so doesn't know whether to defend or attack (see **Immunity**, page 436).

A bone-healthy diet, therefore, should be low in protein and fat, and high in calcium-rich vegetables, such as cooked greens (collards, kale), sesame seeds, molasses, broccoli, and tofu. Some other sources of calcium include sardines, beans, and amaranth (a grain). Avoid sodas (carbonated beverages are high in phosphates that leach calcium from the bones), smoking, and alcohol.

osteoporosis

Most people know that osteoporosis is a disease that makes bones disintegrate and break easily. What most people don't know is that it's preventable. A lifetime of bone-building activity (see below), plus sufficient calcium, cuts a person's risk of getting osteoporosis in half. So yes, it's avoidable and also treatable, but as of yet there is no cure.

Medical experts don't really know why some people suffer from osteoporosis and others don't. As we get older, some bone loss is normal. But osteoporosis is not. Animals, for instance, don't get this disease.

Osteoporosis occurs when there's a disruption in what is called the bone remodeling system. Bones, like some houses, undergo a constant tearing down and rebuilding process. To make themselves stronger, bones need three things: nutrients (calcium, magnesium, vitamin D), weight-bearing exercise, and hormones (sufficient levels of estrogen, progesterone, and testosterone). Without enough of any of the above, too much old bone is destroyed and new bone can't be built fast enough. So osteoporosis sets in, like termites, silently eating away at the body's foundation. For many women, the first sign of osteoporosis is a loss in height. But many don't know they've got it until they fall and fracture a bone. By then the disease is at an advanced stage and harder to treat.

The Truth About Osteoporosis

• Contrary to popular opinion, it's *not* simply the result of insufficient calcium. Nor will calcium cure osteoporosis.

• It's not just a woman's disease, even though half of all women get it and eight out of ten osteoporosis patients are women. It also affects 30 percent of men over seventy-five.

• It's not just an old person's disease. Young people (especially overexercisers and undereaters) and women who miss periods are at high risk even before menopause. During this time, some women lose 50 percent of their bone mass!

• It's not just a thin woman's disease. Overweight, inactive women are also at risk.

Risk Factors You Can't Control

- Being female: 80 percent of all osteoporosis patients are women.
- Experiencing an early menopause or hysterectomy
- Being postmenopausal: After menopause and the drop in estrogen, women can lose up to 20 percent of their bone mass

within five to seven years. Then, bone loss slows down to 1 to 2 percent a year.

- Being Caucasian or Asian: Women of these ethnic backgrounds are more than twice as likely to get osteoporosis as African-American women, whose chances for getting the disease are one in five. Hispanic women are also at risk.
- Being petite or small-boned: Having small bones to begin with means that any deterioration does more total harm.
- Having a family history of osteoporosis

Risk Factors You Can Control

- Not getting enough calcium, magnesium, and vitamin D
- Not taking estrogen replacement or other medications after menopause
- Excessive dieting, especially the eating disorders bulimia and anorexia
- Excessive exercise, especially when it interrupts the menstrual cycle (Ballet dancers and gymnasts, who often starve themselves, are at especially high risk.)
- Smoking cigarettes, which inhibits the absorption of calcium: Female smokers also tend to experience menopause five to seven years sooner.
- Drinking alcohol, which disrupts the bone-remodeling process
- Drinking caffeine and carbonated sodas: Two or more cups of coffee are believed to inhibit calcium absorption. Carbonated sodas contain phosphates (plus caffeine) that pull calcium from bones.
- Not getting enough exercise, especially weight-bearing exercise

- Eating too much protein, which leaches calcium from bones
- Taking certain medications, such as cortisone, thyroid hormones, anticonvulsants, and steroids

Exercise and Osteoporosis: The Four Stages of Prevention

Preventing bone loss with exercise should be a lifelong process.

Stage 1. Children, teenagers, and adults in their twenties need to play, run around, and do sports to make bones stronger. High-impact activities such as running, soccer, dancing, gymnastics, track and field, basketball, and volleyball build strong bones. Young adults eighteen and older should also add weight training. All of these activities sufficiently "load" the bones so fully grown adults (approximately age thirty) can arrive at the apex of bone growth in peak condition. (Intense weight training before the age of eighteen can actually stunt bone growth.)

Stage 2. Adults in their thirties and forties (especially premenopausal women) typically need to switch from high- to lower-impact activities to avoid injury. (Connective tissues aren't as forgiving at this age.) Bones may also start to decay but activity slows the process, while overdoing exercise and dieting can speed bone loss. Choose activities like jogging (preferably on dirt trails), walking, hiking, low-impact aerobic dance, step classes, skating, cross-country skiing (outside or on a machine), and, of course, weight lifting.

Stage 3. Women who are preperi- or postmenopausal but who are not high-risk candidates for osteoporosis (confirm this with a bone-density test) can continue with low-impact exercise—walking, step classes, cross-country skiing (preferably indoor), and, of course, weight lifting. But women at this age, usually between fifty and sixty-five, should avoid high-risk sports like in-line skating, downhill skiing, horseback riding, or full-contact karate, where the risk of crashing into someone or falling down is high.

Stage 4. Anyone with fragile bones (again, this is best confirmed with a bone-density exam) should switch to low-impact exercise like walking and/or nonimpact exercise like cycling (on an indoor bike), swimming, water aerobics, deep-water running, and weight lifting. Both men and women with low bone density should avoid all contact sports and any sports where the risk of falling is high. They might also avoid sports like tennis or basketball where sudden shifts in balance could cause a fall (unless they've been playing all their lives and the games are easy). Sudden twists in the torso (as in golf) should also be avoided.

Bone-Density Exams

The best way to get a true assessment of your bone health is with a bone-mineral-density exam (or BMD). This is the only way to get a true reading of your bone health and to what extent, if any, you have osteoporosis. Healthy bones with no high risk of fracture are considered normal. Bones with below-normal density at the spine or hip (but not at high risk for fracture) fall within a measurement of −1 to −3. Bones with very low density and a high risk of fracture fall within a measurement of −3 and worse (−4, etc.).

Most BMD's take less than twenty minutes, are painless, and use very small doses of radia-tion. Although there are more than seven types of tests, DEXA (Dual Energy X-ray Absorptiometry) is the most common. Your doctor can determine which method is best for you. X rays are not recommended as reliable methods of detection since they will show deterioration only when 25 to 40 percent of bone loss has already occurred.

More and more doctors are recommending that young women between ages thirty-five and forty-five have a BMD as a baseline so that this information will be available as a comparison and action can be taken in time to prevent gross bone loss.

What the tests measure is your total bone mass and how densely it's put together. This is compared to the bones of other people your age and people around thirty years old at peak bone health.

This information enables doctors to determine how much bone you've already lost, predict the rate of decay, and prescribe appropriate preventions and treatments.

Unfortunately, not all insurance companies cover this test, but most of them cost less than $250 (a small price to pay compared to treatments). To find out about bone-scanning facilities in your area, call the National Osteoporosis Foundation's Act Against Osteoporosis at 800-464-6700 or write the NOF, Dept. MQ, PO Box 96616, Washington, DC 20077.

Estrogen's Role in Osteoporosis

Estrogen helps bones absorb calcium and slows the breakdown of old bone tissue. After menopause, estrogen levels drop by more than 60 percent and bones break down faster.

After menopause, the so-called male hormones progesterone and testosterone (which women produce in the ovaries with estrogen) also drop by 50 percent. Since the male hormones stimulate the growth of new bone tissue, a drop here slows the rebuilding process. Hormone replacement therapies often include both male and female hormones, both of which preserve and repair bones.

However, many women confronting menopause fear taking hormone replacement therapy, especially estrogen, because of the reported increased risk of breast and uterine cancer. Yet while only 4 percent of women over fifty die each year of breast cancer, about 50 percent get osteoporosis. So, although hormone replacement therapy may be controversial, the bottom line is it can dramatically improve bone health.

What to Do If You Have Osteoporosis

The following are warning signs that osteoporosis has begun to set in:

- A loss of more than ¼ inch in height: Women with osteoporosis, on an average, lose 2½ total inches in height.
- Severe back pain, usually the result of fractured vertebrae.
- Stooped posture: This can also be the result of vertebral fractures.

Osteoporosis is not a death sentence. Women with this disease can continue to live active lives. Some medications and/or hormone treatments, plus weight-bearing exercise (preferably under the guidance of a medical professional) and adequate calcium not only slow bone loss but can increase bone density even after the disease has set in.

FDA approved medications include:

Fosamax: Approved both for prevention and treatment, it's been shown to increase bone density in the spine and hip and therefore reduce the threat of fractures in those areas. Often recommended for women who can't or don't want to take estrogen. Side effects include stomach pain, nausea, and heartburn.

Calcitonin: This is a natural hormone that helps in the bone-remodeling process, usually prescribed for women five years past the last menstrual period. Slows bone loss and increases bone density in the spine. Taken by injection or nasal spray. Side effects of injection include rash, nausea, and frequent urination, while side effects of the nasal spray have been limited to a runny nose.

Estrogen replacement therapy is prescribed for both prevention and treatment of osteoporosis. Usually given with the hormone progestin to decrease the risk of cancer of the uterus. Estrogen replacement therapy both slows bone loss and increases bone density in the hip and spine, therefore reducing risk of fractures. Side effects include nausea, bloating, and breast tenderness.

breathing

Novice lifters often wonder how to breathe while lifting weights. The standard answer to this question is to exhale as you exert (push, pull, lift) and inhale as you lower the weight. An easy way to remember this is "ex on ex."

The funny thing is many people do this backward, and inhale when they exert. It is strangely tempting to hold your breath when you lift, a fear reaction. But this creates internal stress and can incite a nasty little reaction in the nose and mouth called a Valsalva maneuver (increased pressure in the thoracic cavity), which may:

- Increase your risk of getting a hernia
- Reduce blood flow to the heart
- Reduce the flow of oxygen to the brain
- Make you dizzy—and even pass out!

Exhaling as you work creates an internal cushion for your organs. Psychologically, it also helps focus your efforts, the way yelling gives added impact to a karate kick.

If you can just remember to breathe naturally while you train, chances are good you'll eventually work your way around to exhaling on exertion (see also **Oxygen,** page 214).

Impeccable breathing technique

- Inhale through the nose. Put your nose hairs to work—they're very good at filtering out unwanted dirt and dust particles in the air. Take a nice big lung and belly full of air *before* you start hurling any weights.
- Exhale through the mouth, audibly or silently (that part's up to you). Synchronize your breath with your lift (don't run out of breath before the lift is over or have too much breath left over at the end of each lift).
- Establish a rhythm between your in- and exhalations to match the speed of your lifts. If your lifts last two seconds, so should your exhalations. If your lowerings last four seconds, so should your inhalations.
- Don't completely empty or fill your belly and lungs with each breath. That could make you hyperventilate. Don't force your breath. Keep your breathing full but relaxed.

buttocks

The gluteus muscles, or glutes, are some of the largest and most powerful muscles in the body.

Gluteus maximus

The gluteus maximus is the largest and shapeliest of the three muscles. It's what gives the rounded shape to the buttocks and runs from the pelvis (the sacrum and iliac crest at the top of the pelvic bone) to the thigh bone and the cartilagelike structure on the side of the leg called the iliotibial band. This muscle gets worked in big push-off moves like squats, stair climbing, and cycling.

Gluteus medius and minimus

The gluteus medius and minimus are much smaller muscles and start higher on the hip. These primarily assist when taking the leg out to the side (abduction), but also work when turning the legs inward (internal rotation) and when walking, running, and dancing. Many of the exercises that work the glutes or buttocks also work the muscles of the hips and thighs.

The squat is the grandmother of all buttocks exercises and can be varied in numerous ways.

the free squat

Targets all three muscle groups

For a freestanding squat, take a slightly wider than hip-width stance. Most women get a deeper range of motion with toes slightly turned out. Start with a good neutral spine, chest lifted, knees soft. (You can do this with no weight, holding dumbbells, or a bar on the base of your neck.) Sit back in your hips, as if onto a chair, keeping your spine neutral. Press into your heels to stand up.

Caveats: Avoid rounding your back or lifting your heels off the floor. Avoid locking your knees or arching your lower back as you return to the standing position. Be sure to avoid heavy weights compressing down on your spine until you've built up the strength to handle this. Even then, be careful.

Better lifting tips: As you bend your knees, lift your chest forward for counterbalance. As

you straighten your legs, squeeze your buttocks together and hold the contraction in the glutes. If you can't squat with your heels down, raise heels on two 5-pound plates.

Smith machine squat

Targets all three muscle groups

The Smith machine features a bar that slides up and down two parallel poles. Squatting here lets you keep your torso upright (anatomically impossible with a free squat) and is more comfortable for most people's spines and knees. Place the bar on the fleshy part at the base of your neck, unrack the weights, and walk far enough forward so that when

you sit back, your knees make a 90-degree angle. Keep your chest lifted as above.

Caveats: Even though you're "held" in position by the machine, be careful not to drop your torso forward, exceed the 90-degree angle with your knees, or raise your heels.

Better lifting tips: As you straighten your legs, press through the heels and hips. Keep hips under shoulders as you straighten your legs.

sit back squats

Targets gluteus maximus and quadriceps

This one's harder than it looks. Hold on to a fixed pole, walk your feet right up to the pole and then open your legs about hip-width apart. Bend your knees and sit back into your hips, keeping your spine upright and arms straight until knees are bent to a 90-degree angle. Press your heels into the floor and stand only halfway up to keep constant tension on the muscles. This exercise is a good alternative if you don't have access to a Smith machine. This is very safe for knees and lower back since the force of your weight is sitting back into the hips. (For more squat variations, see **Squats,** page 130.)

Caveats: Beware of moving quickly or "dropping" your weight down. Avoid rounding your lower back as you come halfway up.

Better lifting tips: You should be able to wiggle your toes in your shoes—a good litmus test to make sure you're pressing into heels.

grand pliés

Targets gluteus medius and minimus

Stand with your feet twice as wide as your hips. Turn your toes out to the 10 and 2 o'clock positions. Open toes and heels a total of 5 times and you're in position for grand pliés. Bend your knees to lower your torso. Ideally, you want your knees bent to a 90-degree angle. You may need to start with demi, or half, pliés.

Caveats: Be sure that your knees stay over your heels (not your toes) as you lower. Also, keep buttocks *above* knees and heels down.

Better lifting tips: Keep your torso stable and your hips directly under your shoulders as you lower.

stationary lunges

Targets all three muscle groups and quadriceps

Traditional lunges involve stepping forward and down at the same time (tough on knees!), then pressing up and back (tough on lower back!). Although touted as a "killer bun exercise," very few mortals have the torso stability, grace, and precision to do this effectively. A safer alternative is the stationary lunge. Take a long, cross-country-ski stance—that is, both knees bent, back heel up, feet hip-distance apart. Keep spine vertical as you bend the knees (lowering torso like an elevator) until the back knee almost touches the floor. As you come up, keep both knees slightly bent both for stability and to keep tension constant. (For more lunge variations, see **Lunges,** page 84.)

Caveats: Avoid taking front knee out over the toes. Also, a common mistake is to try to put the back heel down. This can cause you to lose balance and overstretch your Achilles tendon.

Better lifting tips: Do this slowly to keep a constant tension on the muscles; press into the heel of the front foot to rise.

hip extension

Targets all three muscle groups and hamstrings

Pressing the leg back actually uses both glutes and hamstring, but the primary focus is in the buttocks. You can do this freestanding or in a "multihip machine." Stand upright and lean forward slightly (maintaining neutral spine). Bend the knee of the working leg and soften the knee of the supporting leg for balance. Press the foot back so that your shin is parallel to the floor, keeping your torso still. Bring working knee back in line with supporting knee each time.

Caveats: Avoid pressing so far back that you arch your lower back. If this is uncomfortable or still difficult to do, incline forward a bit more.

Better lifting tips: As you extend the leg back, hold it for a second or two and imagine yourself holding a pencil at the point where the gluteus maximus meets the thigh.

(Also see pages 74–78 for additional moves that work the hip and thighs, or quadriceps, abductors, adductors, and hamstrings.)

calves

Gastroc and Soleus

Calves consist of two main muscles. The gastrocnemius, or gastroc, is the bulbous, fleshy muscle visible on the surface; the soleus lies underneath. The gastroc gives the calf its shape, while the soleus gives it size. Both muscles work to point and flex the foot at the ankle joint, so it is used in all sorts of moves. In the weight room, however, straight-leg heel raises target the gastroc while bent-knee heel raises address the soleus.

Calf muscles are the second most densely woven muscles in the body (the jaw is the densest). Densely woven fibers give calves endurance to propel us around all day without lactic acid burn. (In the head, they keep our jaws moving all day, talking and eating without "feeling the burn.") Because calves are so rugged, they can take a lot of punishment without showing any signs of improvement. To make calves bigger or more shapely takes high reps or heavy weight, plus grit, determination, and a high tolerance for pain.

straight-leg heel raise

Targets gastroc

Stand up straight with one or both toes on a raised platform. (You can do this in a standing calf machine or without any weight. Simply hold on to something for balance.) With your legs straight but not locked at the knee, raise your heels as high as possible and then lower them down to below the platform. An ideal range of motion would be from 2 to 4 o'clock.

Caveats: Avoid going too fast, locking knees, or using only a small range of motion.

Better lifting tips: When working calves, wear shoes with enough flexibility in the ball of the foot so you can fully raise and lower the heel. Many people work calves in their socks (as long as you don't need ankle support to push heavy weights).

bent-knee heel raise

Targets soleus

If you don't have access to a seated calf-raise machine, you can do this with a barbell across your knees and toes mounted on a riser that allows heels to drop. Raise the heels (to contract the calf muscles) as high as you can, and then lower the heels (to stretch the calf muscles) as far as possible below the riser.

Caveats: Make sure your feet are securely placed on the riser and aren't in danger of slipping off.

Better lifting tips: Use as full a range of motion as possible. If using a machine that lifts your seat as you raise your heels, maintain a slight forward lean in the torso (to avoid the sense that you're on a rocking horse and to better isolate the calves).

chest

Pectorals, or pecs, have worked their way into common terminology as have glutes and abs. Good pecs are usually prized on men. But strong pectoral muscles help women, too. They assist all pushing, throwing, and hugging moves and also add cleavage, independent of breast size. With stronger pecs, even small-breasted women can build cleavage.

The pectoral muscles fan out from a narrow point at the shoulder joint and widen all the way to the clavicles (the bones that run from shoulder to throat), the sternum (breast bone), and ribs. Bodybuilders have long trained the chest in three parts (upper, middle, and lower), changing the angle of the torso to address different areas.

Upper Pectorals

An incline bench set at a 45-degree angle works the upper portion of the muscle, elongating the cleavage.

Center Pectorals

A flat bench focuses work in the center part of the chest, which is good for overall strength.

Lower Pectorals

A decline bench (with your head below your hips) focuses work in the lower part of the chest. This part of the muscle is covered with breast tissue in women, so working this area won't yield visible results.

It's also virtually impossible to move the pecs without involving the front portion of the shoulder (the anterior deltoid). Therefore, adding additional exercises like front raises for the "front delts" when you work your chest is redundant and can lead to overuse injury (see **Shoulders,** page 123).

Chest exercises come in two main varieties: presses and flyes. Presses use two joints—elbows and shoulders. Flyes use only the shoulders. Many people fail to make this distinction and turn dumbbell or cable exercises into hybrid press-flyes. But it's important to know the difference so you use them intelligently:

Presses. You can use heavier weight when doing presses because two joints are doing the work.

Do presses first (after a warm-up) when you've got lots of strength (usually at the beginning of a week) and you want to push heavier weight, or perhaps increase your personal best.

Flyes. Use a lighter weight when doing flyes because all the weight hangs off delicate shoulder joints.

Do flyes first when you're not so strong and want to "prefatigue" your pecs, so you don't have to use your normal heavier weight to effectively exhaust the chest.

Basic exercises for the chest

Whatever equipment you use—barbells, dumbbells, machines, cables, resistance bands, or body weight—the main rules about chest work are these:

- Whether seated, lying supine, or lying prone, keep the spine in neutral alignment. Don't move your hips, or round or arch your back.
- As you press the weight, or close arms in a flye, LIFT THE CHEST! Collapsing the chest as you contract the pectorals (a common mistake) transfers much of the work to the shoulders.
- Keep your shoulders down and back as much as possible to minimize shoulder involvement.
- Don't lock your elbows as you press. Save your elbow tendons!
- If you're nagged by constant shoulder pain, you may be suffering from a rotator cuff injury, which is often caused by overzealous and persistently heavy training. Back off of heavy weights at the first sign of shoulder pain or you may have to back off chest exercises for several months in order to heal.

push-ups

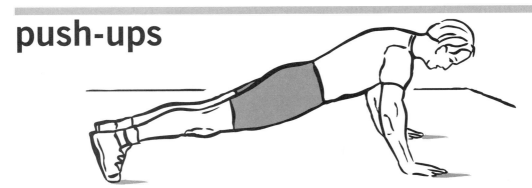

Targets pectorals, arms, and back

Push-ups don't have to be as horrible as most of us remember from gym class or movies about basic training. Whether you do them on your knees or toes, hold the spine in neutral so hips are below the shoulders as you're perched up, ready to lower. Arms should hang in a straight line from the shoulders; neck should be long and in line with the spine. Lower chest only as far as shoulder comfort will allow. Remember to keep your chest lifted as you press up.

Caveats: Don't let hips sag to the floor. As you bend your elbows, your chest should be the lowest point.

Better lifting tips: If this bothers your wrists, spread fingers out and balance on fingertips or use a fist, with knuckles down (not good if you wear rings).

machine press

Targets pectorals

A machine press is one of the safest places for a beginner to start chest work (since there's no worry about balancing free weights) and a good place for experienced lifters to push more weight. Adjust the seat height so that the handles are below the shoulder joints (otherwise you work too much shoulder). Keep feet flat on the floor, abs and lower back slightly contracted to help maintain spinal integrity.

Press arms forward so they're straight but not locked. Slowly bend arms and repeat.

Caveats: Avoid collapsing your chest, throwing shoulders forward, and locking the elbows.

Better lifting tips: Many machines let you vary your grip. The palm-down grip is more challenging for both chest and shoulders. Rotate palms toward each other if you feel any shoulder pain.

flyes

Targets pectorals and front deltoids

Whether you use dumbbells, a machine, cables, or water resistance, work with elbows fixed in a slightly bent position. Left and right arms open to 9 and 3 o'clock positions. As you bring arms together, remember to keep shoulders down and back, and chest lifted.

Caveats: Be careful not to let the weights pull shoulders back beyond the prescribed range of motion. This could cause injury.

Better lifting tips: Avoid banging dumbbells together at the top of this motion. Once weights move beyond 12 o'clock, they fall together with the aid of gravity and momentum. Be sure to stop the weights as arms point to the ceiling, about 12 inches apart, for perfect, strict form.

free weight press

Targets center pectorals, front delts, and triceps

Whether you use a bar or dumbbells, free weights take some getting used to at first, since you provide the stability. Be sure to have someone spot you for your first few times out (and any time you're lifting a challenging weight).

If you're using a bar, have someone help you unrack it. Hold it for a few seconds to feel steady and confident before you lower. If using dumbbells, tuck the weights close to your torso and roll back onto the bench. As you lie down, use the momentum to hoist weights in the air. Your first move with a free weight should always be a lowering, so you don't injure your shoulder joints. Always maintain a neutral spine, especially as you progress into the exercise. Keep your spine steady either with feet on the floor or heels on the bench. With free weights it's critical that you move the weights with slow, controlled motion.

If using a bar, don't bounce the bar off your chest.

If using dumbbells, holding weights with palms facing each other can be the most comfortable position for shoulders.

Caveats: Be careful not to "torque" the bar or do any out-of-control wobbling with dumbbells. Use as much control lowering as lifting.

Better lifting tips: If using a bar, hands should be slightly wider than shoulders. If using dumbbells, press weights up in an *A* shape, then lower so they rest just above the armpits.

compound moves vs. isolations

Compound exercises are complex, multilevel exercises that work more than one muscle group and joint at a time. Examples include squats, bench presses, and lat pull downs.

Isolation exercises primarily work one muscle group and joint at a time. Examples include leg extensions, dumbbell flyes, and lat pull overs.

Some people in the exercise industry have gotten into passionate debates about which is better. Actually, both are valuable and serve different purposes, so a balanced strength routine should contain both.

Compounds

Pros

- Most closely resemble real-life moves, like lifting heavy bags, pushing cars, or pulling big bags of leaves. Thus, they're sometimes called functional exercises.
- Work a bigger area of muscle mass at one time. For your time and effort, you get more results.
- Demand that you use your abdominal, lower back, and pelvic stabilizers to maintain good form.

Cons

- A chain is as strong as its weakest link. The main problem with compounds is the weak link. When you do a bench press for your chest muscles, your smaller muscles, the front deltoids and triceps, give out before your chest gets fully fatigued.
- Hard to perform if you lack torso stability.

Isolations

Pros

- Lets you isolate and fatigue a specific muscle group without being hindered by a weak link. All your work gets focused in the muscle you want to work.
- Useful for beginners or the out-of-shape who lack torso, muscle, and joint stability needed to perform compounds.

Cons

- Work less total muscle mass.

When to do which

Do compounds first when you want to lift more weight—with "fresh" muscles you can work with greater intensity. An example of this would be doing squats before leg curls and extensions, or bench presses before flyes. Seasoned lifters often start a new week's workout with compounds, since they've taken rest and have more energy.

Do isolations first to prefatigue big muscle groups. An example of this would be doing hip extensions, hamstring curls, and leg extensions before squats, or flyes before bench presses so that your tired muscles need less weight to work hard.

Always work big muscle groups first (e.g., the back before biceps) so you don't unnecessarily fatigue the "supporting" muscles before the "starring" muscles have a chance to perform as well as they can.

Muscles	Compounds	Isolations
LEGS	Squats	Hip extension (straight leg)
	Lunges	Leg extension
	Leg press	Hamstring curls
	Hack squat	Leg lifts (abduction)
	Step ups	Inner-thigh lifts (adduction)
BACK	Lat pull down	Pull over
	Seated row	Straight arm press down
CHEST	Bench press	Flyes
SHOULDERS	Overhead press	Lateral raise
	Upright row	Shrugs
BICEPS	Chin-ups, palms in	Barbell curls
TRICEPS	Close-grip bench press	Press downs

contractions

A muscle contraction is a miraculous thing. Lift a frying pan or pick up a two-year-old and you set in motion a beautifully choreographed microscopic event in your muscles. Every time you lift or lower a weight, your muscles push or pull in unison.

This odd behavior is caused by two little protein cells called actin and myosin that live deep inside muscle tissue. In order to make the muscles move, these cells bump heads, which then mesh together like matching puzzle pieces or gears. This generates friction, which allows the muscle fibers (called myofibrils) to move. The muscles then shorten, lengthen, or hold a stationary position. This doesn't happen just once. Even a single repetition causes hundreds of these motions.

Three types of contractions

If you thought strength training was just about lifting weights, read on. Lifting is only one-third of the total equation, which consists of weight lifting, lowering, and holding.

Concentric

This is the most obvious and popular type of contraction. Any time you lift a weight against gravity, your muscles shorten in a concentric contraction. Concentric contractions are sometimes called the positive side of a lift. Interestingly enough, muscles are weakest in concentric contraction.

Eccentric

This is the forgotten side of weight lifting, yet one of the most valuable and most underutilized forms of contraction. This is what happens when the muscle lengthens as you lower a weight with a little assistance from gravity (but hopefully, not too much).

We like eccentric contractions because using them ensures that muscles will get stronger faster. Eccentric and concentric contractions use the same muscles, but eccentrics fatigue those last fibers that the concentrics cannot. They also let you stretch safely with the weight and help you complete the set with more grace and control than if you dropped your weights on the floor.

Muscles are stronger in eccentric than they are in concentric contraction. Besides lowering weights against gravity, other eccentric contractions come from walking downhill or down a flight of stairs, cycling, walking, or running.

Isometric

This interesting form of contraction is basically a standoff between the actin and myosin. The result is no motion. Although no one goes anywhere, lots of energy is expended. Isometrics improve muscle strength, but their value is limited and should be used sparingly.

Bodybuilders use isometric contractions when they're posing in competition. Although it doesn't look hard, flexing can be exhausting. Isometrics also raise blood pressure. So they're not advised for people with hypertension.

Isometrics were made famous in the 1920s by Charles Atlas, the man who claimed he could turn "90-pound weaklings" into muscle-bound he-men with his mail-order course. (Of course, Charles Atlas built his muscles with free weights.) Isometrics were also peddled in the 1960s to a gullible female public with the Mark Eden Bust Developer. (Need we say that attempting to enlarge the breast tissue by squeezing your palms together is a hopeless task?) Isometrics complete the weight lifting, lowering, and holding triad.

How to get stronger safely and quickly

One of the most effective ways to overcome plateaus and push your strength into new territory is to incorporate negatives and holds.

Negatives: After you reach fatigue or muscle failure on your concentric contractions, your muscles can't lift, but they can lower and hold the weight. Here are several variations:

- Have someone help you lift the weight, then lower the weight slowly 3 to 5 times at the end of a regular set or do a set of negatives only.

- Try negative pull-ups. Drag a bench to a pull-up bar, jump up to the bar, then slowly lower yourself. Even if you've never been able to do a regular pull-up, after a few weeks, you'll probably be able to do at least one.

Negatives have gotten a bad rap. Many people believe they create monumental muscle soreness, especially for beginners. It's true that if beginners are too zealous at first, muscle soreness can be extreme and last for several days. But there's no proof that negatives alone are the culprit. Intense training beyond one's level is more likely at fault. Of course, as with all training, it's wise to work with smooth, controlled motion, and if something causes pain, stop.

Holds and peak contractions: Once you fail in eccentric contractions, your muscles still have about 20 percent more strength. Try holding the weight at any part of the motion for at least two seconds. By then your muscles will feel like jelly. This not only builds strength, it builds grit!

If you'd like a gentler approach to isometrics, simply pause for one second in peak contraction (when the muscles are at their hardest, roundest, most blood-engorged point at the top of your concentric contraction). Muscles are often weak here. This brings in additional muscle fibers and also provides a cautious "rest stop" between positives and negatives, which results in better muscle control.

curls

Analyzing every possible strength training exercise one by one can make you crazy. It's much simpler to understand the similarities among all exercises and then apply the general rules. This section, therefore, is the first of several (including **Flex and Extend, Flyes, Lunges, Presses, Pulls,** and **Squats**) that aim to reveal the connections and invisible geometry underlying all strengthening moves.

The major muscles that curl

- Biceps in both arms and legs (i.e., hamstrings)
- Abdominal muscles—but they're in a league of their own.

Motion explained: Curls are single-joint moves that cause muscles to swivel, like the pencil side of a compass, around a single fixed point (a fulcrum). Anytime you perform a curl, you're essentially drawing part of a circle in the air.

So you can easily see the relationship between arm and leg biceps (hamstring) curls, look at each of them done while standing (although this same range of motion applies to biceps exercises in all positions).

What curls have in common

Both begin with arms or feet pointed down to a 6 o'clock position (and legs at 3 o'clock). Both arms and leg (or both legs if prone) should lift at least to a 90-degree angle (9 o'clock), but preferably up another 45 degrees (10 o'clock) to complete a full range of motion with resistance. (Any higher and there's no longer any resistance placed on the muscle.)

To perform curls correctly so the full workload goes into biceps, move only the lower part of the limb (the forearm or shin) and hold the upper part steady.

To do an arm biceps curl properly, avoid moving the elbow either forward or back; doing so allows the shoulders to relieve some of the workload intended for the arms (this is cheating). Also avoid arching your lower back.

To do a leg biceps curl, keep the upper leg steady and avoid moving the knee forward or back. Doing so brings in the hip joint and allows the big, powerful gluteus and lower back muscles to relieve some of the work intended for the leg biceps. (This, too, is cheating.)

Both arm and leg biceps can assist in other moves besides curls, but the workload will be divided. For arm biceps and front delts, hold dumbbells perpendicular to the floor, palms up. Slide arms forward as if presenting a tray of food. For leg biceps and glutes, do standing hip extensions (see **Buttocks,** page 39).

At the top of the lift, both arm and leg biceps can be squeezed in peak contraction (see **Contractions,** page 51) and both arms and legs should be lowered completely so limbs straighten. Avoid hyperextending elbows or knees.

Hamstring curl

Abdominal curls—a special case

Abs are the other muscles that curl. But unlike the biceps muscles, which curl around one joint, these curl around a line of joints in the spine. Abdominals are also the only muscles in the body that can curl both ends toward each other (see **Abdominals,** page 5).

Upper abdominal curls: When you lie on the floor to do crunches, lift your head and shoulders only 30 to 45 degrees off the floor. If you lift higher than that, your stronger hip flexor muscles take over. Bend knees and hips while you do crunches at a 90-degree angle (rest calves on a bench) to subdue your hip flexors. Avoid pulling your head forward. Let your entire upper spine perform the curl, not your neck.

Don't do full sit-ups—they work hip flexors more than abs—and don't do crunches or full sit-ups with legs straight—this puts too much stress on your lower back.

Lower abdominal curls: When you lie on the floor to work your lower abs (actually it's the same rectus abdominis muscle), put your feet on a bench or pull your knees up toward your chest with feet pointing to the ceiling and knees bent. Lift the tailbone 2 to 4 inches, about 20 degrees, off the floor. Try to pull your tailbone toward your nose. Remember: This is a curl. Keep the motion small to focus the work in the abdominals and not the lower back.

Don't do straight-leg lifts and lowers. This is grueling on the lower back, does little to strengthen the abs, and mostly works hip flexors.

If you get ambitious try doing these upper and lower curls simultaneously. In other words, lift shoulders and tailbone for a complete abdominal curl.

Abdominal curl

cycle training
(periodization)

Cycle training is not indoor cycling (that's aerobic). It's a strength-training technique athletes use when training for a specific contest or competitive season. What attracts some people to it is the same thing that turns others off. It's a systematic, highly regimented training schedule meant to bring you to peak form at precisely the time you want. Whether it has value to someone who's training for fitness is a subject of debate.

An example of cycle training for a bodybuilder preparing for a contest might go something like this:

- 1 to 3 months, heavy weights, 6 to 8 reps, for strength
- 1 to 3 months, moderate weights, 8 to 12 reps, for muscle size
- 1 to 3 months, lighter weights, 12 to 15 reps, for muscle endurance
- 1 to 2 weeks active rest and begin cycle again

Someone training for a power-lifting contest might do this in reverse. (Please note: This is meant to serve as an example, not a recommendation.)

Cycles don't have to last a month; they can last a week. The change is good since it doesn't let you adapt to your workout and get stale. But cycle training doesn't always work, even for competitive athletes, who need to be in peak form for hugely varying amounts of time. Adapting to a rigid schedule also doesn't take into account different degrees of strength and endurance. So the regimen can be tough to maintain. It's also easy for seasoned pros to mistime their peak. Theoretically, then, cycle training is a good idea. Practically, however, it has some drawbacks.

Cycle training can be good psychologically because it helps you divide your workouts into manageable chunks of time, instead of feeling trapped forever in a life sentence of exercise. It can also help add variety and raise (and lower) the intensity of your workouts, so you can achieve more equal portions of strength, endurance, intensity, and rest.

This training method appeals most to people who like to keep accurate training diaries, train with a stopwatch (timing sets and rests), know how much weight they can press for a one-rep max, and maintain fairly consistent levels of energy.

Cycle training enables you to get stronger, increase muscle endurance, break through strength plateaus, and use more and different types of muscle fibers.

Cycle training for fitness

Cycle training doesn't only involve weight lifting. You can use cycle training as a form of cross training. Simply emphasize one aspect of your workout for one to four weeks and maintain the others at a lesser intensity.

The endurance or prep phase

- Emphasize cardio (longer workouts, shorter intense workouts, intervals)
- Do muscle endurance workouts (lighter weights, 12 to 15 reps)
- Do light stretches to maintain flexibility

The strength building or high-intensity phase

- Emphasize strength workouts (weights that cause muscle fatigue or failure after 8 to 12 reps, one set each, minimal rest between sets)
- Maintain moderate cardio workouts on rest days
- Keep up light stretches to maintain flexibility

The active rest phase

- Emphasize flexibility training with intensive yoga training (maintain strength by doing static poses)
- Do water exercise to maintain cardiovascular fitness and speed muscle recovery (and heal any unwelcome twinges you picked up along the way)

When you've completed all phases, repeat the entire cycle.

equipment

A lot of fuss is made about the superiority of free weights or various machines. But equipment doesn't make the workout or the physique, you do, with your form, intensity, consistency, and, to a certain extent, your genetics (the length of your limbs, muscles, and tendons). You could spend $2,000 a year on a fancy gym membership, use the most high-tech machines, hire a celebrity trainer, and have the genetic potential of Mr. or Ms. Olympia, but you'll get nothing out of it all if you don't use it properly. On the other hand, you could build weights out of rocks and branches, study weight-lifting technique from muscle magazines, start out shaped like an apple or twig, and build an impressive physique. The X factor is you.

That said, it still helps to know why to choose the various machines.

Free weights

Contrary to popular myth, free weights (barbells and dumbbells) don't build big muscles and machines don't just tone or define. Muscles don't know the difference between free weights and machines. All they understand is load, work, fatigue, and recovery. Stressing muscles is what makes them stronger.

Free weights got their reputation as being "muscle makers" because they've been the tool of choice since the late 1800s for circus "strong men" (and a handful of "strong women"), power lifters, Olympic lifters, and bodybuilders, and are now becoming popular with more people because they're so versatile, readily available, and inexpensive.

Advantages of free weights

- You lift against gravity for a concentric, or positive, contraction and resist gravity as you lower for an eccentric, or negative, contraction (see **Contractions**, page 51). Both contribute to overall strength.
- Dumbbells let you work each limb independently, so you don't favor your stronger side.
- Many of the exercises mimic real-life activities like lifting boxes, pushing cars out of the road, and such.

Disadvantages of free weights

- To use them properly, you have to be the machine and remember to keep your torso stable, go slow enough so you avoid using momentum, and get the benefit of negative contractions.
- In many exercises, you can't exercise a joint and its surrounding muscles through a full range of motion.
- You can stress joints if your range of motion is too big or moves too quick.
- You're almost totally committed to the up and down force of gravity. It's a bad idea to divert weights off that line because it's tough on joints.

- It's time consuming to change plates and safety collars.
- You might need a spotter to help with heavier sets.
- The biggest drawback of freeweights: In some parts of a motion, free weights put no resistance on muscles (a dead zone) while in other parts, they put too much. You might have heard that free weights supply "dynamic constant resistance." This needs translation. Although the force of the weight stays constant, the amount of force on the muscle changes due to the changing relationship with gravity. So you end up with lots of stress on the middle part of the muscle, where they are already stronger, and nothing or too much on the weaker ends.

3 Ways to Get More out of Free Weights

1. Change your relationship to gravity so that the weight will exert the majority of its force on a different part of the muscle group. (For example, change the angle of the bench for chest work.)
2. Avoid straying into unnecessary positions that offer no load on the muscles (like lifting a barbell up to a 12 o'clock position when doing biceps curls). However, some dead zones are unavoidable—you'll still have an almost-dead zone at the 6 to 7 o'clock position.
3. Alternate between free weights and machines.

Machines

To simply talk about "machines" is like saying, "let's talk about cars." There are too many types to mention them all here. Following are some of the most common.

Weight stack or selectorized machines

These are the easiest machines to operate. You pop a pin in a vertical weight stack, sit against a back support, and go (with good form, of course). Thus, most beginners start with these, although they work for everyone.

Most machines in use today owe at least some of their inspiration to the original Universal "multistation" machines (developed in the fifties) and Nautilus machines (developed for widespread use in the seventies). These machines revolutionized weight lifting by offering (at least theoretically) resistance through a full range of motion. (Some machines, however, still have dead zones.)

Nautilus machines took that idea a step farther. The Nautilus shell–shaped cam lightened the resistance at the beginning and ends of the motion, where muscles are weaker, matching a muscle's natural strength curve (this is called dynamic variable resistance). The theory behind this was to give more resistance through a longer range of motion, resulting in better overall muscle development. (To what degree this is actually true is a subject of debate.)

Universal and Nautilus machines are still popular in some gyms and still do the trick. But newer machines have gotten much more sophisticated, offer more varied movement choices, and feel smoother because chains have been replaced with rubber belts. Different machines also offer individual degrees of variable resistance.

Whatever machine you use, make it fit:

- Adjust the seat to make sure you're sitting in the right place—knees should be bent at 90-degree angles and feet should touch the floor.
- On chest presses and pec decks, make sure the handles are just below your shoulder joints (so you can put more load into the chest and less in the shoulders).
- On shoulder press machines, be sure your back is stable as you press overhead; hold on to the inner handles (palms facing each other) if the other handles cause shoulder pain.
- On leg extension and leg curl machines, put the ankle pad directly on the ankle (not on the heel, instep, or up your shin).
- If a seat angle puts you in an uncomfortable position, insert a wedge or pad under your lower back (most gyms have a few of these pads floating around).

Plate-loading machines

Hack squats, leg presses, and some of the most innovative new machines, made by companies like Hammer Strength and Cybex, are "free-weight machines" that combine the best of both. Plate-loading machines dictate your path of motion and allow you to work in angles, which is impossible with free weights. But, as with free weights, you have to control the lift and lower, so the feel is very similar to that of free weights. On the old standard machines, like the leg press, the resistance is constant. Like the Nautilus machines, the resistance is variable on the Hammer Strength and Cybex machines (lighter at the beginning

and end of the motion). (In fact, Hammer Strength machines were created by Gary Jones, the son of Nautilus creator Arthur Jones.) They also let you work each limb independently with "independent movement arms," and offer innovative new angles on old standard exercises.

Cables

Although technically "weight-stack machines," cable equipment deserves a description of its own. Cable machines have come a long way from the heavy, nonadjustable Universal machine overhead and floor cables. The new machines have a smooth feel, with cables coated in plastic or rubber. Some also let you slide the pulleys up or down a pole so you can adjust exactly where you want the resistance to come *from*. Be mindful that if you go to a different gym, 10 pounds on one machine can feel like 30 on another. More pulleys make the weight feel lighter.

A cable station is the most versatile piece of equipment in the gym. All you do is change handles or ankle cuffs and you can work almost every major muscle group.

Like machines, the cables allow you to work in positions off the up and down gravity line and put constant tension on the muscles. But like free weights, you have to be careful to avoid dead zones and you have to work to hold yourself up, especially against the pull of the cable (beginners, take note).

You can work cables standing, seated, kneeling on a bench, or lying on the floor, one or two arms at a time, one leg at a time, and occasionally two.

Hydraulic machines

Keiser is the most widespread manufacturer of these "air pressure machines," popular in some high-end clubs and also sports rehab centers.

The main plus to pneumatics is the smooth feel of the motion. They're also easy on joints and easy to adjust in mid-rep with the twist of a dial. This makes them a great choice for the deconditioned, the elderly, or for people undergoing rehabilitation.

The main drawback is they offer no resistance in the eccentric (negative) part of the lift. Since eccentric contractions contribute greatly to overall strength gains, working on concentric-only equipment can impede progress after a while. (Some home hydraulic machines offer "two-way positive resistance," meaning concentric contractions on the way up and down. We're not sure how this works. Ask before you use or buy.)

Another drawback to air equipment is the dial. Theoretically, you can change pressure in a flash. But when you're not used to it, you can send your resistance from 100 pounds of pressure to nothing with an overzealous flick of the wrist. The little dials can also be hard to read.

A low-budget home gym

If you want to keep it low budget, low tech, and easy to store, consider buying

- a rack of dumbbells (2, 5, 8, 10, 12, 15, 20, 25 pounds)
- an unloaded barbell, a set of plates, and safety collars
- a bench that adjusts from flat to incline
- adjustable ankle weights (that let you add or subtract little weights)
- a big ball for stretching and working ab and lower back stabilizers

- resistance bands
- a pole for balance (Some resistance bands wrap around poles for a unique band and barbell workout.)
- a floor or "sticky" mat for stretching
- some good books and videos on strength training
- cardio equipment (bike, stair machine, etc.) if you don't get your cardio activity elsewhere

A deluxe home gym

You can go moderate to high budget here. If you buy a multistation (which offers flyes, pull downs, leg extensions, curls, etc.), you usually get what you pay for. So beware the incredible bargain. Test every station to make sure

- it's stable (it shouldn't wobble)
- it provides an adequate range of motion for each exercise
- the seats are adjustable and fit you properly (Also, check for quality seat construction. Cheap ones are glued and stapled.)
- the pulleys are no smaller than 4 inches in diameter
- the cables feel smooth (look for cables coated in rubber or plastic)
- the plates and other moving parts don't wobble as you lift
- the handles and attachments are sturdy
- you can change handles (very important)
- the stress points (moving parts, pivots, levers, etc.) land on rubber cushioning
- the weight stack is enclosed in a casing (a nice safety feature)
- it will fit in your floor space and ceiling height
- it's easy to put together

failure

In strength training, the greatest measure of success is how often, how willingly, and how elegantly you fail. Failure is defined as the moment when your muscles absolutely cannot perform another rep. This is not the same thing as when your mind says, "Stop! I don't want to do this anymore." True muscle failure usually happens several reps after that. Of course, the hard part is persisting after your mind has spoken, and ensuring that the muscles "fail with integrity."

Failure is intense, and most personal trainers don't recommend it for beginning weight lifters. It takes some time (consistent training for one to three months) to build an initial base of strength, mental focus, and tolerance for the burning sensation of lactic acid.

But to make gains, even beginners eventually need to confront failure and what it takes to get there. Without pushing at least some sets to failure, you won't get the benefits of a greater percentage of lean body mass, which typically also inspires a drop in body fat, stronger muscles, connective tissues, and bones, and better functional ability.

Failure definitely has a bad reputation. People avoid it in the weight room because they're afraid they'll hurt something in those last, most difficult reps, and because they don't like the pain. But the last reps of a set (when you're doing an average of 8 to 12 reps) are the safest and most valuable.

Here's why:

- In the first reps, your muscles can produce a good amount of force. Because of this, you can push too hard and too fast. This gives your first reps the highest risk of injury.

- With each rep, your fatigue accumulates and you exhaust more muscle fibers, making it harder to produce enough force to hurt yourself. But exhausting the greatest number of fibers is what produces the greatest gains in strength.

- As for the pain, it subsides at the end of the set. Your tolerance increases with time and you even begin to change your perception of it. It's no longer pain but "work," "a pump," "your body's feedback." As long as the pain is in the muscles and not in the joints, you're OK. (When it's in the joints, you need to stop that exercise, change your range of motion and/or your angle, lighten your weights, or do a completely different exercise.)

- Training to failure (or at least extreme fatigue) with a moderate number of reps is actually very safe and effective. In fact, it's the best way to get the most out of your training time.

Contrary to popular myth, explosive, heavy lifts with one rep and a maximum amount of weight do not build strength. (Such lifts can cause skeletal injury, raise blood pressure, require tremendous training to do well, and typically don't fatigue enough muscle fibers to cause noticeable gains in muscle strength or size.) On the other hand, numerous repetitions with light weights that don't inspire failure or even much fatigue do not produce the results most people want either. All those "toning" workouts with little 2-pound dumbbells for 16 or more mediocre reps are a waste of time. Even people with no aspirations to look stronger or more defined, who simply weight train for wellness and general fitness, need to work to failure.

The only people who shouldn't go to failure are the following:

teenagers (Intense training for adolescents is not recommended as it can stunt bone growth.)

the elderly (Failure might put too much stress on untrained muscles, cause fractures in fragile bones, and raise blood pressure. However, elderly people who've trained for years might work to failure with no problem.)

pregnant women (Most pregnant women should focus on maintaining fitness or decreasing intensity throughout a pregnancy.)

people overcoming injuries or illness (It's always a good idea to rehab with low intensity and gradually rebuild strength.)

Are Shorter, Less-Frequent Workouts Efficient?

If you work every set to failure, then you can't do a lot of sets. It's simple economics. The greater your intensity, the shorter your workout, especially if you don't rest between sets. Doing one set to failure also eliminates the need to do multiple sets of the same exercise. You can make sufficient contact with one set (see **Sets and Reps,** page 119). You've already learned that failure is effective. But it's also very efficient. It makes your workouts shorter and less frequent. You don't need to spend as much time strength training, but the time you spend should be totally focused.

If you work to failure, you'll need to take slightly longer rests between workouts. If you train your whole body in one workout, one set to failure, you only need two weight workouts a week. (You may find that your muscles stay sore a little longer when you train with this level of intensity. If a muscle is still sore, it's not yet ready for retraining. Let it heal.)

Plenty of research shows that you can get the same, if not much better, results doing one set per exercise to failure (because you train more muscle fibers) than 2 to 4 sets but not to failure.

The hardest part, for many people, is believing that less can be more.

A successful fail

So what does it take to fail with integrity? First, understand that muscle failure comes in two flavors:

- Concentric muscle failure, which is when you can't lift the weight another rep
- Eccentric muscle failure, which is when you can't lower the weight another rep (see **Contractions,** page 51)

Here's a formula for successful failing that utilizes both:

- Lift the weight slowly with good form until you can't lift it anymore (concentric failure). Use a weight that makes you fail at 8 to 12 reps for upper body, 15 to 20 for legs.
- Then add 3 to 5 more repetitions, but of lowering the weight only (eccentric failure). There are two ways to do this: either work with a partner and have him or her assist on the lifts, while you simply lower the weight; or if you're alone, decrease the weight by about 10 percent and do 3 to 5 more reps, focusing on the negatives (lowering the weight). Take 4 to 8 seconds with each negative. If you really want to fry your muscles, decrease the weight 2 or 3 times and do 3 to 5 reps with each (called a drop set).

If you can't fail, fatigue

Failing is the best way to ensure that you're training with enough intensity. But if failure is too much, then you should at least be working to fatigue—the point where your muscles twitch and feel like they're steaming, but you still have a rep or two left inside you. If you have no conditions that preclude working to failure, you should aim, at least some of the time, to succeed by failing.

flex and extend

If someone asked you to flex your biceps, you'd know what to do, right? You'd bend your elbow at a 90-degree angle, roll up your sleeve, and show off your impressive peak. People think flexing is about simply displaying or contracting muscles. But it's more than that. Flexing is technically about joints. You're in "flexion" anytime you bend a joint so that the angle between two bones decreases. In other words, when you bent your arm to show off your biceps, you reduced your elbow angle from 180 to 90 degrees.

If, on the other hand, someone asked you to flex your triceps, would you know what to do? You'd straighten or extend your arm, because you'd have to go into this straight position to show off your triceps. To flex your triceps (and quads) you have to extend your limbs. If this makes your head swim, don't worry. The main thing you need to know is that flexing and extending are opposites. As you lengthen your limbs, you enlarge the angle between two bones, so the angle changes from, say, 90 to 180 degrees.

Flexing and extending are like Siamese twins. You can't have one without the other, because if you can flex a joint you can also extend it. But typically, when you flex your joints against resistance, you work one muscle group (for example, the biceps), and when you extend, you work the muscle group on the other side (the triceps).

Some examples of opposing muscle groups that flex and extend are:

- Biceps flex/triceps extend
- Hamstrings flex/quads extend
- Abs flex/erector muscles extend
- Hip flexors (psoas, rectus femoris, sartorius) flex/gluteus maximus extends
- Pecs flex/lats extend (although we usually speak of pecs "pressing" and lats "pulling")

Several small muscle groups (those around wrists, neck, ankles, fingers) also flex and extend. And just to confuse you further, shoulders can both flex (with pecs) and extend, as when you raise your arms overhead or lower them by your side. As you can see, unlike curls or flyes where the rules are consistent, the rules for flexing and extending vary because the mechanics and range of motion for each joint are different, so we won't go into detail about the rules for both motions. However, since the terms *flex* and *extend* are commonly used (as in leg extensions, hip flexors, etc.), it helps to know what they describe.

Rules of the road for all flexes

- To flex with integrity, move only the main joint(s). Keep all other joints still.
- Pause in peak contraction and squeeze contracted muscles.

Major Muscles That Flex

Muscle	Sample Exercise
Arm biceps	Biceps curls
Hamstrings (see **Curls,** page 53)	Hamstring curl
Hip (flexors—rectus femoris, psoas)	Walking forward
Shoulder (especially anterior delts)	Front raises
Abdominals (rectus abdominis)	Ab crunches

Rules of the road for all extensions

- Never lock the joints, especially when weight hangs off delicate joints (as in leg extensions).

Major Muscles That Extend

Muscle	Sample Exercise
Triceps	Triceps extensions
Quads	Seated leg extensions
Hips and thighs	Press backs
Shoulder	Dumbbell press
Back (erector spinae)	Hyperextension

flyes

Flyes have fallen out of favor recently. Advocates of the superiority of compound exercises over isolations have, in essence, tried to turn strength workouts into "no flye zones."

The reason people "swat at flyes" is due to the fact that this exercise uses just one joint and a small amount of muscle mass, while a compound move uses many joints and works a bigger muscular area (see **Compound Moves vs. Isolations,** page 49). People hold compounds in great esteem because they theoretically give you greater returns for your efforts.

But what makes a flye unpopular is also what makes it good. In a multijoint move, like a bench press, you have a weak link. Your wrists or triceps give out before the chest gets fully fatigued. With a flye, there's no triceps involvement at all. It's pure chest (and front delt). You address a smaller amount of muscle mass and therefore focus the work where you want it. Flyes, like all isolation exercises, offer the best results mixed with compound moves.

Major muscles that flye

You probably already know about chest flyes. But there are also flyes for all three heads of the delts, which are more commonly known as the front raise—for front delts, the lateral raise—for middle delts, and reverse flyes—for rear delts. (See **Shoulders,** page 123.) All four of these exercises follow the same flye rules.

Rules of the road for basic flyes

- Flyes rotate around shoulders.
- Don't bend your elbow as you move the arm; fix it in a slightly bent position.
- Keep your wrists straight—flopping them back and forth diverts work out of the main muscles.
- Keep your shoulders down and back (exaggerate good posture) as you lift the arms—shrugging involves the trapezius, throws off alignment, and diverts work out of the main muscles.
- Each of the four basic flyes follows a 90-degree range of motion (each arm draws one-quarter of a circle) when you use dumbbells (and with some machines). Don't exceed that angle by more than an inch or two.
- For chest flyes, avoid taking elbows behind the torso—it can stress shoulders.
- For lateral raises, avoid lifting arms above shoulders—it can impinge shoulder joints (which is very painful).
- Also for lateral raises, avoid locking elbows as you raise arms—it stresses elbow tendons and diverts work out of the shoulder.
- For reverse flyes for rear delts, avoid bending elbows or twisting torso, especially when you work one side at a time.

When you use cables, you can increase your range of motion by approximately 20 degrees and keep resistance on the muscles throughout.

- For chest flyes (on high cables), try crossing cables at the wrist as you end each rep.
- For lateral raises (holding low cables), begin with wrists crossed.
- Reverse flyes (holding high cables), are a little tricky to get into: Grab the right cable in left hand, left in right, and lie faceup on a bench. Start with wrists crossed then open.

No Flye Zone

Lots of people, especially in fitness classes, do chest flyes with resistance bands (you put the band behind your back and pull the ends together so hands touch or cross). If you can flex your pecs, then you might think this exercise has merit, but in fact you get the same results without the band.

However, it doesn't do much good since the band doesn't get significantly longer as arms cross, so there's no increased resistance. When it comes to chest work with bands, choose presses over flyes because, with presses, the bands actually stretch.

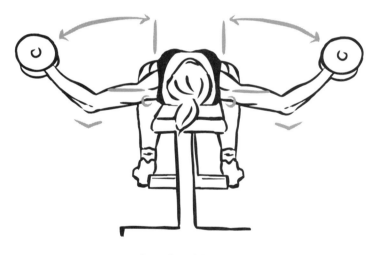

Chest dumbbell flye

gear

You've joined a gym. You're excited about the prospect of pumping iron. But now you must ask yourself the all-important question: What should I wear? Look around and you'll see as many different answers to this question as there are people. The uniform of choice for most female beginners is the big T-shirt over tights—an outfit that's designed to conceal every bulge.

But a big T-shirt over tights doesn't let you see your spine. Since keeping your torso stable is one of the most important things to remember while learning proper form (see **Stabilization,** page 133), you should wear something that more closely hugs the body, even if it's a smaller T-shirt, so you can watch your form.

Here are some suggestions for appropriate gym wear that flatters every woman's body, regardless of shape, size, and age:

- Long black tights pulled up over a leotard. (If you don't like your rear view, tie a sweatshirt around your waist. Take it off when it gets in your way.)
- Jazz pants, a leotard, and an optional tunic
- Stretchy, baggy pants and a tank top
- A support bra
- Dark colors that give a more flattering silhouette

Shoes

In many sports, the shoe question is dizzying. When you buy walking shoes, for instance, the salesperson may ask if you walk on hills, dirt, streets, or in the mall. Whatever your activity and whatever your surface, there's an overwhelming variety of shoes to choose from. Your objective should be to find the one that feels comfortable right away and gives you the support, flexibility, and shock absorption you need for your activity of choice.

With weight lifting, however, most people grab whatever other athletic shoes they have in the closet. Although shoe companies offer weight-lifting shoes, their idea of what people need has varied from shoes that offer lots of shock absorption and ankle support yet zero flexibility in the arch, to shoes that offer tremendous arch flexibility (good for calf raises) and some ankle support but no protection against shock.

In truth, you don't need shock-absorbing shoes since you won't be jumping up and down with barbells. But you may need ankle support for leg and standing exercises and a flexible arch when you do calf exercises. If your other shoes offer what you need, then you don't need a separate shoe especially for weight lifting.

But we'll let you in on a secret. There are still many gym veterans who train in socks, jazz oxfords, martial arts slippers, water walking shoes, and running sandals. Early pictures of Arnold Schwarzenegger show him wearing flip-flops! These days, such a thing is considered a faux pas (especially for a notable athlete—there are endorsements to be had, after all!). Plus, gym owners don't want to be sued if you drop a weight on your toe.

Belts, gloves, wraps, and straps

Back in the early days of grunt gyms, almost every serious weight lifter carried around a gym bag with all sorts of paraphernalia. Lifting belts, gloves, knee wraps, wrist straps, and rosin were just the basics. These days, lifters aren't so accessory laden. Perhaps simplicity has begun to rule in the weight room as well. But let's revisit these former must-haves to see what still has merit and what doesn't:

Belts: Of all weight-lifting gizmos, belts once ranked highest on the cool scale. If you were ultra cool, your belt was made of leather, had a big thick buckle, and your name or initials burned onto the back.

The truth is, a belt offers only a modicum of support for the lower back, and only because it increases intra-abdominal pressure, not because it braces back muscles. It also offers no support when you lie on your back. It can, however, provide some aid for heavy overhead presses, squats, and dead lifts. But few people do these exercises, and if they do, they should lift without the belt to develop the supporting muscles of the lower back and abdominals. Rule of thumb: If you need the belt, you're probably lifting too much.

Gloves: Like belts, gloves aren't as common as they used to be (when people went through them like Gatorade). Gloves, however, do prevent calluses. Fancier gloves also offer built-in wrist wraps. But more and more people seem to enjoy the feel of cool iron on their naked hands.

Wrist straps: There are two types of wrist straps: those with wrist support and those with grip support (with a little "tail" that you wrap around handles, bars, and dumbbells). Wrist bands for generally weak wrists help when you're overcoming an injury. But relying on them can make wrists weaker. Use sparingly.

Wrist straps that offer grip support are a great invention, especially useful when doing back exercises or anytime your grip may give out before your working muscles. It takes a little clever maneuvering to figure out how to use them. Basically, you put your hands through the loops so the little tail is inside your palm. Then you thread the tail around a bar, tug the tail tight, and hold it in place with your whole hand. (Have a gym veteran show you how.) Although these aren't very common, wrist straps can be very helpful.

Knee wraps: If you really need knee wraps, you probably have no business lifting that much weight. It's better to go lighter with strict form and spare your precious knees.

A final word on accessories: For all the time it takes to belt up, put on your gloves, wrap up your wrists, tighten your grip supports, wrap your knees, and then take them all off again between sets (to let your blood flow), you could have done another one or two sets!

gyms

Whether you love them, hate them, or just tolerate them, if you want to get in shape, sooner or later you have to decide if you're going to join a gym, what you will or won't pay for the privilege, and whether or not you'll really go.

Seventy-five percent of all people who belong to gyms and health clubs don't even show up most of the time. Every year, it's the same story. Gyms are deluged in January with customers desperate to work off the holiday pounds. By April, the gyms empty out as people are lured by springtime, the great outdoors, and summer vacation. A second wave of enthusiasm rises after Labor Day but wanes by Thanksgiving, making the average gym membership last about three months.

You don't have to go to a gym to get in shape. Nor do you have to love gyms to join one. But if you belong to one, you might as well go. If you're gym shopping, the most important thing to look for is a gym you'll actually use. All other perks are irrelevant if you won't go. Look for one that's close to your home or office.

Paying for it

- Ask for a week's free pass so you can be sure you like it before you sign up.
- Know your personality and find a club to match it. Are you a neat freak? Do you like

to be pampered? Is your idea of good service a manicure in the women's lounge? If so, then be prepared to pay for this sort of club, usually not called a gym. If you just want to hurl iron, you can pay much less.

- Even if you're already sold on one club, shop around so you know the competition's prices and policies. This is a powerful bargaining tool. Many gym salespeople work on quotas and knock down prices (sometimes without the owners' knowledge) to get you to sign up. Of course, salespeople have been fired for just this kind of deal-making. However, the main thing is for you to know you have some leeway in negotiations.
- Find out if you can get a family discount if you join with a spouse, a buddy discount if you join with a friend, or a corporate discount if you join with a group.
- If you can use the club between 11 A.M. and 4 P.M. you might qualify for a non-prime-time discount.
- Some gyms offer discounts to seniors and teens, although many clubs don't allow children under sixteen to use the weights.
- Beware of salespeople who make you sign up immediately, like it's the last day on earth. If they push you, be prepared to get up and walk, and mean it. This tactic also works when negotiating the price of a car. If the deal isn't there tomorrow, it's no deal.

- Never buy a long-term membership. Gyms have a way of closing overnight and you have no guarantee you'll be there in five years either.

- Many gyms and clubs like to do electronic fund transfers so they're assured they'll get their money. In other words, once you give them a voided check, they'll pull your membership dues out of your bank account every month until you cancel. (We've heard a lot of stories of people who quit a gym but failed to check their bank statements. They didn't realize until much later that they'd paid for several months in membership. By that time, it was too late to rectify the situation. In such a case, it's the member, not the gym, who's at fault.)

- Ask about the cancellation policy. Some gyms won't let you go easily, especially if you want to join another gym, and may drag out your paperwork for at least a month while billing you in full. Find out how much time it takes to terminate your membership.

- If you're going to be away for several weeks or months, most gyms will let you freeze your membership for a small fee (about $10 to $20).

- Find out if they have "sister" gyms in any other parts of the area or country that you can use on your travels.

- Many gyms let you take in one to five guests free per month or year. Don't always assume your visiting relatives have to pay a guest fee. Ask about this policy.

Consider all the costs of your gym membership, not just your monthly dues. Find out if you have to pay extra for:

- Initiation fee: This is a polite term in gym-speak for "putting more money in our pockets for no good reason." Many gyms run specials, making a big deal out of waiving the initiation fee, like they're doing you a big favor. Some who don't run specials will also waive it if you persist. Don't get suckered in by this tactic.

- Parking, child care, training sessions, nutritional counseling, aerobics classes, and "specialty" classes like indoor cycling classes or Tai Chi.

Scouting the floor

If you're still shopping, ask about the equipment. Here are two questions that make you sound savvy:

"What types of equipment do you have?" If they say something like "Hammer Strength, Cybex, BodyMasters, Icarian, Med-X, Nautilus" and your head spins, look impressed anyway. Having a variety of equipment shows that chances are good a person who knows the business picked the equipment piece by piece (a good thing). If they say, "Well, we only have the MusclePump line because it's the best on the market," it means they probably got the whole lot at a discount and it may not be good.

"How many chest press machines do you have?" If they say "one," you'll probably be waiting in

line to use it. If they have several, it shows they have space, money, and are trying to accommodate many members and preferences.

If your membership comes with a free training session, take it. Use the time to get acclimated, learn how to adjust seats and straps, and so on. If a staff trainer suggests a workout to get you started, do not think that this will be your workout for the rest of your life. Some enlightened gyms have numbered the equipment so you don't have to know the difference between a pec deck and a pull over. Figure out your best training time, not just for your schedule but for your age, taste, and personality:

Early mornings before 8, gyms are full of hardworking regulars. You've got to be serious to roll out of bed, glug coffee or Carbo Force, jump into your gym clothes, and go bench press on a cold, gray morning. It's too early for makeup, chitchat, and loud rock and roll.

Late mornings between 8 and 11 are very civilized. You'll find a lot of moms and part-time and self-employed people. One good thing about mornings: You're more likely to stick to your schedule and then you don't have to think about it for the rest of the day.

Lunch times in gyms are fairly quiet. This is a good time if you like a peaceful, although somewhat sleepy atmosphere. Gyms in business districts can be very busy between noon and 2 P.M., however.

After work is a good time if you like spandex and buff, watching glistening young bodies on parade, and a lively social scene. But it can be very tough to actually get onto a machine.

Don't Sweat on the Bench and Other Weight Room Etiquette

PLAY NICELY: Don't bang your weights, show off with how much you can lift, grunt, have loud conversations everyone can hear, sing out loud to a song on your Walkman, scowl at the front-desk people if they're not serving you fast enough, or scowl at anyone else for that matter.

SHARE: If it's busy and people are lined up to use a machine, don't pick this time to do 35 reps in super slo-mo. Tell anyone who's waiting how much time you've got left. If you're doing more than one set, ask if they'd like to work in. If you're the one who's waiting, ask, after they've finished a set, if you can work in. (Don't ever ask someone a question mid-set.) If it looks like they'll be on for a while, or it's awkward to work in because it means changing plates, don't just stand there. Do something. Stretch, hit the floor for a set of abs, or go to another machine and come back.

CLEAN UP AFTER YOURSELF: If you sweat on a bench, wipe it off. Ditto for sneezing.

PUT AWAY YOUR TOYS: Rerack your weights. And don't put 5-pound dumbbells where the 30s are supposed to go. Unload your plates. If you drag a bench across the room, drag it back.

hips and thighs

abductors, adductors, quadriceps, and hamstrings

Few people really think of thighs as having four sides, but they do: front, back, inside, and out. Most thigh muscles also cross the hip joint and originate in the pelvis. Therefore, muscles of the hip and thigh often work in tandem. For instance, when you do squats or pliés, especially with thighs slightly rotated outward, the quadriceps muscles and glutes are the main movers, but the inner thighs also work. When you do hip extensions (leg presses behind you) with a bent knee, glutes are the main movers but hamstrings also work.

That said, take a look at **Buttocks** (see page 39) for more hip and thigh exercises. The following exercises isolate the four sides of the hip muscles into specific groups. These important moves strengthen the muscles responsible for maintaining balance, isolate muscles around the hip joint, and provide additional tone to the thighs.

Abductors

The abductor or tensor fascia latae is the little muscle on the outside of the hip. When it's strong, it lets us do lunges without wobbling and prevents us from toppling over when we walk.

Adductors

The adductor magnus, adductor brevis, or adductor longus refers to the muscles in the inner thighs.

Quadriceps

The rectus femoris, vastus medialis, vastus intermedialis, vastus intermedius, or vastus laterali all refer to the large muscles on the front of the thigh.

Hamstrings

Known in Latin as the biceps femoris, semitendinosus, or semimembranosus, the hamstrings run along the back of the thighs.

leg raises

Targets abductors

Back in the early days of aerobics, floor work used to consist of what seemed like hundreds of leg lifts (leg lifts from hell) to get us to "feel the burn" and trim our thighs. Although we felt the burn, this move did nothing to trim the thighs. It's not a useless exercise, however. What it does work is the abductor on the outside of the hip. This is a pelvic stabilizer.

The best way to do this old standby is on an incline bench, with head at the high end, so the muscle in question can go through a functionally full range of motion. Or lie on a flat bench with hips at the edge so the top leg can hang down. Rest bottom knee on bench or the floor and keep it bent at a 45-degree angle for balance. Lift top leg from 8 to 10 o'clock. If you rotate the toe of the top leg down to the floor, you'll add more work for the gluteus medius and minimus (other abductors) in the hip.

Caveat: Be careful not to pull your top hip back (bad alignment) or turn the leg out as you lift (takes work out of the tensor fascia).

Better lifting tips: Hold yourself up with abdominal strength. Keep neck in line with your spine.

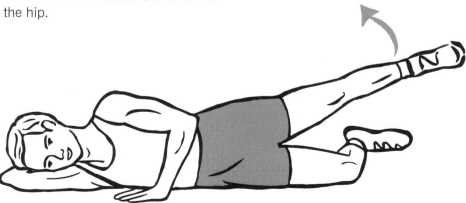

inner-thigh leg lifts

Targets adductors

This is another old standby that can be improved upon. Lie on your incline bench as above or, if on a flat bench, allow the bottom leg to hang down. Rest the top knee on the bench. (You won't have a huge range of motion here.) Lift the bottom leg from approximately 8 to 10 o'clock.

Caveats: If you can't lift the leg higher than 9 o'clock, don't force it up. Build your strength gradually over time.

Better lifting tips: Bend the knee of your working leg to make this easier. Straighten the leg to make this more challenging.

inner-thigh machine

Targets adductors

Most gyms have some sort of inner-thigh machine. To get the most out of it, sit upright in the seat instead of leaning back. If the seat isn't adjustable, put a pad or wedge behind your lower back and hold yourself upright with abdominal strength. Start out with lighter weight and a smaller range of motion than you're used to. Sitting upright is much harder to do but better isolates inner thighs.

Caveats: Beware of slumping your shoulders forward and rounding your lower back.

Better lifting tips: If you're very flexible and want to make this super strict, lean forward slightly (keeping spine in neutral). Lift chest and reach it forward.

leg extensions

Targets quadriceps

Contrary to popular belief, leg extensions don't give you big thighs. They give you stronger legs, stronger knees, and better overall shape (and if your thighs get too large for your liking, use lighter weight and slower, stricter form). Make sure you adjust the seat so the bend in your knee is just beyond the chair and the ankle pads rest on ankles (not shins or instep). Extend feet from a 6 to a 9 o'clock position. Hold for a second or two and slowly lower. If you don't have access to this machine, you can do this, one leg at a time, wearing ankle weights or elastic resistance tied around the ankles (and secured under your other heel), sitting upright in a chair.

Caveats: Don't combine heavy weight, fast motion, and a shortened range of motion.

Better lifting tips: Anchor hips down in the seat, extend legs fully without locking knees, and lower feet all the way under your seat between reps (easier on the knee joint).

hamstring curls

Targets hamstrings

Lie facedown on the hamstring machine, with your hip bones just above the angle on the pad (if you have an old-fashioned flat machine, place a rolled up sweatshirt under your hips). Make sure you adjust the ankle pad (if it adjusts), so it rests on the back of your ankles, not shins or heels. Most machines have your feet lifting from a 4 to a 12 o'clock position.

Caveats: Avoid lifting your knees off the bench, which diverts the work into your lower back.

Better lifting tips: Keep the back of your neck long and in line with your spine. Avoid squeezing the handles too hard.

injuries

As easy as it is to avoid injuries when strength training, it's also easy to overdo it and hurt something, especially when you're just starting out. But as you clock more time and get stronger, your risk of injury should diminish. Otherwise you're doing something wrong. Keep in mind that little twinges and aches are normal. They're also nothing compared to the pains you'd suffer if you never lifted weights.

The following are the most common injuries you can earn in the weight room. (See also **Injuries** in the Cardiovascular Training section, page 194.)

The three most common weight room injuries

Shoulders: rotator cuffs

The rotators are four little muscles that stabilize the shoulder joint. They're especially vulnerable when shoulders are externally rotated, like when you do a tennis serve or bench press. When these muscles get swollen, impingement syndrome results, which makes it very painful to lift your arm out to the side because the rotators and the bursas (little sacs of fluid that cushion joints) get compressed by the shoulder bones.

If you've got this injury: Avoid any motions that cause further pain. You'll keep reinjuring this area and you've got to let it heal. This doesn't mean you have to stop training. But you may

need to change your routine. Add the exercise for external rotation listed under **Shoulders,** page 123. Also avoid the following exercises:

Bench presses, especially with heavy weight. Don't take the bar, dumbbells, machine handles, and so on to your chest. Bring handles or weights to only about 4 inches in front of the chest bone. If this shortened range of motion still causes pain, avoid this exercise until pain has subsided.

Military presses with a bar behind the neck. Behind the neck presses are rotator cuff suicide. Anytime you're that externally rotated and pressing substantial weight, you're asking for trouble. Instead, bring the bar in front of your face, to the top of the chest, and then press.

Lat pull downs behind the head. Although not as deadly as the military press, since you're pulling instead of pressing weight, this can still hurt. Pull the bar to your chest instead.

Lateral raises for shoulders, taking arms above shoulders. End with arms parallel to the floor. Be sure to keep shoulders down as you lift and avoid rotating the weights at the top of the lift, as if you were pouring out two glasses of water. This adds internal rotation, which is also painful.

Upright rows to the chin. This is another uncomfortable position that adds internal rotation. Try lifting the bar only to the chest or avoid uprights altogether.

Knee: pain in the kneecap

Although there are several severe knee disorders, a dull, sharp, or radiating pain in the patella, or kneecap, is the most common (and can be the easiest to fix). The most common cause of this pain is tight hamstrings and calves plus weak quadriceps—very common in runners, because running strengthens muscles in the back of the leg. Quads are supposed to absorb shock but if they're weak, they can't do the job.

If you've got knee pain: Strengthen quads (see Basic Exercises for **Hips and Thighs,** page 74) using the exercises that don't cause further pain. More than other exercises, squats and stationary lunges mimic real-life motions. But avoid bending knees beyond 90 degrees when you do squats or lunges. Leg extensions hurt some people with this condition and help others. Use light weight when you try the leg extension machine to see if it hurts your knees. Be sure to stretch hamstrings and calves (the opposing muscle group) (see **Stretches for Strength Training,** page 137).

If your knees are unstable, your thigh muscles are probably weak, causing your kneecaps to "slide off their tracks." In other words, you might wobble, be knock-kneed, or bowlegged. Over time this can damage cartilage. A medical professional should oversee your therapy if this is the case.

Stair climbing can provide an excellent way to strengthen knees (as long as stair height doesn't exceed 8 inches). Walking down a flight of stairs, however, can be painful. If it isn't, going down stairs (landing gently) can provide an excellent form of eccentric strength training (see **Contractions,** page 51), which best prepares knees to do what they're supposed to do—absorb shock.

Your knee pain could have started in your hip or your ankle. Since the "thigh bone's connected to the knee bone and the knee bone's connected to the shin bone," sometimes one faulty link in a chain of joints can cause pain in another. Try these remedies:

- To stretch hips: Lie on your back. Pull one knee up toward the chest and across the body so it rests on or near the floor. This stretches the hip rotators, which both align and stabilize the hip. Like hamstrings and quads, hip rotators often get tight on runners.
- Check your footfall. Next time you get out of the shower, notice your wet footprints. If your foot rolls excessively out or in, you might want a good pair of orthotics to put in your shoes to balance your weight when you land.

Lower back

Eighty percent of all lower back pain could be prevented with a good strengthening and stretching program. The lower back is at the intersection of several other important muscles, like hips and hamstrings, and it also takes the heat when abdominals are weak.

If your lower back aches, it could be the result of poor posture, poor lifting techniques, a strain, or muscle imbalance. Strengthen muscles around the back. For exercises, see **Abdominals** (especially lower abs), **Back** (especially hyperextensions), **Buttocks** (especially squats and lunges), and **Hips and Thighs** (especially outer and inner thighs), pages 5, 17, 39, and 74.

Move it. Stretch it. Lower backs suffer not because we move too strenuously but because we don't move enough. So many of us sit all day and slouch. Try carefully arching your back and rounding (see the stretch for the lower back under **Stretches for Strength Training,** page 137).

Stabilize it. One of the prime functions of the torso is to hold you still while you move your arms and legs or lift a weight. A wobbly torso is a weak torso. You can strengthen your lower back and abdominals simply by holding yourself still while you exercise arms and legs (see **Stabilization,** page 133).

Be careful when you do little things like wash your face. Be sure you bend forward from the hips, not the lower back, to reach the sink. Learn how to lift heavy objects off the floor with your knees, not your back (see **Lifting Heavy Objects,** page 82).

How to Avoid Injury as You Train

- Lift weights slowly, lower carefully (speed increases the forces around a joint; when the force exceeds your strength, injury occurs).
- Keep your torso stable whenever you lift a weight.
- Always move weights through a full but pain-free range of motion.
- Always warm up before you lift. (A few light sets and stretches or 5 minutes on a bike will do it—see **Warm-ups for Weight Training,** page 144.)
- Cross train—do a variety of activities to avoid overuse injuries.
- Use a weight that's not so heavy it restricts your range of motion.
- Work smarter, not longer. (Long workouts can be exhausting and lead to injury; lots of people injure themselves doing "one more set.")
- Stretch afterward. (If you're tight, your muscles and tendons are more vulnerable if you happen to move too fast or do too big a motion.)
- If you're too loose in the joints, strengthen muscles so you decrease your risk of straining ligaments.

lifting heavy objects

In the weight room, you have to give yourself a leverage *dis*advantage to work a body part. But when you lift things in life, you need to use all the leverage advantages you've got, so you spread out the work and don't hurt yourself.

Always remember, whenever you lift a heavy object, filter the weight through your strongest muscles (your legs), not your weakest (back and arms), and hold it close to your torso.

Lifting a heavy box off the floor uses the same form as a bent-knee dead lift, a power-lifting move. (Bent-knee dead lifts are very good moves for building functional strength, especially if you plan to do a lot of heavy lifting. Power dead lifts are usually done with a long Olympic bar and extra plates that raise the bar 8 inches off the floor. You can use a regular barbell, but if the plates are small, you may want to set the barbell down on an 8-inch riser.)

1. Take a wide stance with the box (or barbell) close to your shins. If you can't get a grip under the box, before you squat down, tilt it away from you and then rest one side of it on your toes to make room for fingers.

2. Squat, keeping heels down, chest up, and lower-back muscles contracted (not rounded).

3. Sit your weight back into your heels and hips and grab the box (or the barbell) in a shoulder-width grip; keep your spine in neutral.

4. Straighten legs and lift. Don't spring up or lock your knees. When upright, keep hugging the box close to your body as you walk forward. Avoid twisting the torso.

If you're using a barbell, the bar should touch the front of the leg as you lift and lower. Some people need extra wrist straps for this exercise and many people like to hold one palm up and one down for a steadier grip.

Lifting a heavy suitcase: Use the same deadlift/squat form as above. Periodically switch sides so you balance out the work. Or better yet, carry two lighter suitcases.

Carrying a heavy shoulder bag: Put your head through the strap, so the weight is more evenly distributed to both sides. If you have to carry it for a while and the strap is long enough, let the bag rest on your lower back, like a backpack.

Moving large pieces of furniture: When you're inspired to redecorate and there's a shortage of large, muscled hunks on hand, here are some moving tips:

If you're moving a big couch, grab one side and deadlift it. (You only need to lift it one inch. Keep arms straight so biceps and wrists don't give out.) Then pivot the couch on one or two legs. Put it down and repeat on the other side until it's in place.

If you must drag it on the floor, it's safest and easiest to put your back up against it and push with your back, legs, and hips. You have much more strength and leverage in this position than if you pushed facing it (your leverage gets too long) or pulled it (your wrists, arms, and back quickly fatigue).

If you need to move a big heavy flat thing, like a filing cabinet, a long distance, get two pieces of 2- to 4-inch pipe or PVC tubing. Lower the filing cabinet toward you, bringing it down on its side and onto one piece of pipe. Roll the second pipe under the other end, either by lifting the low end of the cabinet or putting it next to the first pipe and rolling it down. As you roll the cabinet, you'll have to keep moving the back pipe to the front.

If you're carrying big heavy things up and down stairs and you don't have a dolly, try to be the person on the bottom, especially if you're the weaker of the two. Yes, if the person up top lets go, you're the one who gets flattened. But when you go up stairs, being at the bottom makes it easier to brace the weight on your thighs. If you're on top, try to hold the object behind you, to minimize the strain in your lower back.

When you're going down a flight of stairs, again you want to be the person on the bottom, so you can brace the weight against your body. Hold the object in front or behind, depending on its shape and whichever is most comfortable. If you're on the top, try to brace it on your legs and avoid rounding forward.

If you're carrying children: Women's hips are very good resting places, especially for children. It's a good idea, though, to try not to make this a longtime habit. It's better for your posture to carry a child on your back or close to your chest.

lunges

The lunge is not only a great multimuscle exercise, it's a test of balance and it lets you know right away which of your legs is stronger. Lunges mostly strengthen the quadriceps of the leg in front and the gluteals of the leg in back. If done correctly, lunges both inspire and require strength, finesse, and flexibility.

When most people think of lunges, they think of a step-forward motion, and this *is* the traditional lunge. The problem with this move, however, is that the front knee takes all the stress. Few people can actually execute a flawless step-forward lunge. But the good news is not many people, except those who practice fencing, need this motion in life. The lunge variations below offer more benefits with fewer risks.

Whatever lunge style you choose, remember these pointers:

The rules of the road for all lunges

- Keep heel of the front foot *in contact* with the floor or platform (don't lift it).
- Press *down* into that heel to lift body weight back up.
- Avoid taking knee of front leg *beyond* the toe. The ideal position is *above or behind* the ankle.
- *Lift back heel* off the floor throughout the exercise. (Trying to put it down causes a

loss of balance and overstretches the Achilles tendon.)
- *Bend your back knee,* too. Even in a deep, advanced version of a lunge, keeping the back knee soft allows for greater control through a larger range of motion.
- Keep *spine neutral* (don't round shoulders forward) and actively lift the chest.
- If your knee hurts as you lower, don't go down that far. Work in the *pain-free zone.*
- Perform the motion with confidence for at least *15 repetitions* before adding weight.
- Remember to go slow enough so you work with *muscle, not momentum.*

Step-forward lunge

Add spice to your lunges

- To make lunges more challenging (and to use your buttocks more), *raise* your front foot on a step or platform 6 to 8 inches high. When front foot is raised, you can sink buttocks *below* front knee as long as knee is over or behind ankle. (This doesn't stress the knee and it's an excellent buttocks exercise.)
- Put back foot on a 6- to 8-inch platform to highlight quadriceps of the back leg. A good exercise for the pre-ski season.

- If you have difficulty maintaining balance, gently hold on to the wall, a chair, a ballet barre, or a balance stick.
- To add weight, try holding dumbbells or using a Smith machine (a sliding barbell attached to two fixed poles).
- Try half reps: Lift only halfway up on at least four of your lunges to wake up more muscle fibers and get more work out of doing less.

lunge variations

If you're attached to step-forward lunges, here are our suggestions for helping you achieve a cleaner, safer, more effective form.

The perfect step-forward lunge: Take a hip-distance stance and step forward as far as possible with one leg (like a cross-country ski position), then *stop*! Make sure your back heel lifts off the floor and that both knees are slightly bent. Pausing here helps you to reestablish your balance *before* you lower.

Bend your knees to lower your torso (like an elevator going down). Pause for a moment in the stretched position.

Press into your front heel to lift the torso (like an elevator coming back up). Avoid locking your knees as you lift.

Bring the front foot back and return to starting position.

Alternate legs (easier because legs get a longer rest) or repeat on same leg (harder).

The Groucho lunge variation

This step-forward lunge travels across the room and draws its inspiration from the great man himself. Be sure to "stop" where appropriate and regain your balance.

Step-back lunge: It's much less stressful on the knees if you step *back* into your lunge instead of forward. The step-back motion puts the workload into the hip instead of the knee joint (a much bigger, more stable joint), translating work into the buttocks. Easy to perform well, even for beginners.

Start with feet hip-distance apart. Step back with one leg, onto the ball of your foot, and lower the back knee toward the floor. Keep torso upright as you do this. Bring back leg to meet the front.

Cha-cha lunge variation

Beginners who don't feel confident taking a big step back can take a *half* step back, then another half step back with the same leg in a stationary lunge, returning with a full step forward.

Stationary lunge: Starting in a hip-distance stance, take a long step back. Before you start, check that your feet are parallel, back heel is lifted, both front and back knees slightly bent. Without moving your feet, slowly lower the torso. Pause for a moment in the stretch position. Press into the heel of the front foot to lift (this uses buttocks muscles even more).

Smith machine variation

This exercise works wonderfully with a Smith machine. The apparatus helps hold you in place.

Inclined stationary lunge: Perform the same stationary lunge as before, but incline your torso forward about 45 degrees, keeping the chest *up* and the lower back *slightly arched.* This shifts more of the workload into the buttocks of the front leg. You may need to adjust your stance by bringing your back foot in 2 to 4 inches to feel comfortable.

Lunges to the side: Like step-forward lunges, lunging out to the side can be tough on the knees. This motion, however, can strengthen inner thighs and quadriceps. To make it safe and effective, take a wide, turned-out stance (like ballet's second position). Bend knees to lower into a semi or full plié. Slide 4 to 6 inches to your right, then left, pausing in the stretch. As you shift your weight from side to side, keep the torso upright and press into the heel (of the side your shifting away *from*).

motivation

The only people we know who never lose motivation to exercise are either in denial, taking too many stimulants (in which case they'll crash soon), or getting paid an obscene amount of money to be in shape. Even fitness fanatics have to find ways to stay motivated.

It helps to come to exercise building on your strong points. We're all much too familiar with our faults and shortcomings, and these are the things that get most people to start exercising. But frankly, fears and failing aren't enough to keep you going or lift your spirits. It's easier to be motivated by a positive approach. Start by making three lists. List

1. ten things that inspire you about moving, then choose one and make sure your exercise program contains it
2. ten things you're going to enjoy more once you get into better shape, then choose one and do it today
3. ten things you're already really good at, then choose one and decide how you can use this skill in your exercise

Feed your motivation

Go where the weather suits your clothes

Pick an activity you enjoy. In fact, while you're at it, pick a few. Even if your choices don't seem like formal exercise, find something that will get you off the couch at least three times a week. It can be kite flying or dog walking.

Choose something you can actually do, or at least imagine yourself doing, with some degree of grace and pleasure within a few sessions or classes.

As you begin a regular exercise program, choose something that doesn't wipe you out and lets you build in little rests as you need them.

Don't dwell long in places that offend your senses. Hate the music the teacher plays in that class? Plop on your headphones and hit the bike. Hate the after-work crowd in the weight room? Go before work.

And lastly, do it for you. Don't let an overbearing or overly concerned spouse, friend, or parent steer you into marathon running if you'd really rather be rowing.

Make it easy on yourself

- Remove the usual obstacles. Don't join a gym that's too far from your house or one that your psychotic ex frequents.
- Don't pick something with a high injury quotient. Full-contact kick boxing is not something you want to do every day. What happens if you get pregnant?
- Don't choose an activity that requires a big investment in gear unless you've already spent some time doing it and absolutely know that a shiny new mountain bike, a full suit of fencing equipment, or a belly dancing outfit excites every cell in your body.

Know your personality

If you're a solitary type, find something you can do by yourself without a trainer, instructor, or throngs of people.

If you can't propel yourself onto your feet without prodding, commit to working out with a buddy—or better yet, several buddies—so you let down someone else if you cancel.

Goal making—minute, moderate, and magnificent

Create tiny victories in every workout. For instance, when you go for a walk, build in intervals like "walk to that telephone as fast as possible." After you get there and slow your pace, take a moment to applaud yourself. Notice that you did it before setting another goal, especially if you have an overachieving personality.

Build up endurance and strength gradually. If you're walking, add a minute each time you go out. If you're lifting weights, add another rep.

Write out some easy short-term goals—not "lose ten pounds this month," but "work out three days a week, thirty minutes each." Next month: "four workouts per week."

Hitch your dreams to a very distant star. If you see yourself at age 110 doing Tai Chi by a river at dawn, then by all means hold that vision.

Strength training particulars

- Write it down. All those people walking around with workout cards are keeping track of weights, reps, and exercises. You should do this, too, especially as you start out, so you can chart your improvements. While you're at it, note how food, different types and amounts of exercise, and sleep affect your energy level and attitude. The examined life *can* be fascinating, especially when the subject is you.

- Bored with your routine? Doing the same 40 pounds on the leg curl with no success? *Shake it up, baby.* Do your workout in reverse. Do it slower than humanly possible. Work only one limb at a time.

- If you just can't face the weights one day, free yourself from the shackles of having to work out. Instead, play with some equipment you haven't tried. Or better yet, go work out in a playground.

- Build in constructive rest. When you're burned out, take a break. Don't become a total slug for too long. Stretch. Take easy walks. Let your energy and enthusiasm bubble.

muscles

For some people, the gym is a foreign country, complete with its own language (not to mention strange customs and wild animals). Knowing your "delts" from your "glutes" makes it much easier to get around, find the right machines, work the right body parts, and even converse with the locals.

If you have to write a dissertation on functional anatomy, the following information won't help, since there are over six hundred muscles in the body. What follows is more like a crash course in "the language of muscle."

Major muscles in the legs

Glutes (buttocks)

A.k.a.: gluteus maximus, gluteus medius, gluteus minimus

Where you find them: You're sitting on them.

Claim to fame: The gluteus maximus is the biggest, strongest muscle in the body.

How you work them: For the maximus: squats, grand pliés, lunges, leg presses, hip extensions, running, stair climbing, hurdle jumping, and bounding up into the air. For the medius and minimus: all moves when you step out to the side (hip abduction), as in leg lifts, walking, dancing, skating.

What they'll do for you: The maximus propels all big, powerful, lower-body moves. The medius and minimus also help you balance and walk.

Quads (front of the thighs)

A.k.a.: rectus femoris, vastus medialis, vastus intermedius, vastus laterali

Where you find them: From the hip bone to the knee bone, in the front of your thigh.

Claim to fame: Quads are to the lower body what biceps are to the upper body. When you want to show off lower-body strength, you flex the quads.

How you work them: Leg extensions and cycling. They also get worked in squats, lunges, leg presses, stair climbing, and jumps.

What they'll do for you: Strong quads protect your knees and look great in shorts.

Hamstrings (back of the thighs)

A.k.a.: biceps femoris, semitendinosis, semimembranosus

Where you find them: On the back of the leg, from the hip bone to the knee bone.

Claim to fame: One of the most easily injured leg muscles. They also tend to be tight and much weaker than quads, their opposing muscle group. Since hamstrings take up less leg space than quads, their strength doesn't have to be exactly equal. Tight hamstrings pull your tailbone down, causing a flat back posture (kyphosis).

How you work them: Hamstring curls and hip extension with a bent knee.

What they'll do for you: Strong, flexible hams create better alignment and decrease the risk of hamstring and lower-back injury. They also add a firm, sexy sweep to the back of the thigh.

Adductors (inner thighs)

A.k.a.: adductor longus, adductor brevis, adductor magnus, pectineus, gracilis

Where you find them: They span from the thigh bone to the pubic bone.

Claim to fame: The Thigh Master made these muscles famous, which is amusing since inner-thigh muscles are supporting players, not the stars of the show.

How you work them: Inner-thigh machines or leg lifts. Or lying on your back wearing light ankle weights and opening and closing legs. Adductors also participate when you do squats and grand pliés.

What they'll do for you: They'll let you cross each leg over the center line of the body or hold someone in a leg lock.

Calves (back of the lower legs)

A.k.a.: gastrocnemius, soleus

Where you'll find them: In the back of the leg between the knee and ankle.

Claim to fame: The reason high heels and short skirts were invented.

How you work them: Standing and seated heel raises (see **Calves**, page 43).

What they'll do for you: Help you walk, run, dance.

Also see **Buttocks** (page 39) and **Hips and Thighs** (page 74).

Major muscles in the torso

Lats (outer back)

A.k.a.: latissimus dorsi

Where you find them: All down the back, from the armpit to the tailbone.

Claim to fame: The biggest muscle in the upper body. Developed lats give the torso the famous V taper.

How you work them: All pulling moves: pull-ups, pull downs, rows, and such (see **Back**, page 17).

What they'll do for you: Aside from making your waist appear smaller, they work in all big torso moves: swimming, racquet sports, golf.

Rhomboids (upper back)

Where you find them: In a small section of the upper back, between the spinal vertebrae and the shoulder joint. They lie beneath the trapezius.

Claim to fame: They've never had their fifteen minutes.

How you work them: Pulls and rows to the upper chest. They also see some action when you work the traps and rear delts (see **Back**, page 17).

What they'll do for you: Help you stand upright. They're good posture muscles, especially important if you sit rounded over a computer terminal all day.

Trapezius (neck, shoulders, upper back)

A.k.a.: traps

Where you find them: This muscle starts at the top of the spine, fans out across the shoulders, then forms a point in the lower back.

Claim to fame: Well-developed traps are what give linebackers and wrestlers that big-necked, "don't mess with me" look. For this reason, big thick traps don't do much for women.

How you work them: Shrugs and upright rows (see **Back**, page 17).

What they'll do for you: If you tend to carry your stress like the world on your shoulders, traps can at least help you carry the load and improve hunched-over posture. But go easy on the traps even if you do want the linebacker look. You may be able to shrug 100 pounds, but the next day it might feel as if you've got two bowling balls on your neck.

Erectors (lower back)

A.k.a.: erector spinae

Where you find them: Where your lower back aches, that's where you'll find the erectors. Technically, they run from the tailbone to the top of the rib cage. But we train them where the joints bend the most, in the lower back.

Claim to fame: Most common source of muscle pain. Most lower-back pain disappears with time, exercise, and general movement. It can also be prevented with exercise and proper lifting techniques, both in the weight room and out (see **Lifting Heavy Objects,** page 82).

How you work them: Lower-back hyperextensions, squats, dead lifts, standing, and sitting up straight (see **Back,** page 17).

What they'll do for you: Give you good posture, prevent painful injuries, help you move.

Abs (abdominals)

A.k.a.: rectus abdominis, transverse abs

Where you find them: Hanging out above and below the belt. The biggest ab muscle, the rectus, runs from the breast bone to the pubic bone. When you work "upper" abs with regular crunches and "lower" abs with reverse crunches, you're really just addressing the same muscle from different angles.

Claim to fame: Body part that has inspired the greatest number of weird looking, useless "spot toning" gizmos.

How you work them: For rectus abdominis: crunches, reverse crunches, and holding your spine stable (see **Stabilization,** page 133).

Special caveat: Don't try to work abs with straight leg sit-ups, full sit-ups, or leg raises (lying on your back lowering both feet to the floor).

What they'll do for you: According to those ab gizmo infomercials, strong abs will make all your dreams come true. More humbly, they'll hold you upright, stabilize your torso, and prevent lower-back injury.

Obliques (sides)

A.k.a.: internal obliques, external obliques

Where you find them: These muscles take up a lot of space running from the rib cage to the pubic bone. The fibers of external obliques (the ones closest to your skin) move diagonally across your torso (as if into your jeans' front pockets). The internal obliques move into the other direction (into your back pockets).

Claim to fame: Contrary to popular opinion, these are not your "love handles" (excess fat around your waist earns that distinction). Most of the time, except on very lean bodies, obliques hide under your skin. They're supportive rather than sexy muscles.

How you work them: For external obliques: crunches with a twist to the opposite knee. For internal obliques: crunches with a twist to the same knee.

What they'll do for you: Firm obliques give your torso greater support so you stand up taller and your lower back muscles don't have to pull so hard to hold you upright. Without general overall ab strength (which includes the obliques), you set yourself up for lower back pain.

Pecs (chest)

A.k.a.: pectoralis major, pectoralis minor

Where you find them: From the armpit to the breast bone (sternum).

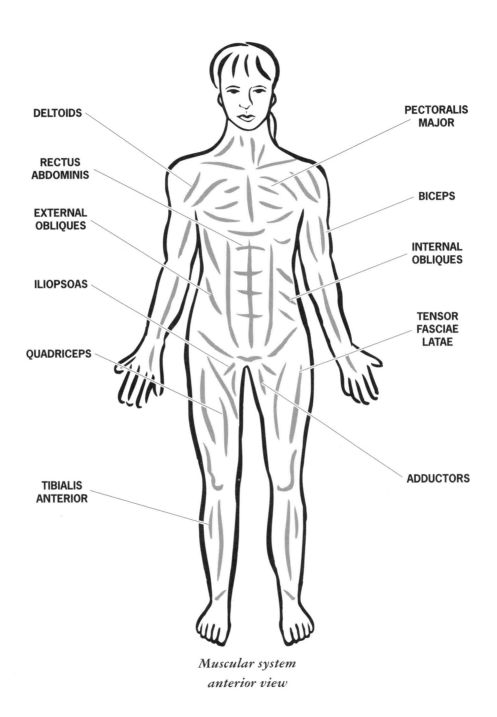

DELTOIDS

RECTUS
ABDOMINIS

EXTERNAL
OBLIQUES

ILIOPSOAS

QUADRICEPS

TIBIALIS
ANTERIOR

PECTORALIS
MAJOR

BICEPS

INTERNAL
OBLIQUES

TENSOR
FASCIAE
LATAE

ADDUCTORS

*Muscular system
anterior view*

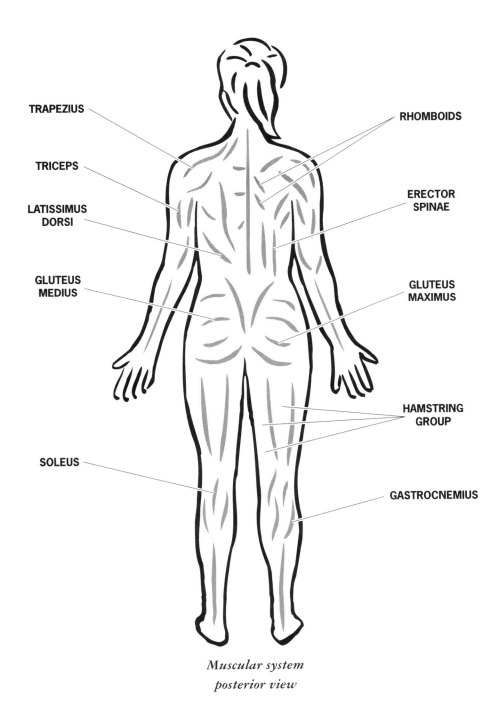

TRAPEZIUS

TRICEPS

LATISSIMUS DORSI

GLUTEUS MEDIUS

RHOMBOIDS

ERECTOR SPINAE

GLUTEUS MAXIMUS

HAMSTRING GROUP

SOLEUS

GASTROCNEMIUS

Muscular system posterior view

Claim to fame: One of the most overworked muscles in the gym, often at the expense of the lats, erectors, rhomboids, and rear delts. High on the vanity scale for men and women.

How you work them: Presses, flyes, also throwing and hugging (see **Chest,** "Basic Exercises for the Chest," page 45).

What they'll do for you: Improve your posture, your profile, and any move where you push or throw. What they won't do for women is make breasts larger. Pecs are muscles. Breasts are balls of fat sitting on that muscle. Firm pecs may let breasts ride a little higher on the chest. But, if anything, breasts will get smaller as pecs get stronger because stronger muscles speed metabolism, which helps people shed fat, and, sadly, breast fat is among the first to go. (So the next time you see a super-buffed, ultra-lean female who's also impressively endowed you'll know that she bought them.)

Delts (shoulders)

A.k.a.: deltoids anterior, medial, posterior (or front, lateral, and rear)

Where you'll find them: All around the shoulder joint and several inches down the arm.

Claim to fame: A major intersection of upper-body muscles. Easily held in the wrong position when working, thus a major reason for bad form and injury.

How you work them: Although the delts contain several smaller muscles, they're usually worked in three main groups. Work front delts with all chest exercises and front raises. Work middle delts with lateral raises. Work rear delts with rear delt flyes. Shoulders also house the rotator cuff muscles, probably the most injured muscle in the upper body (see **Shoulders,** page 123).

What they'll do for you: Strong delts can prevent injuries to shoulders and help you strengthen other upper-body muscles.

Special caveat: Since the shoulder joint has a delicate design, don't train delts with excessively heavy weight and don't overtrain front delts. For better-balanced shoulder strength, favor your middle and rear delts in shoulder training, since your front delts work with pecs.

Biceps (front of the arm)

A.k.a.: biceps brachi, brachialis, brachioradialis

Where you'll find them: Popping up on the front of the arm, from the shoulder to the elbow.

Claim to fame: The most displayed muscle.

How you work them: Curls, all pulling exercises for the back that use elbows, and climbing (see **Arms,** page 14).

What they'll do for you: Help you lift a heavy suitcase, climb a rock face, and let you roll up your T-shirt sleeves and flex with macho pride.

Triceps (underside of the upper arm)

A.k.a.: the long, lateral, and medial heads. All together these create a horseshoe shape.

Where you'll find them: The long head is on the arm's underbelly (it's the one that jiggles the most). The medial head lies under the long head. The lateral head is closer to the front of the body. All run from the shoulder to the elbow.

Claim to fame: Considered the "upper body's version of the thigh" since the upper arm is a main fat storage area.

How you work them: All presses and extensions (see **Arms,** page 14). They also assist in all throwing and pushing moves.

What they'll do for you: Make your arm look defined when hanging straight. Also give you basic "push" strength.

neutral spine

Neutral spine is strength training's ready position. It's nothing more than doing what you should do naturally—stand in an upright, supported posture, letting the spine assume its normal S curve. This boils down to three main points.

1. Let your lower back arch a little. Contrary to popular belief, don't flatten the lower back. A flat lower back does not give any torso support and makes the disks vulnerable to injury, especially if you bend forward. On the other hand, don't overdo your arch. Find the middle zone (see "Assume the Position," page 96).

2. Once you set the lower back into position, your upper back usually falls into place—with an arch in the upper back that moves in the opposite direction from the lower back. Lift the chest slightly to adjust your spine if you're not sure you're in the right position.

3. Balance your weight evenly between forward and back, right and left. If you ran a plumb line (a string with a weight tied to the end) from the center of your head, it should fall along the center of your torso, your hips, knees, and ankles.

Neutral spine is the safest position to be in when you're exposing your body to excess stresses or strains, as you do in weight lifting. Being in neutral lets you takes the downward forces of gravity, plus any weird position you get into, and focus that force in a place your body can handle it best—in the body's center of gravity, about two inches below the belly button and inside the pelvic bone. Neutral spine protects your torso, your joints, muscles, and connective tissues (ligaments and tendons).

Although neutral is natural, it can feel very odd at first and takes some training to get into, especially if you've got weak posture or bad postural habits. If you're embarking on a weight-training program, the first thing you should learn (and be taught), before you ever lift a weight, is how to hold neutral. Otherwise you program your body to learn the exercises with bad form and thereby increase the risk of injury. It's also much harder to break this pattern than to learn it right the first time.

You need neutral not only when you're standing still but also when you move. An athlete or dancer who twists, turns, and contorts constantly returns to neutral. After a while, it becomes unconscious.

Holding neutral while lifting weights both requires and improves balance. It's a workout in itself because both the lower back and abdominal muscles work hard to hold the torso upright and stable (see also **Posture**, page 100 and **Stabilization**, page 133).

Assume the position

1. Take a hip-distance stance. If you're unsteady, take a wider stance. A wide base of support makes it easier to maintain balance. If your balance is good, stand with feet a little closer. A narrow base of support actually helps you increase torso strength.
2. Rock forward onto the balls of your feet, then back on your heels. Find the middle point and stay there.
3. Feel grounded in your feet and legs. Soften your knees.
4. Carefully round your back and then arch. Find the middle spot between these two extremes and hold it. Feel your abdominal and lower-back muscles contract to hold you upright.
5. Lift your chest slightly upward, as if you had a hand supporting you just under your shoulder blades.
6. Slide your chin back toward your neck and lengthen the back of the neck, as if opening a little window there.

What happens if you never find neutral?

If getting in neutral feels extremely foreign, then you know you'd better practice it, all the time. Unless you have a skeletal deformity, like scoliosis (a lateral S curve of the spine), most deviations from neutral can be corrected. It's a matter of retraining muscles and connective tissues. (Also see **Posture**, page 100.)

But if you decide that instead of training yourself, you'll simply slump, then you make a temporary problem permanent. Unless you retrain the soft tissues—your connective tissue and muscles—your bones will adapt. Once your bad posture works its way into the bones, it's too late to fix it.

pain

The old dictum "no pain, no gain" has been replaced with a kinder, gentler phrase: "no strain, all gain." Somewhere between these two extremes is the truth. Strength training doesn't have to be painful to be effective. But if it doesn't cause some discomfort, it's probably not going to make you stronger.

As for how much pain you have to go through, first you have to define pain and understand that everyone has different thresholds. There are also several different types of pain. You need to know how to distinguish them. Finally, you also have to decide which you'd rather endure, the little aches and pains of training or the debilitating pain that comes from never exercising.

Good pain

Good pain is another name for the famous "burn" that happens while you lift weights. It's hot, uncomfortable, and gets more uncomfortable the longer and harder your set. The pain is the result of lactic acid leaking out of your muscle cells and irritating nearby nerve endings. The best thing about good pain is it disappears as soon as you finish the exercise. As you spend more time working out, this reaction occurs a little later and your tolerance for it increases. Some people enjoy this sensation because they know they're working hard. If you can hang in

there with it, it won't damage you. Some immediate soreness, however, can be caused by microtraumas (tears) in the muscle or connective tissue. If the pain persists, don't ignore it (see **Injuries,** page 79).

Other ways to identify good pain:

- It happens in the muscles, not the joints or connective tissues
- It's localized in the body part you're working
- You feel it in both limbs at the same time

Delayed onset muscle soreness

Another type of good pain is that stiff, sore feeling you get in your muscles 24 to 72 hours after a workout (official name: delayed onset muscle soreness). It's thought to be caused mostly by small tears, or microtraumas, in the muscle fibers. The resulting tenderness is a signal that your muscles are undergoing a healing process because you did a fairly intense workout—good for you!

Although some people believe it's unnecessary to train so hard that it creates soreness, others aren't satisfied unless they feel this. The sensible path lies somewhere in between. You don't need to get so sore that you can't walk or get up. Then again, no soreness means you probably didn't work hard enough.

You typically get the sorest at the beginning of a weight-lifting program. It's a little like the old saying, "If you want to make an omelet, you've got to break some eggs." You also get more sore when you try something new or simply overdo it. But if you keep up any activity, your muscles will adapt and won't get so sore.

Many people also believe that "negative" training—lowering more weight than you can lift—causes excessive soreness. Although this isn't the only culprit, it certainly contributes to it (for more on this, see **Contractions**, page 51).

When a muscle is still sore, gentle limbering moves or stretches can warm and comfort the area. But you should wait until the soreness has completely disappeared before training those same muscles with any intensity. Otherwise, you will interrupt the healing process, your muscles won't get stronger, and you risk hurting yourself.

Bad pain

Bad pain is unmistakable. It's sudden, it grabs your attention, and you know instantly something is wrong. It can also be dull, throbbing, radiating, and chronic. Sometimes it comes as a warning and other times it ushers in a full-blown injury. If the pain is in the muscle, you're better off than if it's in or near the joints, because muscles heal faster than connective tissue. In both cases, you should back off any move that causes pain and treat the injury (see, under **Injuries,** "Common Sports-Related Injuries," page 196). Other clues: If you're working both limbs and one hurts, it's a bad pain. If the pain lingers when you stop the exercise, it's a bad pain.

You've got to be able to tell bad pain from good and stop or change what you're doing if necessary.

Training around an injury

It happens. You fall off your skates, get in a car accident, or suffer for some stupid training method you practiced in ignorance or youth. But even injury doesn't have to sideline you from strength training. All your hard work can vanish very quickly, since muscles start to lose strength and size two to four days after their last workout.

Because you can control where and how much resistance you apply to a muscle, strength training can be part of a very effective rehab program. Even if you can't work an injured area, you can reap benefits in other parts of your body. The main rule about training with an injury is avoid pain. Don't reinjure it. You have to train around it, not against it.

- Choose exercises that don't cause pain. If pull downs behind your neck bother your shoulders, do them to the front. If squats bother your back, try a horizontal leg press.
- Use lighter weight. If the 15-pound dumbbells kill your shoulders on dumbbell flyes, try the 10s or 5s. This puts less stress on the ligaments.
- Slow down. Going slow forces you to use muscle, not momentum, which puts less stress on the joints.
- Change the angle of attack. If a flat bench press hurts your shoulders but an incline doesn't, do the incline.

- Change your grip. Many people with shoulder rotator cuff pain have no problem on a machine or dumbbell bench or shoulder press if they use a palms-together grip. Also, a very wide grip on a barbell or pulldown bar can cause unnecessary shoulder pain. Try a grip that's shoulder width.

- Go through a smaller range of motion. If you can bench press through all but the last 4 inches above your chest without pain, choose the pain-free range of motion. Ever so cautiously, increase the range as the injury heals.

- Work the good side. If you broke your foot and can only work one leg (with leg extensions, hamstring curls, maybe a one-legged horizontal leg press), then do it. Your other leg will get stronger too, not as strong but it will respond. This is one of the body's most fascinating little miracles, called bilateral transfer. Studies have shown that the muscle fibers on the injured, nonworking side can also get stronger when the other side works. Following this same principle, your upper body can get a little stronger if you only work legs. Scientists aren't entirely sure whether it's due to neurons in both or all limbs adapting to the load, because the muscle fibers on the nonworking side go into little sympathetic, isometric contractions or because of something we don't yet understand. But it happens and it makes you appreciate the body's wisdom at work.

posture

Having good posture does more than make your mother happy. It affects your physical and mental health, and your self-esteem.

Most postural problems are temporary and correctable, usually a matter of strengthening and stretching muscles and connective tissue. But if bad posture is allowed to get worse the bones will adapt, and then you can't fix it. Stretching and strengthening can bring relief.

The spine contains the spinal cord, which, along with the brain, governs the central nervous system. The spinal cord sends sensory messages to the brain, while the brain sends motor signals down the spinal cord to various parts of the body. It's the mind-body super-highway.

Therefore, good posture is more than just poise. It's the best way to maintain this critical "communication pathway." Bad posture makes the spinal cord vulnerable. It also makes the spine weaker and less flexible.

Although good posture is simple to define, sometimes it's not so easy to achieve. Maintain the natural curves in the spine (see **Neutral Spine,** page 95) with

- a slight arch in the lower back
- a lifted chest (pulls shoulders back)
- a long neck, lifted head, and level chin, slightly pulled back

Keep the abs, lower back, hamstrings, hip flexors, chest, shoulders, and upper-back muscles at least moderately strong and flexible.

Three common postural problems

Lordosis (sway back)

Lordosis is caused by weak abdominals, hamstrings, and buttocks, and tight (or shortened) erectors (lower-back muscles) and hip flexors (the ones that help lift the knee). The prescription for lordosis is to strengthen the abdominals (with crunches and lower-ab exercises—see **Abdominals,** page 5), the hamstrings (with hamstring curls—see **Hips and Thighs,** page 74), and the buttocks (with squats, lunges, hip extension, etc.—see **Buttocks,** page 39).

Lordosis should also be countered with stretching focused on the lower back (lie on the floor, pull knees to chest—see, under **Stretches for Strength Training,** "Erector Spinae Stretch," page 140) and hip flexors (lie face up on a bench. Pull one knee to chest. Let the other leg hang off the end of the bench—see, under **Stretches for Strength Training,** "Hip Flexor Stretch," page 139).

Kyphosis (flat lower back, sunken chest)

Kyphosis is the result of weak hip flexors (front of hip/thigh), erectors (lower back), and mid- and low trapezius (middle back), as well as tight (or shortened) hamstrings, abs (rectus and obliques), and chest.

The prescription for kyphosis is to strengthen the hip flexors (walk up stairs or hills), the lower back (with hyperextensions—see the exercises under **Back,** page 17), and the trapezius (with pull downs to the chest and upright rows—see the exercises under **Back,** page 14).

Kyphosis should also be countered with stretching focused on the hamstrings (see, under **Stretches for Strength Training,** "Hamstring Stretch," page 139), the abs (for rectus: Lie on the floor or on a big stretching ball and extend your arms overhead; for obliques: Take a wide stance, hold one hand on your hip, and lift your other arm overhead, reaching to the opposite side); and the chest: Place hands behind head or lower back and lift chest (see, under **Stretches for Strength Training,** "Chest/Front Shoulder Stretch," on page 138).

Scoliosis (a lateral S curve of the spine)

Scoliosis is a sideways spinal curve, and usually it first shows up in adolescent girls. Medical professionals aren't sure what causes it or why females get it more often than males. Some believe it's genetic; others think it stems from emotional problems or malnutrition.

There are two types of scoliosis: functional and structural. Functional scoliosis is usually caused by a muscular imbalance and can be easily corrected.

Structural scoliosis occurs when the bones grow into a curve. This is much harder to treat, but not a lost cause. It also turns the rib cage, so that one side of the rib cage sticks out in the back, makes one hip higher than the other and one leg longer (although it's hard to say which causes which), and pulls the muscles tight on one side of the curve and loose on the other. When the curve is a full *S* shape, the muscles beneath are tight and those on top are loose, although not all scoliosis is shaped this way.

One way to tell if a case of scoliosis is functional or structural is to change the spine's relationship to gravity. The person in doubt should bend forward at the hips (bending the knees) and round the spine forward, bracing hands on knees or the floor. Someone else should run their hands down the spine. If the spine straightens out, it's functional. If it doesn't, it's structural. Sometimes, the spine will straighten slightly, indicating that it's a little of both.

When scoliosis is caught early enough, chiropractors and physical therapists can recommend various treatments, all of which require discipline—exercise, yoga, massage, wearing a lift in the shoe, and wearing a back brace.

Sometimes surgery is recommended. But it's painful and recovery is long. The spine is typically opened from neck to tailbone and a rod is inserted along the spine. It can require being in bed and a body cast for up to a year (a devastating thing for anybody, let alone a budding adolescent girl). So, if the doctor presents a choice between surgery and any of the above, choose noninvasive methods if you can. Most cases of scoliosis, however, do not develop to this degree of severity.

The weight-training posture

The posture to use for strength training is good posture, tweaked up a notch (see **Neutral Spine,** page 95):

- Find neutral spine.
- Contract the abdominals (so they hold you steady).
- Contract the lower-back muscles (so the spine feels protected).
- Soften your knees (to balance on muscles, not joints).
- Pull your shoulders back and down.
- Lift your chest (this is a very proud stance and it may feel odd at first).
- Lengthen the neck and pull up the head.

Good Posture Tips

Aside from standing and sitting up straight, these things can help posture:

- Sit in a back-healthy chair. (If you don't have a fancy "ergonomic" chair, then support your lower back with a pillow.)
- Wear supportive, comfortable shoes (not high heels!).
- If your feet roll in or out, see a podiatrist for special shoe inserts.
- Work in a well-lit area and bring your work or a book to you, rather than leaning forward.
- Avoid rounding over to lift things.
- If you sit for long periods at work, get up, walk around, and stretch.

presses

Presses are big, im-press-ive movements that use multiple joints and muscles and eat up lots of energy fast. For that reason, presses can feel a bit op-press-ive (sometimes de-press-ing). But the payback for your effort is great (if you can just press on) because presses are compound moves, and compounds work more total muscle mass. In short, if you stick with them, presses give you a lot in return.

Major muscles that press

A press is basically a push. Our main push muscles are big, flashy, and sexy:

- Chest (as in chest press)
- Shoulders (as in shoulder press) and
- Legs—quads, hamstrings, buttocks (as in leg press)

Little muscles, like triceps and calves, also assist in these presses and even have little presses of their own (as in triceps press-downs and calf presses). But, technically, these last two are really extensions, not presses (see **Flex and Extend,** page 65).

Leg press

A perfectly executed press is a beautiful thing, a complex orchestration of designated muscles and joints. But you can ruin it fast by lifting up out of your seat, squirming, or doing any of the not-so-elegant moves listed below.

Rules of the road for all presses

- Keep your hips and butt down on the seat or bench. Lifting up is cheating (you divert the work into the back or shoulders). Cheating is only acceptable when you do it consciously, you're experienced, lack a spotter, and your muscles are failing.

- Use a shoulder-width grip or hip-distance stance. When feet or hands are too wide, you limit your range of motion and subject your shoulders or hips to an uneven force, coming in at an angle. Keep joints "stacked" on top of each other, in nice parallel lines.

- With chest and shoulder presses you have the option of using dumbbells. You can bring weights together in a point (but avoid clanging weights together—that's too much momentum). *A*-shaped presses let you press more weight. Try both versions.

- Don't lock your elbows or knees. Locking out takes the work out of the muscles (which need it), puts stress on the joints (which don't), and is basically a resting move. You can straighten your legs on a leg press, for instance, and sit there for several minutes, carrying on a nice, easy conversation.

- Go slowly into those good, deep negatives. Never let the weight come crashing down onto you or bounce through the lowest part of the lift, which is very dangerous, especially for ligaments.

- Press up through the heels or heels of the hands to keep the force going evenly through other joints.

- Don't throw shoulders or hips forward as you press. Keep your shoulders down and hips still.

- You can do all presses with one or two limbs at a time.

- In upper-body presses, elbows bend to 90 degrees or just beyond, if you have the strength, flexibility, and absence of pain to go there.

- In lower-body presses, knees bend to 90 degrees or just beyond, if you have the strength and flexibility, and feet are high enough on the plate so the knees don't take the force.

pulls

A pull is the opposite of a press. Pull muscles aren't as conspicuous or as sexy as push muscles. They're mostly on the back and underside of our bodies where they're difficult to see in the mirror and to show off. They are the very important behind-the-scenes muscles that provide the foundation for our posture.

Major muscles that pull

The main pull muscles are in the back: the lats, traps, and rhomboids. Every back exercise is a pull: pull-ups, pull downs, rows (low pulls, high pulls), chins, and pull overs. All use the shoulder and elbow joints (except for the pull over, which uses only the shoulder), but not the lower back, hips, wrists, and neck (which you have to hold still).

Biceps are also pull muscles and assist most back exercises. Hamstrings, too, are pull muscles, but by themselves they are single-joint moves (see **Curls**, page 53). We'll deal here with the more complex back pulls because this motion is the most poorly performed and misunderstood of all strengthening exercises. For many people, making a few simple adjustments could improve the effectiveness of the exercises—and remedy the epidemic of back pain and weakness suffered by eight out of ten Americans.

The golden rule of pulling

If you can do this one thing, you're on the road to pull-muscle mastery. Here it is, the secret of successful pulling: *Initiate all pulls from the back first!* What does this mean?

To understand, play this game. The rule is: You can't bend your elbows. Sit upright and raise both hands over your head, as if you were grabbing a pull-down bar. Lower and pull back the shoulders. They won't move very far. Could you do it? Did you bend your elbows? In fancy gym-speak, this is called depressing and retracting your scapula.

Now repeat the same move with your arms out in front of you. Whatever your angle of pull, initiate the movement in your back muscles by pulling shoulder blades down and back.

If you don't do this, three bad things can happen:

1. You'll tend to slump forward, lose your neutral spine, and, in this position, won't even be able to contract the back muscles completely.
2. Your arms will do all the work and the biceps (much smaller than all those big back muscles) will fatigue before the back muscles get any benefit.
3. You will put your shoulder joints in a vulnerable position, especially when you hang weight off them.

As you're learning how to pull, break the motion down this way: First, pull the shoulders down and back so you contract the back muscles. Then bend your arms. Also, lift the chest and hold that squeeze for a full second. To release, straighten the arms. Then stretch your back.

As you get better at this, the movement will become more fluid, like a choreographed dance between shoulders, back, and arms. This motion actually has a catchy name: the scapulohumeral rhythm.

Pull-down to chest

Rules of the road for back pulls

- Don't round your spine as you pull. Keep it in neutral (with lower-back muscles contracted slightly) or you won't be able to effectively contract your lats, rhomboids, and trapezius.

- As you pull any bar, handle, or dumbbell to your chest, lift your chest to meet the bar. This will engage the trapezius and keep your shoulders and neck in a safe position.

- If your shoulder blades pop up or forward, it is a sign of bad form and fatigue. Stop or finish the exercise with lighter weight.

- Avoid very wide grips. They limit your range of motion and put an uncomfortable, uneven angle on the shoulders.

- Vary your grips for various degrees of biceps assistance. An underhand grip (with palms up) is easiest. In this position, biceps provide the most leverage. A parallel grip, with palms facing each other, is harder. Slightly rotated, biceps provide less leverage. An overhand grip (with palms down) is hardest. In this position the biceps provide the least amount of leverage (because the biceps tendon wraps around one of the bones in the forearm). If your grip gives out before your back muscles do, wear wrist straps to help you hold on.

resistance

Lifting weights is not the only way to build muscle. If you can push, pull, drag, curl, or stretch something, you can build strength. Elastic bands, water, even your own body weight will give good resistance, but as with weights, you have to know how to use them.

Bands and tubing

Bands and tubing have been around a long time and started as physical rehabilitation tools. Bands run the gamut from minimalist to fairly sophisticated, with handles, poles, and straps so you can loop the band through doorjambs, around aerobic steps, and so on. These add-ons give you more options. But you can also get a good workout from simple strips of latex.

How to get the most out of your bands

- Use progressive resistance by choking up on the band, using two bands at once, or using a thicker resistance (at least for a few reps, then finish with easier resistance).
- Check bands for rips and tears before using—a sudden snap is nasty.
- If standing on one end of the band and lifting the other, stand on it with your heels. Bands can slip through your instep and fly up in your face.
- Every few weeks put bands or cords in a plastic bag, sprinkle in baby powder and shake to prolong the life of your "rubber gym."

- Make sure you can wrap the bands around the poles or somehow adjust resistance if you use bands that come with poles.

Body weight

If you were alone on an island with no weight-lifting equipment and all the time in the world, you could get stronger not only from climbing coconut trees, swinging on vines, and swimming for your dinner, you could do: push-ups, pull-ups, dips, squats, lunges, standing leg exercises, ab crunches, and a clever combination of isometrically held postures

But again, the drawback with body weight is that if you want to get stronger, you have to add more resistance. Here's how to do it:

- Go slowly. If you're doing squats in 2 seconds, slow down to 10 seconds. Eliminate momentum and work harder.
- Add holds or small, gentle pulses at various parts of the lift.
- Change the angle. For instance, on a stationary lunge, try inclining your torso 45 degrees forward to better target the buttocks.

Some Advantages and Drawbacks of "Pumping Rubber"

Advantages	Drawbacks
They come in different strengths and you can double them up for more resistance, so they work for any fitness level; seniors use them and bodybuilders pump up with them.	It's tough to measure your progress. (In the weight room you know how much you're lifting; with bands, there's no easy way to measure.)
You can exercise muscles from many angles, without worrying too much about the downward pull of gravity.	Without handles, bands can be tough on hands. Try an overhand, thumbless grip so bands don't cut between thumbs and forefingers.
You can work every major muscle group in your body with one little band (and have even more fun with two).	Handles, though comfortable, also confine you to a certain range of motion; don't hesitate to hold the elastic for more resistance.
You can do many of the same exercises you do with free weights and machines (lateral raises, triceps extensions, biceps curls, chest presses, squats, calf presses, etc.).	
You can often get more resistance through a full range of motion with a band than you can with free weights.	

Water: 3-D resistance

Water can be a great strengthening tool. You can work muscles from a huge variety of angles not possible on land. When you're using a free weight, machine, or band, you are attaching the resistance to the end of your limbs. But in water, the resistance surrounds the entire limb. This is not only good for strengthening, it helps rehabilitate injured or overtrained muscles, joints, and connective tissue. Best of all, the water lets you work opposing muscle groups in one move. For instance, with flyes, you work chest and rear delts. You can't do this on land either.

The main drawback to working with water is, again, the need to add progressive resistance. You can do this a few ways:

- Increase your speed.
- Increase your "drag" (by cupping your hands, spreading fingers slightly, wearing webbed gloves, and/or adding ankle gear).
- Lengthen and widen your levers. (This means that a straight limb disperses more water than a very bent one, so if you want to work even harder, slightly bend your knees or elbows, because a wider lever disperses more water than a narrow one.)

Resistance gizmos

The good news is that most people realize the need for strength. The bad news is that it's birthed a bizarre collection of resistance-training devices. When you find yourself bombarded with sales pitches, here are some questions to ask before you buy (see also **Equipment,** page 58):

- Does it give resistance through a full, or at least decent, range of motion? (For example, the Thigh Master gives a specific, short range of motion—not appropriate for all people or muscle groups, not even the inner thigh.)
- Can you increase the resistance or are you stuck with a set amount? And if you have to buy add-ons, how much more will you have to spend?
- Does it work more than one muscle group?

rest and recovery

Getting stronger, leaner, and healthier is a three-part system: one part exercise, one part food, and one part rest. How much you need of each is relative to how fit you are, what you're doing now, and what you're trying to achieve. What isn't relative is that everyone needs a balance of all three.

Exercise stimulates a physiological response. You don't get stronger during workouts, but later, when you rest. If you exercise too much, you interrupt this healing cycle and become prone to injury. If you don't exercise enough, you don't stimulate the strength-building response.

Rest between strength workouts

When you strength train, you create microscopic tears in muscle fibers, which take at least two days to heal. That's why you shouldn't train the same muscles two days in a row.

If you train hard, you may need to take four or five days off. (If muscles are very sore, gentle limbering moves and stretches can ease your pain—see **Pain,** page 97). A good rule of thumb is to wait until soreness goes away before doing another intense workout. If your workouts aren't that hard and you don't get sore, you can come back sooner (or you might want to reevaluate your workouts and increase the intensity if appropriate).

The American College of Sports Medicine recommends strength training the whole body every other day, three times a week. They believe that twice weekly workouts can also be effective but give only 80 percent of the strength gains you get from three.

Roger Schwab, on the other hand, author of *Strength of a Woman* (Bryn Mawr, Penn.: Main Line Publications, 1997) and owner of Main Line Health and Fitness, prefers two or even only one workout a week to give muscles more time to rest. Schwab supervised a twelve-week circuit-style weight-training study with ten "unconditioned" women, some training two times a week, others training three. After the twelve weeks, the women who trained three times a week started to lose strength, while the two-times-a-week group continued to improve. The moral of this story: If you want to get stronger and train smarter, train less, train harder, rest more.

The power of rest

Progress is cyclical, not linear. Nobody can maintain high energy all the time and no one keeps getting stronger indefinitely. Strength curves, like learning curves, follow a natural rhythm. Sometimes we grow in spurts and learn quickly, other times we just have to process the information, rest, and adapt.

Here's how to tap the power of rest:

- If you're making gradual strength gains over a long period of time, then you're getting enough rest. Keep it up.
- If you're stuck on a strength plateau, try building in an extra day or two of rest and increase the weight, at least for 8 reps.
- If you're in a growth spurt, making big strength gains, don't assume it'll last forever. Pull back before you hit burnout. Don't go for more than three weeks of all-out intensity without taking at least a week or two of rest.

Resting between sets

How long you rest between sets is usually based on how hard you're working. Beepers go off in the gym all the time, letting someone, somewhere know rest time is over (a dreaded sound).

The traditional belief about rest time is:

- 15 to 20 reps of light weight (muscle endurance), rest for 20 to 30 seconds;
- 8 to 12 reps of moderate weight (for building strength and size), rest for 30 seconds to a minute;
- 1 to 6 reps of heavy weight (for building strength and power), rest for up to 5 minutes.

Active Rest

If you're dedicated to exercise, you know that being told to rest can make you crazy. Rest doesn't mean you have to sit on your butt all day. If you've got to have it (exercise, that is), then try active rest. This is a fancy term for cross training, which mixes light days with hard days (see **Cross Training,** page 167). It goes something like this:

- Push the weights hard on Monday.
- Ease up on Tuesday with a walk or bike ride.
- Take a yoga or dance class on Wednesday.
- On Thursday hit the weights again.
- Take Friday off or take a gentle walk or jog.
- On Saturday do some upbeat cardio.
- On Sunday sit around so you can be ready for the gym on Monday!

Other forms of active rest include working with lighter weights, not to failure; walking instead of running; and aquatic exercise instead of land-based. You can also stretch, work in the garden, play with kids, or walk the dog.

Taking rests between sets can be good when you feel tired or dizzy, or if you simply perform better with built-in downtime. But if resting makes you antsy, skip it or do it differently. Resting also takes your heart rate way down. If you don't rest you get a slight aerobic benefit.

As an alternative to resting, work a different body part; go from a leg exercise to the back or chest. Let one muscle group rest while you work another. Or stretch between sets—specifically, stretch the muscle you just worked.

Athletes at rest and in motion

If you're an athlete with a specific season of competitions or performances, adjust your training to suit these demands. When you have to be at your peak on the playing field or stage, you can't train very hard. It's maintenance time. This doesn't mean you should stop weight training altogether. Simply go lighter and less frequently to keep up strength and prevent injury. Save your big gains in strength for the off-season.

routines for all levels

Since each person's strength, schedule, preferences, and types of equipment are different, it's impossible to provide specific weights, reps, and numbers of sets for everyone. Therefore, we've focused on exercises and the muscles they work. These are explained in detail in basic exercises, but even so, space does not permit us to show all variations of all exercises. Substitute a complementary exercise for a specific body part as long as you know that it works. But keep to the muscle order specified, since each routine is designed in a logical sequence—large muscle groups first and muscles that work synergistically (push, pull, or opposing muscle groups) following one another.

Research has shown that people can make impressive strength gains from twice-weekly workouts, with one set per exercise. (For a full rundown on how to determine the optimum number of sets and reps, amount of weight, and number of strength workouts to do each week, see **Sets and Reps,** page 119).

The American College of Sports Medicine also recommends:

- 2 to 3 strength workouts per week, consisting of 10 exercises for major muscle groups. (If you want to do more than 10, aim for 12 to 14. Avoid doing more than 20 exercises as this is too stressful on the body and impedes recovery.)
- 1 set of 8 to 12 reps at moderate to high intensity sufficient enough to produce considerable muscle fatigue or failure and, therefore, strength gains.
- Workouts that last from 30 minutes to an hour.

Since the glucose that fuels a strength workout generally fizzles in 45 minutes to an hour, workouts that last longer than an hour mean either that you're not working hard enough in each set, or your rests between exercises are too long. Three full-body workouts per week may even be too many as muscles need at least 48 to 72 hours of recovery time (and muscles get strong in recovery, not in workouts).

Many people, however, want more results in a shorter period of time and so spend hours each week in the weight room splitting up body parts (the following routines cater to them as well). The splits also work well for people who like to zero in on body parts, rather than trying to get an all-over pump. It's very easy to go overboard with training. Muscles need recovery time to perform better and get stronger, and carbohydrate stores need about 48 hours to be completely replenished after intense workouts. So although various muscle groups may be ready to go, the fuel reserves may be too low to inspire a workout of any value.

The best way to get strong, no matter how you do it, is in short, intense workouts, followed by sufficient rest, proper nutrition, and complimentary activities that don't further impede your recovery. Going out for a long run the day after a leg workout, for example, impedes progress. A wiser choice might be a swim, a walk at a moderate intensity, or a session of yoga.

If you decide to split body parts, be sure to have at least three months of steady lifting under your belt before doing so. As you gain experience and strength, a true test of progress would have you spending less time in the gym but working harder when you're there.

Save your abs and lower-back exercises for last (but don't forget to do them!). They hold you steady throughout your workout. If they're both weak and tired, you may topple over. By the time you get to them at the end, however, they'll be preexhausted and won't need as much work to get *completely* exhausted.

Full-body gym routine, beginner

Exercise	Muscles Worked
Hip extension in multihip machine	Glutes, hamstrings, quads, lower back
Hamstring curl	Hamstrings
Leg extension	Quads
Sit-back squat	Glutes, hamstrings, quads
Pull downs to the chest	Lats
Machine chest press	Pecs and front delt
Machine shoulder press	Delts
Barbell biceps curl	Biceps
Triceps press-down	Triceps
Lower-back hyper-extension	Erectors
Abdominal stabilizer (see **Stabilization,** page 133)	Abdominals

Full-body gym routine, experienced

Exercise	Muscles Worked
Horizontal squat machine, Smith machine squat (or leg press)	Glutes, quads, hamstrings
In-place lunges (with or without hand weights or in Smith machine)	Glutes, quads, hamstrings
Leg extensions	Quads
Hamstring curls	Hamstrings
Inner-thigh machine	Adductors
Calf raises (standing and/or seated)	Gastroc and/or soleus
Bench press	Pecs and front delt
Chest flyes	Pecs and front delt
Seated row with low cable, narrow grip	Lats
Seated row with high cable, wide grip	Rhomboids
Lateral raises	Medial delts
Dumbbell biceps curls	Biceps
Triceps overhead extension	Triceps
Lower-back hyper-extensions	Erectors
Pelvic tilts for lower abs	Rectus

Full-body routine, at home, using body weight and dumbbells, beginner

Exercise	Muscles Worked
Sit-back squats or free squats, no weight	Glutes, quads, hamstrings
In-place lunges	Glutes, quads, hamstrings
Side leg raises (lie flat)	Abductors
Inner-thigh lifts (lie flat)	Abductors
Push-backs	Pecs and front delts
Lateral raises	Medial delts
Dumbbell biceps curls	Biceps
One-arm triceps extension	Triceps
Pelvic tilts for lower abs	Rectus
Crunches, regular and with twist	Rectus and obliques
Lower-back hyper-extensions	Erectors

Full-body routine, at home, using body weight and dumbbells, experienced

Exercise	Muscles Worked
Standing hip extensions	Glutes, hamstrings
Sit-back squats or free squats	Glutes, quads, hamstrings
Grand pliés	Glutes, quads, hamstrings, adductors
In-place lunges	Glutes, quads, hamstrings
Incline leg raises	Adductors
Incline inner-thigh lifts	Adductors
Push-ups	Pecs and front delt
Shoulder press	Delts
Rear delt flyes	Rear delts
Dumbbell biceps curls	Biceps
One-arm triceps extension	Triceps
Lower-back hyper-extensions	Erectors
Pelvic tilts for lower abs	Rectus
Crunches, regular and with twist	Rectus and obliques

Lower-body routine, gym or at-home workout, experienced

Exercise	Muscles Worked
Leg extensions	Quads
Hamstring curls	Hamstrings
Hip extensions	Glutes, hamstrings
Squats	Glutes, quads, hamstrings
Lunges	Glutes, quads, hamstrings
Incline leg lifts	Abductors
Inner thigh (machine or lying on side)	Adductors
Standing calf raises	Gastroc
Seated calf raises	Soleus

Upper-body routine, gym or at-home workout, experienced

Exercise	Muscles Worked
Pull downs to front	Lats
High pulls	Rhomboids
Upright rows	Trapezius
Chest machine or bench press (bar or dumbbells)	Pecs and front delts
Dumbbell or cable flyes	Pecs and front delts
Seated dumbbell press	Delts
Lateral raises	Medial delts
Rear delt flyes	Rear delts
Barbell biceps curls	Biceps
Triceps press-downs	Triceps
Pelvic tilts for lower abs	Rectus
Crunches, regular and with twist	Rectus and obliques
Hyper-extensions	Erectors

Chest, shoulder, triceps gym workout, experienced

Exercise	Muscles Worked
Bench press, bar, machine, or dumbbells, flat or decline	Pecs and front delt
Bench press, bar, machine, or dumbbells, incline	Pecs and front delt
Flyes, machine, dumbbells, or cable, flat or incline	Pecs and front delt
Standing cable crossovers	Pecs and front delt
Shoulder press, machine, dumbbells, or bar	Delts
Lateral raises, machine, dumbbells, or floor cables	Medial delts
Triceps press-down	Triceps
One-arm triceps extension	Triceps

Back and biceps gym workout, experienced

Exercise	Muscles Worked
Pull downs to chest	Lats
Pull over machine	Lats, trapezius
Seated row, low row with narrow handle	Lats
Seated row, high row with wide handle	Rhomboids
Hyper-extensions	Erectors
Upright row	Trapezius
Rear delt flyes	Rear delts
Barbell biceps curls	Biceps
Dumbbell biceps curls	Biceps

sets and reps

One of the most frequently asked questions about strength training is "How many sets and reps?" There are standard answers, and then there are intriguing ones. The bottom line is that many roads lead to muscle fatigue and strength.

As you experiment with numbers of sets and reps, try to choose methods that serve your changing needs. In other words, as a beginner, you might do many sets and many reps, but as you improve, you'll get more out of doing less.

How many reps?

The standard answer to the rep question is:

- 1 to 6 reps with heavy weight—to build power and brute strength
- 8 to 12 reps with moderate weight—to build strength and muscle size
- 12 to 15 or 20 reps with light weight—to build muscular endurance and some strength

But this doesn't take into account the quality or speed of those reps. The more intriguing and accurate way to count reps is to work specific muscle groups for certain periods of time. These time frames complement the size and capacity of different muscles. Be warned, however, that this approach is both harder and more humbling. But it's very effective. Work

- buttocks (with squats, leg presses, etc.) for 90 seconds to 2 minutes

- legs (hamstring, quads, inner/outer thigh) for 1 minute to 90 seconds
- back, chest, and abs for 45 to 75 seconds
- shoulders, arms, and other small muscles (calves, wrists, neck) for 45 seconds to a minute.

You don't have to use a stopwatch to keep track. Simply time your reps.

The 8-second rep

REPS	BODY PART
11 to 15	buttocks
8 to 11	legs
6 to 9	back, chest, abs
6 to 8	shoulders, arms, etc.

The 6-second rep

REPS	BODY PART
15 to 20	buttocks
10 to 15	legs
8 to 13	back, chest, abs
8 to 10	shoulders, arms, etc.

How many sets?

The American College of Sports Medicine, body-builders, trainers, and gym veterans have been recommending 2 to 3 sets for years, and many have gotten good results. But more and more people are trading quantity for quality and doing fewer sets at a higher intensity. Both multiple and single sets have their pros and cons, and both work. The bottom line is that you want to fatigue the muscles to elicit an anabolic response. How you want to do that is up to you. Keep in mind, the trade-offs have to do with time and energy.

Multiple Sets

Advantages	Drawbacks
With each set, your fatigue accumulates, so you may work more total muscle fibers (the ultimate goal).	You tend not to give your best effort when you know you've got more sets.
You use up more calories in your workout.	They're time consuming.
You don't have to work at such a high intensity to improve.	The high volume of work can easily cause injury, or your muscles can get so fatigued they can't regenerate tissue and actually get weaker and shrink (they become catabolic). If your intensity is very low, you probably won't get results. Even a large quantity of submaximal work will lead to submaximal results.

Single Sets

Advantages	Drawbacks
You cut your workout time in half or by a third, getting comparable results to doing multiple sets (while decreasing risk of overuse injury).	If you can't muster the energy to work hard, shape, a teenager, or a senior citizen, this you might not get enough of a stimulus to make your single set worthwhile.
You're more willing to work to failure (see **Failure,** page 63) because you know you've got only one set.	If you're sick, injured, pregnant, out of may not be the way to go because you shouldn't go to failure.
Single sets lend themselves to shorter or no rest between sets, giving training a slight aerobic benefit.	
This is a safe way to train because during your last, most intense (and most valuable) reps, the fatigued muscle fibers can't generate enough force for you to hurt yourself.	

The Joy of Sets

If you get bored with the straight approach to sets, try some of these classical techniques for increasing "sets appeal." Do them to save time, mix up your workout, alleviate mental and muscle boredom, and make deeper "inroads" into your muscle fibers.

Note: When doing two or more sets back to back, try not to rest for more than 15 seconds between sets to maintain intensity.

Supersets: Two back-to-back sets of different exercises that either work the same muscle group (i.e., bench press and chest flyes) or opposing muscle groups (biceps curls and triceps press-downs).

Triple and giant sets: Same theory as above, but with three or more exercises for the same or opposing muscle groups.

Pyramids—up and down: When you're doing multiple sets of the same exercise, you either increase the weight (pyramid up) or decrease it (pyramid down) with each set.

Drop sets: Start with a heavy weight and, with good form, do as many reps as you can to failure. Then, without resting, decrease the weight and continue. Drop the weight at least once and work to failure with each successively lighter weight.

Run the rack: This is a drop set, using dumbbells (usually found on a rack). As in a drop set, start with a heavier weight and fail, put it down, pick up the next lighter set . . . and so on down the rack. For a good time, try biceps curls starting, say, with 15s and drop to 12½s, 10s, 7½s, 5s. Your biceps will be singing.

Negatives: Have someone assist you on the lift while you simply lower the weight. A good place to do this is pull-ups—more accurately described as "jump ups and then lower yourself down" (see also **Contractions,** page 51).

21s: Divide a movement (like a biceps or hamstring curl) in half. Do 7 lifts in the lower half, followed by 7 lifts in the upper half. Finish with 7 full-range-of-motion lifts. Why someone chose lucky 7s instead of crazy 8s no one knows.

Super slo-mo: This is a catchy phrase for samurai weight lifting—you attack your opponent (the weight) with the willingness to suffer. Super slo-mo's start with 10-second reps, and pass into the great beyond of 15-, 20-, and 30-second reps. Going this slow will frazzle your brain, fry your muscles, and make smoke come out of your ears, all at the speed of a slow Bronco chase. Very surreal.

shoulders

Shoulders are called deltoids, or delts, because they were named after the Greek word *delta,* which describes their triangular shape. Delts are commonly referred to by their three sections—front, middle, and rear (or anterior, medial, and posterior)—and are trained accordingly:

Front delts

These assist in all push moves and in chest work. For this reason they get their workout with pec work. Because these muscles can get overworked with extra exercises, it makes better sense to balance shoulder muscle strength with exercises that focus on middle and rear delts.

Middle delts

The middle delts primarily lift the arm out to the side and provide a finished, "cap" look to the body's outline.

The rear deltoid

The smallest of the three muscles extends the arm back behind the torso and also assists in external rotation (when you touch the back of your head). Stronger rear delts, along with upper back exercises (for rhomboids) help maintain correct posture.

Rotator cuff

Another group of muscles that play a key role in shoulder health are the rotator cuff muscles. These four muscles rotate the arm in and out and hold the shoulders steady when the arm is lifted out to the side. They are small muscles that can be easily injured when made to hold more weight than they can handle. Impingement syndrome, a common condition, occurs when the rotators and bursas (little sacs of fluid that help pad the joints) become swollen, which then causes pain when the arm is pressed forward or lifted out to the side.

Shoulders need to be trained with care. Many people, however, overwork their shoulders with fast moves and heavy weight, unaware (until it's too late) of how vulnerable they are. Nine major muscles and several smaller ones cross the shoulder joint, so shoulder muscles are involved to some degree in *all* upper-body movements, whether as active muscles or stabilizers. The shoulder joint itself is a ball and socket design, much like the hip, although the bones aren't as sturdy. Both hip and shoulder joints allow arms and legs to move in a number of ways:

- Forward and back (flex and extend)
- Away from and across the center of the body (abduct and adduct)
- In circles (circumduct)
- In and out (internally and externally rotate)

All these actions make the shoulder both more crucial and more vulnerable than other joints in the body. The best advice for shoulder training is to work strictly, slowly, and with a weight you can handle. Also, avoid putting your shoulder joints into unnecessarily dangerous positions.

overhead presses

Targets front and middle deltoids

When it's done correctly, the overhead press can be a great shoulder exercise; when it's done incorrectly, it can be a nightmare. Whether you do this with your back supported on a bench, seated on a flat bench, or standing, be sure to keep your spine in strict neutral alignment. Pressing weights overhead can easily compromise your spine.

1. Start with dumbbells slightly above and next to your shoulders.
2. Press weights straight up, keeping shoulders down. To get the most out of light weights (3 to 10 pounds), keep hands parallel as you raise them. To lift heavier weights (5 to 20 pounds), raise weights and bring together overhead.

If you're using a bar, pass the bar *in front* of your face and rest it lightly on the upper chest between reps.

Caveats: Never press a barbell up from behind your head. The most dangerous thing you can do to your rotators is to put weight on them when they're already externally rotated. When using dumbbells, make sure you press weights up, not forward or out to the sides. The farther the weights are from the joint, the more dangerous the move becomes.

Better lifting tips: If using dumbbells, keep weights above shoulder joints. As arms extend, keep elbows soft and avoid shrugging.

lateral raises

Targets front and middle deltoids

1. Standing or seated, hold dumbbells (or crossed cables or resistance bands) down by your side. Before you lift, soften your elbows and press your shoulders down and back.
2. Lift weights to the 3 and 9 o'clock positions.
3. Lower to 6 o'clock. Avoid banging weights together at the bottom as this will propel them up with momentum. Lower with control.

Caveats: Don't lock your elbows. This is a common cheating technique for diverting work out of the deltoids and it strains elbow tendons.

Better lifting tips: Keep your spine and especially your lower back completely still as you lift your arms.

rear delt flyes

Targets rear deltoids

1. Sit or lie facedown on a flat or incline bench (an incline bench, set lower than a 45-degree angle, is more comfortable).
2. Whether seated or prone, lift your arms straight up the line of gravity (don't lift arms on an angle) so hands end up parallel to or slightly behind your back. Use light weight here—these are little muscles. Even 2 pounds get very heavy when form is strict.

Caveats: Make sure this is just a one-joint move. Don't bend elbows as you lift or lower the arms.

Better lifting tips: Be sure to keep your neck in line with your spine.

external rotators

Targets shoulder rotators (rotator cuff)

Shoulder rotators are most commonly injured in the movement of external rotation. The following is a good preventive as well as rehab exercise (as long as it doesn't cause pain).

1. Lie on your side with a very light weight in your upper hand. Fix the elbow into your waist as a fulcrum point.
2. Raise the dumbbell from an 8 to an 11 o'clock position.
3. To work internal rotators, start with the weight at 11 o'clock and slowly bring your bent arm in toward the body to create an internal rotation.

Caveat: Don't get too ambitious with the amount of weight or your range of motion. Keep it light, small, controlled, and pain-free.

Better lifting tips: Support your head with your other hand or rest your head on a rolled up sweatshirt or pillow.

split routines

If you see a group of weight lifters standing around the gym and want to get them all riled up, ask for their theories on split routines. This is gym-speak for "What's the best way to train different body parts—all together or split into separate workouts?" You may hear wildly conflicting opinions about this. At one end of the spectrum is the minimalist approach: 2 (maybe 3, but that's pushing it) full-body workouts per week, end of discussion. At the other end is the elaborate approach: 1 or 2 body parts each day, or even twice a day, 3 to 6 days a week. (This option is overdoing it. There are more sensible split routines.)

Based on common sense and efficiency, full-body routines win, hands down. You save time, energy, and minimize your risk of injury. But from a kinesthetic perspective (a right-brained sensation-oriented approach), split routines often *feel* more satisfying. The trouble is, a split routine puts you in the gym too much, which can lead to burnout, overtraining, injury, and a neglected outside life. However, both full-body and split routines have their merits and drawbacks, and appeal to different personality types.

Whatever way you decide to group your body parts, you should aim to spend *less* time training (not more) but make your training time more concentrated, intense, and satisfying.

Full-body Workouts

Advantages	Drawbacks
You can work harder while training because you've gotten enough rest.	You can't spend adequate time exploring, feeling, and fatiguing all body parts.
You get more rest between workouts so muscles can heal and carbs can be replenished, giving you more energy.	Both your attention and blood flow get dispersed to all muscles, so you don't end up with as localized a pump.
Your body heals as a unit. Training as a unit (rather than training in chunks) is more respectful of this healing process.	
You spend less time in the gym.	

Split Routines

Advantages	Drawbacks
You focus the work in specific body parts and receive physical and psychological satisfaction from working specific muscles fairly hard.	Training several days a week doesn't let you replenish glycogen, which can leave you feeling flat.
You fatigue more muscle fibers in a localized area.	This can easily lead to obsessive overtraining and doesn't leave enough time for other activities.
Allow you to more finely chisel your body.	

How do you decide what's right for you?

The best way to decide between full-body workouts or split routines is to experiment and see which you like best, which serves your schedule, personality, and goals. (For a full rundown on various full-body and split workouts, plus exercises, see **Routines for All Levels,** page 113.) There's also no law that says you can't mix both methods, especially as your needs, life, and time constraints change.

A Compromise Workout

It's possible to morph the focus of a split routine with the efficiency of a full-body workout. Some people do an upper-lower body split routine this way:

- Monday: buttocks and legs
- Thursday: upper body and abs
- 3 or 4 days each week, do a variety of physical activities—riding a bike, playing soccer, skating, rock climbing, yoga, dancing, or martial arts
- 1 day: total rest or light stretches

Although the muscles only get one "serious" workout per week, they often get secondary workouts from other activities. All this activity can still increase the risk of overtraining, but this approach leads to better overall conditioning—and why not have fun with that strength? A seasoned exerciser (as opposed to an obsessive exerciser) often becomes sensitive to the signs of injury and knows when to ease up.

spotting

Spotting is a great gym tradition that helps you get strong with a little help from your friends. One person lifts while the other helps with form, safety (to bail you out when you fail), a few more reps, some negative reps, and well-timed words of encouragement. It's also beneficial to have the emotional support of simply having someone present. Good spotting takes practice and communication. Use words, body language, and be sensitive to each other.

Spotting dos and don'ts

Being a good spotter is like being a bridesmaid. Your job is to let the other person shine. To do this, you have to be 100 percent present.

Do

- Know your limits. If a hulky person wants you to spot a 250-pound bench press and this is beyond your stratosphere of possibility, defer. (If they accidentally drop the bar on their throat, it's your fault.)
- Ask for particulars on how and when they want to be spotted.
- Put yourself in a safe position. Squat down when you need to (especially when spotting a bench press, squat, or pull-up). Keep your knees bent and your lower back in neutral and stable. Try to lift with your whole body (legs and back) and not just arms.

- Help them maintain the intended path of movement. Don't push sideways (unless you're unracking or reracking). This is very annoying.
- Use the finger method. Start by giving one finger's worth of assistance, then 2, then your whole hand. A light touch is best at first. When they're finished, give them an indication of just how much you helped (1 finger or 2 pounds' worth?). People like to know.
- Talk them through it. Some favorite spotting phrases include: "all you," "come on," "good form," "watch that (shoulder, hip, back, etc.)," "one more," "you can do it," "beautiful," and "good job."

Don't

- Help too much or too soon (this is patronizing).
- Block their view in the mirror or put yourself in the path of the weight.
- Acknowledge anyone else's presence. Ignore attractive people strutting by, your favorite song or announcements on the loud speakers, your beeper, and your cell phone.

Dos and don'ts of being spotted

Do

- Tell your spotter how many reps you can do on your own so they know when to jump in, like Mighty Mouse, to save the day.
- Tell them to stand back until you give them a word or a nod if you don't want them to help until you need them.
- Show them where you want them to hold the weight for you. If doing a pull-up, do you want to be pushed up from the knees or the waist? When doing a free-bar bench press, do you want them to squat down and lift the bar from underneath or pull it from above (lifting from underneath is easier on the spotter's body). When doing a dumbbell press (for chest or shoulders), do you want them to hold your elbows or the weights? (Pushing from the elbows feels better for the person lifting and is easier for the spotter.)
- Let them know if you need help racking or unracking the weight.
- If you have any lifting quirks (for example, your hips shake from side to side when you squat), ask them to observe and point out when you do this.

Don't

- Depend on your spotter to do the work for you. If you need the other person to work too hard, your weight is too heavy.
- Assume someone else will know how to spot you. Be clear about how you'd like them to do it.

squats

A squat might look (and sound) like a lowly, basic move. But it can be a beautiful thing, simple yet powerful—a complex orchestration of multiple muscle groups that takes concentration to do correctly. A squat works many muscles at once: buttocks, hamstrings, quads, inner thighs, lower back, and abs. It's even believed to make upper-body muscles strong. Squats are also highly functional—for example, we should use the squat when we pick up suitcases or boxes.

But the squat can be as risky as it is effective. In fact, it becomes an orthopedic time bomb if you do it wrong and with heavy weight. The good news is you don't need to use heavy weight to get the most out of this exercise. You don't even need to do traditional, free-standing squats if they don't work for your body.

Why Heavy Barbell Squats Are a Bad Thing

Putting a heavy barbell on your neck
- compresses vertebrae
- puts damaging shear forces (a side-to-side wobbling) on knees
- puts enormous stress on the lower back
- can cause a ruptured or herniated disc

All the stresses are worse if you're tall. A long torso and legs create a big biomechanical disadvantage. The farther the barbell is from your lower back, the heavier it feels.

Regardless of the squat you choose, the form is essentially the same.

The rules of the road for all squats

- Place your feet hip-distance apart or, at most, double hip-distance. More than that misaligns ankles, knees, and hips, and shortens your range of motion. (A very narrow stance is acceptable but is an advanced move.) With feet close, don't squeeze knees together (this deflects some of the up and down force— that's cheating).

- Because women have wider hips (and more external rotation of the hip), they get a deeper range of motion if they turn out toes slightly, to 11 and 1 o'clock. Men can keep feet parallel.

- Sit hips back (as if sitting down) before you bend your knees. Some people think squats are simply elaborate knee bends. Think hips, then knees.

Sit back into a semi-squat.

- When doing freestanding squats, allow the chest to incline forward slightly but keep your back in neutral (maintaining a slight contraction in the lower back).

- Do not bend your knees more than 90 degrees (too much knee bend rounds the back and strains ligaments in knees and back). A shorter range of motion is OK.

- Keep heels on the floor. If you have short Achilles tendons (usually from wearing high heels) that pull heels up, support heels under two 5-pound plates.

- Press up through the heels, not the balls of your feet. Keep the three main joints (ankles, hips, and shoulders) aligned and balanced above each other.

- Make a smooth transition between the lowering and the lift (no "dropping" or bouncing at the bottom).

- As you straighten legs, squeeze the quads and glutes. Avoid locking knees.

Sit-back squat. For advice on the sit-back squat, see **Buttocks**, *page 39.*

The free squat. For details on the free squat, see **Buttocks**, *page 39.*

squat alternatives

These next two squats require gym equipment. Both change your angle and remove stress from your back and knees. As a variation, try them with ankles and knees squeezed together to work inner thighs. You can also do these exercises one leg at a time. One-legged squats are humbling and difficult. Because you surrender your wide base of support (which adds a biomechanical advantage), you may need to work one leg with less than half your two-legged weight and with less than a full range of motion. Try these variations with caution. The advantage of a one-legged move is that you can't press more with your stronger leg.

The horizontal squat: This machine minimizes stress in both lower back and knees. Be sure, before you lie down, to adjust the sliding pad so you have a full range of motion (knees should bend to a 90-degree angle). Place your feet at the *top* of the foot plate so your kneecaps don't shoot out over your toes. You can vary the width of your stance but remember the Rules of the Road.

Variation: the one-legged horizontal squat

Align your working leg so it's straight in line with your hips. Raise your nonworking leg, so it's ready to spot you at any time.

The hack squat: This viscous-sounding exercise is actually very forgiving. Like the horizontal squat, it offers lower-back support. Although pads rest on your shoulders, this weight doesn't dangerously compress the vertebrae because you're inclined back. Hack machines run the gamut from ridiculously light to absurdly heavy (usually old equipment found in grunt gyms). Know your hack machine and capabilities before you load it with weight and jump on. Put toes on the outside edge of the foot plate to protect your knees. Again, follow the Rules of the Road.

Variation: the one-legged hack squat

If you have access to a light hack squat, try a one-legged version with light weight and half your average range of motion. Make sure your working leg is directly aligned under your hips. Keep your other foot slightly ahead of the working leg so you can spot yourself. *Never* bend your nonworking knee so it touches the foot plate.

stabilization

Stabilization is not the sexiest subject, but don't turn the page! In the world of strength training it is a subject of utmost importance because it gives you functional strength. If you want to make progress, you've got to hold your torso, hips, and shoulders still while you move arms and legs. If you can't do this, you've got no business hoisting heavy metal. Building strength is like building a house. You build a good foundation before you decorate the bedroom. So before you start training the "look-good muscles," make sure you can stabilize

- the torso (abdominals and lower back)
- the pelvis (abductors and adductors)
- the shoulder girdle (pecs, lats, and the other muscles that stabilize the shoulder)

If these areas are weak and wobbly (and on most out-of-shape people, they are), you can strengthen them three ways:

1. Start with the stability exercises below, two or three times a week for about two weeks before you do any other exercises.
2. Strengthen the stabilizing muscles (especially in the hips and torso) with weight or resistance (see basic exercises for **Abdominals, Back,** and **Hips and Thighs**, pages 5, 17, and 74).
3. Simply hold these areas still while you exercise other parts. (This puts the stabilizers into isometric contraction and builds both muscular strength and endurance.)

Pelvic stabilizers

Without pelvic stabilization, you can fall over. The abductors (upper hip) and adductors (inner thigh) hold the body upright and help you walk. These are the balance muscles of the lower body that play an even more important role as people age (poor stabilization causes falls and fractures).

The abductors are high on the back of the hip, the gluteus medius and minimus. Another abductor, the tensor fascia latae, is located closer to the outer thigh. These muscles literally hold up our hips between foot steps and assist in leg movements such as lunging, walking, running, and dancing.

Ab stabilizer

Anytime you press, pull, twist, throw, dance, jump, etc., you need to anchor into your core muscles to maintain a stable torso. Along with the lower back muscles, ab stabilizers hold the trunk still.

The main abdominal stabilizers are the obliques, the muscles on the sides of the torso. The rectus abdominis, the central abdominal muscle, doesn't actually stabilize the torso, especially when the body's upright (if it did, more people would have stronger abs), unless you consciously contract it.

The following exercise gives stabilizing power to *all* the abdominals. What makes this different from a regular crunch is that the abs aren't the main movers but they work very hard to hold you still.

Your mission is to keep your torso *motionless*. You may flatten the lower back into the floor or maintain a neutral spine, whichever is more comfortable. Just pick one position and don't change it. Lie on the floor with your feet and arms up, knees and elbows bent at a 90-degree angle. Simultaneously, extend one leg straight out (but keep it up in the air) and both arms overhead. If this causes lower-back pain, don't lower the leg close to the floor. Return to the starting position before you switch legs. Do as many reps as you can, maintaining form, for at least a minute.

Lower-back stabilizer

Lower-back muscles work to hold you upright when you sit or stand. But anytime you lean the torso forward beyond 60 degrees (halfway forward is 45 degrees), these muscles stop working and the ligaments support the weight of the spine. This can damage ligaments (and is the reason why unsupported forward flexion is such a no-no). Add to this a twisting motion and you've got a recipe for spinal disaster because, in this position, you can easily tear the protective fibers around the vertebrae and cause a herniated or slipped disk. One way to protect yourself is to strengthen the lower-back stabilizers. Another is to avoid unsupported and twisting positions.

Get down on your hands and knees and set your spine in neutral (see **Neutral Spine,** page 95). Lift your opposite arm and leg so they're in line with your spine (no higher). Hold for a full second. Slowly lower and switch sides without noticeably shifting weight onto your other knee. As in the abdominal stabilizer, your mission is to keep your torso motionless as you move arms and legs. Do as many reps as you can, maintaining form, for at least a minute.

Shoulder stabilizers

Shoulders play a part in almost all upper-body movements and exercises. The trick is to hold them still when they're not supposed to move. When you do a biceps curl, for instance, your chest and back muscles should isometrically contract to hold the shoulder girdle steady. If the shoulders are not stable, they're primed for impingement syndrome, a painful inflammation that limits motion and can cause headaches and carpal tunnel syndrome.

The two best ways to strengthen shoulder stabilizers are to hold your shoulders down and back when you perform virtually all upper-body exercises and to strengthen all upper-body muscles.

Upper hip stabilizers

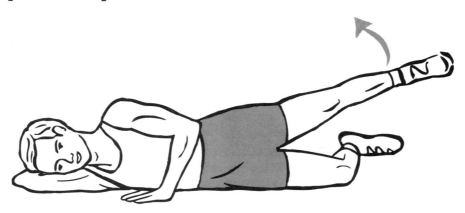

The old standard leg lift is good for strengthening the tensor fascia. Lie on the floor on your side. Bend the bottom knee to a 45-degree angle. Keep the top leg parallel to the floor and lift to a 45-degree angle. (For a greater range of motion, see, under **Hips and Thighs,** "Leg Raises," page 75). To incorporate the gluteus minimus and medius, bring the working leg forward over the supporting knee and rotate the toes so they point down toward the floor. Do as many reps as you can with good form for up to a minute and a half.

The inner thigh muscles, the adductors
These muscles take up a significant amount of thigh space (about a third) and help stabilize the leg when you walk, squat, or lunge.

Lie on your side, put the top knee on the floor and raise the lower leg. (Again, for greater range of motion, see **Hips and Thighs,** page 74). Do as many reps as you can with good form for up to a minute and half.

stretches for strength training

Stronger muscles don't result in a muscle-bound body. That's a myth. It's true that if you overdevelop certain muscles and never stretch them, you'll look lopsided, feel stiff, and walk funny. But stronger muscles are usually more elastic than weak muscles and therefore stretch farther. They can also do this without stressing ligaments and tendons (see **Ligaments,** page 204, and **Tendons,** page 243).

You can stretch before, during, and/or after your strength workouts. Each achieves a slightly different effect.

Before: It's best to do 5 minutes of easy aerobics (on a bike, for instance) before your first stretch because warm muscles stretch farther than cool ones (see **Warm-Ups for Weight Training,** page 144). But many people opt for stretches only. In general, keep preworkout stretches gentle, static (no bouncing!), and short (there's no need to stretch for more than 10 seconds). Use this time to mentally prepare for your workout.

During: Stretching between sets is a good way to make constructive use of rest time, especially when you do 2 or 3 sets of the same exercise. Your workout then becomes a kind of muscle yoga. If you choose to stretch between sets, try to stretch the muscle you just worked. However, you might want to save your lying-down stretches for last so you don't have to keep dropping to the floor.

After: Stretching after your workout lets you iron out all the remaining kinks. Muscles are now thoroughly warm and full of pumped blood and lactic acid. Stretching removes excess waste products from the muscles, which helps prevent soreness. After exercise is also the time when you can make permanent improvements in flexibility. Hold each stretch for 10 to 30 seconds (or more) and exhale to relax further.

lat stretch

1. Hold on to something you can't pull over, such as a pole or fixed piece of machinery.
2. With feet hip-distance apart, knees bent, and back in neutral, pull away from the pole and stretch one side. Repeat on the other side. Don't pull too hard on your shoulder joint.

triceps/rear shoulder stretch

Cross one arm in front of the chest and gently pull the elbow toward the opposite shoulder.

chest/front shoulder stretch

Do this standing or seated.
1. Put your hands on the back of your head, palms forward and elbows up.
2. Press the chest forward, hold shoulders down and pull elbows back. Pull elbows back only as far as is comfortable.

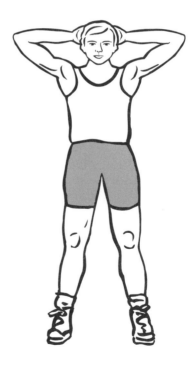

hamstring stretch

1. Lie on your back and bend one knee so that your foot is flat on the floor.
2. Extend your other leg up to the ceiling and hold on to the back of that leg. If you can't reach with your hands, use a small towel around your leg to pull the leg in. Your stretching leg doesn't need to be completely straight. As you gain flexibility, you can try to straighten the leg.
3. For an even greater stretch, flex the heel to the ceiling.

hip flexor stretch

1. Lie down on your back on a bench with one hip at the edge.
2. Pull that side's knee to your chest (for your lower back and for balance) and let the weight of the leg stretch the front of your hip (this is also a good stretch after step aerobics or stair climbing).

quad stretch

1. Stand on one leg, raise the other leg and grab onto the foot.
2. Pull the heel *away* from, not into, the buttocks.

erector spinae (lower back) stretch

1. Lie on your back.
2. Pull both knees toward your shoulders and grab the soles of your feet or behind your knees. Let your tailbone lift off the floor.

abdominal stretch

1. Lying on your back, extend your arms overhead and your legs straight along the floor.

2. Gently arch the lower back. This stretches abdominals from pubic bone to breast bone.

calf stretch

1. Stand with your toes on a riser or step (and your heels hanging off) and hold on to something so you don't fall over.

2. Lower one heel at a time below the step and hold the stretch. Repeat with the other foot.

trainers

It's true that anybody with half a bicep and a clipboard can call themselves a trainer (also a personal-wellness coach or fitness facilitator). Since no single governing agency sets the standards for trainers, the field has its share of shady characters.

But, if you're wondering "Should I hire a trainer?" ask yourself this: "Would I fly a plane without lessons?" Pushing weight around is dangerous if you don't know what you're doing, and a good trainer isn't hard to find.

When you join a gym, you're often entitled to a few free training sessions. Take them so you know how to navigate the floor, adjust seats, and lift weights properly. Some "floor" trainers are very good, and do this to build an independent training business. Some are hustlers. Some are trainers-in-training (everyone's got to start somewhere). You might get lucky with an assigned trainer. But to get quality training you have to seek it out.

When you're shopping for a trainer

Many people find a trainer by joining a gym and watching several trainers in action before making a choice. If you do this, notice if the trainer is instructing or just counting. What's the trainer's bench-side manner? Some people hire trainers on looks alone because they think "Maybe I can look like them." Considering everyone's genetic differences, this usually isn't possible. A trainer's impressive physique also doesn't ensure that a good teacher dwells within. Education, communication, and patience are more valuable assets.

Education and professionalism

Professionally minded trainers often display brochures that list certifications, specialties, education, training philosophies, and fees. In the past decade, hundreds of certifying organizations have come and gone. The best ones are still around. Although certification doesn't guarantee that a trainer is knowledgeable or can communicate, it does at least show that he or she had to sit, study, pass a test, and take continuing education to stay up-to-date. Still, lots of trainers remain uncertified. Avoid them. The leading certifying organizations are:

ACSM, the American College of Sports Medicine. Considered the Rolls-Royce of training certifications, their test is designed for trainers, exercise physiologists, and physicians and consists of practical and written elements. It's also famous for being tough (many trainers fail it a few times). ACSM has no phone hotline listing ACSM certified trainers. But ACSM certified trainers are encouraged to advertise as such in all promotional materials. For more on ACSM and hot topics on fitness, visit their website at www.acsm.org/sportsmed.

ACE, the American Council on Exercise. This organization offers a very thorough personal training certification (also aerobic and weight management certifications). To find ACE certified trainers in your area, call 1-800-825-3636. If you give them your zip code, they'll supply you with the names, background, and fees of three trainers. For other info about ACE, plus info on fitness, visit their website at www.ace-fitness.org.

NSCA, the National Strength and Conditioning Association. This organization sports two certifications: the CSCS, or Certified Strength and Conditioning Specialist (which includes sports conditioning), and the Personal Trainer exam, a favorite among trainers because it's more specifically geared to strength-training technique than the exams of other organizations. NSCA doesn't have a phone hotline for certified trainers, but you can visit their website for more info and educational materials at www.colosoft.com/nsca.

AFAA, the Aerobics and Fitness Association of America. This was one of the pioneer certifying organizations and it now offers several types of certifications. For a list of AFAA certified trainers in your area, call the Fitness Practitioners hotline at 1-800-YOURBOD (928-7263). For more info and educational materials, visit their website at www.afaa.com.

A degree in exercise science or physiology is one of the best means of certification, since it shows ongoing education and not just cramming for a test. Carrying liability insurance is another sign of professionalism; trainers carry this coverage in case someone drops a dumbbell on their foot, though such occurrences are rare.

A Trainer Should

- Take a full medical history and lifestyle evaluation, and design a program to help you achieve your goals, especially if you have any medical concerns.
- Address postural quirks (teach you neutral spine and stabilization) and modify exercises for weaknesses and/or past injuries.
- Design a full program for you, not just weights but cardio and stretching as well.
- Assess your current level of strength, cardiovascular fitness, and flexibility and monitor your progress.
- Update your program every few weeks or months.
- Train you so that ultimately you don't need them anymore. (A really good trainer will "graduate" you so you can work out without them!)

Fees

Fees range from $25 to $250 an hour, but the high-end prices are found mostly in Hollywood and Manhattan. A top-of-the-line trainer (without the celebrity clients, who inflate fees), usually makes between $40 and $75 a session, more for traveling to your home. Novice trainers usually charge the lowest fees. Be sure to find out if that fee is per hour or session, so you don't pay more if the session runs long. Many trainers offer free or discounted first sessions— ask. When you find someone you want to hire, ask him or her about discounts for a series. (Be sure to ask how long those unused sessions are good for. Don't expect to use a session three years after you paid for it.)

Extra questions for your trainer

- Do they have any additional specialties you might be interested in: massage therapy, martial arts, or the Alexander technique, for example?
- Can they offer simple nutritional guidance, such as meal or menu planning?
- Do they give you a body-fat test? Take measurements?
- Do they do unusual things, such as videotaping your workout so you can see your lifting technique?
- Will they design a portable workout with equipment you can take when you travel?
- Will they offer you discounts if you refer your friends?
- Can they also recommend other good trainers, in case you want more information from a different perspective?

What a trainer looks for in you

This is a two-way relationship. Just because you're paying doesn't mean you'll both be happy. Trainers have been known to fire problem clients. A trainer isn't there to do the work for you—he or she is there to guide you. To be a good client, you should:

- Be curious and willing to learn; ask questions and write down the answers and the workout in a format you understand.
- Take responsibility for learning how to adjust the seats, unrack and rerack weights, and so on.
- Be punctual—if you're half an hour late, you lose.
- Not cancel an hour before your workout unless it's an absolute emergency. Some trainers, like doctors, have a twenty-four-hour cancellation policy and charge in full if you cancel on short notice.
- Treat the trainer and the work with respect. Trainers don't like to be grouped with all the other hired help.
- Not turn it into a therapy session. Many clients pour their hearts out to trainers, and many trainers listen and pour their hearts out in return. Sometimes this is what people need on an exceptionally rough day. But the trainer didn't go to school for counseling. The more you talk, the less you work.

warm-ups for weight training

There are many ways to warm up for a strength workout, but there's really no ultimate warm-up. A warm-up should simply prepare both your body and mind for work. The three most popular ways to warm up are listed below. You can keep it simple or combine them. Just make sure your warm-up doesn't exceed 8 minutes or it becomes counterproductive.

The cardio warm-up

Five minutes on a bike, treadmill, stair machine, or other cardio machine at a low intensity will increase your blood flow, raise your body temperature, and lubricate joints and muscles. It also serves as a good mental buffer. Once you break a light sweat, you're warm. Some people like to follow this with light stretches (and even a light warm-up set) before lifting.

Light stretches

If you like to stretch before strength training, it's ideal after 5 minutes of cardio since warm muscles stretch farther. Keep stretches gentle and short—there's no need to hold them for longer than 10 seconds. Save your flexibility-enhancing stretches for post-workout.

Of course, you can do warm-up stretches without the cardio. But the muscles won't be as warm, so don't try to stretch too far. Stretching alone before the workout will moderately increase your flexibility but not your body temperature. Another option is to mix rhythmic limbering motions (as in an aerobic class warm-up) with stretches to make muscles warmer.

The areas that might need stretching most before a workout are: the lower back, the shoulders and the hamstrings. (See **Stretches for Strength Training**, page 137.)

Light sets

Although some trainers consider this politically incorrect, you can do away with the cardio warm-up and light stretching and simply perform one or two *very light* warm-up sets. Choose an exercise for a major muscle group: buttocks/legs, back, or chest (a leg press, pull down, or chest press, for example). Warming the big muscles will warm the small ones, too.

Use light resistance, high reps, and slow, controlled motion to get blood flowing. Don't push to fatigue (save that for the workout).

Once you've completed one or two warm-up sets, you can do some light stretches. Just make sure you feel completely warm and prepared before you work at higher intensity. You *don't* need a warm-up set for each individual exercise (lots of people do this). Remember: Many sets at a submax intensity don't make you strong.

weights and aerobics:

which to do first?

There's no easy answer to this question. It depends on what you're trying to achieve, your schedule, your preferences, and what ultimately works best for you.

Of course, this question only comes up when you do both on the same day. But it's not a bad idea to do half an hour of weights and half an hour of aerobics on the same day, two or three days a week, especially if that's all the time you have for any kind of exercise but you can give a full hour to exercising on those days (and maybe another 5 or 10 minutes for stretching).

The advantages of doing it this way are

• You work and rest your body as one unit.

• Your muscles get more total recovery time between workouts.

• You're not at high risk for overtraining or burning out.

The disadvantages are you might not get enough time to explore and enjoy different types of workouts, and if you're a fidgety type, you might get antsy on off days without any, even very gentle, exercise.

Doing your weights, aerobics, and possibly your flexibility workouts on separate days has its advantages in that you have more time to devote to different types of workouts. Of course, the big disadvantage is you don't get enough rest and you can easily overtrain and lose motivation.

All of this brings us back to the original question: Assuming you choose weights and aerobics on the same day, which should you do first?

For weight loss and fitness

Do weights first. With fresh muscles and a clear state of mind, you can focus better on form and working hard. Lifting weights takes skill and concentration. Get the tough stuff over with first. Lifting weights and aerobics both use glucose (stored carbohydrates) for fuel, although aerobic activity burns glucose (and fat) in the presence of oxygen and weight training does not (see **Aerobic vs. Anaerobic,** page 150). It's best to come to your weight workout with a full tank of glucose, which will start to dwindle after 45 minutes. If you do 30 minutes of weights, without resting between sets, you'll also get a moderate *cardio* benefit from your workout. If you do aerobics after weights, you'll start using fat for fuel sooner and therefore begin burning more fat.

To clarify this last point, if you do aerobics first, you'll spend approximately 20 minutes burning through your glucose (more if you're not fit, less if you are) and only get about 10 minutes of fat burning. By the time you hit the weights, your glucose will be down so you might feel too fatigued to train with enthusiasm.

Still, some people swear by cardio first because it energizes them for weights. If this is the case with you and you like the results you're getting, don't argue with success. But if you're not happy with your progress, switch to weights first.

Training for an endurance event

If you're preparing for a marathon, a hiking expedition, or a bicycle trip through Europe, do your cardio workout first because your endurance training is the most important. Supplement this with weight training one to three times a week in your spare time (especially for those muscles that will assist your event or are completely neglected). Don't forget to build in rest time. And don't neglect your flexibility, either. Stretching can speed recovery and minimize soreness.

Training for skill

If you're on a soccer team, playing in a tennis match, dancing in a performance, swimming, diving, or doing just about any athletic activity that has a high skill quotient, practice skills first, when your energy is highest. It's tough to improve skills when you're worn out from a workout.

Skill-building exercises often (but don't always) have built-in cardio and strength benefits. It's up to you or your coach to supplement your sport with complementary workouts to improve performance and total fitness. Schedule additional strength and endurance workouts after practice or on days off.

women and muscle

Realities and Myths

Despite an overwhelming amount of information and evidence to the contrary, many women are still afraid that strength training will give them big muscles. Worrying about this makes as much sense as worrying about becoming too happy, healthy, beautiful, and rich. The female body just isn't programmed to grow "manly" muscles. Genetics, hormones, body fat, and body type all prevent that. Even if you *want* to grow big muscles, you'll soon discover that without dangerous steroids it's virtually impossible.

How Mother Nature Grows Muscle on Women

Women's muscles get leaner, not bigger, with an average increase in size of a quarter to a half inch, even after years of training. Although women can get stronger indefinitely, muscles respond by getting denser, not bigger. Many women notice their waists, hips, thighs, and buttocks get smaller as they get stronger. Shoulders may appear a bit larger and squarer (sometimes merely the result of improved posture) and arms may get more defined as less fat hangs off the underarm.

But stronger muscles weigh more. Because muscle weighs more than fat, some women notice that training makes them *gain weight* (and this is a tough psychological barrier to break). A body-fat test is a more accurate measure of progress than a scale.

• Women with 15 to 20 percent body fat may notice an immediate weight gain after a few weeks of training.

• Women with 20 to 30 percent body fat may maintain a steady weight for a while but notice their waist lines shrinking.

• Women with more than 30 percent body fat may experience an immediate weight *loss*.

Also remember: Lean muscles look bigger. As body fat drops to between 15 and 20 percent, muscles start to peek out from under the protective glaze of body fat.

Some women still get bigger than they'd like, especially if they have an endomorphic or mesomorphic body type (see **Body Types,** page 22). A body-fat test can confirm if this size increase is muscle or fat.

• To shrink muscle, simply ease up on training for a while.

• To shrink fat, strength train more intensely, two or three days a week. Make cardio workouts longer and moderate (45 to 60 minutes) or more vigorous for 30 minutes so you expend more total calories. Eat four or five times a day, 400 to 500 calories at each meal, and don't eat a big dinner.

Why Women Can't Build Big Muscles

For a woman to succeed at building big muscles, without the help of anabolic steroids, she literally has to be a genetic freak. The chances of this happening are about one in a million.

• Most women (and men) have short muscles and long tendons. This makes it very tough to build large, curvaceous muscles, since too much of the limb is made of flat connective tissue (see **Tendons,** page 243). Very few mortals have long, full muscles and short tendons.

• Women don't have enough testosterone. Although women's bodies naturally produce this male, growth-inspiring hormone (just as men's bodies produce female hormones), men have about 100 times more of it. Some women produce more testosterone than others. But that's still not enough to give women a natural anabolic edge.

• Women have more body fat. Most women have between 20 and 30 percent body fat. Fat hides muscle. It also means that women possess a smaller ratio of lean muscle to fat, so less muscle mass is available for use (although women are as strong as men when compared, according to this percentage of lean muscle).

cardiovascular
training

aerobic vs. anaerobic

Aerobic exercise is any type of sustained, rhythmic movement of low to moderate intensity that uses large muscles and is continued for more than fifteen minutes. Activities include walking, swimming, biking, running, and aerobic dance—basically any continuous motion that creates a demand on the heart and lungs to deliver oxygen into the bloodstream, where food is metabolized as fuel. Aerobic exercisers can sustain activity for anywhere from fifteen minutes to several hours, depending on level of fitness.

The main fuels for aerobics are glucose (stored sugars from carbohydrates) and fatty acids (stored fat from foods). Amino acids, which result as the body digests protein, are used very sparingly as aerobic energy. Their job is to build and repair muscles and cells.

Anaerobic exercise (literally, exercise that doesn't require oxygen) typically refers to stop-and-start activities such as weight lifting, sprinting, or a game of doubles tennis when you wait to hit the ball. Such motion requires quick bursts of energy followed by a lull.

As in aerobic exercise, the fuel that makes this possible comes from glycogen (the stored sugars that are the by-products of carbohydrates). But this glycogen doesn't need oxygen to convert it to fuel—it's immediately available in the muscles and liver. The downside is that anaerobic exercisers like sprinters typically run out of gas after a very brief period of time, as little as a few seconds. Weight lifters, for example, can do a series of several small sets lasting from thirty to sixty seconds each, but with thirty-second rests between sets, they can keep going for about forty-five minutes before experiencing full-out glycogen depletion. (For a more complete definition of *anaerobic,* see page 12.)

Where do we get energy for exercise?

Our energy for both exercise and life comes from food. But before food can be converted into energy, it must be broken down into a chemical compound the body can use (much the way a refinery turns crude oil into gas). The body's crude oil is food. Its gasoline is called ATP—adenosine triphosphate.

When we eat, our food is either absorbed into busy, active cells, where it will be metabolized, via ATP, into energy; or it is stored in the body for later use (stored sugars go into the liver or muscles, while stored fat ends up as body fat).

The body's energy system is even more complex than this. Like a car with three tanks of different fuels, it switches among the various fuel systems as different activities demand. Thus, it's possible to use anaerobic-energy systems during an aerobic workout and vice versa.

The anaerobic-energy system

Phosphagen—for quick, all-out sprints

- Fuels very quick, all-out exertions that last 1 to 15 seconds before fatigue sets in
- Used when lifting a heavy weight one time, jumping over a log, running up to 100 yards, or when beginning a workout
- Energy comes as a molecule and is broken apart to help produce ATP. It's immediately available (because it doesn't require oxygen) but in limited supply.
- Fuel used—creatine phosphate

Anaerobic glycolysis (glucose)—for slightly longer activities

- Fuels moderately short actions, from 1 to 3 minutes
- Used when lifting weights for several repetitions or sprinting a quarter mile
- Energy is immediately available but in limited supply
- Fuel used—glucose (the by-product of carbohydrates), the *only* fuel in this process
- Fatigue sets in when lactic acid builds up (and you feel the burn) after about 30 to 45 seconds. After a short rest (30 to 60 seconds), lactic acid dissipates, thus making it more comfortable to return to activity. Full glycogen depletion happens after about 45 minutes in the weight room, rest time included.

The aerobic-energy system

Aerobic glycolysis (glucose)—when your body burns sugar

- Fuels medium distance, sustained workouts, usually under 20 minutes
- Is utilized in workouts of *high intensity and short duration,* and in the beginning of a longer workout, after the first 3 minutes
- Requires less oxygen than fat and is easier to metabolize. So when intensity increases, the body uses glucose instead of fat.
- Needs oxygen to be efficiently utilized (and it takes 5 to 10 minutes of warm-up time to create the oxygen-rich internal atmosphere)
- Fuel used—glucose formed by carbohydrates
- Fatigue sets in rapidly if the cardiovascular system is not capable of delivering oxygen to the cells, where food is turned to energy (i.e., if someone's not in shape)
- Glycogen can help sustain an aerobic workout for up to 2 hours (Marathoners who "hit the wall" at 2 hours experience the aerobic version of glycogen depletion. With an empty glycogen fuel tank, making it to the finish line becomes mind over matter.)

Fatty acids—when the body burns both fat and glucose

- Fuels longer aerobic workouts (more than 20 minutes) of moderate intensity. This same "double fuel system" operates when the body is at rest. (Start to exercise at a rigorous pace, however, and working muscles demand more fuel. At high intensity, the body uses mostly glucose because glucose needs less oxygen than fat to be used as fuel. Switch back to a gentler pace, and both are used.)

- The energy from fatty acids isn't immediately available. It takes approximately 20 minutes to create the right oxygen-rich atmosphere, which then triggers the sympathetic nervous system to release fat from the usual storage areas (buttocks, thighs, abdomen, etc.). Only under these conditions does fat fuel the work.

- Fatigue sets in based on a person's level of fitness. Long, slow workouts, in the lower end of the target range (see **Target Heart Rates,** page 239), can be sustained for several hours.

Health benefits of aerobic exercise

- Decrease in body fat
- Lower resting heart rate
- Lower blood pressure
- Decrease in LDL (bad) cholesterol
- Increase in HDL (good) cholesterol
- Increased life expectancy
- Some improvement in bone density
- Decreased stress, overall well-being

Health benefits of anaerobic exercise (especially strength training)

- Improved ratio of muscle to fat
- Faster metabolism
- Stronger bones and connective tissue
- Prevents back pain and other injuries
- Relieves stress

Some Frequently Asked Questions About Aerobic Exercise

Which is Better, Anaerobic or Aerobic? You need both—aerobic for heart, lungs, and fat burning, and anaerobic for strengthening muscles, bones, and speeding metabolism by improving the ratio of muscle to fat. In an ideal world, you should do two strength-training workouts per week for the whole body, and three aerobic workouts, averaging thirty minutes each to gain and maintain fitness. Some workouts, like an uphill hike or a power step and sculpt class, use movements that combine quicker, harder (anaerobic) activities that add strength with slower, more sustained (aerobic) motions that use both glucose and stored fat for fuel.

What Sort of Aerobic Workout Will Burn the Most Fat? Workouts that are moderately long, slow, and cover distance (otherwise called LSDs) are most effective for fat burning.

Why Do Shorter Intervals of Higher Intensity? High-intensity intervals (sprinting up a hill, bounding up a flight of stairs, etc.) help add an anaerobic element of strength and increase aerobic capacity, a more rapid and efficient delivery of oxygen to muscles and cells. In short, intervals can help make you more fit.

Do I Have to Do Formal Workouts to Get Aerobic Exercise? No! Try making daily chores aerobic. Try cardio house cleaning, dog walking, gardening, or playground time with your kids.

An aerobic workout

Warm-up

Always warm up for at least 5 minutes with low-intensity moves before launching into a full-blown aerobic workout. Warm-ups let your cardiovascular system slowly adjust to the work ahead and warm and loosen muscles and joints.

Warm-up moves should be similar to your main exercise (i.e., if you walk for fitness, warm up at a lower intensity) at approximately 35 to 50 percent of your maximum heart rate (see **Target Heart Rates,** page 239). These movements should be low impact with a small to moderate range of motion and can include light stretching. Save your deep stretches for after the cool-down.

The body of your workout

After warming up, gradually increase intensity for the sustained aerobic part of your workout. Ideally you want to work at between 55 and 85 percent of your target heart rate. In other words, the work should be hard enough so you feel your heart beating, but not so hard that you can't talk. This portion of the workout should last between 15 and 45 minutes.

If you're new to exercise and can't sustain aerobics for long, try working at this level for 10 minutes, adding 2 minutes each week until you're comfortable at a greater length. If you need to do shorter workouts because of time constraints, try breaking it up into two 20-minute workouts. Take a brisk walk before breakfast and another after dinner, with warm-ups and cool-downs. The main body of these mini-workouts should be 15 minutes to gain aerobic endurance. But doing anything is better than doing nothing!

Cool-down

Always end your aerobic workout with 5 minutes of winding down, similar to your warm-up, but in reverse. This returns the heart to the lower end of the target zone and allows the blood to return from where it has pooled in the extremities. Failing to cool down could make you faint. Be sure, also, to keep your head above your heart during the cool-down so you don't get dizzy. After five minutes, you can stand or move to the floor for calisthenics or deeper stretches (see also **Stretching,** page 234).

The Fitt Principle

Four factors influence the effectiveness of your fitness program, and all can be varied according to what works for you. These four things are often called the FITT Principle.

Frequency: How frequent are your aerobic workouts? Ideal: 3 to 5 days a week.

Intensity: How hard do you exercise? Ideal: at 55 to 85 percent of your maximum heart rate.

Time: How long are your workouts? Ideal: 15 to 60 minutes (not including the warm-up and cool-down).

Type: What type of aerobic exercise do you do? Ideal: A blend of rhythmic, continuous motions works best so you can avoid boredom and muscle over- or underuse. Just changing one of these factors can dramatically effect your metabolism and energy.

The Ten Commandments of Aerobic Exercise

If you do the following, you set the stage for more efficient and enjoyable exercise.

1. FIND ACTIVITIES YOU ENJOY enough to actually *do* on a regular basis. If you can't find one that appeals to you, go out and do something you *think* you could like some day and fake it. In other words, keep showing up and the pleasure will come.

2. DRESS APPROPRIATELY. Wear shoes that suit the various terrains you will cover and your movement styles and needs for ankle, knee, and hip support. Wear layers in cold temperatures, loose cotton in the heat. Women should wear a sports bra, and men should wear a jock strap or briefs.

3. WARM YOURSELF SUFFICIENTLY. Designate at least 5 minutes for gentle motions, full-body movements, and light stretches, held for 10 seconds each, before zooming off into the body of your workout (see, under **Stretching,** "Best Pre- and Postaerobic Stretches," page 234). Keep your heart rate at 35 to 50 percent of maximum as you warm up.

4. WORK WITHIN YOUR TARGET HEART ZONE during the main portion of the workout to assure better use of oxygen and fat for fuel. You should be able to sing or speak with relative ease, mixed with some deep breathing. If it's too easy, rev up; too hard, bring it down.

5. STAY IN THAT ZONE for 10 (for beginners) to 60 minutes (for experienced exercisers). Optimal cardio-enhancing, endorphin-producing, and fat-burning time for the average female is 30 to 45 minutes from the start of a warm-up to the last moment of cool-down, three to five days a week. Males need only 20 to 30 minutes to achieve this.

6. LISTEN TO YOUR BODY. More exercise isn't always better. Avoid burnout and don't push it when you can't talk, feel excessively fatigued, or sense an illness coming on (don't work out when you're sick). Trade in quantity for quality: increase the intensity or create a fine-tuned mind-body-spirit connection. Learn to get more out of less.

7. DRINK WATER before, during, and after your workout. Keep water handy and drink it before you're thirsty, while sweating, and guzzle it when you're done working out. When it's excessively hot, pour some water on your head.

8. AVOID OVERHEATING. If exercising outdoors, don't do it in high humidity, blazing temperatures, or the midday sun. Choose morning, evening, or shade. If exercising indoors in a hot space, have fans handy or spray yourself with water.

9. COOL DOWN. Cool down with gentle motions, a heart rate at 35 to 50 percent of maximum, for 3 to 5 minutes. Follow with sculpting, floor work, or final stretches. Hold these stretches for more than 10 seconds each to permanently increase flexibility.

10. RESPECT THE WARNING SIGNALS OF OVERUSE. Do not draw from the same well every day or the well will run dry. Find other activities that move you so your workouts will continue to be fun and healthy.

body fat

Body fat is more than a substance. It's also a highly charged emotional and political issue—as well as a possible indicator of overall health.

Although many people have become fat phobic, body fat is a critical ingredient in a healthy life. Body fat provides warmth, stimulates nerve function, and insulates internal organs. Women need a minimum of 10 to 15 percent fat, men 3 to 5 percent, just to survive. Adding an additional 10 to 15 percent above that improves body function and adds curves to our bones and roses to our cheeks. Problems arise (both psychological and physiological) when body fat percentages go higher than this.

Women's body fat

Men and women both possess around *30 billion fat cells*—but that's where the similarities end. Men's fat cells are smaller and contain more of the enzyme that *releases* fat from the cells. Women have bigger fat cells and more of the enzyme that makes cells *store fat.* That's why it's easier for men to do less exercise and get faster results. Depressing as this may sound, this is critical information for waging the battle against female fat (see "If You Want to Be a Contender . . . ," page 158).

Women are fatter for one main reason: to maintain a healthy, warm atmosphere for giving birth, to propagate the species. This female fat-storage ability dates back to our cave-dwelling ancestors and has helped women survive cold winters, famines, and droughts. Not coincidentally, female fat stores have enough reserve energy to see women through nine months of minimal food supplies. Evolution hasn't yet caught up to our mostly centrally heated, sedentary lives.

Consequently, women have become very good at storing fat. About half of our stored fat is *internal* and surrounds and protects our organs. The other half is stored directly under the skin as *subcutaneous* fat. This is the fat that looks like rice kernels when pinched. Although it's called cellulite, it's basically just fat with a high water content. No special creams, body wraps, diets, or supplements will get rid of it. The only way to win the war against fat is by shrinking and decreasing the number of fat cells the old-fashioned way, with low-fat eating and regular exercise.

Most women store fat in the hips and thighs and are pear-shaped (see **Body Types,** page 22). As most women already know, stored hip and thigh fat is the first to go on and the last to leave because the fat-storage enzymes in that part of the body are the most rugged. It takes persistence, but with effort and intention, the fat *will* eventually begin to disappear here (once it's come off the breasts, upper arms, and face).

Apple-shaped women, however, store excess fat around the abdomen, and therefore, like men with beer bellies, are at higher risk for diseases related to body fat such as Type II diabetes and coronary heart disease.

Being fat is not a disease

Being fat is a result of many things: genetics, lifestyle, culture, psychology, even economic status. Although having a high percentage of body fat (obesity) is often regarded as a disease, it isn't one and doesn't necessarily increase the risk of early death, as some headlines have led us to believe. It can exacerbate existing health problems and possibly be the cause of disorders such as high blood pressure, high cholesterol, coronary heart disease, high blood triglycerides, and diabetes, as well as muscular and skeletal problems. It can also be the result of these disorders. But it is entirely possible both to have these health problems without being fat and to be fat without showing any presence of any disease.

Much research remains to be done on this subject, but it may be revealed that being fat is better for long-term health than chronic dieting.

Body fat and health

How much a body weighs says less about its probable fitness and rate of metabolism than what that body is made of. A 5-foot, 4-inch woman who weighs 140 pounds, for instance, with 17 percent body fat is probably fitter than a woman of the same height who weighs 100 pounds and has 35 percent body fat. Percentages of body fat determine the ratio of body fat (essential and stored) to lean body mass (muscles, bones, connective tissue). Lean body mass is active tissue that uses up calories just sitting there, while fat mostly sits there waiting to be called into action when other fuel reserves run low. The greater the amount of lean body mass, the speedier the metabolism.

Most women could stand to put on more lean body mass. When women start training with weights and building muscle, they often gain weight because muscle weighs more than fat. But since so many women have been schooled to think in terms of pounds and not body composition or percentages of body fat, they tend to think putting on or not losing weight is bad, thus, they can fail to recognize the progress they've made.

Instead of relying on a scale to assess fitness, it's better to judge the way clothes fit, look in the mirror, and/or take body fat tests.

Although there is no standard for acceptable percentages of body fat in terms of appearance or health, experts agree on how the percentages of fat on the facing page reflect various degrees of health.

Fat Facts

- The best way to lose fat is slowly, about .5 percent a month, with a steady lifestyle of exercise and healthy eating habits—not a diet!
- The majority of women are about 30 percent body fat. To get down to 22 percent (the amount at which thigh muscles begin to reappear) could take up to sixteen months.
- If you want to go the surgical route, liposuction can cost several thousand dollars (and it's not covered by insurance). Approximately 30 percent of all liposuction patients experience a "regrowth" of fat.

Body Fat Percentage Chart for Men and Women

Description	Women (in percents)	Men (in percents)
Essential fat (required for normal function of organs)	9–12	3–5
Very lean (most common in competitive athletes)	13–17	6–12
Lean, healthy (but not average!)	18–22	13–17
Slightly overfat	23–25	18–20
Fat	26–32	21–24
Obese	32+	25+

Adapted from both the ACE Aerobics Instructors Manual, 1993, revised 1996, published by ACE, and the AFAA manual, Fitness Theory and Practice, co-published by AFAA and Reebok University, 1993.

Age-Based Body-Fat Chart for Women

Most of us don't need a chart to tell us that we tend to put on fat as we age. It's normal, a result of less overall activity. But age-related fat is not destiny, merely a result of lifestyle. Here's a chart that takes slowing down into consideration.

Age	Extremely Fit (in percents)	Very Fit (in percents)	Healthy (in percents)	Unhealthy (in percents)
20–29	19	22	25	30
30–39	20	23	26	31
40–49	22	26	29	33
50–59	26	29	33	36
60+	27	30	34	37

If You Want to Be a Contender in the Fight Against Fat . . .

If you want to seriously challenge your body fat, you need to understand your adversary. Make sure you're following these guidelines:

Do	Don't
Eat 4 or 5 small meals every day (stoke your metabolism)	Diet, ever again
Stick to about 500 calories per meal (what your body uses before it stores the rest as fat)	Overeat at one sitting
Eat your meals when it's light out	Eat big, late dinners
Stick with 15–30 percent fat	Eat a high-fat diet
Aim for three aerobic workouts per week, 45 minutes in duration, or break it up into two 20-minute workouts per day	Miss your aerobic workouts
Add some lean body mass with one to three strength workouts per week	Skimp on strength training
Relax the reins from time to time, enjoy some chocolate, keep a sense of humor, and love yourself as you are	Get obsessed with fat

Methods for measuring body fat

Hydrostatic weighing: Also called the dunk test, this underwater weighing method is considered the most accurate. It works under the premise that "fat floats" and "muscle sinks." Therefore your weight on land is measured against your weight in the water. By determining body density, an accurate body-fat measurement can be figured. This test requires expensive equipment and trained staff.

Bioelectrical impedance analysis: Also called the zap test, this works under the premise that lean body mass conducts more energy than fat. Electrodes are placed on the skin and electrical currents are measured. A quick-and-easy test, but the equipment is expensive. Also not recommended for people who are very lean or obese (because accuracy is harder to determine in the high and low ranges) or for the elderly.

Skinfold calipers: Also called the pinch test, this is the most popular and uses the least expensive equipment. In fact, you can buy your own calipers. Skinfold measurements are taken at various sites, and then the numbers are run through a fairly complex formula. Computerized calipers figure these numbers into the body-fat total, taking into account a person's sex and age.

Approximate your percentage of body fat

Even the most sophisticated tests can be as much as 5 points off, up or down. Factors such as who takes the test, body temperature, what you ate for your last meal, and if you just worked out can all change the numbers. Here's a way to figure out your body-fat percentage in the privacy of your home, with no one pinching you, dunking you underwater, or taping electrodes to your skin.

The following isn't any more accurate, but it gives you an approximate number without the fancy equipment (and at least gives you a place to begin). Approximate yours in the chart below. The formula is based on your BMI, or Body Mass Index, used by professionals in the health care field.

1. Multiply your weight in pounds, by 700 (i.e., $132 \times 700 = 92,400$)

2. Divide that number by your height in inches (i.e., $5'7'' = 67$ inches. 92,400 divided by $67 = 1,379$)

3. Divide that result by your height in inches again (i.e., 1,379 divided by $67 = 20.5\%$ body fat)

(Remember: This is an approximation. It may also be an overestimation for a very muscular individual or pregnant women.)

Your waist-to-hip ratio

Another way to figure if you're within the "acceptable" range of body fat is to figure your hip to waist ratio.

Take your waist measurement _____

Divide that by your hip measurement _____

Healthy numbers for women are less than .80. Healthy numbers for men are less than .95.

burning fat in cardio workouts

There are three rules to becoming a lean, fat-burning machine.

1. Regular cardio workouts of low to moderate intensity and medium to long duration
2. More lean muscle, gained with a weight-training program, because an improved ratio of muscle to fat creates a faster metabolism and more rapid utilization of fat
3. Several small, low-fat meals eaten throughout the day inspire fat cells to more readily release fatty acids and stabilize energy

Most people anxious to burn fat tend to pray at the altar of aerobics, and thus focus on rule #1, while neglecting #2 and #3—and thus fail to get the results they seek. However, while #2 and #3 are very important, this section deals with cardiovascular fitness, so the focus here will be fat burning the aerobic way.

How do you burn fat?

Think of your body as having two main fuel tanks to propel you through an aerobic workout. For the first 20 minutes or so, your body uses fast-burning fuel, glucose (your stored sugars from the pasta you ate last night). Once this fuel begins to run low, your slow-burning fuel, fat, kicks in. A fitter person might use fat a lit-tle sooner. A not-so-fit person might take even longer (remember, a not-so-fit person becomes fit with training!).

The main thing to remember in the war against fat, especially *female* fat, is that fat burning doesn't really start until *after* an average of 20 minutes into your workout (which includes a warm-up and stretches). Men can do slightly shorter cardio workouts of 15 to 25 minutes and burn fat, but women's fat cells are more reluctant to give it up. This isn't fair. But women who want to burn fat should continue with cardio for 10 to 25 more minutes.

Go slower, longer

It's been bandied about that longer, slower, easier workouts burn more fat than harder, more intense workouts. This is partly true and partly misleading.

It's true that if the workout is too intense, too long, and elicits an off-the-chart heart rate, you burn sugar, not fat. But few mere mortals can keep up such an intensity for long. Usually we do this only in quick bursts, like an intense weight-training set or a sprint to catch a plane.

It's also true that at a relatively low intensity (about 60 percent of maximum heart rate) the body uses a greater percentage of fat as fuel than it does at higher heart rates.

But burning more fat by working at a low intensity just doesn't add up. The real issue is the *total calories* you burn during a workout and *how long* you can keep it up. If you walk on a flat surface at 4 mph for 60 minutes, you burn about 300 calories. About 80 percent of that (240 calories) comes from fat.

If you run at 8 mph for 30 minutes you burn about 450 calories. Approximately 60 percent of those calories come from fat, or 270 fat calories. So in the shorter, tougher workout, you've not only burned more fat calories but *more total calories* and you've probably also helped boost your aerobic capacity (increased your body's ability to use oxygen). But shorter and tougher isn't necessarily better. Choose whichever way works for you.

The ultimate fat-burning cardio workout

- It's long, slow, relatively easy, and lasts 45 to 60 minutes *or*
- It's shorter, more intense, and lasts 30 to 45 minutes.
- It's easy enough so you never get completely out of breath, but intense enough so you feel your heart beating faster.
- It takes place *three times a week.* Twice a week isn't enough to keep the body sufficiently conditioned to release fat; four or five fat-burning cardio workouts a week are OK as long as you don't feel exhausted and overtrained. But since lean muscle helps speed your metabolism (and therefore inspires a quicker and faster usage of fat for fuel) you might substitute at least one of those aerobic workout slots

for strength training, if you aren't already including one or two weight workouts per week. (See **Cross Training,** page 167, to add a cardio element to strength training.) And don't forget flexibility. All that activity tightens muscles unless you stretch.
- It happens *no more than five times* a week. Overdoing aerobics can create orthopedic damage, which may not show up until months or years down the line.
- It's got *variety.* If you do only the treadmill for 45 minutes three days a week and aren't getting results, switch machines. Try 15 minutes each on the rowing machine and stationary bike, then do the treadmill. Cross training aerobically helps you recruit different muscle fibers.
- It's *fun* and you love it or at least you love what it does for you.

If you're doing everything right but not seeing results

- Try a different activity entirely, either a different aerobic activity, weight training, or a new sport.
- Stick it out for 5 more minutes than usual.
- Add another workout day.
- Subtract a workout day. (Perhaps you're overtrained. Listen to your body instead of imposing your will.)
- Substitute a regular aerobic workout with intervals (see **Intervals,** page 199).
- Don't give up.

Preparing to Burn

If you're a beginner, it takes persistence, dedication, and about three to six months of regular cardio workouts for the body to adapt this new thing called exercise. Your physiology won't change unless you show it that you're serious. You'll definitely feel better as soon as you begin an aerobic exercise program. But don't expect big changes right away, especially if your body fat is above 30 percent. Think of your first three to six months as the time you prepare to burn. You also won't see changes in your buttocks and thighs until body fat drops to 18 to 22 percent. So hang in there.

If even long, relatively easy workouts are too much at first, start with 15- to 25-minute workouts to break in to fitness. Add a minute per workout.

What zone are you in?

Taking your heart rate to determine if you're in your optimal fat-burning zone can be a nuisance and inaccurate if you slow down, miscount, or can't find your pulse. The best indication of how hard or easy to work out is your voice. If you can't talk while working out, you're working too hard and burning sugar, not fat. But if talking is too easy, you're probably not working hard enough. If talking is somewhere in between—not flowing but not labored—then you're in your fat-burning zone.

(But if you love numbers and want to take your pulse, see **Target Heart Rates,** page 239.)

calories and exercise

Calories are units of measurement. How many calories a food contains or are consumed during exercise gives an indication of the efficiency of that food or activity compared to others. (For a definition of what a calorie is and the different amounts found in various types of food, see the Diet and Nutrition section.)

The amount of calories consumed *in exercise* is based on how much oxygen passes through the body. For instance, when you walk briskly, about 1 quart of oxygen is consumed each minute; therefore, your body uses about 5 calories. When you jog, oxygen consumption jumps to 2 quarts a minute, and calorie usage in that time goes up to 10. More oxygen equals more calories. (But remember, working harder aerobically means you can get out of breath—experience an oxygen deficit—and thus be more apt to burn sugar, not fat.) To receive the same training benefits from walking as from jogging, you'd need to walk for twice the time you would run.

Do you consume or save calories?

Caloric needs and usages are individual, dependent on levels of activity, lifestyle, and, most important, body composition. Muscles are calorie *consumers,* feeding on calories even while at rest. Fat is what results when calories are stored.

People who are calorie consumers

- have a higher ratio of muscle to fat
- exercise regularly
- have a more active lifestyle in general
- eat what their bodies need at one time and not much more

People who are calorie savers

- have a higher ratio of fat to muscle
- don't exercise
- have a sedentary lifestyle
- eat more food than their bodies can store at one time and thus convert excess calories to fat

But each individual also experiences a large variance in caloric requirements as daily activities and circumstances change. On an average day, with 45 minutes of exercise, you might need 1,700 calories. On a highly active day, say one in which you take a two-hour hike, you may need 2,000 calories. On a rest day, you may take no exercise and sit all day working and therefore need only 1,400 calories. Other factors that can increase your body's caloric needs include more activity and exercise, menstruation, pregnancy, and stress.

Calories used in exercise

People are concerned with the number of calories used during different types of exercise—and yes, the body uses more than its normal share during exercise. But exercise typically lasts only 30 to 60 minutes. The more important number is how many calories are used the rest of the day (i.e., how rapidly food is metabolized). The number of calories used in exercise, however, can boost the amount of calories used for the rest of the day.

The body also uses about three-quarters of its calories in the daylight (from about 6 A.M. to 6 P.M.) and the other one-quarter at night (from 6 P.M. to 6 A.M.). If we keep this in mind, and eat three-quarters of our calories when the body is most active and make our last meal the smallest one, we feed the body calories when it is most apt to use them for fuel and not convert them into fat.

General calorie requirements for different body weights

To find your approximate daily caloric requirement, multiply your body weight by 13—for example: $134 \times 13 = 1,742$ calories per day.

The daily caloric requirements for your body weight will vary according to your body composition (with more muscle and activity, you can and should eat more). But remember: It's not just the total number of calories you eat but whether those calories come from protein, carbohydrates, or fat (see **Calories,** page 281).

If you want to maintain your weight and exercise regularly, allow 25 to 35 percent of your calories to come from fat.

If you want to lose 1 to 25 pounds and exercise regularly, allow 20 to 30 percent of your calories to come from fat.

If you want to lose more than 25 pounds and exercise regularly, allow 10 to 25 percent of your calories to come from fat.

Calorie Consumption of Different Activities

The following chart lists average calorie consumption for a 130-pound woman. Numbers will vary depending on level of intensity, outside conditions (heat, terrain, etc.), and individual physiology.

Activity	Calories expended per 30 minutes
Aerobic dancing	294
Basketball	243
Bicycling, 15 mph	304
Circuit weight training	325
Cross-country skiing	250
Golf (walking the links)	150
In-line skating	258
Running, 10-minute mile	314
Swimming, freestyle	213
Tennis, singles	200
Walking, 15-minute mile	126
Walking, hills	177
Water aerobics	120

circulation

Blood is tissue (like muscle and bone) but in fluid form. It's made up of live tissue (the platelets and white and red blood cells), nonliving tissue (blood plasma), and more than 90 percent water. The normal adult body contains about 8 percent blood. Women possess 4 to 5 liters, men 5 to 6 liters.

Blood is the body's good soldier—it reports for duty wherever it's needed. At rest, the majority of our blood remains in the torso to regulate organ function. A good deal also stays in the brain to oversee mental faculties. After eating, it moves to the stomach to assist digestion.

Blood tends to pool in the center of the body, which is why we get cold hands and feet when we sit for long periods of time. But once we start to move around, the blood moves from the abdomen to the extremities, to accommodate working muscles, and to the skin, to disperse the built-up heat. During the hardest part of aerobic exercise, blood flow increases to about a gallon a minute. After the workout, a 5- to 10-minute cool-down (with moves of decreasing intensity) ushers blood out of the extremities and veins and back to the heart, muscles, and brain. A sudden stop can cause dizziness.

Cardiac output

Cardiac output is a measurement of how much blood (the stroke volume, which must be measured in the lab) is pumped out with each heart-beat (measured in beats per minute). A fit person can deliver *more* blood to the cells that need it in less time than an unfit person. In other words, a healthy heart does more work with less effort.

Aerobic exercise increases cardiac output. Even after just three months of regular aerobic training, a once unconditioned heart can pump more blood at a lower heart rate. Thus, *resting* heart rate *decreases* because more blood can be processed with each contraction. But a healthy heart can also work harder, closer to the maximum heart rate, and still be working aerobically (using oxygen and burning fat for fuel). An unfit person at that same heart rate would just be burning glucose.

A fit body responds to increased physical demands by creating more capillaries in the active muscles, which, in turn, pull oxygen (or fuel) from the blood. The active cells also create more enzymes, which increase the oxygen-utilizing ability of the blood.

Think of it this way: Before getting into shape aerobically, the body is like an old factory with little modern machinery, too many workers standing around idle, and a stockpile of garbage (fat) that gets bigger every day. After regular exercise, the factory gets renovated. New, more effective machines are brought in (a better heart pump, more efficient blood valves, more active cells), the workers learn how to work harder with less effort, and each day, the garbage is burned off and used to propel the machines, so the stockpile is whittled down.

How do you improve circulation?

The answer is easy: move around. Moving gets blood flowing to extremities. This is both a short- and long-term fix. In the short term, movement can warm chilly fingers and toes. In the long term, the cumulative effect of *regular* movement (during formal and informal exercise) can improve the blood's ability to travel more effectively through the body.

Blood Pressure Ranges*

Healthy, optimal	120/80 and below
Normal to high	130/85 to 139/89
High or hypertensive	140/90 and higher

For a blood-pressure test, see your local clinic, doctor, or fitness trainer. Many health fairs also offer free blood-pressure screenings.

Blood pressure

During standard, clinical stress tests on treadmills, one of the things technicians measure is blood pressure and its response to exercise to indicate a person's health. Blood pressure combines two measurements: the **systolic,** which is the amount of pressure generated by the blood being pumped *out of the heart;* and the **diastolic,** which is the amount of resistance of the small arteries *during the pause between heartbeats* and against which the heart must work.

During exercise, systolic pressure should increase to meet the oxygen demands of the muscles. Diastolic pressure should stay the same or decline somewhat because blood vessels open and therefore allow an easier transport of blood. This creates less resistance, so the overall resting pressure can be lower.

The Transportation System

Blood is the body's mass-transit system. Nutrients, oxygen, and waste products all ride the bloodstream to the appropriate places around the body. Like a big terminal in the center of a city, the heart receives and spits out all the visitors. But the veins and arteries are the tunnels where all the blood travels. The following is a simplified blood transit map:

VEINS take blood *to* the heart.

ARTERIES, which are bigger and thicker than veins, take blood *away* from the heart. From the arteries, smaller tracks branch off: **arterioles** (smaller arteries) and **capillaries** are very important little arteries where the main *exchange* of nutrients takes place in the blood. This is where the arteries and veins meet and trade substances.

PULMONARY ARTERIES transport blood *to the lungs* where carbon dioxide is released.

PULMONARY VEINS (there are four), take the newly oxygenated blood *from the lungs* back to the heart.

THE HEART *receives all the blood* from the rest of the body (except for the lungs) in the **right atrium;** the **left ventricle** squirts blood out to the entire body. The **superior vena cava** is the main route for all blood that flows *above the heart.* The **inferior vena cava** is the main route for all the blood that flows *below the heart.*

cross training

The term *cross training* didn't enter the fitness vocabulary until the late 1980s. Before that, even many health and medical organizations recommended only one sort of activity (usually aerobic) to satisfy people's total fitness needs. Thus, people followed various fitness fads (jogging, tennis, aerobics), thinking that was all they needed. But injuries gained from overuse, research findings (regarding the importance of stronger muscles and bones for longevity), and increased awareness in general have made people aware of the importance and necessity of cross training.

Any fitness program that claims to be truly complete *must* involve cross training. In other words, it must contain the three components of fitness:

- Cardiovascular. Any type of continuous, rhythmic motion that uses large muscles and increases the body's demand for oxygen. An aerobic workout mostly taxes heart and lungs (although some strength and flexibility work can be involved).
- Strength. The maximum force created by a single muscle or group of muscles. A strength workout mostly taxes muscles, connective tissue, and bones (although some cardiovascular and stretching can be involved).
- Flexibility. A muscle's ability to move around a joint and stretch. A stretching workout mostly elongates muscles

(although some strength and cardiovascular work can be involved).

The benefits of cross training are both physical and mental. Cross training

- adds *variety* (which quells boredom and stokes motivation)
- creates a more *balanced* use of muscles (because it prevents overuse of some muscles, underuse of others)
- helps the body get *stronger* and *more aerobically fit* because the body never gets a chance to adapt to the same old routine. Thus, it's always on the lookout (because of new demands you make upon it) to recruit more muscle fibers and nerves.

So how do you cross train? There are many ways to cross train as long as you are willing to be creative and tailor workouts to suit time, energy levels, desires, and needs. However, not all cross-training methods are sensible. The goal of cross training shouldn't be to spend a lot of time working out. The goal should be to work out smarter and get better results (and a lower risk of injury) from training less. (See the following Cross Training Recipes for the benefits and risks of various methods.)

Cross-training recipes

The purist approach

One type at a time. Workouts are separated into three individual chunks. An example of this would be: strength training on Monday, the stair machine on Tuesday, and yoga on Wednesday.

Benefit: If you like to work out every day, it offers safe choices and caters to different moods.

Drawback: Devotes a lot of time to working out.

The mix-and-match approach

Combine any two or three *separate* components in one workout. An example of this would be strength training for 30 minutes (resting between sets), followed by 20 to 30 minutes of cardio (on cardio equipment or aerobic-type dance), followed by stretching. Each segment has a different personality.

Benefit: You get all three components in one session.

Drawback: To get the full benefit of each approach, your workout will probably be about one hour and 15 minutes.

The three-in-one approach

This method combines the three components of fitness at the same time. In other words, no break is necessary to switch from one mode to another. One example of this would be a water-fitness class in which big motions (done properly) can raise the heart rate (cardio) and work muscles from all angles (strength) while increasing flexibility (because in the water, body weight is minimized so muscles stretch farther).

Another example is a circuit-training workout, using moderate weights, with one set to failure and no rest between sets.

Benefit: You get all three done at once without having to switch mental gears.

Drawback: Unless you use proper form, you may achieve none of these benefits successfully.

The T.O.I.L. Method

Cross training need not be complex. You don't really need a coach with a clipboard to design your program. You can cross train yourself if you employ any one of these four (T.O.I.L.) methods.

- Change the TYPE of exercise you do (some or all of the time)
- Change the ORDER of the exercises (if you always start strength workouts with legs, try starting with back exercises)
- Change the INTENSITY by alternating between longer, moderate workouts and shorter workouts at a higher intensity
- Change the LENGTH of your workout by switching, for example, between 25- and 45-minute cardio workouts.

Sport-specific cross training

Cross training can also be used to train within one component of fitness. Although the following cross-training methods employ changing the type of exercise, they don't necessarily add a *complementary* form of exercise. Thus, those who use them can be at risk of overtraining and injury.

Aerobic cross training: By definition, triathletes are aerobic animals, swimming, biking, and running to cross train. A smart triathlete would complement this program with workouts that include strength and flexibility.

Strength cross training: Serious strength trainers often employ techniques from bodybuilding and Olympic and power lifting. A smart strength trainer would include cardiovascular and flexibility training.

Flexibility cross training: Dancers, skaters, gymnasts, and other performers who need to demonstrate impressive flexibility often enhance that flexibility with yoga stretches in water or on land. A smart flexibility athlete should include some strength training (to avoid overstressing joints) and cardiovascular work for endurance.

If You're New to Cross Training

If you're new to fitness, start with cardiovascular work (fast walking, stationary bikes, etc.) for up to six weeks to build endurance. Gradually add one and then two weight training sessions a week. After you've done at least three months of regular exercise, you've built up enough endurance and strength to start getting playful.

eating for cardiovascular fitness

People who regularly participate in endurance sports (running, biking, etc.) used to love the idea of carbo loading. It was a great excuse to pile on the spaghetti for several days before an event. Even people who did a 60-minute aerobics class in the morning borrowed the idea and used it as an excuse to carb up the night before. This "store it up and burn it off" philosophy didn't take into account how the body really worked, and sometimes lead to obsessive approaches to eating and exercise. (Not to mention that any carbs the body didn't use as glycogen were converted to fat.)

Yes, carbs do fuel aerobic workouts. But a better, more efficient, and sensible way to do this is to follow a regular eating pattern consisting of complex carbs, low fat, and moderate protein in amounts the body can use at one time—usually an average of 400 to 500 calories per meal. No special storage meals are necessary. The body stores glycogen on its own.

During cardio workouts, the body relies on fat and sugars (glycogen) stored in the muscle cells for fuel. It takes about 90 minutes of fairly intense activity to seriously deplete glycogen to the point where a trained athlete "hits the wall" and can't function as well. (Winning, at this point, becomes a question of mind over matter. The famous second wind is highly psychological in nature.)

But it isn't only long, strenuous workouts that deplete glycogen stores. Over the course of a week, a trained athlete, fitness enthusiast, or instructor who works out every day for an hour or more can also feel flat at the end of the week. The best way to bounce back from such a burnout is with rest days and meals high in complex carbohydrates.

Complex carbs—breads, pasta, rice, potatoes, vegetables, and fruits—provide more energy over a longer period of time than simple carbs—fruit juice, candy, and pastries (also high in fat)—that give the body a quick energy boost followed by a drop. But even simple sugars used at the right time can be useful.

Do carbs make you fat?

Carbs (like protein and fat) go in and out of nutritional fashion. In the late eighties and early nineties they were granted the status of power food. In the mid-nineties, protein became the food of choice. Meanwhile, fat was branded as poison and nutritional experts recommended daily intakes as varied as 10 to 40 percent (since the average American diet was 50 percent fat, 40 percent was considered an improvement). What we are coming back to is a balanced, commonsense approach to eating that includes all three types of nutrients in amounts that nourish but don't overindulge the body.

Carbs can make you fat if you eat more of them in one sitting than the body will use (because the excess will be converted to fat). But fit people and unfit people use carbs in very different ways.

When unfit people eat carbs, insulin levels increase because unfit muscles require more insulin to convert carbs to glucose. This conversion process isn't very efficient in an unfit person and so more carbs end up stored as fat—and the risks increase for getting Type II diabetes.

When fit people eat carbs, however, they produce very little insulin. Their muscles are more efficient at using the sugars in these foods as fuel, and therefore don't have as much excess to store as fat. Likewise, their muscles use this glycogen more readily (along with fat) during exercise. Fit people's muscles become carbohydrate machines, better at utilizing the sugar in food and burning it as fuel.

So, yes, carbs can make you fat if you're not fit. But if you're fit, they're less likely to do so.

When to eat in relationship to your workout

Carbohydrates pass through the digestive system in about three hours—and thus can be converted to glycogen fairly rapidly. Protein takes twenty-four hours to pass through the intestines. Fat is also slow. So carbs are best for a preworkout meal because they deliver the most energy in the shortest time.

The best time to eat before a workout is about three or four hours prior, so the stomach is empty when the exercise begins. Eating right before a workout won't fuel that activity. Lunch or last night's dinner will do that. But some people (particularly before morning workouts) like to have something in their stomachs to avoid fatigue and perilously rapid drops in blood sugar.

People who work out in the late afternoon might do best to mix a small amount of easily digestible protein (like egg whites) with their carbs, since an all-carb lunch can cause a major mid-afternoon energy drop. Just make sure the amount of protein is small—and try to wait three or four hours before exercising to maximize the amount of energy available to you.

Immediately after exercise (both aerobic and anaerobic), when glycogen levels are lowest (though not necessarily depleted), the body's ability to reabsorb glucose and replenish its fuel stores is reportedly greater than normal. Some call this the glycogen window of opportunity. The best thing to eat right after exercise is a small amount of pure, simple sugar (as in fruit), followed within the hour by a regular meal of mostly carbs and protein.

Good preworkout snacks (three or four hours before exercising)

- Low-fat cereal and nonfat milk
- Small plate of pasta with sliced tomatoes, two scrambled egg whites
- Bowl of vegetable soup and two slices of bread
- Low-fat muffin or bagel

Good immediate postworkout snacks

- Sports drinks or energy bars (don't let the manufacturers fool you; it's not the fancy additives that refresh you, it's the sugar!). Make sure they're low in fat.
- Fruit (grapes, oranges, apples, berries, melon) or fruit juice
- Carrot sticks or juice
- A potato (minus the butter and sour cream—try spooning salsa on top)

endorphins

Endorphins are "feel-good chemicals" that are released in the brain. Most commonly known as the "runner's high," these natural opiates (more powerful than plant opiates like opium and heroine, and without the life-destroying side effects) increase tolerance to pain and create rushes of well-being. Endorphins are linked to several of the body's systems.

The autonomic nervous system is a complex web of neurotransmitters, hormones, and growth regulators. This system regulates such vital functions as heartbeat, breathing, and blood circulation. Most Western scientists believe that we have no direct access or control over the autonomic nervous system, but some practitioners of Eastern meditation disagree.

The enteric nervous system is the sensitive lining of the stomach, esophagus, small intestine, and colon and is comprised of 100 million nerve cells (more than the number in the spinal cord). The vagus nerve directly links the belly to the brain. So there really is such a thing as a gut reaction. This is more than a figure of speech; it's real, with a physiological base. The brain and gut share emotional messages. Thus the brain and the gut mirror each other in how they react to a situation. (Yet sometimes the brain loses its "gut instinct" when it switches into too much logic. Intuitive people know that when the "head brain" malfunctions, the "belly brain" may hold the answer.)

The immune system is a combination of glands, bone marrow, and white blood cells (see **Immunity**, page 436). Some professionals believe that immune-system cells actually communicate with endorphins, and credit them with giving immune cells an extra dose of "fighting spirit."

What creates endorphins?

Endorphins both defend the body against pain and create a pumped-up fearless form of aggression in situations that might normally cause a person to flee. In other words, they're both painkillers and euphoria-enhancers.

Pain: When the nerve receptors receive pain signals (as in exercise or when under extreme duress, as when injured), nerve impulses travel up the spinal cord to the higher centers of the brain (as if for transformation). On the way down, they pass through the midbrain; when they hit the spinal cord, they release endorphins, which are then picked up by receptors in nerve cells adjacent to those that first sent the pain signal. The end result is that the endorphins stop nerve cells from transmitting the pain signal, or from having this signal be fully received, therefore creating a temporary state of well-being.

Euphoria, passion, excitement: When you meet someone attractive and get "butterflies" in the stomach, those are endorphins at work. Or when you're passionate about a cause, or fueled by excitement in your life, it's partly the endorphins that make you feel good.

Aerobic exercise: After about fifteen minutes into a cardio workout, the body raises its own resistance to pain, even minimal pain, so it can continue. The endorphin rush can also be fueled by a person's passionate commitment to exercise.

Chocolate: Chocolate's unique combination of chemicals, sugar, and fat make it the ultimate pleasure food for women. It releases both endorphins and serotonin (a brain chemical that promotes feelings of calm). An occasional little piece of chocolate can do wonders for PMS and moods in general.

Smoking: Nicotine releases endorphins. This feel-good sensation is partly what hooks people, both psychologically and physiologically. Unfortunately, this form of endorphin production can be fatal.

endurance

Endurance is an important asset, not only in the realm of exercise but in life. We need endurance when doing tasks as small as raking leaves as well as for more grand pursuits, such as hiking mountains or giving birth (and raising children!).

Both the cardiovascular system and the muscles have the ability to *endure*—to perform sustained activity for extended periods of time—without suffering excess fatigue. In fact, cardiovascular and muscular endurance have more in common than do muscular endurance and muscular strength.

Cardiovascular endurance

This is synonymous with cardiorespiratory and aerobic endurance. It refers to the ability of the heart, lungs, and circulatory system to maintain a consistent workload at a higher than resting pace. It also includes the lungs' capacity to exchange oxygen and carbon dioxide with the blood, and the blood's ability to transport nutrients into working muscles, as well as removing waste. Brisk walking, swimming, and dancing are all exercises that build cardiovascular endurance.

Some benefits of cardiovascular endurance
- Increased utilization of body fat
- Decreased risk factors associated with high levels of body fat, high blood pressure, and high levels of blood sugar
- Reduction in the frequency and/or severity of sleep problems, depression, anxiety, and diabetes
- Promotes healthy pregnancies, both pre- and postdelivery
- Tends to promote more rapid healing from injury or disease

Muscular endurance

This is the muscles' ability to perform (usually at a consistent pace) over an extended period of time against moderate or minimal resistance. Activities that promote muscular endurance take a fair amount of time to accomplish and therefore are also aerobic (using heart, lungs, and circulatory system). Activities that promote muscle endurance include: performing 20 to 50 reps with light weights, rowing, playing tennis, or raking leaves.

Some benefits of muscular endurance
- Improved cardiovascular system (and the benefits associated with that)
- Improved ability of muscles to perform small to moderate tasks over an extended period of time
- Enhanced performance in various sports

Muscular endurance vs. strength

Muscular strength refers to the maximum amount of weight a muscle can lift for a single repetition (one-rep max). Muscular endurance employs minimal to moderate weight for many repetitions.

Put simply, anything beyond the one-rep max introduces muscular endurance. When resistance is moderate to heavy and causes the lifter to achieve true muscle failure after 8 to 12 repetitions (at approximately 75 percent of his or her one-rep max), then a moderate use of muscle endurance is used to gain strength. (One-rep maxes are not advised for building strength because they're difficult and dangerous, and although they *can* make someone stronger, they do not recruit enough muscle fibers to make a muscle grow in size. However, when a person's one-rep max [pure strength] increases, then muscular endurance rises in relationship to it.)

There are higher degrees of muscle endurance that do nothing to inspire strength (or a change in body shape or increased muscle definition). When many reps are used and weight is minimal, strength gains taper off quickly because few muscle fibers are recruited to perform the activity.

Muscle fiber types and endurance

Slow-twitch fibers are the ones that promote endurance (both muscular and cardiovascular). They fatigue slowly and are very good at delivering oxygen to active tissue. Thus, they propel all endurance activities like running, aerobic dance, and light resistance work.

Fast-twitch fibers promote faster motions (anaerobic activities). They fatigue quickly and are very bad at delivering oxygen to active tissue. Thus, they propel all short-lived activities like sprinting or lifting heavier weights.

Some people have a greater percentage of one type of fiber over the other. This may be one reason why certain people seem to be born distance runners or power lifters. Most people, however, have an equal portion of both, plus **intermediate fibers** that seem capable of adapting to either type of activity.

This distribution of fibers is genetic. However, there is much debate over how much we can alter our percentage of fibers (or perhaps train our intermediate fibers) to adapt to the activities we do most often.

energy

Energy and exercise

Although any food that contains calories essentially provides energy, the best energy source for aerobic (and anaerobic) workouts comes from glycogen. Glycogen, also called glucose, is a form of sugar that results when the body converts carbohydrates into fuel. Therefore, the best meal of choice to fuel a workout is one that's high in complex carbs, low in fat (no more than 20 percent), and—depending on when you eat that meal—easily digestible protein (like egg whites).

Carbs are the preferred energy source for organs and active cells. When eaten in amounts the body can utilize (400 to 500 calories every three to five hours), they become glucose in the blood, which then gets transferred to the capillaries, where it's then redirected as fuel to working muscles, the liver, the lungs, and/or brain. Any excess gets stored for later use as fat.

Protein is not an effective energy source. The amino acids in protein are often called the building blocks of muscle. If a muscle is in need of growth or repair (after a fairly intense workout), the amino acids rush in to work. If there's no need for the repairing power of protein, it gets stored away for later use as fat.

Fat is *not* a readily available energy source—it's available as energy only after glycogen has been at least partially depleted, although the fatty acids in fat cells will be released more quickly as fuel in a fit person than in someone who seldom or never works out. The greater the amount of body fat, the greater the chance that body fat won't be converted into energy.

Why exercise gives you more energy

Everyone who works out knows that, in the long run, exercise gives you energy. But why—since exercise uses energy? Many reasons:

- The body is meant to be used, not neglected. So when all the working parts *work* (instead of sitting around idle), they use both the readily available energy (glycogen) and the stored energy (fat). In short, the body becomes energy-efficient.

- People who exercise often stop overeating—either consciously because they want to make a positive change or naturally because their bodies reach a sense of balance between calories in and calories out. When people stop overeating, blood is no longer tied up in digestion and instead goes into the brain and working muscles.

- People who exercise regularly become more in tune with how to best fuel their bodies. Some exercisers find that energy remains stable with four or five small meals throughout the day. This keeps blood-sugar levels constant. High blood sugar and hyperactivity result when you eat too much sugar at one time. Low blood sugar and fatigue result when you go too long without eating.

equipment

The latest greatest cardio equipment consists of good old standbys like bikes, treadmills, and stairs. Newer inventions (like riders and air gliders) offer some unusual movement alternatives—and may appeal to people who want something different—but they don't necessarily deliver a good workout, especially to the already fit. Choosing the right equipment, however, is a personal matter, as individual as choosing a mate. The best machine is the one you will use.

Cycling

Cycling outdoors is a great way to get around and enjoy the outdoors, but there's no way to ensure it'll be a great workout, not with weaving through traffic, stopping at lights, fixing flat tires, breathing carbon monoxide, and coasting down hills. Workout-wise, indoor cycling is a better bet. Cycling is also nonimpact, so it's especially good for people with arthritis and pregnant women.

Some general info about cycling

- Set the seat height so one leg straightens but the knee stays slightly bent (too low a seat puts continual stress on the knee; too high makes the knee lock and hyperextend).
- Women find the seat more comfortable when tilted slightly down.
- Men find the seat more comfortable

tilted slightly up, and they should also beware of riding on hard seats for long periods of time—it can numb testicles!

- Handlebars should be positioned so you can bend and rest elbows on them.

Cycling alternatives

Recumbents

Advantages: Good for people with back and knee problems (the back gets support, the knees don't hyperextend). Also works the hamstrings and buttocks more than upright bicycles do. This position lets you relax and keep both hands free for reading.

Disadvantages: The temptation to sit back and relax can make this a less effective workout.

Regular uprights. These run the gamut from fancy computerized bikes to bikes with strap resistance, air resistance, and flywheels. You can even buy a "wind" or "magnetic trainer" that raises your back wheel and turns your outdoor bike into a stationary cycle.

Advantages: Because upright stationary bikes make you sit up straight, they use more energy, resulting in a tougher workout.

Disadvantages: Lack of back support. Knees and hips can easily bend beyond 90 degrees.

Indoor cycling classes. These classes usually feature flywheel bikes made by Schwinn, Reebok, and Keiser to take cycling "down a road less traveled" (although it's getting more crowded).

Advantages: Instructors guide participants on fantastic journeys over imaginary hills and down country roads. They also give alignment cues and encourage singular focus. These classes relieve the boredom typically experienced with bikes and push people to improve aerobic capacity by standing up and setting the resistance higher. Plus bikes are adjustable, so everyone can work at their own pace. Some classes even use heart monitors so participants know what "zone" they're in. Most include strength and stretching to improve muscle balance in areas typically stressed or neglected while cycling: knees, lower back, neck, forearms, and wrists. Caloric expenditure averages 450 to 500 an hour in these classes—higher than other stationary bikes.

Disadvantages: Nonfit people might get caught up in the moment and work too hard, leading to dehydration and overheating. But a good instructor should encourage them to work less.

How to spice up your bike ride

- Listen to music and add arm work, as if dancing or pumping weights (just be sure to keep your torso stable if you lift your arms overhead).
- Do *slow* strengthening exercises with elastic resistance (also maintaining a stable torso); bands are easier to control than dumbbells.
- Stand up, as if you're pedaling uphill.

Stair climbing

One of the most popular machines in the gym, stair machines can provide a hefty aerobic workout. "Steppers" come in two varieties, both of which can tone buttocks and thighs when you take deep-enough steps and calves if you get on your toes (stretch heels down afterward).

The escalator model

Advantages: More like real hill climbing because you have to pick up your foot with each step. A functionally real motion—difficult, especially if you do two steps at one time.

Disadvantages: Because the step height is preset, steps might not accommodate everyone's knees.

The hydraulic

Advantages: Easier to use for beginners because the machine assists your upward step.

Disadvantages: Because it assists your upward step, it doesn't mimic real-life stepping and is not as effective over the long haul.

How to ride the stairs

- Stand up straight. Leaning forward on the bars removes at least 25 percent of your weight, decreasing your workload by 20 to 70 percent.
- Take deep steps. Setting the machine on full speed and taking itty-bitty steps is not as effective a workout as slowing down and going through a fuller range of motion.
- Swing arms for greater cardio benefit and to improve balance.

How to spice up your stair workout

- Take diagonal or backward steps
- Alternate big slow steps with small fast ones
- Move your arms

Treadmills

Treadmills keep gaining in popularity. Although most people still prefer trekking in the great outdoors, treadmills, like bikes, offer a more controlled, sometimes better workout. For instance, you can set a steady incline and never worry about knee pain when you go downhill. Most treadmills have a cushioned bottom that absorbs half the impact, making running on a treadmill a softer surface—and easier on your legs—than a city street.

Treadmills come in two varieties.

Manual

Or should we say "pedual." Each footfall turns the belt so *you* become the motor.

Advantages: They're inexpensive, effective, have fewer parts to break down, and often fold up for storage.

Disadvantages: Since you control the speed, it's natural to slow down your pace and not realize it. These can also be noisy and flimsy.

Electric

Motorized, computerized treadmills give you more options (heart-rate readings, calories expended, etc.) and people prefer their more rugged design.

Advantages: Once you set the pace, you have to keep up with it. This can motivate you to work harder. Most feature a stop button for sudden dismounts.

Disadvantages: Creates a strange dizzy feeling when you get off. The ground, by comparison, feels like it's still spinning.

How to ride a treadmill

- Because you're not actually going anywhere, there's no wind resistance. This makes it easier to walk a flat 4-mph pace on a treadmill than on the road. So to get the same benefit you'd get at a similar speed outside, increase the incline 2 to 4 percent.
- Avoid leaning on the rails. Use your arms for a better workout.

Setting the speed

- Walking: 0 to 4 mph
- Fast walking/jogging: 4 to 6 mph
- Running: 6+ mph

Note: Putting the engine on full-tilt boogie is a good way to burn out an engine, so don't push yourself too hard.

How to spice up treadmill time

- Don't just vary speed, vary the incline (many lift up to 15 percent)
- Use visualizations: See yourself going up a mountain, down a road; be conscious of landing on your heel, then springing off your toe (pushing the belt behind you).
- Vary arm position from swinging straight (slower) to punching forward from the waist (faster)
- Get a walking audio that'll talk you through a workout

Cross-country ski machines

Cross-country ski machines often get the highest calorie-per-hour rating, mostly because they add resistance to both the upper and lower body at the same time. They also put very little stress on the knees and lower body, since the heels never strike the ground, making this very low impact. Real cross-country skiers rank among the most fit of all aerobic athletes. The problem with the machines is not everyone can coordinate the moves.

Cross-country machines come in two varieties.

Arms and legs work independently

The original models work arms and legs as separate units. These are still good, still popular. The arms pull a cord through a pulley.

Advantages: You get a better workout because arm and leg motions are separate. You can also set the machine to an appropriate resistance and stride.

Disadvantages: The motion and body position take getting used to. It's best to start with the legs and get that movement down before adding arms.

Arms and legs work together

These are newer models. Arms and legs work together and the arms work vertical levers, just like ski poles.

Advantages: The machine sets the cadence for arms and legs, ensuring a full range of motion. Good for people who can't achieve coordination on the older model.

Disadvantages: Because leg motion dictates the pole movement, the workout isn't as effective. It does the work instead of you.

How to ride a cross-country ski machine

This takes coordination, patience, and practice (a few hours!).

- Get the leg motion first, then add the arms.
- Stand upright and lean into the hip pad.
- Lift your heel as you push back.

How to spice up cross-country skiing

- Watch videos of snowy trails. It's not easy to read or do much else.

Rowers

Rowing machines tend to languish unused in gym corners. But rowing ergometers probably deliver more of a full-body workout than any other piece of equipment, even more, perhaps, than "independent" cross-country ski machines (and the learning curve isn't as steep).

If you look at people who row for sport, you find very developed upper and lower bodies. It's hard to argue, then, that rowing doesn't build strength, although technically this activity should mostly build cardio and muscle endurance. Many rowers also enjoy the full-body motion for legs and upper body.

Rowing machines come in many varieties: flywheel, piston, airwheel. Flywheels feel the most sturdy and professional.

Advantages: Rowing is a compound motion, a beautiful synchronization of arms and legs. Back and legs get a thorough workout. It's also essential training if you ever aspire to scull through glassy waters before dawn.

Disadvantages: Without proper form, lower backs take the stress, and these machines can be noisy.

How to row

- Sit up as straight as you can to avoid "breaking" at the lower back.
- Pull bar with your whole body and in this order: legs, back, arms. Slightly push the chest forward to meet the bar (to avoid hunching over).
- Make sure the angle of the ankle brace isn't too severe (could be uncomfortable and mess up your stroke). Set the seat so your legs stretch out completely with each stroke.
- Keep motion continuous.
- Make sure the seat rolls smoothly—if it sticks, it's time for service.

How to spice up rowing time

- Get into the rhythm. Let music set the pace like a metronome (very hypnotic).
- Be your own coxswain; say the word *stroke* at every pull.

Ellipticals

The newest kid on the block is the elliptical machine. This is a clever cross between cycling, stair climbing, running, and cross-country skiing. People line up at gyms to get on them.

This machine is popular because it has a lot going for it. It uses both arms and legs and so delivers a more effective cardio workout than legs alone (i.e., stair machines). It's weight bearing (good for women) but extremely low impact (about the same as walking). The unique walk-pedal action uses four to five times the amount of muscular activity as walking but the motion still feels easy and natural—and it delivers the same cardio benefits as running,

Elliptical machine

without the pain. The motion is very safe on knees because it is a "closed chain." In other words, your feet stay in contact with the pedals the whole time and the knees can't bend to a dangerous angle (your motion is set).

It offers a lot of variety. You can move both forward and back, vary the resistance, and also use it without the arms, if that's your pleasure.

- If you go forward, you'll get a better cardio workout than you do going backward.
- Going forward you work the glutes and hamstrings.
- Going back, you work the quads and calves.
- If you keep elbows close to your side, you work the biceps and triceps.
- If you extend your arms to straight, you work the pecs and upper back.

How to "pedal-walk"

- Imagine that you're standing up straight, as if walking. Your body will naturally incline forward. Let it do so from the hips. Don't arch the back.
- The machine fits most people. If working with your arms extended throws you off balance, keep them bent.
- Don't be afraid to lift your heels off the pedals, but don't lift your whole foot.
- Hold on to the arm rails if you need to lighten up the work.

Advantages: An effective, low-impact, full-body cardio workout. Uses muscles from many angles. Has many speeds and resistance levels.

Disadvantages: As with walking, torso muscles don't get used much. You have to consciously hold yourself upright to involve and strengthen abdominal stabilizers.

How to spice up your elliptical time

- Change speed and direction.
- Use it with arms and without.

The Great Calorie Burn-Off

Which machine burns the most calories? Researchers from various universities and even the American Medical Association continue to crown new winners all the time. The top contenders have been the cross-country ski machine, the rowing machine, and the treadmill. Stay tuned as the research turns . . .

The following numbers are *averages,* based on 130- to 180-pound individuals (men and women) working at a moderate pace. Keep in mind that you can increase or lower calorie expenditure depending on metabolism (how much lean muscle you have vs. fat), gender, size, and how vigorously you use a machine.

Machine	Calories per Hour	Speed
Cycling	420–550	10–12 mph
Indoor cycling class	485–593	
Stair machine (hydraulic)	375–562	50–75 feet per min.
Treadmill	420–520	5–6 mph
Rowing machine	420–600	
Cross-country ski machine	475–650	

Machine-hop your way to fitness

If you hate machines but your gym has them and you feel obligated to make full use of the gym, try machine hopping with this boredom-beating 40- to 60-minute workout:

- Treadmill: warm up 10 minutes, moderate to fast walk
- Stair machine: 10 minutes total. One-minute intervals of long slow strides mixed with faster pace
- Cross-country ski machine (if you can do it): 10 minutes of long strides and/or
- Rowing machine: 10 minutes at a steady, somewhat hard pace
- Optional treadmill: 10-minute run
- Bike: 10-minute cool-down

Rules for Smart Home-Gym Shopping

- Don't buy without testing it first.
- If you buy it from the TV, make sure you can return it for a full refund.
- Beware of phony claims: No ab-butt machine in the world will help you "lose five inches in weeks."
- Beware the machine that does it all: aerobics, strength, flexibility—especially when it's designed for only one part of the body.
- Beware of any machines that overuse some parts of your body while neglecting others, and come with programs that recommend you do the workout six days a week (which would lead to overuse injuries).

exercise
addiction

People in the industrialized West are famous for overdoing it. The logic seems to be: If a little of something is good, then a lot of it must be much better. And this is where we get into trouble with all kinds of substances—food, alcohol, money, sex, and even exercise.

Unlike other types of addiction, exercise addiction is not always easy to recognize. There is sometimes a fine line between the focused, goal-oriented athlete or fitness enthusiast and the exercise addict. From the outside, both seem healthy and disciplined. But the athlete or enthusiast can be more realistic about results, build in rest, and handle a missed workout or two; the addict cannot.

Exercise addiction is usually defined as when a person puts exercise above just about everything else—work, family, friends, and so on. It often goes hand in hand with a poor body image and eating disorders. The exercise addict is driven to excel not so much at exercise but with the *results* of exercise. For some, that's an unrealistically thin (and unhealthy!) body; for others, it's exceptionally large and defined muscles. Some yearn to excel in competitive or performance-oriented sports (such as body-building) where body image is factored into performances and scores.

The exercise addict uses exercise as a form of atonement rather than as a source of pleasure or a means to balanced health. Exercise represents the purge side of a binge-purge cycle, while eating (in both large and small quantities) represents excess, guilt, and fear. This addiction is often a symptom of other serious underlying psychological problems. Yet because exercise addiction is often closely related to eating disorders (particularly anorexia—self-starvation), it could create serious health problems, or even lead to death! Therefore, it cannot be ignored or handled lightly. Anyone who displays signs of exercise addiction should receive professional counseling both to modify present behavior and, farther down the road, to address the deeper, underlying psychological problems that contributed to the addiction in the first place.

Signs of addiction

- Excessive exercise (two hours on the stair machine, two or three classes a day, two hours in the weight room every day, etc.). Such amounts of exercise go far beyond the requirements for health. At best, they bring diminishing returns. At worst, they set the person up for injury, physical collapse, and psychological failure.

- No rest days. Rest is an essential part of the eat-exercise-rest cycle. Without rest, the body can't repair itself. A person who doesn't get adequate rest is therefore nullifying all other efforts to attain health.
- Extreme distress at missing a workout. Depression can be severe, bordering on suicidal.
- Continuing to exercise despite an injury.
- Unrealistically negative body image. The person feels or complains about being fat when body weight is normal or below the norm.
- Constant attention to body weight or body fat that is often accompanied by an ongoing inner (and sometimes outer) dialogue about amounts of food consumed in relationship to exercise.
- Physical signs of anxiety, such as hair loss, weight fluctuations, bloated face or hands.
- Physical and psychological manifestations of overtraining, including loss of sleep and/or appetite, negative or highly changeable moods, higher resting pulse rate, worsening athletic performance, and overuse injuries to muscles, tendons, ligaments, and joints.

What to do if you know an exercise addict

- Express concern for their health in a private, nonjudgmental manner.
- Be prepared to supply them with a list of practitioners who address exercise addiction and eating disorders in private and group settings.
- Avoid making any self-deprecating comments about your own body to make that person feel better (such comments will only fuel the obsession with negative body images).
- Be prepared to be rebuffed. Take rejection in a neutral manner and end the conversation by stating that your help is always there when she or he needs it.

flexibility

Of the three components of fitness—aerobic, strength, and flexibility—flexibility is often the most neglected. Many people know they *should* stretch, but they don't or they tack on stretches at the end of a workout and, when in a time crunch, skip them. Yet complete fitness can't be achieved without flexibility.

Flexibility is defined as a muscle's ability to move around a joint in a normal range of motion. It's *not* a matter of how far a muscle can be pulled, but how *well* a muscle (specifically the connective tissue inside the muscle) can move a joint.

Why is this important?

What flexibility can do for you

- Maintain mobility
- Prevent injury
- Increase range of motion in a joint
- Ease degeneration of a joint (i.e., arthritis)
- Release tension
- Correct postural imbalances
- Enhance performance in other activities
- Decrease postexercise soreness
- Remove waste products from muscles
- Improve balance
- Ease lower-back pain (Lower-back stretches can involve not only the lumbar spine but hamstrings, hip flexors, and pelvic stabilizers.)
- Increase nerve impulse movement in the brain (faster reaction time)

The best way to stretch

- Before and after every type of workout, aerobic or anaerobic (see below)
- When muscles are warm
- In a comfortable, static position (never bounce!) for 10 to 30 seconds
- Within a normal range of motion for each joint (see "Stretching the Limits," below)
- Within *your* comfortable range of motion (avoid comparing your flexibility to someone else's)
- Without excessive outside force (imposed either by a person or inanimate object)
- Exhaling to relax and stretch farther
- Maintaining a safe back position (see **Neutral Spine,** page 95)
- One muscle group at a time (for beginners) rather than the whole body, to maintain better alignment
- Every day—elongated muscles stay that way for only a few hours to a day.

Stretch before and after aerobics

According to the American College of Sports Medicine (ACSM), stretching before your workout isn't necessary. The ACSM also says you should *never* stretch muscles when they're cold (that's like pulling on cold taffy). If you like to stretch before your workout (and many people do—for their minds and muscles), do it after three to five minutes of a rhythmic, moving warm-up to heat muscles. Keep preworkout stretches easy and brief. Stretch the muscles you'll be using the most. Standing stretches are most appropriate here.

Save your long, deep stretches for after the workout. These stretches can help remove waste products from muscles, prevent soreness that typically occurs twenty-four to seventy-two hours after a workout, and help you make lasting flexibility gains.

For recommended pre- and postworkout stretches, see **Stretching**, page 234.

Stretching the Limits

There is such a thing as being too flexible. Some yoga practitioners, ex-gymnasts, dancers, and other "flexibility athletes" can stretch far beyond a "normal" range of motion. Ligaments (a tissue that connects bone to bone—also a hard substance, like cartilage, and therefore not resilient) can end up overstretched and injured when muscles aren't strong enough to hold joints in place. This predisposes or causes joint degeneration. It also decreases coordination.

Why do muscles get so tight?

Muscles get tight for all sorts of reasons. Some of the main ones are:

- **Underuse.** The less active you are, the more muscles adapt to inertia by shortening.
- **Overuse.** Muscles healing from activity respond by becoming sore and stiff. This can be worked out by warming muscles with gentle motion, stretches, massage, and rest.
- **Age.** Age can both directly and indirectly causes tightness. Directly speaking, an aging body (over twenty-five!) typically creates more rugged connective tissue in the muscle, which makes them more difficult to stretch. Lack of moisture in the soft tissue also decreases the amount of nutrients that flow to muscles, resulting in more tightness. Regular stretching, however, can reduce these two effects. Indirectly, aging often gives way to inactivity and thus creates tightness from underuse.
- **Muscle imbalances.** When one muscle group (for instance, abdominals) is much weaker than its opposing muscle group (lower back), the lower-back muscles can become very tight. Stretching can improve alignment and muscle balance.
- **Body structure.** Due to genetics, some bodies are put together in a way that inhibits flexibility, either due to the thickness of the connective tissue within muscles, the structure of the joints, or the tendons around a joint. Men are also typically tighter than women, particularly in the lower back, hips, and shoulders. Women have more elastic connective tissue in the pelvis to allow for expansion in childbirth.

glucose

How the body converts and stores glucose

Glucose is the body's favorite fuel. It's abundant and readily available to energize all sorts of activities, both aerobic and anaerobic, and rest. (For information on **Blood Glucose** and **Diabetes,** see pages 274 and 275.) The body converts all carbohydrates (breads, pasta, potatoes, fruit) to this simple sugar. But before the carbs can be used as energy, they have to be converted to a form the cells can use.

That's where ATP comes in. ATP, or adenosine triphosphate, is a complicated chemical compound (actually a phosphagen molecule) that either turns glucose (also fat and protein derivatives) into immediately available energy, or puts it away for later use.

Stored glucose or glycogen is stored in the liver and muscles. The process that converts glycogen into energy via ATP is called glycolysis. This can happen with or without oxygen. That's why glycogen can be the main fuel source for both aerobic and anaerobic workouts.

It's easier for the body to use glycogen than fat. When workloads become intense, the body makes it easier for itself and burns sugar; oxygen delivery suffers with more work, and glucose uses less oxygen than fat. Fat is a denser fuel with 9 available calories per gram; carbohydrates have only 4 calories per gram. Thus, carbs act more like kindling (where fat acts more like a log) and burn up more easily. (For tips on how to burn fat in exercise, see **Burning Fat in Cardio Workouts,** page 160.)

The fuel factory

Since the ATP process is complex, it may help to visualize this procedure as a huge, highly organized factory with one main product—energy! Here's what happens on the assembly line.

When food (the raw material for production) lands in the stomach for digestion, it is broken down into the three nutrients—carbs, protein, or fat.

The carbohydrates are turned into glucose, the protein into amino acids, and the fat into fatty acids. Then, depending on your energy needs, each nutrient is either put into immediate use or into storage for later. The nutrients tagged for immediate use get put into the big ATP pathway, where they will be immediately sent off and consumed by billions of eager, hard-working cells. This call to action to the ATP is set off by muscle contractions.

The majority of the fuel to make this happen will come from carbohydrates and get used in the form of glucose, either in a bubbling, oxygen-rich atmosphere or with no oxygen at all. When the glucose supply begins to run low, the body calls on its fat deposits. If that fails (as it sometimes does during times of extreme hardship, like diets), then the protein department surrenders some of its supply as energy, even though that's not its job. (When protein gets used for fuel, it comes out of the muscles, so muscle power is depleted.)

What isn't immediately used gets stored in the body. Carbohydrates are stored in the form of glycogen. Fat is stored in fat cells as body fat, or adipose tissue. And protein is stored as amino acids.

The body functions best when supply and demand are balanced.

Glucose in action

Glucose works differently in aerobic and anaerobic situations.

Aerobic glycolysis

With a steady supply of oxygen, glucose becomes a long-distance fuel for activities of easy to moderate intensity, usually lasting longer than five minutes. Oxygen is the key. Without it, the body doesn't produce ATP, which means no energy.

But with oxygen, glucose and ATP together create energy, carbon dioxide, water (sweat), and heat (which is energy lost). This glucose-ATP relationship occurs in the mitochondria, little "power centers" of the cells that contain enzymes that use oxygen to make energy. (It's in these same mitochondria that fatty acids are converted into fuel.)

The relationship between glucose and ATP in aerobic glycolysis is considered a "complete" relationship because most of the energy is used in the activity. Minimal waste dissipates in heat and sweat.

This process is limited by the body's capacity to move oxygen around quickly enough to working muscles, but improves with training.

Anaerobic glycolysis

Glucose is also the fuel of choice for short bursts of greater intensity, lasting between 45 and 90 seconds (like sprints or a weight-lifting set). (Shorter actions are fueled by phosphagen—see, under **Aerobic vs. Anaerobic,** "The Aerobic-Energy System," page 151.)

Glucose is broken down with ATP but *without* oxygen. Anaerobic glycolysis is considered "incomplete" because high amounts of waste (lactic acid) are created in its wake. When circulation can't transport the waste out of the muscles fast enough, the burn gets intense.

Lactic acid always results. But with training, a person can adapt to it by creating it a little later and tolerating it more.

How to avoid hitting the wall

Competitive bodybuilders do a dangerous, nasty (and arguably unnecessary) little nutritional trick called carb depleting before contests. Since carbs supply a healthy rounded appearance to muscles, the idea behind carb depletion is to deprive the body, for up to five days, of the sugars it craves. Anyone who's done this (or gone on low-carb diets) will agree it's hell. Energy levels plummet. Brain function diminishes. The person becomes scattered, forgetful, irritable, and explosive. But on the fifth day, when carb loading begins, everything changes. Muscles pump up at the slightest bit of exercise. Moods soar.

Bodybuilders may do this willingly, but they aren't the only ones who suffer from "glycogen-depletion hell." Here are tips on how to avoid it:

- Don't run marathons. Two hours of continuous, relatively high-intensity activity can seriously deplete glycogen. Between the twentieth and twenty-second mile most runners hit the dreaded "wall." If you must run marathons, give yourself several days of rest afterward to rebuild stores of glycogen.
- Avoid exercising intensely for several days in a row without rest.
- Eat your carbs.

heart

Design and health

The heart is a hollow, fist-sized muscular organ that is responsible for the flow of blood—and therefore nutrients and waste products—throughout the entire body. The intricate design of this strong, persistent pump is remarkable in its efficiency—when it's healthy.

The heart is basically four mini-pumps in one: two atria and two ventricles. The atria act like mini–primer pumps while the ventricles do the heavy, powerful work. The two atria chambers are at the top of the heart; the two ventricles are at the bottom.

Blood from the body enters the right atrium, which sends it to the right ventricle. The right ventricle, in turn, sends the blood to the lungs for the purpose of releasing waste (carbon dioxide) and picking up nutrients (oxygen). From the lungs, the blood goes back to the heart, this time to the left atrium. From there, it enters the left ventricle, which sends the blood back to the body through the aorta.

The blood travels to the heart through veins; the outgoing blood travels through arteries. Blood enters the heart through two large veins— the upper, or superior, vena cava, which brings blood from body parts above the heart, and the lower, or inferior, vena cava, which brings blood from below the heart. (For more information on how blood flows, see **Circulation**, page 166.)

How it works

The pumping action of the heart actually begins with the heart muscle relaxing, allowing blood from the body (including the lungs) to enter the heart. The first beat is the heart contracting, sending blood from the atria to the ventricles. The second beat, the stronger one, is the contraction that sends the blood out of the ventricles to the lungs (from the right ventricle) and to the body (from the left ventricle). (For an explanation of blood pressure, see page 166.)

People who take regular aerobic exercise often have lower resting heart rates than those who don't. When the heart is fit, it can stay in the resting phase (diastolic) for longer periods of time. This also allows the ventricles to enlarge to hold more blood and also propel more blood out again in a more efficient manner. Thus, the heart doesn't have to work so hard to process the same amount of blood.

Cardiovascular disease

It's been said that a machine is only as strong as its weakest link. The heart is no exception. Cardiovascular disease, or diseases of the heart and circulatory system (inextricably linked), kill more people in the United States than all other types of death combined. Congestive heart failure, heart attack, stroke, hypertension, vascular disease, and/or diseases of the heart valves can result when the cardiovascular system breaks down.

The most prevalent form of cardiovascular disease is coronary heart disease (CHD). This almost always is the result of a buildup of fatty acids in the artery walls (called artherosclerosis), which impedes normal blood flow. (Arteriosclerosis is a slightly different condition, commonly known as "hardening of the arteries.") When blood clots occur in a person with CHD, blood flow can be cut off all together. When this effects blood flow to the brain, stroke occurs. When it effects the arteries to the heart, heart attack results.

Are you at risk?

The major contributing factors to cardiovascular disease include:

- Smoking
- High intake of saturated fats
- High percentage of bad cholesterol (LDL)
- Low percentage of good cholesterol (HDL)
- Hypertension
- Inactivity
- Family history
- Uncontrolled diabetes
- Stress
- Age (men thirty-five and older and post-menopausal women are at higher risk)

A word about cholesterol

Having high cholesterol isn't always an indication of being at high risk. There are two types of cholesterol: one is "bad" (dietary) and the other is "good" (manufactured in the body).

The bad kind—LDL (low-density lipoproteins). These come from saturated fats in food and leave a residue in the arteries as they travel through the blood.

The good kind—HDL (high-density lipoproteins). These are manufactured in the body and clean up waste inside the arteries.

Premenopausal women have higher amounts of HDLs than men of the same age, thus their risk of contracting coronary heart disease is decreased until after menopause. Regular exercise along with a low-fat diet can significantly increase the level of (good) HDLs in the blood.

In determining whether someone is at high risk, physicians measure the ratio of good (or bad) cholesterol against total cholesterol.

Good Cholesterol vs. Bad Cholesterol

	HDL (good)	LDL (bad)	Total
Low	below 35*	below 130	below 200
Borderline	35–60	130–159	200–240
High	60+	160+	240+

*A low *amount of HDL is* bad, *since HDLs help clean out the arteries. A person with a low HDL ratio is at higher risk for CHD. Therefore HDL level should be at least 60.*

injuries

Anyone enamored of exercise and athletics knows that injuries are not only painful but highly frustrating, especially when they sideline activity for long periods of time and could have been easily prevented. Unfortunately, exercise-related injuries from mild to severe are all too common. Most injuries occur in muscles, bones, tendons, and ligaments.

Muscle injuries: When a muscle gets pulled or tears, scar tissue grows in the injured area, and unlike muscle, new scar tissue doesn't stretch. For the injured muscle to regain elasticity, scar tissue has to gradually stretch and get stronger with exercise.

Tendon injuries: Tendons attach muscle to bone. They're easily injured and, because their blood flow is much smaller than muscles, heal slowly.

Ligament injuries: Ligaments attach bone to bone. When ligaments are overstretched, they don't stretch back because, like tendons, they're not elastic. Thus, they can make joints floppy and unsupported. Ligaments heal slowly. But the best preventive and rehab involves strengthening the nearby muscles.

Bone injuries: Bones break in two ways: They get tiny cracks (stress fractures) or they break. People can walk around with stress fractures and not know it, but a break is impossible to ignore. Although a broken bone can seem like the most drastic injury, at least bones, of all the tissue in the body, have the ability to heal themselves (without scarring or weakness) as long as they're properly set.

Injuries come in two varieties:

Chronic: These result from repetitive stress that can build up over weeks, months, or years.

Acute. This is a sudden, critical injury, usually brought on by a sudden occurrence, which may also be a chronic injury reaching critical mass.

Don't ignore the warning signs of an injury

If you experience any of the symptoms below, stop the aggravating activity, rest, and, if severe, see a physician:

Pain, in a specific area: If you can pinpoint the pain to a particular spot on the bone about one-half to one inch wide, it could be a stress fracture.

Pain, radiating: Shooting pains can be nerve-related.

Weakness: In a specific muscle group, especially if that weakness is pronounced compared to a corresponding body part, may signal problems.

Restricted range of motion: Whenever you can't perform a pain-free range-of-motion exercise, a problem is brewing inside.

Swelling: The body's way of defending and healing itself is an indication that some sort of injury has already occurred.

Treating an injury

Physicians often recommend treating many injuries the same way—with R.I.C.E. (*Rest, Ice, Compression, Elevation*).

Rest: This stops the activity that caused the injury in the first place, prevents reinjury, and thus speeds healing.

Ice: Ice reduces secondary swelling. The body immediately responds to a blow or tear by swelling. White blood cells troop to the location and initiate healing by restricting motion and protecting it from further blows. However, when the first stage of swelling isn't treated, the body goes into secondary-swelling mode, which slows the healing process and could prevent full function in the injured area. Immediately after an injury, ice for 20 to 30 minutes, as often as you can, continuously for 24 to 78 hours. Never put ice directly onto skin. Put an insulating wrap around the ice bag or limb to prevent frostbite (this makes icing more tolerable).

Compression: Wraps, Ace bandages, and supports can also reduce swelling and prevent reinjury without weakening the muscles that support the area. Always wrap from the biggest part of the injured muscle to the smallest.

Elevation: Clever use of gravity can reduce painful throbbing. Try raising the injured area to or above the heart. This is especially useful at night when throbbing sometimes becomes more pronounced.

Cross train to prevent injury

Many injuries result from bad habits: repetitive exercise routines, bad form, unsafe exercise posture, muscle imbalances, weakness, and inflexibility. They also accumulate silently, particularly as a result of years of jumping motions like running or high-impact aerobics. Sudden falls or blows can also cause a potential injury to blossom into a full-blown disability. Although it's hard to undo the sins of the past, the following tips can help to prevent injuries:

- Reduce impact in all activities.
- Avoid dangerous sports or situations. Always pad up to minimize injuries from falls off bikes, skates, horses, etc.
- Get adequate rest, particularly of overused areas like knees and shoulders.
- Gradually strengthen the muscles around bothersome joints by adding strength-training exercises (stronger muscles are better able to withstand stress).
- Don't do too much too soon (that could stress tendons and ligaments, which take much longer than muscles to heal).
- Balance your muscle strength—for instance, hamstrings should have about 65 percent of the strength quad muscles do. So if you lift 55 pounds on leg extensions, you should be able to lift 35 pounds on the hamstring curl.
- Gently stretch the most active muscles before a strenuous workout—hold stretches longer after the workout.
- Don't work through sharp pain. Stop! "Good pain" is muscle pain that happens on both sides of the body at once and comes on slowly. "Bad pain" is in the joints, usually occurs on one side of the body, and comes on suddenly.
- Avoid exercises that promote joint pain; find painless alternatives.

Common sports-related injuries

Lower-body injuries

Calves: Achilles tendinitis—small tears in the tendon that connects the calf muscle to the heel, causing painful swelling.

Major causes: Excessive jumping or running without stretching.

Preventions: Stretch calf muscles and Achilles.

Note: To stretch Achilles, do a regular calf stretch keeping the heel on the floor or hang down a step. Then slightly bend the knee (keeping heel down) to stretch the Achilles. This is especially important for women who wear high heels, which shorten the Achilles.

Treatments: Ice and rest. Add gentle stretches. Avoid the activity that caused the injury.

Ankle sprains—an overstretched or torn ligament in the ankle. Most common sprain occurs on the outside, caused by "twisting an ankle."

Major causes: Quick moves in reaction to a slippery floor, an unexpected stop or curb, a bad landing off a jump.

Preventions: If you have weak ankles and do things like run on rocky terrain, tape ankles before you go. Also make sure you wear the right shoe for the surface you're training on.

Treatments: Use R.I.C.E., icing every 3 to 4 hours for up to 30 minutes. Don't put weight on it.

Knees: chrondomalacia—a degeneration of cartilage in the kneecap.

Major causes: Running, jumping, or lifting weights with poor body position; especially occurs in women whose wider hips don't allow a linear stacking of ankles, knees, and hips.

Preventions: Avoid high-impact moves or heavy weight lifting, especially the leg extension exercise.

Treatments: Ice, rest, and, after it's healed, gradually return to strength training with lower weights. If pain persists, there might be a fracture.

Knees: torn meniscus—a tear in a cartilage-type band under kneecap.

Major causes: Sudden twisting, flexing, or extending motions.

Preventions: Avoid quick changes of direction and improper body position while exercising. Avoid squats and stretches that twist the knee. Strengthen quadriceps muscle.

Treatments: Ice, rest, stop weight-bearing activity. Sometimes this heals itself, other times surgery is necessary.

Muscle strain—an overstretched or torn muscle. Can be a simple muscle ache or disabling.

Major causes: A sudden move or stress particularly when muscle isn't properly warmed up.

Preventions: A thorough cardio warm-up (gentle motions) followed by static stretches of the most active muscles, before and after the workout.

Treatments: Ice and rest. If the strain is mild, light exercise may be permitted as long as it's within a pain-free zone. Some severe strains can take several months to heal.

Feet: plantar fascitis—a swelling on the bottom of the feet, just where the heel meets the arch (a strip of tissue called the plantar fascia). Usually most sensitive first thing in the morning and dissipates through the day.

Major causes: Excessive impact, compounded by a nonresilient surface and nonsupportive shoes.

Preventions: Shoes with strong but flexible arch supports. Avoid high-impact moves, weight-bearing moves (like walking) for long periods of time, and stretch foot and calf muscles daily.

Treatments: Orthotics, ice, and avoidance of high-impact or heavy weight-bearing moves.

Stress fracture—a hairline crack in a bone that is not always visible in an X ray. Untreated stress fractures lead to broken bones. Most exercise-related stress fractures occur below the knees.

Major causes: These progress quietly over time from repeated stress on the bone and gradually get worse and worse, particularly with weight-bearing exercise, especially high impact.

Preventions: Cross train. Repetitive motions wear down the bone over time. Wear good shoes and train on a soft, yielding surface like dirt or a sprung-wood floor.

Treatments: Cessation of all impact moves. Arch supports can provide some relief, as can soft rounded pads placed on the most sensitive point of the bone. Ice after exercise or with pain.

Mid-body injuries

Lower back—this most common and debilitating of injuries is most often the result of a muscle spasm.

Major causes: Poor posture, improper lifting techniques, weak abdominal muscles, inflexible back muscles, sudden twisting moves, viral illness, even emotions can put muscles into spasm.

Preventions: Exercises that strengthen abdominals, obliques, lower back, and pelvic stabilizers. With pelvic stability the hamstrings and gluteals (leg extensors) can work more efficiently and keep lower-back muscles from always handling the load. Hamstring flexibility is also very important because tight hamstrings can pull the lower back out of proper alignment. General relaxation techniques like yoga or meditation.

Treatments: Most back injuries heal with time. Rest, ice, and gentle stretches until pain goes away. As pain subsides, add strength and stretching exercises mentioned above.

If injury is mild to moderate: Lie on the floor with knees up; ice under lower back if pain is bad. To stretch, remove ice and lift tailbone off the floor (pelvic tilt). Avoid uncomfortable sitting positions and unnecessary risky movements like bending forward at the waist.

If injury is severe: Do all of the above but ice every few hours for as long as pain is intense and stretch slowly and carefully but only if it offers relief, not more pain. Take anti-inflammatories (ibuprofen or aspirin), apply a topical balm like Ben-Gay (the tingling takes your mind off the pain and gives the nervous system a rest). See a chiropractor, massage therapist, or acupuncturist if necessary. As pain subsides, add strengthening exercises and wear a supportive back belt if you have to do any job-related lifting.

Upper-body injuries

Bursitis—a swelling of the bursas, little fluid-filled sacs that pad potentially sensitive areas where tendons might rub bones.

Major causes: High activity or overuse in a particular joint (elbows, shoulders, knees).

Preventions: Proper exercise technique and a light weight-training program. Also stopping any activity that may have caused the swelling in the first place.

Treatments: Ice and rest. Bursitis typically subsides with rest. Return to exercise with light activity.

Arms: carpal tunnel—a painful swelling in the wrist caused when nerves become constricted in tight "tunnels" that run through the wrist.

Major causes: Repetitive actions like typing that compress the nerves.

Preventions: Take frequent rests and move wrists and fingers on the job if work causes the problem. Avoid supporting your weight on wrists or hands (as in push-ups) or squeezing things (like weights) too tight.

Treatments: Ice and rest after flare-ups. Wear wrist braces to protect wrists when work requires the repetitive action. If typing is the culprit, get padded wrist supports or a slanted keyboard, sold in computer supply stores.

Shoulders: rotator cuff—four muscles that support and surround the shoulder joint. An injury to the external rotators is perhaps the most common upper-body injury.

Major causes: A sudden forceful move, a fall onto the shoulder, or repetitive activities—especially throwing and weight lifting.

Preventions: Stretch before major activity like a moderate to heavy bench press. Include rotator strengtheners in a weight-training program.

Treatments: Ice when painful. Avoid aggravating it further (no tennis serves, ball throwing, or heavy bench pressing until it's pain-free). Begin rehabilitation with full-range-of-motion moves (like a bench press) without weight or a tennis serve without a racquet. Gradually add light weight or slowly perform these similar motions under water, adding speed as injury heels.

Elbows: tennis elbow—pain in the outside of the elbow where forearm muscles attach and descend down to the wrist.

Major causes: Racquet sports or work-related activities.

Preventions: Stretch forearms, wrists, and shoulders. Strengthen working muscles with light weights. Avoid sharp, sudden bending of elbows or wrists, especially holding weight.

Treatments: Ice after exercise. Wear an elbow brace. Avoid range of motion in arm exercises that cause pain.

intervals

Interval training can make you fitter and leaner, faster. Intervals make you work harder for short periods of time, and can be both aerobic and anaerobic. The idea is to do short bursts of activity (as in sports), followed by rest periods that are twice as long.

Try doing intervals every fourth workout. In other words, walk faster for short periods of time (alternating with "recovery" intervals at a slower pace) so you feel only slightly winded, not completely out of breath. If intervals feel too difficult, modify your workload by working only slightly harder. People with high blood pressure, heart conditions, and high levels of body fat should avoid intervals.

A sample interval program for walking would be:

5 minutes—warm up at a slow to moderate pace (easy)

10 minutes—moderate steady pace (somewhat hard)

10 to 15 minutes—a 1-minute faster-paced interval (moderately hard to hard) combined with a 2-minute slower recovery interval (somewhat hard to moderately hard)

Repeat interval cycle 3 to 5 times.

5 minutes—cool down at a moderate pace (easy)

More seasoned exercisers can do harder intervals for two or three minutes. Just remember to rest twice as long as you worked.

joints

Articulation and mobility

A joint is a meeting point between two bones. Ligaments (nonstretchable material, like cartilage) bridge and stabilize this connection.

A few joints (in the skull and ribs, for instance) have very small ranges of motion. These nonmobile joints are the fibrous and cartilagenous joints. Most of the joints involved in exercise, however, are synovial, which means they provide a substantial range of motion. To properly care for these joints, it helps to first understand how they're put together. Synovial joints have distinguishing characteristics:

- They're hollow in places
- The ends are coated with cartilage
- They're surrounded by a sheath (called a joint capsule) of densely woven connective tissue, which is lined inside with a thin membrane
- That membrane squirts out synovial fluid as a way to nourish the joint
- Stress, injury, and repetitive actions can release too much of this fluid and cause swelling
- Synovial joints also occasionally contain an extra "shock absorber" called a meniscus. The meniscus in the knee is perhaps the most well known and most often torn (see **Injuries,** page 194). The meniscus is a fibrous band at the base of the kneecap (the patella) that adds extra support to the basically unstable knee joint.

Joint trouble?

Joints are most often injured from being hypermobile or not mobile enough. Both of these states can be caused from an imbalance of activity—either too much repetitive action (especially with improper form or excessive force) or not enough activity at all.

Hypermobility is most often seen in dancers, gymnasts, yoga practitioners, or other highly flexible people who may have impressive extensions but don't have the muscle strength to support the flexible joints. Without sufficient muscle strength, the nonelastic ligaments get stretched out of shape (and don't return to previous lengths), thus the joints lack stability and support. The best remedy is to add strength work and to avoid overstretching.

Hypomobility typically results from a past injury (leaving inflexible scar tissue on the muscle, which takes a long time to regain flexibility. It is also caused by arthritis and age. Aging joints continue to repattern themselves according to demands placed on them. When joints don't receive the message to stay flexible, the amount of lubricating collagen diminishes.

Both of these conditions can lead to further injuries. Because joints act like links in a chain, when one is injured, others are affected. (That's why you can hurt your knee and feel discomfort in your hip.) This is one reason why proper alignment is so important.

A Joint-Friendly Warm-up

Keep all movements slow, controlled, and as much as possible use full range of motion. Avoid any movements that cause pain. Repeat each move at least 8 times in each direction.

1. Roll shoulders backward and forward (together and one at a time).

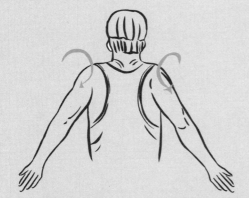

2. Interlace fingers, take arms in front of body, parallel to the floor, and make small gentle circles at the body's center line. Repeat, twisting your body to the right, then left.

3. Release arms and bend the head to the right shoulder, then to the front, and finally to the left shoulder (avoid rolling head backward).

4. Reach up to the ceiling, alternating sides, lengthening up from the waist, and circle (and reverse). Keep elbows bent if this causes joint pain.

5. Bend and straighten arms (as if doing barbell curls).

6. Roll wrists in both directions. Wiggle fingers.

7. Stand in semi-squat position, hands on knees. Round and arch lower back.

9. Stand with knees slightly bent. Put your weight onto your right leg and lift the left leg from 6 to 8 o'clock position, keep hips down; repeat on the other side.

8. Sit back in semi squats.

10. Stand with feet together, and tap your right toe on the floor behind you. Repeat with left toe, as if walking backward, but stay in place.

11. Stand on right leg, circle left ankle; change feet.

Arthritis

Extreme joint trouble is usually caused by arthritis, a burning and immobilizing pain. There are two types of arthritis:

Osteoarthritis: This is the more common, age-related variety, often attributed to injury or general wear and tear. This type of arthritis can begin to show up around age forty and affects most people over age seventy-five. Whether wear and tear is the real cause is a subject for debate (see below). As the cartilage deteriorates, the protective padding between joints diminishes, thus causing a painful grinding friction between bones. Even the synovial fluid that nourishes the joint can begin to dry up.

Rheumatoid arthritis: This is the rarer variety of arthritis, and it's actually a disease of the immune system (see **Immunity,** page 436). This disease inflames the synovial membrane and suppresses the release of synovial fluid, leading to pain and limited motion. It most commonly affects women of childbearing years. Rheumatoid arthritis typically gets worse under stress yet has also been known to disappear suddenly, thus showing the relationship between nerves and the disease. To find relief, do all of the below and relax, meditate, do nonpainful stretches, laugh—do something calming to improve mind-body-emotional health.

The inflammation produced by both types of arthritis can possibly be decreased by eating certain types of oils and avoiding others.

Eat fish oils (omega-3 fatty acids), found in sardines, salmon, and other oily fish. These stimulate the hormones that help reduce swelling.

Don't eat polyunsaturated vegetable oils or margarine. These stimulate the hormones that increase swelling.

And supplement your diet with ginger, which is believed to be a natural anti-inflammatory.

Joint Care for Lifelong Activity

Perhaps one of the best preventions against arthritis is an exercise program that emphasizes

- proper posture
- balanced muscle strength
- normal and healthy but not excessive flexibility
- regular full-range-of-motion mobility exercises for all joints
- nonimpact motions
- smooth, controlled movements, especially when lifting weights
- sufficient warm-ups and cool-downs
- relaxation

ligaments

Ligaments are made of long, fibrous, non-stretchy tissue and connect bone to bone, stabilizing the joints. Their ability to stretch and hold the joints with sufficient strength is a result of both genetics (the design of joints and fibrous tissue) and training. Proper strength and flexibility exercise can greatly influence the ligaments' "tensile strength" and their ability to expand and contract (although ligaments and tendons, which attach muscles to bones, take longer than muscles to achieve strength and flexibility because they're made of denser material). Likewise, improper exercise technique can damage ligaments, often beyond repair.

Hips and ankles have the most numerous and therefore strongest ligaments in the body, while shoulders and knees have the fewest and therefore weakest ligaments.

Ligaments typically aren't subjected to dangerous situations in normal exercise routines. However, sudden sharp moves (like twisting an ankle) and general lack of coordination (wild, uncontrolled motion) can sprain (tear or overstretch) ligaments. All ligament injuries are called sprains.

The greatest risk to ligaments occurs when joints are stretched beyond a natural range of motion and muscles don't have the strength to hold the joints in place. This happens to some dancers, gymnasts, and yoga practitioners (see **Joints,** page 200). However, some circus performers, for instance, can do incredible feats of flexibility that would tear a normal person's ligaments. But because their muscles have the strength to support and control the ligaments through all their motions, they aren't at as high a risk. Sufficient strength, proper body position, and high coordination protect the ligaments when the body stretches beyond its normal limits.

Pregnant women are at high risk for ligament injury. During pregnancy the body produces the hormone relaxin, which loosens ligaments to allow the baby to pass through the birth canal. Unfortunately, all the ligaments loosen. So pregnant women (particularly flexible ones) have to take special care not to stretch too far or they could sprain a ligament.

Once ligaments become sprained, they take a long time to heal because, unlike muscles, they have no blood flow, which would send nutrients to speed up repair. It is often said that it's better to break a bone than to tear a ligament because once stretched or torn, they stay weak and lax and, therefore, leave a person in a permanent high state of risk. Also, when bones heal, they often heal themselves completely.

One of the best preventives against ligament injury is making sure that all joints are properly warmed up before each and every workout (see, under **Joints,** "A Joint-Friendly Warm-up," page 201).

metabolism

The word *metabolism* encompasses the entire chemical process that converts carbohydrates and fats into energy and uses protein to build, fix, and grow new tissue. Metabolism never stops. What does change, however, is the speed at which it does its job and the amount of energy it processes at one time.

Most of the time, the metabolism is spent in a creative mode—building, repairing, and restructuring. This is **anabolic metabolism.** But under duress and fear, the normal processes of supplying energy, building, and repairing shut down and the body switches into **catabolic metabolism,** when it essentially feeds off its own tissues in order to survive. Any stress that causes this syndrome interferes with metabolism by halting digestion, raising blood pressure, and tensing the muscles and breath. If our fear responses are short-lived (jumping out of the path of a car or defending against attack) these reactions do little harm and mostly *protect* us. However, when the response continues (when dieting or in a chronic nervous state), the effects of a catabolic metabolism can be devastating, leading to many potential diseases (hypertension, muscle deterioration, nerve damage, circulatory problems, etc.).

The obvious choice here is to remain in anabolic metabolism as much as possible with a balance of exercise, proper nutrition, and a calm state of mind.

Exercise and metabolism

Aerobic exercise speeds metabolism by

- sending oxygen to active tissues (mostly muscles and organs), which sets off a series of energy events
- speeding up the removal of wastes, leaving less stress on the body
- putting the body into a steady state— where the delivery of oxygen keeps up with the demand—and heart rate, blood flow, and oxygen output reach stable levels.
- burning more fat than glycogen (sugar) calories. As fitness increases, the body uses this reserve fat energy sooner, and thus utilizes more.

Anaerobic or strength work increases metabolism by increasing the body's caloric needs. It does this by altering the ratio of lean muscle to fat. Because lean muscle is metabolically active tissue (i.e., it uses up more caloric energy than fat does, even when sitting still), its energy needs are greater. Muscles typically consume about 25 percent of all the body's ingested calories. When lean muscle mass increases, that rate of consumption goes up. Even a simple twice-a-week strength program can raise the metabolic rate by 300 to 400 more calories per day (which doesn't include the 200 to 300 calories used up in the activity).

Age and metabolism

Without activity, muscle mass typically decreases at a rate of about half a pound every year, or 5 to 10 percent per decade. Thus the metabolism decreases by about 2 to 5 percent per decade, resulting in an increase in body fat. By age sixty-five, it's possible to have lost half of all lean muscle mass and to have doubled the amount of body fat.

Loss of lean muscle mass from disuse is one of the main reasons why the metabolism slows so much with age. In other words, perhaps *some* (but a very small percentage) of the decelerating metabolism has to do with the wisdom of slowing down. But the majority of it comes from failing to use the body the way it was intended. Tribal cultures all over the world, where physical labor is maintained throughout a lifetime, create able-bodied, lean, muscular old people. In other words, the major damage to metabolism that goes with aging can be prevented with activity.

When the metabolism is slow, the result is an internal atmosphere that is more susceptible to disease. One of the most common diseases of metabolism is adult-onset, or Type II, diabetes. This (noninsulin-injecting) type of diabetes affects 90 percent of all diabetics and occurs when the body can no longer efficiently create or use insulin (the hormone that regulates the breakdown of carbohydrates). Being overweight is the main cause.

If you want to prolong your active years and slow the aging process, boost your metabolism. The best way to do this is with a balance of sound nutrition and exercise.

How to boost your metabolism

- Do 3 to 4 aerobic workouts per week, at moderate intensity, working up to 45 minutes of cardio per session (for more information, see **Burning Fat in Cardio Workouts,** page 160).

- Increase your lean muscle mass with 1 to 2 weight-training workouts per week. You can give your weight workouts an aerobic component by not resting between sets (see **Cross Training,** page 167).

- Eat a high-carb, low- to moderate-protein, low-fat diet.

- Eat what your body uses and no more to limit fat storage, which means eating frequent, small meals of about 400 to 500 calories, 4 to 5 times a day.

- Don't go hungry for too long. Waiting too long to eat causes you to "inhale" more food than your body will use at one time.

- Work with your natural metabolic cycles. Eat more of your food in the earlier part of the day, not late at night when the metabolism slows down.

- Adjust your food intake to match your activity level. A day of high exertion requires more energy to replenish glycogen stores.

muscles

In an aerobic workout, muscles play a supporting role. They lift, flex, curl, and reach with one major purpose: to raise the heart rate and increase cardiovascular endurance. The residual muscular endurance and strength that occur are of secondary importance to the flush of oxygenated blood. However, since the heart, lungs, and circulatory system can't get what they need without the muscles' work, it makes sense to give muscles the best possible care.

Caring for your muscles

All cardiovascular workouts should follow the same gradual increase and decrease in intensity on muscles as used in aerobics classes, whether that workout is a jog on a treadmill, a swim, or a walk in the park. The aerobics-class format *intelligently* prepares muscles to work optimally, increases coordination and flexibility, balances muscle strength, and adequately prepares and then relaxes the muscles, all of which lead to better aerobic performance.

The warm-up

Part 1. Isolations (2 or 3 minutes): Think of this as joint limbering, a time to prepare the neuromuscular system for what's ahead. This also provides a good mental prep time, opening up mind-body communication. Isolations don't need to last longer than 2 or 3 minutes. Think of moving from head to toe or toe to head and move each joint or series of joints; focus on those joints that will be most active in your workout. (See, under **Joints**, "A Joint-Friendly Warm-up," page 201.) For instance, if you're walking, be sure to warm up feet, ankles, knees, hips, and lower back. If you're swimming, warm shoulders, chest, and back.

Part 2. Rehearsal (5 to 8 minutes): Think of these moves as a mini-version of what you'll be doing later. If you're walking, walk at a slow to moderate pace. If swimming, swim slowly. The idea here is to work the whole body—legs, arms, torso—and warm the muscles by increasing the blood flow. This *isn't* the time for lengthy stretches or isolations.

Part 3. Optional light stretches (2 or 3 minutes): If you do this step, do standing stretches to keep heart rate elevated. Think of these as "prep stretches" rather than "serious stretches" (save them until after the workout).

The body of the workout

How well or poorly a muscle responds during a workout (and how satisfied you are with the process) dictates the amount of pleasure, frustration, or pain you'll get from a workout. The recipe for long-term muscular success and satisfaction in cardio workouts boils down to three things:

- A high degree of coordination
- Low impact
- Minimized momentum

Coordination: Some people seem to have more of this than others. Why is that? Are muscles smart, independent of our degree of education? Yes and no. Muscles are told what to do by sensory receptors located in muscles, joint capsules, tendons, ligaments, and the inner ear. This interwoven system promotes muscular learning, called proprioception.

People with high levels of proprioception have a more pronounced "mind-body connection" and therefore experience movement in a much more internal (less logical), more satisfying manner. They are keenly aware of body placement, the textures of their muscles, and how the subtlest shift changes the feeling of the motion. In short, they become enraptured in the process. Someone with this degree of "kinesthetic intelligence" is not unlike a musician who has mastered an instrument. This level of proprioception can be learned.

Those who struggle in the back of an aerobics class, unable to follow the choreography, aren't "uncoordinated." In fact, many of these same people excel at other physical activities. But in a classroom situation, they switch into a mental gear rather than one that encourages mind-body communication. Enchancing proprioception isn't difficult. It's really about learning to move. You'll have to rediscover this any time you take up a new type of motion.

How to improve coordination

- Become aware of your unconscious body habits. If you stick out your chin and slump, pull your chin in and stand up straight. If, when you stand, you lock your knees or stick your hip out to one side, soften your knees and stick your hip out to the other side. (If you don't know your unconscious habits, ask someone who knows you.) This retrains proprioceptors and increases awareness in previously unconscious areas. This is both an unlearning and a repatterning process that contributes to muscle balance, improved performance, and satisfaction.

- Do it your way. Break down a movement into little parts. Do it slowly. Make a dance or a game out of it. Don't try to follow a teacher. Reinvent the activity to suit your body.

- Don't *think* a move, feel it. If counts and directions are involved (such as "move right, kick 2, step 2-3-4") use the words as *rhythms,* not directions. Even trained dancers have a hard time switching from brain to body that effectively. Rhythm speaks the body's language; words do not.

- Remove any anxiety about doing it right. In fact, consciously try to do it *wrong.* Give yourself permission to do it as badly as you possibly can. You may be surprised at the results. Surrendering perfection spurs creative spontaneity.

- Don't practice in front of a mirror. (It's too easy to judge performance.) Learn to move from the *inside.*

- When you start to get too mentally involved, stretch and go home.

Momentum: When you were a kid, did you ever run full-tilt down a hill? It was exhilarating, but it was also hard to stop. Momentum is seductive. It takes over and carries you. But too much can rob the muscles of a work opportunity, and can be dangerous. The greater the speed, the more muscles lose control and the more force you need to stop.

In an exercise situation, momentum is fun and useful in things like figure skating, hurdling, kicking a ball. But add weight, and the ligaments and joints strain to support the increasing force.

In cardio workouts, some degree of momentum is necessary for simply overcoming inertia. But if you're adding hand weights to a step class, for instance, be very careful not to move at a pace that exceeds 130 beats per minute. Moving weights quickly to achieve a cardiovascular training effect puts connective tissue at risk. A smarter way to do the job is to put down the weights and make bigger arm motions.

Impact: It's a good thing that high-impact sports like old-fashioned aerobics and running have been losing favor, because impact is a bad thing for the skeleton. When you run or jump, you lift both feet off the ground at the same time and then land with three to five times your body weight. Gravity multiplies the downward force and the body compensates by meeting the hard surface with its version of equal and opposite reactions. Some adaptations occur. Runners get stronger leg bones, for instance. But some injuries brew for years and then show up all at once, resulting in a very bad day (that can last for years).

Common impact injuries include: shin splints, stress fractures, plantar fasciitis, knee and back instability and injury (see **Injuries,** page 194).

How to prevent impact-related injuries

- Do nonimpact cardio workouts, like cycling or water aerobics.
- Try low-impact moves like walking or low-impact aerobics classes.
- Vary your workouts to avoid overuse injuries (see **Cross Training,** page 167).
- Try a dance class.
- Strengthen muscles that support weak joints (for instance, thigh muscles support vulnerable knees).
- If you must run, run on soft surfaces like dirt trails, wear supportive shoes, and mix in intervals of fast walking.

Cool down

After your cardio workout, it's important to cool down.

- **Reduce intensity (5 minutes):** Just like in Part 2 of the warm-up, end your cardio workout with smaller, easier moves. Keep moving to allow blood to flow back into the heart and brain—otherwise it pools in the legs. During a workout, arteries open to accommodate extra blood flow. Suddenly reducing the blood flow can lead to a sudden decrease in blood pressure (creating dizziness, even fainting). During this part of the cool-down, the head should be kept above the heart.
- **Optional conditioning exercises (10 to 15 minutes):** Additional strengthening exercises for abdominals, buttocks, arms, and such work best here.
- **End with a final stretch (5 to 10 minutes):** If you want to increase flexibility, now, when muscles are warmest, is the best time. The stretching you do here can lead to permanent improvements. Just be sure to hold each stretch for at least 10 seconds (no bouncing), and avoid overstretching joints (see **Flexibility,** page 187). Stretching helps reduce soreness.

Optimal Muscle Care for Any Aerobic Workout

Warm Up

Part 1	isolations (shrugs, shoulder rolls)	2–3 min.
Part 2	aerobic rehearsal	5 min.
Part 3 (optional)	gentle stretches	2 min.

Body of Workout

	gradually increase then maintain intensity	20–30 min.

Cool Down

Part 1	reduce intensity	5 min.
Part 2	muscular work (optional)	10–15 min.
Part 3	final stretches	5 min.

outside conditions

If you like to exercise outdoors, it's important to know how to work with the conditions. Sudden changes in heat, cold, or altitude can be dangerous. Typically, the body needs about a week to adapt to such differences.

However, extreme conditions don't pose the only threats to health. Even a slight rise in humidity, a sudden shift in temperature, a jog in the noonday sun, or a hike at a higher altitude can be threatening unless you know how to avoid trouble.

Exercising in the heat

The body already gets hot during exercise. When it's hotter than normal, the blood vessels expand to let more blood pass to the skin, where it causes sweat. Evaporating sweat is the body's cooling system. In high humidity, the sweat doesn't evaporate, so the body can't stay cool. The core temperature rises, causing headaches, dizziness, muscle cramps, and disorientation. Extreme overheating can lead to irregular heartbeats, even coma and sudden death. When the humidity's low but the heat is high, these same conditions can occur. Fortunately, these extreme reactions can all be prevented.

Beating the heat

- Don't work out in the midday sun. Choose cool times like early morning and evening or exercise indoors.
- Be aware that you can be susceptible to dehydration and other heat-related disorders when the humidity goes above 80 percent and the temperature is as low as 70 degrees (even with low humidity).
- If you must exercise outdoors in hot or humid weather, reduce the intensity of your exercise by as much as half if you're not acclimated to the conditions. As you become acclimated (after about five days), gradually increase intensity and duration a little more each session.
- You should already be so well hydrated before your workout that your urine runs clear. (Without water, your circulation doesn't work.)
- Drink 17 ounces of water 2 hours before exercising, if possible (especially before a long endurance event).
- Drink 8 ounces or more of water 15 minutes before your workout.
- Drink 4 to 8 ounces of water every 10 to 20 minutes during your workout.
- Drink another 8 ounces after a workout.

- Spritz, spray, or dunk yourself in water. This "external sweat" cools you down and keeps your body from working so hard.
- Wear loose, light-colored clothing, preferably cotton (which breathes) or high-tech fabrics designed to leach sweat off your skin.
- Wear a light-colored hat with a shade brim.
- Wear a sport-friendly sunblock that lets your skin breathe.
- Don't wear rubberized pants hoping to drop "water weight."
- Don't take salt tablets. The amount of salt lost during sweat is minimal compared to water (so replacement isn't necessary).
- Avoid alcohol before and after exercise as it opens blood vessels, which can increase body temperature.
- Give yourself an adequate warm-up. Heat alone won't warm your muscles.
- If your workouts last more than 45 minutes, give yourself rests before finishing.
- Monitor your heart rate and avoid working in the high part or above your target zone.
- If you suffer or witness anyone suffering from heat exhaustion or heat stroke (disorientation, pulse above 100, profuse sweating or no sweating), call the paramedics. Until they arrive, wrap the person in cool wet towels or sheets, apply ice or sponge on cold water (especially to the neck, under the arms, and the groin area), use fans and keep them in a cool, dark, breezy area. This is a very dangerous, potentially fatal condition.

Bracing for the cold

Because activity warms your body, exercising in the cold isn't the problem. Problems occur when you get chilled afterward or suffer prolonged exposure.

- Wear layers of clothing, so they can be removed and put back on as you need them.
- Wear wool or polypropylene next to your skin. These fabrics "breathe" and can keep your body warm even if they get wet. When cotton gets sweaty, it chills the skin. Synthetic fabrics that don't breathe also cause sweat to pool on the skin and drain body heat after exercise.
- Bring a nylon wind breaker to wear before and after exercise and during your warm-ups and cool-downs. Don't wear it during exercise as it might make you sweat too much and cause you to overheat.
- Wear a hat, and if you don't need it during the workout, be sure to wear it before and after.
- If it's extremely cold, cover ears and nose.
- Wear gloves or mittens.
- Wear good wool socks and, if possible, water-resistant shoes.
- Drink plenty of water to avoid dehydration. Humidity is typically low when it's cold. This causes the kidneys to work harder to produce more urine, and more water vapor is lost as you exhale.
- Get out of wet clothes as quickly as possible.

Exercising in higher altitudes

The air indeed gets thin at higher altitudes because there's less oxygen. Even very fit athletes need to curtail their training above 5,000 feet, and the higher the altitude, the harder it gets. The body can't deliver as much oxygen to working muscles because there's less oxygen to be had. It can take one to several weeks to adapt to altitudes, and some people never adapt at all. Generally, though, most people feel better after about five days.

Altitude sickness can create headaches, dizziness, moodiness, and sleep difficulties. In extreme situations (as in mountain climbing expeditions), it causes lungs to bleed (pulmonary edema) and the only way to stop this potentially fatal condition is to come back down.

How to acclimate yourself to the air up there

- Give yourself at least five days to acclimate your body to the reduced level of oxygen. Don't try to exercise at the pace you do at sea level during this time.

- Begin with light activities, at least 50 percent less than normal. Gradually add duration or intensity with each day.

- If you feel dizzy or short of breath, immediately decrease the intensity.

- Give yourself longer than usual warm-ups and cool-downs.

- Enjoy the short-lived feeling of invincibility. When you come back down again after acclimating to the altitude, you'll probably feel full of boundless energy. Unfortunately, the enhanced oxygen-carrying ability of your body is only temporary. It adapts to sea level again in a few weeks.

A Word About Air Pollution

It's hard to get an invigorating workout and bad for your health when your lungs fill with polluted air. To minimize your exposure to common pollutants (like carbon monoxide), which can cause fatigue and decrease aerobic capacity:

- Don't run on city streets where there's a lot of traffic, especially truck and bus traffic. Find a park or side street.
- Don't exercise outdoors when the Pollution Standard Index (PSI) is above 100 for unfit people, 150 for those who are fit. Your local weather report should provide these numbers.

oxygen

Humans can live a few days without water, several weeks, even months, without food, but only a few minutes without oxygen. Oxygen is the most vital nutrient of all, necessary for sustaining all human functions. Yet we often take it for granted, and even deny ourselves rich oxygenated breaths because we get tense and forget to breathe deeply. Yet fortunately for us, breathing goes on regardless, automatically, unconsciously.

What is this powerful chemical called oxygen? What does it do for us and how does it travel through our bodies?

Oxygen is a tasteless, odorless, colorless gas that is carried through the body by red blood cells (in a protein-iron compound called hemoglobin). Oxygen makes life possible both when we rest and when we exercise. It's the air to the flame that ignites the fire that sets off a complex series of events.

An in-depth analysis of how oxygen works is beyond the scope of this section. And keeping it simple may provide a more vivid understanding of how the body uses it at rest and at work.

Oxygen's incredible journey

Oxygen enters the body on a breath. We inhale the oxygen that plants expel. (Likewise, plants absorb the carbon dioxide we exhale. This symbiotic relationship sustains life on the planet.)

Oxygenation: As we inhale, oxygen molecules pour into the lungs, our temporary holding tanks. (How much air we take in depends on our lung capacity or respiratory ventilation—the number of breaths we take each minute and the depth of each breath. People with asthma and emphysema can't take deep breaths and thus can't propel as much oxygen through their systems.)

In the lungs, the oxygen is sent into the bloodstream, where it catches a ride on the hemoglobin molecules in red blood cells. These red blood cells are like chauffeured limousines that take the V.I.P. oxygen where it needs to go. (The higher the hemoglobin count in the blood, the better the blood's oxygen-transport service will be. When the hemoglobin count is low, which occurs in anemia, less oxygen is delivered.)

Delivery: The delivery system is somewhat charitable, based on need (like the squeaky wheel getting the oil). During rest, most oxygen goes to the heart and brain. After eating, oxygenated blood goes to the digestive system. In exercise, it goes to working muscles and cells (although it always maintains its flow to heart and brain).

Moderate, sustained exercise is aerobic because it increases the need for and speedy delivery of oxygenated blood. Thus, the lungs and heart work harder and the amount of blood carrying oxygen (the cardiac output) increases.

Energy: Inside active cells (in muscles, organs, skin) are energy-production plants called mitochondria. When oxygen arrives in this part of the cell, it completes the energy-making process by taking stored carbohydrates (glucose) and fatty acids (body fat that's been transformed and is waiting to be put to use), and puts them into a form the body can use, called ATP (adenosine triphosphate). ATP is responsible for fueling all muscle contractions. In its wake it leaves waste products consisting of water (sweat) and carbon dioxide (exhaled breath).

Extraction: How much oxygen is pulled from the blood and put to use is determined by slow-twitch muscle fibers (which are responsible for firing endurance activities of relatively moderate intensity). These fibers contain enzymes designed to pull oxygen from the blood. (Oxygen extraction actually takes place in the capillaries.) (For more on muscle fibers, see, under **Endurance,** "Muscle Fiber Types and Endurance," page 176. For further explanations of aerobic energy production, see **Aerobic vs. Anaerobic** [page 150], **Circulation** [page 165], **Energy** [page 177], **Burning Fat in Cardio Workouts** [page 160], **Heart** [page 192], and **Carbohydrates** [page 283].

What's your VO2 max?

Each of us can increase the intensity of our workouts and reach a certain point when we're no longer working aerobically (i.e., burning glucose and fat in the presence of oxygen). Instead, we start burning sugar, *without* oxygen, and thus work anaerobically and with no burning of fat. The body does this to conserve itself because, when demand is high, it takes less energy to burn sugar than fat. That's because each gram of carbohydrate equals 4 calories, while each gram of fat equals 9.

The point at which the body transfers to sugar burning is different for everybody. It depends on the maximum amount of oxygen—the maximal oxygen consumption (VO2 max)—your body can process efficiently to maintain supply and demand. An untrained person reaches his or her maximum sooner (thus, unfit people need to work at lower intensities to stay aerobic and burn fat). With training, however, the body reaches its maximum much later, and can thus work harder and still remain aerobic. Oxygen consumption, delivery, and extraction also improve with fitness.

It is possible to determine your VO2 max. Such tests are complicated and often need to be done in the presence of a doctor. Clinics, hospitals, and research facilities have trained staff who can administer the test.

To determine your *estimated* maximum heart rate (the rate you *don't* want to train at), based on age, see **Target Heart Rates,** page 239. However, individual maximum heart rates will vary. Older people should see their physicians to determine a safe training rate.

Although VO2 max typically declines with age, it is possible to improve aerobic capacity at any age.

Breath, the pulse of life

The constant shift between inhaled oxygen and exhaled carbon dioxide is in sync with the empty-full movement cycles of other natural bodies—oceans, planets, seasons.

Oxygen is more than aerobic fuel. It both vitalizes and soothes us, and because we can inhale it both consciously or not, it provides a bridge between our voluntary and involuntary nervous systems. Practitioners of yoga, meditation, and other consciousness-expanding systems believe we can influence the workings of our involuntary nervous system. Deep breaths can indeed lower blood pressure, slow heart rate, and speed digestion. Anyone who's ever focused on breathing even for just 10 seconds knows how hard it can be to keep the mind there.

As babies, we naturally take full belly breaths. But as we get older (more nervous and wired), our breathing gets shallower. We cut off our oxygen supply, the best tonic we can take to stay calm and energized.

A few simple breaths change our state of mind and therefore our physiology. Whenever you feel tired, frazzled, or simply want to remember something, take at least three breaths.

The best way to prime your belly for deep breathing:

- Exhale all your carbon dioxide and then push out even more, until you feel your muscles strain somewhat to expel it all.
- Take a deep breath through the nose (nose hairs warm the breath and help filter out little particles).
- Again, focus on exhaling completely, although you don't have to consciously push out each breath.

As you exercise, stay aware of your breath: During aerobic workouts, your breath should be deep but steady, not strained. Focus on letting go of stale air. Inhale invigorating clean oxygen.

When you work out anaerobically (without oxygen), don't forget to breathe: Exhale as you exert because the passing air creates intra-abdominal pressure that helps protect trunk muscles and organs. Holding your breath at this time can hinder the return of blood to the heart, reduce oxygen supply to the brain, and make you faint. This nasty little occurrence is called the Valsalva maneuver.

Oxygen is still free and abundant and is perhaps the most important nutrient on the planet. Enjoy some today!

pregnancy and exercise

All by itself, pregnancy is a workout. It could be called the ultimate endurance event because even at rest a pregnant woman's heart rate, blood flow, body temperature, metabolism, consumption of oxygen and glucose all increase, as they do during aerobic exercise. But it's also the ultimate in progressive resistance (i.e., strength training) because every day that baby's weight gets heavier and heavier. Theoretically, this should make a woman stronger all over as muscles adapt to the greater load. But for most women it doesn't really work this way.

Pregnancy isn't a time to *get* in shape; it's a time to maintain and pull back. It helps to be in shape *before* getting pregnant, because cardiovascular and muscular fitness make adapting to pregnancy and recovering much easier. But even very fit women discover that it's difficult and ill advised to try to maintain prepregnancy fitness levels. It's a time to nurture new life, listen to the body, and exercise common sense.

That said, the benefits of a carefully monitored prenatal fitness regimen are numerous: Exercise can ease postural problems and other ailments such as constipation, varicose veins, leg cramps, poor circulation, swelling, fatigue, and insomnia. In addition to maintaining cardiovascular and muscular endurance and strength, a good exercise program can prevent too much weight gain. And regular exercise will give new mothers the strength to carry their babies and equipment.

The following information is in line with exercise prescriptions and warnings for pre- and postnatal women, as sanctioned by the American College of Obstetrics and Gynecology (ACOG).

Note: All women, regardless of fitness levels, must have their doctor's approval before embarking on or continuing an exercise program, and should continue to check in with the doctor and modify the exercise throughout the term and beyond.

Beginners: Nonexercising women who get pregnant, then decide to start an exercise program need to use caution. The workload should be very easy. The harder part of a cardio workout shouldn't last more than 15 to 20 minutes (not including an 8- to 10-minute warm-up and a 5- to 8-minute cool-down at easy intensity).

Weight workouts should include light weights that promote muscle endurance rather than strength without stressing the joints.

Experienced exercisers: Pregnancy is not a time to make fitness gains. It's a time to maintain and ease up. Many fitness enthusiasts continue to push themselves during workouts and this can be dangerous. Women who experience no discomfort can maintain cardio workouts for the same duration but should lighten intensity.

Strength workouts should be maintained but at a lower intensity, without putting undue stress on joints.

Low vs. Nonimpact

The best way to go? Many fit pregnant women like to continue with the same low-impact activities they did before getting pregnant—step aerobics, walking, dancing. But even very fit women feel the need to decline intensity by 10 to 50 percent, progressively (especially in the first and third trimester). Yet many feel much more capable of maintaining long-duration, low-intensity, nonimpact exercise, like cycling and water exercise (see "Take It to the Water," opposite). For some women, switching from weight-bearing to non-weight-bearing exercise during this time makes exercise much more palatable.

Three Rules of the Road

Whatever form of exercise you choose during pregnancy, always do these three things.

Stay cool: *Do not* get overheated. Your internal temperature is already higher than normal and the baby's temperature is one degree hotter than yours. Excessive heat can cause birth defects by damaging the baby's nervous system. This is especially important during the first three critical months of fetal development, when women don't yet "feel pregnant" and don't realize the possible damage they could do. Never exercise in hot or humid places. Wear cool, loose, cotton clothes when you work out.

Stay hydrated: Dehydration can cause early labor. Drink water before, during, and after workouts. Build walking to the bathroom into your workout.

Stay nourished: A pregnant woman needs an additional 300 calories above normal intake—more if she's exercising. A developing baby consumes a lot of glucose, therefore a pregnant woman needs to eat and keep energy levels steady to avoid becoming hypoglycemic. A pregnant woman should eat several small meals and snacks throughout the day with carbohydrates for energy, protein for building the baby's body, and a fat intake of about 30 percent for creation of essential fatty acids.

Warning Signs

Stop exercising immediately (and call your doctor) if any of these symptoms occur:

- Any kind of pain
- Bleeding
- Contractions
- Lightheadedness
- Nausea
- Heart palpitations
- Unusual swelling
- Overheating

If you have any of the following conditions, your doctor may advise you not to exercise at all:

- Early labor in past or present pregnancy
- Bleeding in second and third trimester
- Hypertension
- Thyroid diseases
- Cardiac (heart), vascular (blood), or pulmonary (lung) disease
- Diabetes
- Anemia
- Irregular heartbeats

Don't Go Above 140 Beats Per Minute

Pregnant women reach their maximum aerobic capacity much sooner than nonpregnant women. Their needs for oxygen increase at rest (thus, even simple breathing can feel harder, especially as the growing baby compresses the diaphragm). During exercise, less oxygen is available for working muscles and cells.

Heart rates above 140 can cause exhaustion and overheating. Higher heart rates (especially for longer durations) may also cause more than 50 percent of the blood to flow away from the uterus, which can be dangerous to the baby.

Take It to the Water

Water provides the perfect environment for the pregnant woman. Gravity is decreased, the body weighs a fraction of its normal self, joints are no longer under strain, swelling goes down, and moods go up. Most important, the heart can work at a moderately hard pace and keep up aerobic fitness without overheating.

Water pressure impacting the body actually assists blood flow back into the heart. The heart gets outside help but you still get the same benefits. Your water-adjusted heart rate is about 10 to 15 percent less than it would be doing the same activities on land. Still, don't go above 140.

Swimming (the crawl or breast stroke) increases the blood flow to the uterus (healthy for the baby). Vertical exercise is also good either in shallow water (about nipple height) or deep water, wearing a deep-water flotation belt with the buckle *under* the belly for extra support. Water temperature should feel cool when you first get in but warm shortly after. (For more details, see **Water Exercise,** page 250.)

Muscles, Joints, and Bones

A complete pre- and postnatal exercise program should contain cardio work and exercises that promote strength and balance in muscles and joints most affected by pregnancy.

Don't

- Stretch too far. The hormone relaxin has loosened up ligaments to prepare for birth. This makes for vulnerable loose joints. Avoid the temptation to take stretches too far, especially if you're very flexible. Stretch only to the point of mild tension. All the joints are affected but hips are the most vulnerable.
- Lie on your back for any length of time and avoid abdominal work lying on your back after the first trimester. This position reduces blood flow to the heart (the venous return), which can reduce total cardiac output, blood pressure, and blood flow to the uterus.
- Put excess weight on your wrists. Swelling of extremities can affect the nerves in the wrists and cause carpal tunnel syndrome. If wrists are sore, avoid positions such as push-ups or putting weight on all fours for long periods.
- Jump or bounce. Avoid high-impact exercise. With relaxin softening the ligaments, impact puts joints at risk.
- Play contact sports or participate in any activities (like skating or skiing) where you might suddenly lose your balance and fall.

- Move, twist, or get up suddenly. All sudden moves, particularly with one hip lifted (out of alignment), can sprain a ligament.
- Sit, stand, or walk for too long. Prolonged sessions of all of these can create back pain. If sitting, get up and/or raise one foot on a box (periodically switch sides). Cardiac output can decrease if you stand for too long. Likewise, raise one foot on a box. If walking long distances, take breaks.

Do

- Wear a supportive bra. Aside from adding comfort, this also improves posture by correcting the urge to lean forward.
- Wear supportive shoes to protect vulnerable joints.
- Favor low-impact aerobics like dance or cycling or nonimpact aerobics like water exercise.
- Empty your bladder before working out.
- Add grace and balance-enhancing moves to your workout. This is a good time for ballet, Tai Chi, belly dance, or other types of gentle movement that improve body image and balance—especially good for letting muscles adapt to a new center of gravity.

Postpartum Prescription

You may be pregnant for nine months, but your body thinks it's pregnant for much longer than that. Postpartum is like pregnancy in reverse. It takes time for the body to wind down. Your uterus can take six weeks to several months to return to normal. Relaxin can stay in your body for up to a year, so joints remain vulnerable. The pelvic floor gets stretched in a big way. Without strengthening exercises (Kegels), you could have a prolapsed uterus (because it has no support) and leak urine.

Your transverse abdominals stretch like a balloon during pregnancy. Without exercises to retone this muscle group, the lower back is susceptible to injury and posture slumps, the torso remains unstable, and the belly muscles could "pooch" out indefinitely.

Most women are anxious to get back to their prepregnancy figures. It's important to wait for your doctor's OK before beginning *vigorous* exercise. This may be six weeks with a vaginal delivery or twelve weeks with a C-section. In the meantime:

- Restart your activity with walking. Take half-hour walks three times a week (it's a good opportunity to get out with the stroller and meet other mothers).
- Once you get your physician's permission to exercise more vigorously, work up gradually to aerobics—20 to 60 minutes, three times a week.
- Empty your bladder and nurse or pump breast milk before exercising.

- Be patient and don't push yourself too hard. Focus on being healthy, not thin.
- Don't try to lose more than 4 pounds a month, especially if you're nursing. Nursing makes you retain extra body fat. Once you stop, the last 5 to 10 pounds will magically disappear.
- Eat enough to maintain energy. Nursing uses up 500 to 800 extra calories a day. Exercise may take another 300. An average woman eats about 1,800 a day. A nursing active woman may need 2,500 calories a day.

- Lack of sleep and food can set you up for postpartum depression.
- Get support. Family and friends give you the connections you need.

exercises and stretches every pregnant woman should know

Carrying a baby in your body can do a number on posture and muscle tension and strength. The following standing stretches address some of the most commonly stressed and weakened areas:

Hip flexor. Stand with feet parallel, hip-distance apart, and in a long "split" stance as if cross-country skiing. Take a step forward into a semi-lunge position. Slightly bend both knees, so the back heel is lifted, and press the hip (of the back leg) forward. Lift your chest as you do this but be sure not to arch the lower back. Hold for at least 10 seconds and switch sides.

Hamstring. Stand with feet parallel, hip-distance apart, and in a long "split" stance. Put one leg forward and lift the toes. Sit back into the hip of the other leg and incline chest forward from 15 to 45 degrees. Put hands on thighs but not over the kneecap (to protect the joint). To get the most out of this stretch, reach forward with an open chest and avoid rounding the back. Torso doesn't have to be far forward to make this effective.

Chest. Stand with feet hip-distance apart. Lace fingers together behind the lower back and gently raise the arms without overstretching the shoulders, elbows, or wrists.

Lower back. Take a wider than hip-distance stance and bend the knees. Incline torso forward and rest hands on thighs in semi-"huddle" position—or lean forward onto a table. Gently round and straighten lower back. Also, draw imaginary circles with your tailbone, moving clockwise and counterclockwise.

Kegels. Kegels work your pelvic-floor muscles, as when you stop and start the flow of urine. You can vary these by (1) tightening the muscle for 10 seconds and (2) doing "elevators," in which you lift the contractions higher, going up about five floors. Doctors recommend doing a hundred Kegels a day. You can do them when sitting or doing other exercises. Avoid doing them as you urinate.

Semi-recumbent abs. Lying on your back after the first trimester cuts off blood supply to the uterus. Modifying the position by shifting weight to your left side allows blood to return to the heart and reduces the pressure on the linea alba (the band that runs down the center of your abs, which splits during pregnancy. See "Recti Splinting" opposite). In this position, do your regular crunches, also pelvic tilts. Start to gain awareness of your transverse abs as well (these get stretched during pregnancy). Try to pull the belly button down to the floor, as if hollowing out the inside of a bowl.

(See also exercises under **Back** and **Shoulders,** pages 14 and 5.)

postpartum abdominal exercise

Wait until you've stopped bleeding to do this.

Recti splinting. During pregnancy, abdominal muscles separate to some degree. Before performing exercises for your abs, you should figure out how much they have separated. To do this, lie on your back with knees up. Lift your head and put your finger vertically below the navel, then press finger gently down.

- A separation of one finger is normal. Go ahead and do regular ab work (see page 5).
- If it's 2 fingers, do the recti splinting exercise but avoid twisting motions.
- If it's wider than 2 fingers, don't do any traditional crunches or other abdominal work. Instead, breathe into the belly and do pelvic tilts. Wait until split goes down to 2 fingers before splinting.

The splint. With knees bent, feet on the floor, inhale, cross your hands over your belly, and lift your head. Exhale, squeezing the right and left sides of your belly together, and harden your abdominals as if receiving a punch.

quickie
workouts

If you're pressed for time and only have 5 to 20 minutes to work out, is it really worth the effort? Yes! Something can be better than nothing. If you use the time intelligently you can get much more than half a workout. You can make fitness *gains.*

Most fitness professionals agree that the best cardiovascular benefits (more fat burned and improved cardiorespiratory performance) occur during 30- to 45-minute aerobic sessions. Most people don't even *start* to burn fat until approximately 20 minutes into a cardio workout. Stopping at 20 minutes, then, seems to defeat the purpose, as does breaking a workout into two 20-minute segments hours apart.

For a fit, time-crunched person, however, a quickie cardio workout keeps the body conditioned to exercise during times of travel or heavy workloads. Fit people tend to burn fat sooner than nonfit people, so some fat is burned in a shorter workout. But mostly, the time spent exercising oxygenates the blood, clears the mind, and relieves stress.

For someone new to aerobic exercise, a short workout is one of the best ways to acclimate the body to the increased demands for energy. Putting more frequent, shorter, light stresses on the body is a much gentler way to start with an aerobic fitness program, rather than dragging through a 45-minute workout. Someone just starting out should try two or even three brisk walks a day—before breakfast, before lunch, after dinner—at a comfortable but invigorating pace (warming up at a slower pace for about 5 minutes and cooling down for 3 minutes—in a 20-minute walk, that leaves 12 minutes of somewhat hard intensity).

Shorter doesn't necessarily mean harder

A short workout doesn't have to be of high intensity to be effective. In fact, it's a bad idea to rush to "get it all in" if it means you put your body at risk. Be sure to

- warm up sufficiently so you adequately prepare muscles and joints.
- don't elevate the heart rate too quickly.
- don't maintain a heart rate above your maximum (see **Target Heart Rates,** page 239). (Make sure you can talk throughout. Otherwise you're no longer in the fat-burning range.)
- don't forget to cool down at a moderate intensity.
- be sure to stretch your most active muscles.

Shorter duration does lend itself to higher intensity, as long as you follow all the precautions above. During the 12 minutes of somewhat hard intensity, push yourself a bit to increase your aerobic capacity. This helps beginners get in shape faster and experienced exercisers push themselves to new limits.

A word on intervals: Make sure that your higher-intensity intervals make you only slightly winded, not completely out of breath. And be sure you feel rested enough in recovery intervals before shifting back into higher gear.

A Quickie Interval Program (for Any Cardio Activity)

5 minutes—warm up at a slow to moderate pace

12 minutes total—somewhat hard aerobics alternating between a 1-minute moderate interval and a 1-minute faster pace (for a total of six times)

3 minutes—cool down at moderate pace

1 minute—stretches

Quick workouts don't have to be aerobic

If you've got 20 minutes: Try a weight workout with no rests between sets, pushing each set to failure, or close to it. Twenty minutes is enough time for a whole upper- or lower-body workout. Be sure your first set is a warm-up and uses large muscles to send blood to the rest of the body. (Muscles progressively warm up with more repetitions. The safest reps actually come at the end of the set, when you're less capable of pushing too hard.)

Do a yoga stretch series. Start with standing stretches, then go down to the floor on all fours. End on your back.

If you've got 15 minutes: Pick one to three muscle groups for a strength workout. Pick muscles that work together synergistically—all "push" muscles (chest, shoulders, triceps) or "pull" muscles (back and biceps). Or you can try opposing muscle groups, such as back and chest; biceps, triceps; abdominals and lower back; or quads and hamstrings.

Do Chi Kung or Tai Chi exercises.

Do yoga stretches.

If you've got 10 minutes: Do joint limbering exercises (see **Joints,** page 200).

Do abdominal exercises.

Do standing balance exercises.

Do yoga floor stretches.

If you've got 5 minutes: Do deep-breathing exercises.

Get up, walk around, and stretch.

special medical conditions and working out

Special medical conditions shouldn't necessarily preclude you from exercise. In fact, exercise often tops the list of prescribed treatments (and preventions) for all sorts of ailments. If you have any of these conditions, please check with your doctor before following the guidelines below to make sure your individual needs are being met.

Anemia

Almost half of all women are anemic, possessing what advertisers used to call "iron-poor blood." Much of this is caused by loss of blood through menstruation and an iron-deficient diet. Anemic women lack sufficient oxygen-carrying hemoglobin molecules in their red blood cells. Therefore, the circulatory system doesn't produce or deliver enough oxygen, the muscles don't get the fuel they need, and all-over aerobic capacity is diminished.

Symptoms include

- Fatigue
- Pale, washed-out skin

Exercise guidelines

- Train aerobically at a lower intensity.
- Avoid high-intensity aerobic training since it could lead to the further destruction of red blood cells.
- There is no reason to avoid anaerobic strength training. But once again, keep intensity light to moderate and avoid overtraining or exhaustion.

Arthritis

Arthritis is a deterioration of the joints, resulting in pain and decreased range of motion, function, and flexibility. It is not necessarily an inevitability of old age (see **Joints**, page 200). Nor is there any evidence that exercise causes it, although an injured joint might be more prone to arthritis pain. Actually, there are two types of arthritis:

Osteoarthritis: This is the more common old-age variety and it's further divided into four categories from Class 1, mildly inconvenienced, to Class 4, fully incapacitated. A physician-approved program takes these different capabilities into consideration.

Rheumatoid arthritis: This is a rarer, autoimmune disease (see **Immunity,** page 436).

Most people with arthritis respond well to regular moderate exercise, which can

- offer pain relief
- increase range of motion
- improve functional movement
- improve neuromuscular coordination
- prevent further degeneration

Arthritics should

- favor low-impact (i.e., walking, dancing) or nonimpact aerobic exercise (water exercise in *warm* water, cycling)—at least 4 times a week.
- do joint-mobility exercises every day—whether attached to an aerobic workout, by itself, or as part of a yoga-stretch or strength workout (see, under **Joints,** "A Joint-Friendly Warm-up," page 201).
- use 10-minute warm-ups to adequately prepare joints. (Beginners should keep the "work" portion of aerobics to 10 to 15 minutes. Cool-downs should also be about 10 minutes.)
- take rests or minimize range of motion if pain occurs. (Don't push through pain. Avoid it; work around it.)
- stretch the muscles that attach to the most-affected joints.
- always maintain good alignment during exercise. (Misalignment—especially with added resistance—can further exacerbate painful joints.)
- strengthen muscles with *proper* weight-training techniques to increase joint range of motion.

- strength train at a low intensity.
- increase flexibility with a regular stretching program—either after aerobic workouts or in separate sessions.
- relieve painful joints in hot tubs.
- ice "hot" joints during flare-ups.

Arthritics should *not*

- exercise with extreme joint pain. (Instead, rest for a few days to let pain subside.)
- do any high-impact exercise, such as running.
- do water exercise in cold water.

Asthma

Asthma constricts breathing passages and turns a simple breath into hard labor. No one really knows what causes it—cold, smoke, pollutants, cat hair, stress. It can appear and disappear without warning.

The majority of asthmatics suffer attacks *during* exercise (known as exercise-induced asthma, or EIA), but exercise can improve asthmatic conditions for others. Still, asthmatics can and should exercise. In fact, higher fitness levels tend to increase the point at which wheezing occurs. People with asthma should:

- have a bronchodilating inhaler handy at all times and use it at the first signs of wheezing (using it about 20 minutes before a workout can also decrease the risk of EIA).
- do long warm-ups and cool-downs for aerobic workouts.

- avoid exercising outside during extreme cold, heat, or high levels of pollution or pollen.
- slow down when intensity causes labored breathing.
- drink plenty of water before, during, and after workouts to keep the respiratory tract secreting fluid.
- during anaerobic strength workouts, take longer rests between sets if breathing passages become constricted.

Cardiovascular disease

Cardiovascular disease (CVD) kills more people each year than all other diseases combined. This generic term covers all diseases of the heart, blood vessels, and arteries that can result in coronary heart disease, heart attack, stroke, hypertension, vascular disease, and other ailments. The most common form of CVD is coronary heart disease (CHD), which is most always caused by artherosclerosis—a buildup of plaque on artery walls caused by excess fat and cholesterol in the diet and genetics.

Coronary heart disease used to be thought of as a man's disease—and being male over thirty-five with a family history of CHD is a major risk factor. However, postmenopausal women are also at risk. Before menopause, estrogen helps keep arteries clear. But once these hormones subside, the heart becomes more vulnerable. One in two women over fifty-five will be affected by CHD. Each year five times as many women die of this disease than breast cancer.

Regular exercise plays an important part in heart health by
- helping to maintain a healthy body weight (which reduces risk of hypertension, adult-onset diabetes, and can encourage other healthy behaviors).
- making the heart a more efficient pump.
- reducing the amount of "bad" cholesterol.
- toning and clearing the arteries.
- improving arrhythmia.
- increasing the likelihood of surviving a heart attack.

The heart can give warnings that it's in trouble—with pain, numbness, and shortness of breath—but it can also give no warnings at all. Therefore, everyone, especially anyone with any of the above risk factors, should be screened by a physician (preferably with a treadmill test) before undertaking an exercise program.

Aerobic exercise guidelines
- Start with a low-intensity aerobic workout (like walking) and gradually increase intensity.
- Work within physician-monitored levels of exertion.
- Build up to 30 minutes a day, 5 days a week.
- Be sure to take adequate time to warm up and cool down.

Diabetes

By itself, having diabetes is not a curse. When it coexists with a healthy lifestyle it requires being aware of what's going on in the body at all times. Diabetes is basically a disease of metabolism—inefficient conversions of carbohydrates, proteins, and fats. There are two types of diabetes.

Type I: Insulin-dependent diabetes mellitus (or childhood-onset diabetes).

Type II: Noninsulin dependent diabetes mellitus (or adult-onset diabetes). More than 80 percent of all people with diabetes fall under this category—often caused by being overweight, especially from fat stored around the abdomen. Also caused by genetics.

People with either type of diabetes can benefit from exercise because increased fitness can reduce the risk of heart disease and stabilize levels of blood glucose.

People suffering from both types should

- exercise two hours after a meal.
- monitor blood-sugar levels before and after exercise (and during exercise, when beginning a program).
- avoid working out when insulin activity is at its peak.
- make aerobic workouts a priority over strength or flexibility workouts. (But if time permits and desire is there, add strength and stretching workouts as recommended by a physician. However, be sure to carefully follow the eating, injecting, and sugar guidelines prescribed by a physician.)

People with **Type I** should

- plan exercise, injections, and eating all at consistent times each day to stabilize insulin levels.
- do aerobic exercise 5 to 7 days a week for 20 to 40 minutes at a low to high intensity.
- avoid injections into major muscle groups that will be used during exercise (i.e., don't inject thigh before a step class).
- carry some form of fast-acting sugar (like orange juice or candy) in case of rapid drops in blood sugar.
- eat a light-carb snack before and during long workouts.

In Type II diabetics, exercise replaces injections because it has an insulinlike effect of its own. In addition, exercise can also help Type II's to

- lower cholesterol.
- maintain healthy body weight.
- make muscles more receptive to blood glucose.
- reduce the amount of fat circulating in the blood.

People with **Type II** should

- do aerobic exercise 4 to 5 days a week.
- build up to 40 to 60 minutes (to facilitate fat burning).
- maintain a low to moderate intensity.
- carry candy or juice in case of rapid plunges in blood sugar.

sports

Some people work out their whole lives and never do sports. And some people play sports and never work out. You can easily exercise without sport. But it's not a good idea to do sports without exercise. Yes, you can get fit playing sports. But it depends on the sport and how you play it. Most sports combine aerobics with quick anaerobic bursts. In the long run, this can create lopsided fitness.

So before you run onto the court or playing field, know what that sport is doing for you so you don't kid yourself into thinking you're getting everything you need. And fill in the training gaps with complementary exercises.

Basketball

Basketball is a full-body workout and a contact sport without pads. In other words, it's more rugged than it looks. To play more than a pickup game, get in shape. The better your game, the greater the fitness benefits.

Fitness benefits: 80 percent anaerobic (lots of quick energy bursts), 20 percent aerobic. More aerobic when you run down the court, less when you block, jump, or pass.

Approximate calories per hour: 400 to 800

Most used muscles: You use them all—legs to defend, jump, and run; chest, shoulders, and arms to throw, pass, and dribble; back to pull the ball out of someone's hands; and abs and lower back to stabilize torso as you fake out an opponent.

Most neglected: Not applicable

Most common injuries: Impact injuries from falls or collisions.

What you need for conditioning:

- Endurance. Combine regular cardio workouts with short-distance sprints (the time it takes to run the length of the court). If you run for cardio, run on soft surfaces to avoid shin splints.
- Practice quick changes of direction for agility and speed.
- Do full-body weight workouts. Some good exercises include: squats, lat pulls, chest presses, shoulder presses, triceps press-downs, dumbbell curls.
- Stay strong and flexible to prevent injury.

Cycling: road or mountain biking

Outdoor cycling is a great way to get around and a true nonimpact sport (until you fall off). But it's not a great workout when you go downhill.

Fitness benefits: 75 percent aerobic, 25 percent anaerobic, especially when you're on a steep incline

Approximate calories per hour: 500 to 700—more if you're a speed demon

Most used muscles: Quads, glutes, and hamstrings

Most neglected: Abs, upper body

Most common injuries: Aside from falling injuries, knee pain (seat too low?) and hamstring pain (seat too high?)

What you need for conditioning:

- For cycling muscles, do step-ups, squats, stair machine (take long strides).
- To strengthen neglected muscles (and to be more comfortable while riding), do ab and lower-back exercises, chest presses, lat pulls, triceps press-downs (and biceps curls for muscle balance). Circuit-type strength workouts are good for cyclists.
- Cross train with swimming (trains cycling's unused muscles), running (walk down hills to prevent knee injury), skating, and stair climbing.
- Stretch to prevent injuries.
- Alternate between long, fat-burning rides (1 plus hours) and short rides with intervals to build strength.

Golf

Although golf is probably the most aggravating sport around, it's not exactly athletic. If you hire a caddy and ride in a golf cart, you'll get into better shape walking through the mall.

Fitness benefits: Zilch unless you walk the links and carry your bag. The swing is one quick anaerobic second (swings average about one every three minutes). Walking is aerobic. Riding in a cart is not.

Approximate calories per hour: 200 to 270 (walking alone is 300)

Most used muscles: Back, shoulders, chest, spine, and hips for the swing, and legs when walking

Most neglected: Abdominals and arms

Most common injuries: Shoulder rotators and blisters on hands. Also bruised egos.

What you need for conditioning:

- Balance—you can't hit the ball if you fall over. Train hip and torso stabilizers (with inner- and outer-thigh exercises, lower-back extensions, and ab work).
- The swing is a full-body motion, requiring flexibility, precision, and concentration. Before you play, take a club in both hands behind your lower back and gently lift arms. Also lift club overhead, with both hands, then alternate tilting one side higher.
- Get your cardiovascular and muscle conditioning from other sources and do full-body stretches when not on the links.

In-line skating

It's a sport, a recreation, a workout, a phenomenon! Many ex-runners have traded in their running shoes for skates and discovered that while running made them groan, skating makes them smile.

Fitness benefits: 20 percent anaerobic, 80 percent aerobic. Make it more anaerobic by sprinting, more aerobic by skating with even strides.

Approximate calories per hour: 300 to 600, depending on whether you skate on flats or hills, if there's a head wind, and your weight and speed

Most used muscles: Quads, hamstrings, buttocks, torso

Most neglected: Shoulders, arms, calves

Most common injuries: Broken wrists, sprained elbows, and torn rotators—all from falling

What you need for conditioning:

- A base of cardiovascular endurance and lower-body muscle strength.
- A full upper-body weight workout (to add muscle balance).
- Don't even think about skating without helmet, wrist, elbow, and knee pads. They also make butt pads.
- Take a lesson. Learn how to lean forward into your skates and brake.
- Avoid sidewalks, curbs, traffic, and bumps until you've built up some confidence.

Skiing or snow boarding

Although skiing clears the head and lifts the spirit, unless you're very good, it's not a great workout. Don't expect to ski into shape. Get in shape before you hit the slopes.

Fitness benefits: 40 percent anaerobic, 60 percent aerobic. More aerobic if you're at high altitude, also if you slalom. Less if you simply cruise down the kiddy slope.

Approximate calories per hour: 250 to 500

Most used muscles: Quads, calves, hip stabilizers, torso stabilizers

Most neglected: Arms and shoulders

Most common injuries: Broken arms and legs from falling

What you need for conditioning:

- Endurance training. Start pre-ski conditioning at least twelve weeks before you hit the slopes.
- Cross train with running or fast walking (test your agility and speed by stepping over sticks, sidewalk cracks, etc.).

- Train your ski muscles with squats, lunges (especially if you telemark), leg extensions, hamstring curls, wall sits (sit with back against the wall, knees at a right angle), lower-back and ab exercises.
- Train upper body to prevent muscle imbalances.
- If you ski moguls, prepare your knees by doing plyometric jumps. Pull both knees to chest and land on a soft surface (no concrete).
- Stretch for all-over flexibility.

Soccer

This is the number one game in the world, played by all ages. All you need is a ball and space.

Fitness benefits: 60 to 80 percent anaerobic, 40 to 20 percent aerobic. This highly explosive game is full of quick changes of direction and sudden bursts of energy.

Approximate calories per hour: 300 to 750

Most used muscles: Legs and torso

Most neglected: Upper body

Most common injuries: Pulled groin, pulled hamstring, sprained ankle

What you need for conditioning:

- Stamina—you can win a game simply by outlasting an opponent. Try long-distance running, interspersed with running backward, sideways, zigzags, sprints.
- Full-body weight workouts—leg exercises should focus on explosive strength and muscle endurance in quads, buttocks, hamstrings, inner and outer thigh,

calves. Torso strength should focus on lower back and abs, especially obliques. Upper-body strength workouts will add balance.

- All-over flexibility is important—especially in calves and Achilles tendons.
- Be ambidextrous. Practice dribbling and juggling with both feet.
- Dribble without looking at the ball.

Swimming

People think swimming keeps you fat. True, the heart doesn't beat as quickly in the water and you don't sweat as easily (though you can sweat). But swimming does condition heart, lungs, and muscles—the perfect stimulus for burning fat.

Fitness benefits: 40 percent anaerobic, 60 percent aerobic. A novice swimmer's workout is mostly anaerobic. An experienced swimmer's workout is mostly aerobic.

Approximate calories per hour: 240 to 480

Most used muscles: Back, chest, shoulders, abdominals

Most neglected: Legs

Most common injuries: Shoulder rotators

What you need for conditioning:

- Strong lats, shoulders, and good lung capacity.
- To be a really good swimmer, take lessons. Even experienced swimmers need pointers.
- To address muscles from different angles, combine freestyle, backstroke, breast stroke, and, if you can, butterfly.
- Except for the frog kick, swimming

doesn't work legs through a full range of motion. Do additional leg exercises.

- Strengthen and stretch shoulder rotators to prevent overuse injuries.
- Add sprints for greater strength and aerobic capacity.
- Get yourself some short swim fins, a kickboard, and webbed gloves for upper- and lower-body drills.

Tennis

Tennis peaked in popularity in the eighties. But just because it's been dwarfed by other sports doesn't mean its beauty has diminished.

Fitness benefits: 60 to 70 percent anaerobic, 40 to 30 percent aerobic. Keep moving to up the aerobics.

Approximate calories per hour: singles, 450; doubles, 200

Most used muscles: Legs, torso, and racquet arm

Most neglected: The unused arm

Most common injuries: Tennis elbow and shoulder

What you need for conditioning:

- A full-body weight workout—especially the unused arm, legs, and torso.
- Gently strengthen and stretch the muscles around the weakest links—wrists, elbows, shoulder rotators.
- Extra cardio workouts for endurance
- All-over flexibility
- Quick reflexes. Practice eye-hand coordination drills.
- To strengthen your stroke, take an old beat-up tennis racquet into the pool and practice swings in both directions.

stretching

Best pre- and postaerobic stretches

In the quest to burn fat (or build muscle) most people skimp on stretches. This is a mistake because flexibility is a key ingredient for enjoying exercise and being more mobile and functional in life (especially as you get older). Muscles contain "stretch receptors" that constantly inform the nervous system about the body's overall level of tension. Chronically tight muscles throw off alignment and send signals to the brain that the body is under stress.

Stretching before and after workouts prepares muscles, ligaments, tendons, and joints, as well as increases performance, improves range of motion, prevents injury, enhances moods, and eases the mind and body in and out of exercise.

Stretch this way

Pre-warm-up, optional (2 or 3 minutes): Begin with gentle isolations such as shoulder rolls, small and gentle hip rotations (see, under **Joints**, "A Joint-Friendly Warm-up," page 201) to stimulate areas you're about to work.

Warm-up (5 minutes): Bigger, full-body moves. If walking, for instance, walk at an easy to moderate pace, swinging arms.

Warm-up stretches (about 2 minutes total): Hold each preaerobic stretch for at least 10 seconds. Choose stretches for your tightest and most active muscles. But be sure to balance stretches (don't just stretch quads, stretch the hamstrings on the other side, too).

Cardio workout (10 to 45 minutes): Start at a moderate intensity. Work up to somewhat hard and sustain—or do intervals (see **Cross Training**, page 167).

Cool-down (3 to 5 minutes): Bring the pace back down (still moving rhythmically).

Final stretches: Repeat warm-up stretches or switch to floor stretches. Either way, hold each stretch for at least 20 seconds. With warm muscles, this is your chance to permanently improve flexibility.

stretches

The following stretches are classic all-around stretches for any whole-body aerobic activity, but they are especially useful for walking, running, dancing, aerobics, or step. For a swimming workout, focus on torso and upper-body stretches. Stretches should target the muscles that'll be used most.

1. Lower back. Stand with feet hip-distance apart. Crouch into a semi-squat position, with knees bent and hips pushing back (think of lifting your tailbone to the ceiling). Put your hands on your knees (or on a table, fence, etc.) for support. Round your lower back so the tailbone points to the floor, then straighten the back.

2. Standing hamstring. Take the same position as above but extend one leg forward and flex your toes up to the ceiling. Your leg need not be straight for a good stretch. The secret to this stretch is to *push your chest forward and sit hips back* (keeping your lower back slightly arched—tailbone to the ceiling again). Be sure not to push your hands down onto the knee of your extended leg. Switch legs. This is an especially important stretch if you have a "sway" back.

3. Calf. Slide one leg behind the other (in a lunge position). The front knee should stay bent as you lower the back heel to the ground. Lean forward 25 to 35 degrees (so your torso is in line with your back leg). Move to the next 2 exercises without changing legs.

4. Hip flexor. Raise the back heel off the floor and bend the back knee. Keep the front knee bent as you bring your torso upright and press forward with the back hip (i.e., pelvic tilt). This is an especially important stretch if you have a "flat" lower back.

5. Achilles/soleus. Bring your back leg forward a half step then shift your weight back onto it. Keep the back heel down as you bend the back knee. Repeat stretches 3, 4, and 5 on the other leg. This is an especially important stretch if you wear high heels.

6. Quads. Get your balance on one leg (hold on to a wall, chair, pole, etc.) by softening your supporting knee and sinking your weight down. Hold the other foot behind you. Imagine you're holding a balloon between your knees. Don't drop it as you gently pull the foot behind you (not all the way up to your buttocks, this is a dangerous angle). The thigh you're stretching should stay as close to vertical as possible and the pelvis shouldn't move (your hips should be forward).

7. Shoulder extension. Reach both arms directly overhead. Fingers can be laced together or be open. Be sure to keep torso steady (don't overarch the lower back). But you can also use this to stretch your abdominals and intercostals (rib muscles). "Lift" the rib cage. An especially important stretch before aerobics, dance, or other movement with much arm motion.

8. Upper back/trapezius/neck. Hug yourself. Let your head hang forward as you hold shoulders and relax upper back. Be sure to hold abdominals and lower back steady as you do this.

9. Chest. Clasp hands behind your back and push chest forward. Keep chin tucked under, knees slightly bent, and lower back and abs steady as you do this. An especially good stretch if you typically hunch forward.

10. Torso. Take a stance wider than hip distance. Soften knees. Hold one hand on the hip. Extend other arm first to the ceiling (keeping shoulder down), then approximately to 1 or 11 o'clock. Lengthen up through the rib cage (not just the arm) and aim for a clean perpendicular line from fingertips down to your hips.

target heart rates

When aerobics classes first became popular, taking heart rates was de rigeur. Every fifteen minutes, the aerobics instructor would yell "start" and everyone would walk around with their fingers at their throats counting pulses until she yelled "stop." Then everyone would compare that heart rate to a number on a wall chart to see if they were in "the training zone." Back in the high-impact eighties, a high pulse was a trophy. Today, moderation is not only a more sensible way to go, for many aging athletes it's a necessity.

Counting heartbeats is still a good way to monitor exertion, but it can be a workout interruptus that slows you down just as the endorphins start to kick in. There are other techniques for measuring intensity. However, before we get to those, let's revisit good old-fashioned pulse-taking (because it's free and easy).

Idiot-proof pulse taking: the 6-second count
Back in the early days of aerobics, there was much debate about whether a 6-, 10-, or 15-second count was most accurate, and if the counting should begin at 0 or 1. After all these years, most people agree that the 6-second count is the easiest, although perhaps not the most precise. Count your first pulse as 0, 1, 2, etc., for 6 seconds (starting at zero accounts for

catching your first heartbeat in mid-pulse). Add a 0 on the end of that number and, voila, you get your pulse. If you counted 6 pulses in 6 seconds, your heart rate would be 60; and so on.

Your resting heart rate

Your resting heart rate gives a good indication of your overall level of fitness. The higher your resting heart rate, the lower your level of fitness. Resting heart rates range from 40 (in trained athletes, yogis, and very mellow people) to 100 (less fit, nervous, or overexercised people).

- Average resting heart rates for men: 70 to 75 beats per minute
- Average resting heart rates for women: 75 to 80 beats per minute

The best time to record your resting heart rate is first thing in the morning (but not just after the alarm goes off or when a child's scream yanks you from sleep). Use the 6-second idiot-proof method above or, for a more accurate reading, take a 30-second count and multiply by 2.

To determine your training zone: subtract your age from 220 (220 minus your age = your maximum heart rate). (Don't try to work out at this heart rate—you can't sustain it, you won't be burning fat, and you could hurt yourself.)

To get your training heart zone, multiply your maximum heart rate by the number below that corresponds to your fitness level.

.40 to .60 (beginners): This is your zone if you: live a sedentary life, are over sixty and display any of the major risk factors for coronary heart disease, have over 30 percent body fat, or are pregnant. *(Note:* If you're in this group, you should definitely get your doctor's approval before beginning a fitness program.)

.55 to .65 (semi-regular exercisers): If you haven't been working out on a regular basis, but look fit or are stepping up from the previous level, this is the appropriate zone for you.

.70 to .85 (experienced, dedicated exercisers): Only push yourself to this zone if you've been working out aerobically at least three times per week for more than six months.

Warm-up and cool-down pulse rates

Always warm up for at least 5 minutes with low-intensity moves. These can be similar to your main exercise (i.e., if you walk for fitness, warm up at a lower intensity), at an intensity of 35 to 50 percent of your maximum. Always end your aerobic workout with 5 minutes of winding down similar to your warm-up, at the same 35 to 50 percent of maximum.

Taking your pulse

Keep moving rhythmically (don't abruptly stop). Press lightly with middle and forefinger on the inside of your wrist. (Pressing into the carotid artery on the neck is no longer recommended.)

How hard are you working?

The aerobics industry responded to the pulse-taking problem by allowing exercisers to rate their own levels of exertion. Borg's scale of perceived exertion (RPE) is an industry standard and lets people subjectively measure their intensity—using a scale of 1 to 10 and verbal descriptions of each level.

Note: The verbal descriptions in the far-right column are ours, not Borg's.

0	No activity	No movement at all
1	Very easy	Barely moving
2	Easy	Moving at a slow pace
3	Easy to moderate	Picking up the pace a bit
4	Moderate	Not too slow, not too fast
5	Medium	Halfway between sleeping and all-out effort
6	Moderately hard	Starting to sweat
7	Hard	Definitely working, huffing and puffing
8	Very hard	Pushing the envelope
9	Very, very hard	Beginning to "hit the wall"
10	All-out effort	Reaching the upper limits

Most aerobic workouts should

- start at a level of 2 to 4
- maintain a working intensity between 4 and 8
- cool down between 2 and 4

The problem with perceived exertion is that not everyone agrees on what moderate, hard, or very hard feels like. Many people both over- and underestimate their levels of exertion. Despite all this subjectivity, the good thing about perceived exertion is that it's relative. As you become more fit, what once seemed very hard becomes moderate and a new perception of very hard takes its place (in other words, you become more fit).

Talk test

This is the friendliest of exertion-testing techniques. It's also very "right brained," in that no numbers are involved. Talk to yourself during the "work" part of your workout.

- If you can talk with ease, your elocution is beyond reproach, and you can tell witty stories with perfect timing, you're not working hard enough.
- If you're panting so much that you can't spit out your name, address, and phone number, you're working too hard.
- You should be able to speak, sing, or "whistle while you work." You know you're working hard enough when you prefer short phrases or snippets of songs rather than whole dialogues, and you punctuate your words with deep breaths.

Pulse monitor

The most left-brained (i.e., logical, accurate, and foolproof) way to monitor intensity is with a heart-rate monitor. Many companies make wrist devices (with accompanying bands to wear around the chest) that accurately measure pulse. Most are waterproof (you can wear them in the pool) and some even beep when you go out of your training zone. A pulse meter lets you check your pulse without slowing down. Plus, there's no confusion about when or where to take your pulse, or concern about how many seconds to keep up the count—and whether it will be accurate.

Recovery heart rate

Like your resting heart rate, your heart rate immediately after a cardio workout is another indication of fitness. The faster the recovery, the fitter your heart. Take your pulse immediately after the "hard" phase of a workout and again one minute later. Your pulse should drop by 20 to 40 bpms in that minute.

Target Heart Rates for Beginners and People with Medical Concerns
40 to 60 Percent of Maximum

Age	Max	Training Zone
20	200	80–120
25	195	78–117
30	190	76–114
35	185	74–111
40	180	72–108
45	175	70–105
50	170	68–102
55	165	66–99
60	160	64–96
65	155	62–93
70	150	60–90
75	145	58–87
80	140	56–84

Target Heart Rates for Apparently Healthy Adults in Below-Average Condition

55 to 65 Percent of Maximum

Age	Max	Training Zone
20	200	110–130
25	195	108–127
30	190	105–124
35	185	102–120
40	180	99–117
45	175	96–114
50	170	94–111
55	165	91–107
60	160	88–104
65	155	85–101
70	150	83–98
75	145	80–94
80	140	77–91

Target Heart Rates for Aerobically Fit Adults

70 to 85 Percent of Maximum

Age	Max	Training Zone
20	200	140–170
25	195	136–166
30	190	133–161
35	185	129–157
40	180	126–153
45	175	122–149
50	170	119–144
55	165	115–140
60	160	112–136
65	155	108–132
70	150	104–128
75	145	100–124
80	140	96–120

tendons

Tendons are fibrous, densely woven connective tissue that attach muscles to bones. They're not as soft as muscle and not as hard as bones, so they're equally suited to serve both. Every weight-bearing move that strengthens a muscle also strengthens tendons, which in turn sends strength down to the bones. When tendons get stronger, they get thicker and can withstand greater levels of force. So, a person with strong, flexible tendons can better tolerate irritations or sudden forceful moves without risk of sustaining injury.

Tendons support and stabilize muscles because they are attached to the end of and woven through muscle fibers; they occasionally cross over a joint. Without activity, tendons tighten and shrink. A good strength and stretching program, however, can keep tendons supple and strong.

Just about every muscle has a tendon at each end that attaches directly to a bone. However, the ends of the trapezius, the serratus, the gluteus maximus, and the deltoids all attach directly to the bone, without tendons.

Your attachments: Another thing that affects tendon and muscle strength is *where* tendons are attached to the bones. The farther the attachment from the joint, the greater your leverage advantage.

The Long and Short of It

Flex your biceps as if you want to show off your muscle. Now feel where the lower end of the biceps, closest to the elbow, begins to rise up (into an impressive peak?). Measure the distance between the elbow joint and the foothills of your Mt. Biceps.

- If it's 1 inch or less you've got short tendons (and long muscles).
- If it's 2 inches you've got medium tendons (and medium muscles).
- If it's 3 inches you've got long tendons (and short muscles).

Of course, there's not much you can do about this, since tendon and muscle length are all genetically predetermined (although strength is not; that's something you can control). So how does tendon length affect your life?

With short tendons and long muscles, you'll have a leverage advantage because you've got more active tissue (i.e., less fibrous stuff) to haul that barbell. So if you have a friend who's your size and about equal to you in strength but has long tendons and short muscles, you can challenge that person to a biceps curl contest and probably win easy money. On the other hand, if you're the one with the long tendons and short muscles, you need to be patient with your progress (and don't take up any challenges of strength).

Golgi tendon organs

Tendons come equipped with little sensing devices that essentially search for trouble and prevent injuries. These little sensory nerves, called Golgi tendon organs, act as guardian angels. When the tendon senses tension, either from a sudden action or wear and tear from repetitive use, it goes into protection mode and essentially forces the muscle to which it is attached to relax. The muscles suddenly give out. This is mostly involuntary, although as you get stronger, this "sudden death" takes longer to occur.

It is possible, with extreme intention, to override the Golgi reflex, but it's not a good idea. Mothers who lift cars off trapped babies are bypassing this reflex. So are competitive bodybuilders, who are so intent on ignoring the pain and winning the prize that their biceps tendons snap and roll up like an old window shade. Tendon injuries are painful, debilitating, and take a long time to heal because there's no healing blood flowing through them.

How to avoid tendon injuries

Tendons, like muscles, can get strained. (Ligaments and joints, on the other hand, get sprained.) Strains range from first-degree mild tears to third degree, like the window-shade variety above. Tendonitis is also a common injury, which occurs from overuse. Inflammation, discomfort, and pain are all warning signals to avoid repetitive stresses and take a rest.

The tendons most susceptible to tendonitis and strains are

- the Achilles tendon (between the ankle and calf on the back of the leg)
- shin splints (on the front of the lower leg)
- knees
- elbows

The best ways to prevent tendon injuries are to
- warm up sufficiently
- wear shoes that cushion impact and offer proper support
- stretch regularly so you have sufficient flexibility to handle sudden, unexpected changes in tendon length
- strengthen the muscles that attach to susceptible tendons so the muscles protect the tendons
- not wear high heels all the time (it causes Achilles tendonitis). If you must wear heels frequently, be sure to stretch.

If it's too late to prevent injury

If you didn't do all of the above and you've got tendonitis, what should you do?

R.I.C.E.: Rest, Ice, Compression, Elevation. In other words, sit or lie down; put an ice pack on the pain; wrap it tightly (especially when you have to apply any force to the injured tendon); and raise that part of you onto a pillow or chair, preferably above your heart (blood flow makes throbbing pain worse, especially at night). While you're at it, take some aspirin to bring down the swelling (see **Injuries,** page 194). Do this for at least the first forty-eight hours after the initial injury and again whenever it starts to hurt.

Don't stretch the tendon while it's injured.

If it's Achilles tendonitis, try wearing a cushioned heel lift as you ease back into activity.

walking

Hands down, the easiest, no excuses, put-on-your-shoes-and-go cardio workout is walking. All you need is a good pair of shoes and the ability to put one foot in front of the other. It's popular, the risk of injury is low, you get to be outside, and you can walk with friends or just listen to music. It's the best way to get back into shape, especially for people who are overweight, have been sedentary a long time, or are over sixty. Twenty minutes of walking three times a week is all it takes to lower your risk of heart disease and pull yourself out of total inactivity—the precursor to bad health. Still, several misconceptions about walking remain. Walking a mile takes about half the amount of energy as running a mile. So to get the same benefits from walking as from running, you have to walk twice as far. But that's only if you're maintaining a 5 mph pace during the hardest part of your walk. Much slower than that and fitness gains are minimal.

The good news is that walking is

- low impact, so it's a much better choice even for hard-core joggers who refuse to stop hobbling through their running workouts.
- weight bearing. The "mild shock" that travels up through the muscles and skeleton helps thicken bones. However, walking doesn't necessarily tone your arms or abdominals. So you may want to add additional strength training for your upper body and torso.

Walk this way: tips for better walking

- Beginners should start walking for 20 minutes, 3 to 5 days a week. Add time (increase to 45 minutes) before adding intensity. As you get a few months into a longer walking groove, add intensity by adding faster intervals or hills.
- Start at a slow pace, approximately 3 mph, and gradually build speed for 5 minutes. Keep your arms swinging at your side in opposition to legs.
- When you're warm, stretch your calves, Achilles, and lower back. If you have time, add stretches for quads, hamstrings, and hip flexors (see **Stretching,** page 234). Hold each stretch for 10 seconds.
- As you begin the "work" portion, pick up the pace to 4, then 5 mph (if you listen to music, tempos of 130 to 145 beats per minute should get you moving).
- Keep an upright posture as you speed up. Walk with chest lifted, head up, inclining slightly forward from the ankles (not the hips or lower back). With every step, push off with the ball of your foot as if you were trying to kick up some dust.
- As you accelerate, shorten your steps. Bend your arms at the elbows and punch forward (swinging arms at this tempo gets strenuous for shoulders).

- You should feel as if you're almost running or at least walking somewhere in a big hurry. Breath should be deep but you should still be able to talk.
- To alleviate boredom, play games with yourself: speed up to that telephone pole, then ease up to the end of the block. Walk diagonally, sideways, backward (make sure you've checked for big holes and curbs in advance). Step over sidewalk cracks.
- As you wind up the workout, cool down as you warmed up. Repeat the same stretches you started with but hold them longer.
- Be sure to wear shoes with adequate support, especially in the heel and ankle. Many walkers like running and hiking shoes, but walking shoes are getting more sophisticated (and fashionable) all the time. Be sure your soles match your terrain. If you like crumbly slopes, wear waffle bottoms.
  A few warnings:
- If you walk in the sun, don't forget your hat and sunblock.
- If you wear a portable stereo, keep the volume low enough so that you can hear traffic.
- If you walk at night (in safe neighborhoods only, please) wear some sort of reflector so others can see you.

water

Water is one of the most important substances we put into our bodies, but almost no one drinks as much as they should. Here's why it's so vital. Although the body is made up of 60 percent water, it can't manufacture or store it. It has to get it from the outside. If the incoming water supply dwindles, waste products languish in the system and chemical processes that support life slow down or stop.

During exercise or strenuous activity, the body's demand for water becomes even greater. So it's especially important when you exercise to make sure that you drink enough water and ward off dehydration.

When you exercise, water performs the following functions:

- Carries fuel (i.e., glucose) to working muscles
- Carts away waste products, such as carbon dioxide and lactic acid
- Excretes the waste through urine
- Keeps the body cool with sweat (warm, moist skin meeting circulating air acts as a cooling system)
- Keeps blood circulating through the heart, lungs, veins, arteries, capillaries, etc.
- Lubricates the joints
- Keeps the nervous system operating more efficiently and reduces the excess stress on the body caused by exertion

How much water do you need?

The old standard suggestion of 6 to 8 8-ounce glasses of water a day is still good. But people who exercise may need more like 2 or 3 quarts, especially when it's hot and humid outside (and during illness).

Get in the habit of carrying a water bottle. It's easy to measure, handy to cart around especially during workouts, and saves waiting in line at the water fountain—where it never seems polite to guzzle what you really need when others are waiting.

Drink cool water when you're hot. Cool water empties out of the stomach and enters the system faster. Drink warmer water (room temperature or warm uncaffeinated tea or broth) when exercising outside in the cold.

Drink *before* you're thirsty. People who drink to satisfy thirst replace only about half of what they need. An intelligent, by the book, "hydration schedule" for a workout looks something like this:

- 17 ounces of water *2 hours before* your workout
- 8 ounces or more *15 minutes before* your workout
- 4 to 8 ounces *every 10 to 20 minutes during* your workout
- another 8 ounces *after* your workout

Dehydration

When you don't drink enough water your

- heart rate increases
- body temperature rises
- neuromuscular responses slow down—resulting in bad coordination

You might either sweat profusely or stop sweating altogether, which is more dangerous because your body can't cool itself. You're at risk for becoming dehydrated even if you only lose 2 to 3 percent of your body weight. For instance, a 130-pound woman only needs to lose 2½ to 4 pounds of water weight to be dehydrated (easy to drop on a hot, humid day).

How do you know how much water you're losing? Weigh yourself before and after workouts. Drink enough water so you replace that water weight loss with the same volume of water. Otherwise, you could be inadequately hydrated for your *next* workout.

Check the color of your urine. If it's dark yellow, you're probably somewhat dehydrated. If it's clear, you're probably OK. However, you can drink alcohol and caffeine and have light, frequent urine but still be somewhat dehydrated. You can also be well hydrated but have dark urine if you're taking a lot of vitamins.

Alcohol, coffee, and caffeinated sodas are diuretics. In other words, they cause you to urinate more frequently. This stresses the kidneys and removes necessary water from the body.

If you're feeling puffy and bloated from holding water, you're probably dehydrated. That's your body's way of trying to hold on to what it's got. The best way to beat the water weight feeling is to drink more water!

Water vs. sports drinks

There's much debate among fitness pros, nutritionists, and manufacturers on the pros and cons of special sports drinks that contain added carbs, electrolytes, proteins, and such.

If your cardio workouts last 45 minutes or less, you probably don't need a sports drink. Water is the best thing. Your body loses more water through sweat than it does electrolytes or carbs. Water is also absorbed into the system much faster than a sugary drink.

However, if your cardio workout lasts more than 45 minutes, then a sports drink might be a good energy source. But the drink should have just the right amount of carbs. So what's the right amount? Six to 8 percent sugar seems to be optimal. Anything with 5 percent or less doesn't contain enough energy and is almost useless. Anything above 8 or 10 percent (soda or juice) is too sugary and can cause intestinal cramps and nausea. Read the label to make sure your sports drink has the right amount.

Water, Water Everywhere but Not a Drop to Drink

Water may be the juice of life but how clean is it? What's the best water to drink? And how do we know what's in it?

Most water companies will provide you with a detailed description of what's in your tap water and may even suggest which purifiers are best for your water. But no water company can be accountable for the lead in your pipes.

Bottled water is not guaranteed pure as it may say on the label. It may also taste funny if it comes in plastic containers—plus it's expensive.

To remove two of the most common drinking water pollutants, chlorine and lead, try the following:

For chlorine: Let the water sit for several hours in a bowl or pitcher with a wide opening. Chlorine rises into the air. Another way to remove chlorine is to whip the water in a blender without a lid, since this also sends some chlorine back into the atmosphere.

For lead: Let the water run till it's clear and rust free before drinking.

water exercise

Although water exercise is gentle enough for absolutely everybody, it can provide an intense form of training. The key is not the water but how you use it.

When you stand in chest- to shoulder-high water or float in the deep end, you instantly shed about 90 percent of your body weight. Suddenly you weigh what you did when you were a small child.

The temptation is to take advantage of this weightlessness and float and bob around. Classes that have you jump up and down in the shallow end and wave your arms in the air may be fun for this reason, but they don't give a smart, effective workout. Using water this way is like walking into a gym and rolling the weights on the floor. Diverting perhaps, but what's the point?

When you swim for speed, the idea is to cut through the water and minimize drag (that's why competitive swimmers shave their bodies). Although swimming can be a great workout, it's not so easy to master (see, under **Sports**, "Swimming," page 233). Working vertically in the water increases your resistance by 75 percent and it's easier for most people to do (and you don't have to mess with goggles or wet your hair). It can also give you a much better leg workout than swimming does. The best way to take advantage of the water is stay *under the water line* so you use its viscosity.

Water has twelve times the density of air. So moving through it is like pushing thousands of little dumbbells in all directions. And since gravity is minimized and in some cases reversed, you can work *two* muscle groups with *one* move, a move that on land would only target one. For instance:

- When you run in the water, you use quads and hamstrings; when you run on land, your hamstrings are favored.
- When you hold your arms out to the side in the water and push forward and back (i.e., do a flye), you work chest and upper back; on land, you'd only work one muscle group (and you'd have to lie on your back to work your chest, on your front to work your upper back).

Water not only gives you these toning two-for-ones, it can also give you three workouts at the same time:

- Cardio
- Muscle toning
- Flexibility, because when you work with lighter limbs, your range of motion increases both as you move and during static stretches.

Good candidates for water fitness

- Cross trainers—get training variety
- Runners—add mileage without extra pounding
- Overweight people—get a great workout and feel graceful and protected in the water
- Injured people—heal faster in the water; some even return to activity stronger than before the injury
- Pregnant women—maintain a lower heart rate and thus keep a safer, lower body temperature for the baby; also protects "softened" joints
- People with multiple sclerosis—maintain a lower body temperature (M.S. mostly affects the nerves. Although aerobic exercise is important, avoiding exhaustion can prevent further damage to the nervous system.)
- People with arthritis—achieve greater joint range of motion, without pain
- Nonswimmers—feel comfortable in the water, without having to go under

Good pool rules

Whether you choose shallow water exercise or deep, the same properties of water apply. To use the water intelligently, make sure you do the following:

- Work with equal force in all directions. For instance, if you lift your knee, be sure to push your leg back down with the same intensity. Your knee lift will be "buoyancy assisted" (the opposite of "gravity assisted"), so that part of the move will be easier. To work hamstrings and gluteus, push your leg down.

- Keep an upright posture and a stable torso. One of the very best ways to build torso stability is to walk fast or run forward and back in the water (avoiding bobbing up and down). You can do this in shallow or deep water, but in the deep you need a flotation belt or vest (see below).
- Bend elbows and knees to make moves easier (short levers)
- Straighten elbows and knees to make moves harder (long levers)
- Slightly bend elbows and knees to make moves hard (long, wide levers push more water)
- Cup hands (or wear webbed gloves or paddles) and point and flick your feet (or add foot or ankle cuffs or flippers when appropriate) to increase resistance (increases area of "surface drag").
- It's generally a good idea to warm up with less resistance (shorter levers) and add resistance (longer, wider levers) as you go.

Water-adjusted heart rate

Heart rates are typically 10 to 15 percent lower in water than on land—a little lower in cold water, higher in warm. In other words, a pulse of 140 in the pool equals between 154 and 161 on land. But that doesn't mean you're not getting as good a cardio workout in the water. It just means that your heart is working a little less vigorously but still receiving the benefits of a harder workout. Here's why:

- The force of the water impacting your body from all angles actually assists the return blood flow (the venous return) to the heart. The water gives it a little outside help, like an additional pump.

- Since your body weight is a fraction of its normal self, your heart doesn't work so hard to *lift* your limbs. But it can work hard to lower them and push them through resistance.
- In water, your body loses heat very quickly (about four times faster than in the air). A lower body temperature results in a lower heart rate. (This is why you shouldn't stop to take your pulse in the water. Keep moving as best you can.)
- Although your heart doesn't work as hard, your lungs actually work harder. Water pressure impacting the lungs makes it harder to fill them with air. Ultimately, this improves respiration.

Heart Rate Chart for Water Exercise

Age	Min. HR	Max. HR
20–29	124	179
30–39	119	161
40–49	114	152
50–59	108	143
60–69	103	134
70+	98	125

Water temperature

Swimmers tend to like bracing, cold water, 76 to 84 degrees F°. Rehabilitation pools can be 86 to 90 degrees, like a bath. Water exercise classes work best in a moderate water temperature, 84 to 86. But since water exercise classes tend to share the pool with swimmers or rehab people, it's not easy to get that perfect temperature. So,

if your pool is cold, warm up vigorously. Don't let your body temperature drop suddenly. And don't stand around, keep your arms or legs moving for toning work, and when stretching, "scull" the water with one or both hands. If you get cold, get out.

If your pool is hot, you can easily overheat if your moves are too vigorous. So keep your workout gentle. However, a warm pool provides a great opportunity for static stretching.

Water workout gear

Webbed gloves and paddles: Webbed gloves not only make you look like the creature from the black lagoon (albeit, the gloves come in bright colors), they can really add upper-body work. What a great design. With the spread of your fingers, you control how much resistance you get. Paddles are a little more awkward and uncomfortable; the only way to change resistance is to turn them.

Noodles: This clever invention gets high points for versatility and price. Noodles generally sell for under $5. Originally a kid's toy, clever aqua-fitness instructors recruited noodles to add buoyancy for deep water and resistance for upper-body work. You can wrap them around you like an inner tube to stay afloat or move the "ends" to create more resistance.

Floating dumbbells and steps: These two pieces of equipment were adopted into water fitness because they are familiar to dry-land exercisers. Both have limitations.

Since the dumbbells float, you get your workout by trying to keep them under water. Again, any upward motion is buoyancy assisted.

In other words, if you do a biceps curl, the upward part of the motion offers little work (you get some surface drag but the weight still pops up by itself). The real work comes as you lower it back down (and work the triceps). Some people experience shoulder pain from trying to hold them down. (Gloves are more versatile.)

As for the aqua step (now passing out of fashion), again, all upward moves are buoyancy assisted. The work comes as you step down, forward, or back. Steps were also known to skid around pool bottoms and were hard to see in murky water. They rate high on the gimmick scale and you can accomplish similar work on a flat surface.

Deep-water flotation belts: The deep-water vest and belt originally started as rehab tools for overtrained runners. (Horse trainers had a similar idea for racehorses.) Running, dancing, and playing in the deep turned out to be a great workout alternative. The belt holds you upright while you push the water in all directions. It's a little like dancing suspended in a vat of Jell-O. (You can also add webbed gloves or foot gear for more resistance.)

Foot and ankle gear: Buoyant foot gear and ankle cuffs add extra leg resistance and can be worn alone or with other gear—for deep- or shallow-water workouts. (But if the foot gear is designed so you *step* on it, you're better off wearing those in deep water.) Some people like to use buoyant foot gear and dumbbells together or foot gear and deep-water belts.

Waterproof pouches for portable stereos: At last, music in the pool! A few companies make waterproof pouches for cassette players and radios. The headphones are usually covered in rubber. Although a great invention, few are truly leak-proof. It's best to double bag your stereo in a Ziploc. These pouches are usually listed for sale in the back of swimming magazines or in catalogs for swimmers.

Shoes: If you walk, run, or jump on sloped, cracked, and craggy pool bottoms, you'll want shoes. Old sneakers will do or you can get fancy aquatic shoes. Most major athletic shoe companies make them and many discount stores sell cheap knock-offs.

Clothing: An itsy-bitsy bikini doesn't work in water exercise. You'll spend all your energy keeping it on. Find a good swimsuit with straps that don't fall down. A dark color works best, since all suits will fade and disintegrate in chlorine. (We've all seen unsuspecting people get out of the pool, unaware that everyone could see through their pale peek-a-boo suits.) In cool water, an old pair of Lycra tights and/or a long-sleeve top can help keep you warm. Some companies now manufacture bathing suits for women who've had mastectomies. Suits are another thing you can find in the back of swim magazines.

diet and nutrition

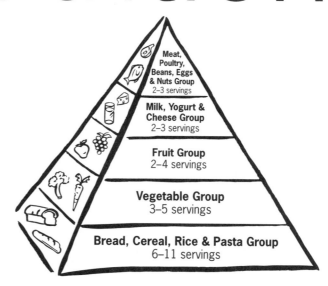

Meat,
Poultry,
Beans, Eggs
& Nuts Group
2–3 servings

Milk, Yogurt &
Cheese Group
2–3 servings

Fruit Group
2–4 servings

Vegetable Group
3–5 servings

Bread, Cereal, Rice & Pasta Group
6–11 servings

An Important Component of Complete Fitness

Food gives us sustenance, energy, and lots of pleasure. If we eat right, it builds our bones and our brains and keeps our internal systems running smoothly. If we're not careful, though, or at least mindful of our choices, it can clog our arteries, overwork our organs, and break down the finely tuned machinery of our bodies.

Good nutrition is an essential part of complete fitness whether your goal is to lose weight or build muscle, lower your blood pressure or increase your HDLs (see page 288 for an explanation of "good" cholesterol), or simply to maintain excellent health. The following section provides details on the nutrients we can't live without as well as the substances we should live with less of. There are entries that explain—in plain English—what happens to all kinds of food once it enters the body. And there is a wealth of information on the healing powers of vitamins and minerals—and a healthy, balanced diet.

alcohol

Alcohol is naturally produced when certain carbohydrates ferment (or break down anaerobically). For thousands of years, people have been fermenting grapes, apples, berries, and grains. From them we get wine, ciders, beer, and hard liquor (which is simply alcohol that has been distilled or processed to be more concentrated).

Chemists call the alcohol in beverages ethanol, a compound composed of two carbons and one hydroxyl group (hydrogen-oxygen bond). *Proof* is the term used to describe the percentage or strength of alcohol in a liquid. One hundred proof contains 50 percent alcohol; 50 proof, 25 percent alcohol. Each of these common drinks deliver about ½ ounce of pure ethanol:

- 3 to 4 ounces of wine
- 12 ounces of beer
- 10 ounces of wine cooler
- 1 ounce of hard liquor (vodka, whiskey, gin, or rum)

Empty calories

Because it does not contribute to growth, maintenance, or repair of cells, alcohol is not considered a nutrient. In fact, in high levels it acts more like a toxin, doing more harm than anything else. Though it does contribute energy—7 calories per gram—these calories are empty, with no nutritional value.

Recently there has been some evidence that drinking alcoholic beverages can interfere with the way your body regulates appetite, triggering some people to overeat. This can be a prob-

lem, particularly if the foods eaten, such as chips, dips, and nuts (common accompaniments to alcoholic beverages), are high in fat. Since alcohol is burned before fat, excess intake can lead to weight gain.

Furthermore, people who regularly drink alcohol (5 to 6 drinks per week) are more likely to gain weight around the middle (commonly known as a "beer belly")—pounds that carry a higher health risk than fat accumulated in other areas of the body. The more you drink, the higher your waist-hip ratio and therefore the larger your belly (this is particularly true for men). Liquor and beer seem to effect the belly more than wine.

What happens to alcohol once you drink it?
First, it travels to the stomach, where some of it is broken down. The rest of its tiny molecules are absorbed right through the stomach wall and directly into the bloodstream. The more alcohol you drink, the faster it is absorbed and the higher the concentration in the bloodstream. Food slows down absorption by blocking the molecules from reaching the cell wall. That's why it's best to always drink on a full stomach or while eating.

Once in the bloodstream, alcohol goes directly to the liver where its absorption takes precedence over all other functions. There it is broken down, at the expense of breaking down fatty acids. The fats that aren't being broken down then accumulate, leading to a condition called fatty liver. Most times this condition is reversible, but long-term heavy drinking can do irreparable damage, eventually leading to serious liver problems such as cirrhosis.

Since the liver can only process about one drink an hour, drinking too fast can quickly lead to high levels of alcohol in the blood and intoxication. Every organ in the body is affected by alcohol, but the brain is particularly susceptible to its influence. Alcohol has a sedative effect on the brain, first removing inhibitions and later impairing judgment and reasoning.

Short-term effects of alcohol consumption

Increases urinary output: Alcohol depresses the hormone that allows the kidneys to reabsorb water. The result is excess water loss. To make up for it, the body stimulates your thirst mechanism; unfortunately, this usually only leads to more drinking. Alcohol's dehydrating effects are often felt the morning after a bout of drinking. Not only does it contribute to fatigue and general malaise, but dehydration of brain cells may also be partly responsible for the headache or hangover that heavy drinkers experience.

Impairs muscle coordination and delays reaction time: This is a direct result of alcohol's influence on the brain. Further drinking will cause even more of an effect and lead to slurred speech, blurry vision, staggering, and eventually unconsciousness.

Diminishes judgment and reasoning: Alcohol relaxes and relieves stress by lowering inhibitions. At the same time, it sedates the brain centers responsible for reasoning and judgment, often causing a display of unchecked emotions.

Long-term effects of alcohol consumption

Malnutrition: The more people drink, the more likely they are to eat poorly. This is mostly because alcohol replaces food and all the important nutrients it provides. In fact, the more people drink the less likely they are to eat at all.

Even if adequate amounts of nutrients are taken in, alcohol can impair digestion and absorption of food, so the nutrients will not be utilized.

As far as vitamins go, heavy drinkers or alcoholics tend to be deficient in the B vitamins (especially B_6, B_{12}, folate, and thiamin), vitamin D, and vitamin A. They also tend to lack calcium, magnesium, iron, and zinc.

Cancer: It is a well-known fact that heavy drinkers have a greater chance of developing cancer of the mouth and esophagus than light drinkers. Still, some studies have found that even two drinks a day may substantially increase risk for these cancers. Combine drinking with smoking and the result can be lethal.

Breast cancer is another illness that has been directly linked to alcohol. According to a National Cancer Institute study, as little as one drink a day can increase breast cancer risk among women; have two a day and the risk can rise by as much as 70 percent. (But the study also found that *when* you drink makes a difference. Alcohol consumed five years prior to diagnosis had more significant impact than alcohol consumed ten years prior.)

How does alcohol promote breast cancer? Scientists think it may boost levels of estrogen, but dietary patterns may also have something to do with it. Drinkers tend to eat less protective foods like fruits and vegetables than nondrinkers, further increasing their risk.

Liver disease: Years of heavy drinking can lead to hepatitis, an inflammation of the liver, and eventually to cirrhosis. Cirrhosis is a condition whereby liver cells die and harden, forming scar tissue and permanently damaging the liver. Chronic alcohol abuse is the most common cause of cirrhosis in this country.

What Is a Drink?
The Dietary Guidelines count as one drink:
- 12 ounces of regular beer
- 5 ounces of wine
- 1½ ounces of 80 proof distilled spirits

Possible benefits of alcohol

Back in the early nineties, red wine made headlines for its purported role in the prevention of heart disease. It was called the French paradox because red wine was credited for allowing the French to consume a high-fat diet while still having low rates of coronary heart disease. But the French also have lower levels of stress, and very different eating patterns than we do (they usually drink wine with meals and often eat their biggest meal during the day, rather than in the evening).

Indeed, later studies have shown that it was really the alcohol itself that reduced the risk of heart disease, and not specifically red wine. These findings showed that white wine, beer, or spirits will give the same heart-healthy advantage as red wine. But some scientists are still unconvinced that all alcohol is the same, particularly since red wine does contain substances called flavonoids, which act as antioxidants, blocking "bad" LDLs from forming artery-clogging plaque. So far, however, there is no consistent evidence favoring one alcoholic drink over another.

How does alcohol help fight heart disease?

- It raises HDLs—the "good" cholesterol.
- It prevents LDLs—"bad" cholesterol—from oxidizing
- It thins out the blood, making blood cells less likely to clump together and clog arteries.

Despite these benefits, health experts stop short of recommending alcohol as a way to stave off heart disease; there are just too many negative effects associated with alcohol consumption. In other words, people who don't normally drink alcohol shouldn't start.

In addition to an increased risk for malnutrition, cancer, and liver disease, alcohol consumption is also associated with high blood pressure, stroke, and birth defects (women who drink while pregnant can have children with lower IQs or learning disabilities). Overall mortality rates for drinkers are also much higher. This is primarily due to the contributing role alcohol plays in many traffic accidents, suicides, and violence.

This is not to say that moderate drinking is in any way dangerous. For people who like to imbibe on occasion, the 1995 USDA Dietary Guidelines recommend no more than one drink per day for women and two drinks per day for men. If you are pregnant or trying to conceive, have a high risk for breast cancer, or are taking prescription medicine, consult your physician before consuming any alcohol.

Drinking Buddies

Although a man and a woman may drink like equals, when it comes to "holding" their liquor it is the male who usually wins out. Women definitely become drunk faster than men (meaning they have higher blood-alcohol concentration levels). Most people attribute this to sheer size—it takes more alcohol to intoxicate men because they weigh more—but that's not the only reason for the inequity.

Research shows women tend to have less of an enzyme called alcohol dehydrogenase, the enzyme responsible for alcohol breakdown in the stomach. So more alcohol has a chance to enter the bloodstream and go to the head.

Body composition also plays a role. Women have proportionally more body fat and less water than men, meaning the alcohol is more diluted in men, thereby dulling its effects.

allergies

Although food allergies are blamed for a variety of ailments by up to 25 percent of the population, in truth only about 1 to 2 percent of adults and 5 percent of children suffer from true food allergies. That's good news, because genuine food allergies can be quite devastating and sometimes even fatal. Food intolerances are much more common, and usually less severe.

Food allergy vs. intolerance

The difference between a food allergy and food intolerance lies not so much in the physical symptoms but with the mechanism responsible for the reaction. Food allergies trigger an immune system response and produce antibodies that can affect a number of vital functions in the body. Specifically, it is the large protein portion of the food that causes the immune system to react.

Food intolerances, although potentially serious, do not involve this system. Like food allergies, they also can cause wheezing, hives, stomachaches, headaches, diarrhea, and many other problems, but this time the offending agent can be almost anything—a flavor enhancer like MSG, a mineral like sulfur, or even a sugar like lactose. Since they do not involve the immune system, many food intolerances tend to be localized in nature.

Allergic reactions

The severest kind of allergic reaction is food-induced anaphylaxis, the systemic generalized shock involving multiple organs. In severe cases and if not treated immediately, it can lead to death from respiratory failure.

Although any food is capable of causing anaphylaxis, the foods that are responsible for about 90 percent of all allergic reactions are

- peanuts
- other tree nuts like Brazil nuts, cashews, or almonds
- wheat
- milk
- eggs
- fish and shellfish
- soy

As a group, children tend to be more allergic to foods than adults, and some people (adults or children) can eventually outgrow allergies to soy, cow's milk, eggs, and wheat. Other allergies, like those from peanuts, tree nuts, fish, and shellfish, people never outgrow. Unfortunately, these are also the foods most likely to cause the severest allergic reactions. What's more, extremely sensitive individuals can react simply from using the same pan or dish used previously to cook or serve a trigger food.

Symptoms of anaphylactic shock

When it comes to food-induced anaphylactic shock—the allergic reaction caused by food—symptoms can appear in as little as five minutes after eating the offending food, or it can take one or two days. While anyone with a food allergy can go into anaphylactic shock, people suffering from asthma are often at greatest risk. Here is a list of common symptoms:

- Itching in and around the mouth
- Wheezing and hoarseness
- Shortness of breath or a tightening of the throat
- Hives
- Nausea
- Cramping or vomiting
- A sense of impending doom
- A drop in blood pressure
- Swelling of the eyelids, hands, lips, or feet
- Loss of consciousness

Hidden food allergens

Many foods contain hidden ingredients that can cause an allergic reaction in sensitive individuals. Canned tuna fish, for example, may contain vegetable broth or hydrolyzed vegetable protein, which can be detrimental to people on a soy-free diet. Similarly, chocolate and chocolate products, which may contain milk solids, should be avoided by people sensitive to milk. Consequently, it is necessary to read all food labels carefully when using any processed food products, especially canned or frozen items. For an allergic person, even the tiniest amount of a food can set off a severe allergic reaction.

Treating food allergies

By far the best way to treat a food allergy is to avoid the offending food altogether. Desensitizing allergy shots do not work because they themselves can trigger an allergic reaction. People who are at risk for severe allergic reactions or have a history of asthma may need to carry an emergency dose of epinephrine (available as Epi-Pen or Ana-Kit), which can be self-administered immediately.

Epinephrine is a hormone that reduces swelling, lowers blood pressure, and prevents people from going into shock. Its effects are similar to antihistamines but stronger. For food allergy sufferers it is a lifesaver.

Common allergen ingredient names

Determining if a food contains an allergen is not as easy as it looks. Many times the food appears in a different form with a different name. To help quell the confusion, here is a list of the seven potentially dangerous allergens and their alternative names. Beware of red-flag items as well, since these foods will also most likely contain the offending ingredient.

Peanuts

A.k.a. or found in: Cold-pressed peanut oil, mixed nuts, Nu-nuts artificial nuts, peanuts, peanut butter, peanut flour.
Red flags: Asian food (Chinese, Thai, Vietnamese, etc.), baked goods (especially cookies), candy, chili, egg rolls, marzipan, and soups.

Wheat

A.k.a. or found in: Bran, enriched flour, farina, gluten, graham flour, high-gluten flour, wheat bran, wheat germ, wheat gluten, whole wheat flour, wheat starch, vital gluten.

Red flags: Gelatinized starch, modified food starch, modified starch, vegetable gum, and vegetable starch.

Tree nuts

A.k.a. or found in: Almonds, Brazil nuts, cashews, chestnuts, filberts/hazelnuts, giandiju (chocolate-nut mixture), hickory nuts, macadamia nuts, marzipan or almond paste, Nu-nuts artificial nuts, nut butters, nut oils, nut pastes, walnuts, pecans, pine nuts, pistachios.

Red flags: Chocolate and candy mixtures.

Beware: Peanuts Are Everywhere!

Peanut allergies are on the rise. Scientists think this may be related to an increase in peanut-containing products being incorporated into the food supply. For instance, peanuts can be found in Chinese food, chili, gravy, ice cream, enriched cocoa, and in a powdered form as a thickener. The increase may also have to do with the fact that more children are being exposed to peanuts and peanut products at an early age.

Milk

A.k.a. or found in: Artificial butter flavor, butter, butter fat, buttermilk, casein, caseinates, cheese, cream, curds, dry milk solids, lactalbumin, lactalbumin phosphate, lactose, margarine, milk, rennet casein, sour cream, sour cream solids, sour milk solids, whey, yogurt.

Red flags: Caramel color, caramel flavoring, high-protein flour, and natural flavoring.

Note: A "D" on the product label indicates the presence of milk protein.

Eggs

A.k.a. or found in: Albumin, eggs, eggnog, egg whites, egg yolks, mayonnaise, ovalbumin, ovomucoid, Simplesse.

Red flags: Yellow color or shiny glaze on baked goods may indicate the presence of eggs.

Fish

A.k.a. or found in: Anchovies, caviar, fish by-products, imitation shellfish, roe, surimi.

Red flags: Worcestershire sauce and Caesar salad dressing may contain anchovies.

Cooking for someone with food allergies

Many people believe avoiding a specific food or foods when cooking is all it takes to prepare a safe meal. But it is not that simple. Preparing foods free from allergens takes careful planning and special attention not only to the ingredients but to all other aspects of serving and preparing food. Here are some helpful suggestions:

- Foods for someone with food allergies should be prepared and served with absolutely no direct or indirect contact with the threatening food. This means preparing foods from scratch rather than just removing a harmful ingredient from an already-prepared dish. Scraping the nuts or sauce off an entrée will still leave potentially fatal fragments of the food on the dish.

  Another golden rule is always to use fresh ingredients, even if the ingredient will not be eaten. For example, always fry using oil that hasn't been used to cook anything else. Cooking french fries in oil that has been used to fry fish is not only a bad kitchen practice, it can also be dangerous to a person with a hypersensitivity to fish.

- Utensils should be completely clean and unused so there is no cross contamination. Pots, pans, spoons, knives, and other equipment should always be washed thoroughly before using. Be particularly careful when using spoons to stir or mix a sauce or soup.

- Be extra cautious with sauces, dressings, and garnishes. Since knowing exactly what's in some prepared sauces may be impossible, it is best to avoid these ingredients altogether. If you must serve them, be sure to offer them on the side rather than with the entrée.

Dining out with a food allergy

Since it is often difficult to know how restaurant food was prepared or what ingredients it contains, dining out can be extremely stressful and dangerous for a person with food allergies. Whenever possible, order foods that are simple, plain, and unadorned with garnishes, dressings, or sauces. Since many food protein additives are now used in commercially prepared products, even sauces or salad dressings straight from the bottle can be potentially dangerous. It is best to avoid "secret" sauces and dishes with a lot of ingredients, which may be hard to keep track of. Most important, make the server as well as the manager (and if possible the chef) aware of any food allergy you have and be sure to ask plenty of questions. People with a shellfish allergy will react to something prepared in a shellfish broth, and those who are allergic to nuts are also allergic to nut oils. So be very specific with your inquiries. If you ask, some establishments may even show you the ingredient label of certain products.

antioxidants

When antioxidants first came onto the scene, they were the darlings of the nutrition community. Highly celebrated substances touted as magic bullets, able to stave off illness and slow down the degenerative effects of aging, they seemed to be the answer to all our health problems.

But antioxidants are not the cure-all they were once thought to be. After many years of intense investigation, we now know antioxidants may be potent protectors against a variety of diseases from heart disease to cataracts, but we also know that, depending on how they are taken, some can be of no help at all and may even cause harm.

Fending off free radicals

What exactly are antioxidants? They're chemical substances found in a wide variety of foods. What's more important is what they do: shield us from harmful oxygen molecules called free radicals. Free radicals are damaged molecules that roam around the body looking for other molecules to latch onto. This bonding process damages the cell and causes a series of chain reactions (particularly if the free radicals harm the DNA or genetic blueprint of the cell). Scientists think free radicals contribute to the general decline in health seen with aging and to the development of certain diseases.

How can we stop free radicals? It's not easy. They're are all around us—inside and out. Naturally produced in the body as a by-product of many cell reactions, they are also generated by outside influences such as air pollution or chemical contaminants we eat or breathe. It's the job of antioxidants to neutralize these free radicals and halt their damaging effects.

The big three

The most abundant supply of antioxidants can be found in the plant kingdom, with generous amounts in fruits, vegetables, cereal grains, legumes, seeds, and nuts. Animal foods also contain a fair share of antioxidants, particularly red meat, chicken, and oysters, which have the antioxidant minerals zinc and selenium.

Originally, researchers thought only three nutrients were major antioxidants in the diet: vitamin C, vitamin E, and beta-carotene, a precursor of vitamin A. Consequently, most of the scientific research in the last few decades centered on these three nutrients. But minerals like zinc, selenium, manganese, and copper also have strong antioxidant properties, and researchers eventually started investigating them as well.

Scientists have recently uncovered a whole slew of other compounds working as antioxidants in the body; these are the phytochemicals, a class of compounds found only in plants.

These newest members of the antioxidant group seem to hold the most promise for combating disease. Although not all phytochemicals are antioxidants, a good majority are, and some are believed to be just as potent if not more potent than the "big three." Scientists are only just beginning to unlock the secrets behind these plant chemicals.

What we don't know

Since antioxidants block the harmful effects of free radicals, which pose a number of risks, over the long term their use should decrease our susceptibility to various chronic and debilitating diseases. By promoting general good health, they should also help mitigate the effects of illnesses such as arthritis.

Unfortunately, what antioxidants theoretically do and what they actually do are not always the same thing. Over the years, research findings using man-made supplements have been inconsistent, sparking a heated debate about the efficacy of antioxidants in general. And there are other complicating factors:

- Most of the studies that have linked antioxidants to reduced risk of disease were epidemiological, meaning they studied the dietary intakes of whole populations. What they found were that diets high in fruits and vegetables—and consequently, antioxidants—had lower rates of illness.

- Today, we know there are hundreds of other compounds in foods that can interact with antioxidants to make them more effective or less effective. Furthermore, most foods contain more than one kind of antioxidant—canteloupe, for example, contains vitamin C, beta-carotene, and a wealth of phytochemicals that may have antioxidant properties. For this reason scientists are beginning to speculate that antioxidants may work best in combination with other antioxidants. So a dose of vitamin E and C may be much more advantageous than vitamin C alone.

- No one knows for sure what size dose or duration of supplementation with antioxidants will yield a benefit. So, in research, supplementation patterns vary greatly, further confounding results. (Researchers tend to use large amounts of antioxidants to ensure a measurable effect.)

For all these reasons nutritionists are hesitant to recommend taking antioxidant supplements as a way to prevent illness. Instead of taking supplements, the best advice is to eat foods high in these valuable nutrients. Except for vitamin E, ample quantities of all of the antioxidants can easily be obtained in the diet. Vitamin E is naturally found in plant oils and foods like sunflower seeds, peanut oil, avocado, and wheat germ. To get its protective effect (it has been shown to improve immune function and ward off heart disease), you need to consume large quantities, which can only be achieved with a supplement.

Antioxidants against disease

Despite spotty research on antioxidant supplements, we do know that some antioxidants can help protect against certain diseases.

Alzheimer's: There is now strong evidence that large doses of vitamin E can slow down Alzheimer's disease by delaying its progressive debilitating symptoms. Researchers think the vitamin acts by reducing oxidative damage to brain cells.

Arthritis: In preliminary research, eating foods rich in the antioxidant vitamin C may slow the progression of osteoarthritis.

Cancer: Many nutritionists believe antioxidants, particularly beta-carotene, can reduce the risk of a variety of cancers including colon, lung, and breast cancer by neutralizing free radicals. Since beta-carotene may work in conjunction with other carotenoids to offer protection, whole foods containing the antioxidant are probably a better source than supplements.

Note: Despite beta-carotene's promise as a cancer fighter, a large well-controlled study a few years back discovered that beta-carotene supplements actually increased the risk of lung cancer in smokers.

Diabetes: Antioxidants may help mitigate the effects of high blood-glucose levels in diabetics, thus curbing the serious health complications many of them face throughout life. Both vitamin C and E have shown potential in this area.

Eye disease: The retina contains high concentrations of vitamin C, which protects the eye from harmful cataracts. (Cataracts cloud the normally clear lens of the eye.) Vitamin C, vitamin E, and carotenoids in general (including beta-carotene) sweep away the free radicals that can oxidize proteins and cause damage to the eye.

Vitamin A is also essential for eye health. Adequate amounts protect the macula, a part of the eye that is crucial for vision. Research shows a diet high in fruits and vegetables rich in vitamin A can significantly decrease the risk of macular degeneration, a condition that can cause blindness in the elderly.

Heart disease: LDL, bad cholesterol, can cause heart disease when oxidized. By removing free radicals, vitamins E, C, and beta-carotene reduce the chances of LDL picking up an oxygen molecule and becoming oxidized, therefore lowering the risk of heart disease. Several studies support this theory.

In addition to oxidizing LDL, free radicals are also thought to damage blood vessel walls, making them more prone to plaque buildup, which can result in a blockage and ultimately a heart attack. Vitamin E has been shown to help ward off heart disease in this way, too.

artificial sweeteners

When artificial sweeteners first hit the market in the early 1970s, they were designed to offer people with diabetes (and dieters) an alternative to the sugar they couldn't (or shouldn't) have, providing all the taste without the calories. Now, the popularity of artificial sweeteners has created a $1.5-billion-a-year market worldwide.

Most of these sweeteners have carved out a niche in the reduced-fat, low-calorie, light-foods category, an area that has shown tremendous growth over the last few years. According to the Calorie Control Council, a whopping 92 percent of adult Americans (over 179 million people) consume low-calorie, reduced-fat, and light products on a regular basis (at least once every two weeks); 78 percent of Americans choose only low-calorie/sugar-free brands.

With such high demand, artificial sweeteners have become a common sight in our food supply, appearing in everything from yogurt to chewing gum. Soft drinks account for the largest share of artificial sweetener usage, representing 70 to 80 percent of the non-nutritive sweetener market (this includes carbonated, noncarbonated, and fruit-based drinks). In fact, most of the growth in the artificial sweetener market can be directly attributable to our soaring soda intake.

The safety question

Despite the prevalence of artificial sweeteners, questions about their safety still linger. No one really knows what kind of effect taking large quantities of artificial sweeteners for long periods of time will have on us. Furthermore, several sweeteners have been linked to an increased risk of cancer related to tumor growth, and some are believed to cause adverse reactions in sensitive individuals (though allegations of sensitivity are based only on anecdotal evidence).

In 1970, the Food and Drug Administration banned the artificial sweetener cyclamate due to concerns about its safety. However, cyclamate is deemed safe by fifty other countries around the world, including Canada. Here in the United States there have been repeated attempts to get the FDA to reapprove it, but so far they have all failed.

What are artificial sweeteners?

Artificial sweeteners are non-nutritive, high-intensity sweeteners that provide zero calories at most intake levels and are much sweeter than ordinary refined table sugar. In the United States the three major non-nutritive sweeteners are aspartame, saccharin, and acesulfame K. This is likely to change soon as new products enter the market and competition increases.

Aspartame

Aspartame is about two hundred times sweeter than regular table sugar. It is made from two amino acids (the building blocks of protein) and so, like protein, contains 4 calories per gram. However, since such small amounts are needed to sweeten products, it is virtually noncaloric.

Made by the NutraSweet company, aspartame is currently the most popular high-intensity artificial sweetener in the United States (in 1995 we ate or drank 19 million pounds of the stuff). Since aspartame loses its sweetness when it is heated, it is best used in cold dishes, though it can be successfully added at the end of cooking. Manufacturers have recently come out with an encapsulated form that can be heated and is now available for commercially baked products.

As far as safety goes, aspartame contains phenylalanine, an amino acid that cannot be tolerated by people with a rare genetic disorder called phenylketonuria (PKU). Thus, all products with aspartame must bear a label stating that they contain this substance.

In addition, there have been a number of complaints of adverse reactions—everything from headaches to seizures—reported by individuals, but so far there is no scientific data to support any of these claims.

Acesulfame K

Acesulfame K, or acesulfame potassium, is a noncaloric sweetener known by the brand name Sunette. It is about two hundred times sweeter than table sugar, but unlike aspartame, it can be heated. Taste-wise, acesulfame K is reputed to have a bitter aftertaste when used in large quantities. Many manufacturers get around this problem by blending it with other low-calorie sweeteners.

Currently, acesulfame K can be found in a number of candies, baked goods, frozen desserts, and sauces but not in soda. Petitions for the right to use it in soft drinks are now under review at the FDA, and manufacturers expect to begin using this sweetener in soda soon.

As far as safety goes, the FDA has given this artificial sweetener a clean bill of health. Some public interest groups, though, claim the sweetener was inadequately tested and may increase your cancer risk.

Saccharin

First discovered in the late 1800s, saccharin has been used as a sugar substitute for nearly a century. As a noncaloric sweetener, it is about three hundred times sweeter than table sugar, but it does sometimes have a perceptible flavor and bitter aftertaste.

Although it ranks second in the U.S. sweetener market, in the world it is the most popular, used in a wide range of foods and beverages as well as nonfood items like toothpaste.

In the late 1970s, saccharin was reported to cause bladder cancer in rats exposed to very high doses. As a result of this research, the FDA proposed a ban in 1977, but strong public opposition put it back on the market, this time with a warning label. Every few years, saccharin's safety is reevaluated by Congress.

Sweeteners of the future

In an effort to gain a bigger share in this growing market, many companies are busy developing other high-intensity sweeteners. Here are just a few of the new and improved nonnutritive sweeteners awaiting FDA approval:

Alitame: Two thousand times sweeter than table sugar, alitame is made from the amino acid aspartic acid.

Sucralose: A high-quality sweetener, six hundred times sweeter than table sugar, sucralose goes by the brand name Splenda. It was approved for use in the U.S. by the FDA in April 1998.

Sweetener 2000: Made by the Monsanto company (the same company that makes Nutra-Sweet), this sweetener is said to be eight thousand times sweeter than sugar.

basic
food groups

In 1992 the United States Department of Agriculture (USDA) introduced the five basic food groups of the Food Guide Pyramid. Like the basic four food groups it replaced, the new pyramid broke food down into recommended categories—the bread, cereal, and grain group; the vegetable group; the fruit group; the meat, beans, eggs, and nut group; and the milk, yogurt, and cheese group—and was based on Dietary Guidelines for Americans. However, there are some major differences between the old groupings and the new, reflecting a new attitude about the way we look at nutrition and diet.

Over the years more and more scientific evidence has accumulated about the benefits of eating fruits and vegetables. As a result, the Food Guide Pyramid places more importance on these two foods, and creates two separate groups: one for fruits, one for vegetables. The number of recommended servings has been increased, too.

Concern about the impact of high-fat and saturated-fat intake on health has also led to an emphasis on lean choices in all of the food groups, separating out fats, oils, and sweets so consumers can be more conscious of their consumption. The Pyramid now advises us to get the majority of our calories from the fruit, vegetable, and grain groups and specifically recommends a minimum number of servings for each group in amounts that are higher than in years past. Dairy products and meat, although still important, should not be the cornerstones of our diet, as once thought.

How the Pyramid Works

The Pyramid is flexible enough to fit into almost any lifestyle or dietary pattern. Calorie levels range from the very low end of 1,600 calories (for the minimum number of servings) to the very high end of about 2,800 calories per day (for the maximum number of servings listed). How many calories or servings you take in depends on your height, weight, and activity level. All diets, however, should include a wide variety of foods and follow the basic pattern of 15 percent protein, 55 percent carbohydrates, and no more than 30 percent fat.

Pyramid Power

Visually, the Food Guide Pyramid is a powerful tool, illustrating how most of our calories should be coming from the bottom half of the Pyramid—fruits, vegetables, and complex carbohydrates—while only a small portion should come from the top. There are no recommended servings for fats, oils, and sweets because most people get too much as it is. Instead, the Food Guide Pyramid simply recommends "Use Sparingly."

Each of the five food groups includes a number range for servings. Because people have a hard time estimating serving sizes, the USDA has tried to give as many examples as possible. Here's what they've come up with:

Bread, cereal, rice, and pasta group—6 to 11 servings: This is the starch, or complex carbohydrate group. Because carbohydrates are the primary source of energy for the body, they should be the largest group in terms of calorie consumption.

Best choices: whole grains, pastas, rice, and bread that are high in fiber and contain little fat. Avoid baked goods like croissants, high-fat muffins, and pastries. Also beware of sauces and spreads often used to flavor these starches.

What counts as a serving:
- 1 slice of bread
- 1 ounce of ready-to-eat cereal
- $\frac{1}{2}$ cup of rice or pasta
- $\frac{1}{2}$ bagel

Vegetable group—3 to 5 servings: A healthy diet includes a variety of different types of vegetables. Nutritionists recommend eating some of these vegetables several times a week:
- Dark-green leafy vegetables like spinach, broccoli, and Romaine lettuce
- Deep-yellow or orange vegetables like carrots, sweet potatoes, yellow peppers, and squash
- Starchy vegetables like potatoes and corn
- Legumes or dried beans or peas like navy, pinto, or black beans

Vegetables provide a number of important vitamins and minerals like vitamin A, C, folate, iron, and magnesium. They're also naturally low in fat and high in fiber.

Best choices: Fresh, frozen, or canned, if low in sodium.

What counts as a serving:
- 1 cup of raw leafy vegetables
- $\frac{1}{2}$ cup of other vegetables cooked or raw
- $\frac{3}{4}$ cup of vegetable juice

Fruit group—2 to 4 servings: Again, variety is the key. Include fresh, frozen, canned, or dried fruit in your diet, as well as fruit juices. Try to eat citrus, melons, and berries on a regular basis.

Nutritionally, fruits, like vegetables, are high in fiber and low in fat. They also provide substantial amounts of vitamins like C and minerals such as potassium.

Best choices: Eat whole fruits as often as possible and pass up fruits canned in heavy syrup or sweetened fruit juices.

What counts as a serving:
- 1 medium apple, banana, or orange
- $\frac{1}{2}$ cup chopped, cooked, or canned fruit
- $\frac{3}{4}$ cup of fruit juice

Milk, yogurt, and cheese group—2 to 3 servings: This is the dairy group, most notable for its contribution of calcium to the diet. It also provides plenty of protein, vitamins, and minerals. *Best choices:* Choose low-fat dairy products like skim milk, light sour cream, nonfat yogurt, or light cream cheese whenever possible.

What counts as a serving:

- 1 cup of milk or yogurt
- 1½ ounces of natural cheese (about a 1-inch cube)
- 2 ounces of processed cheese

Meat, poultry, fish, dried beans, eggs, and nuts—2 to 3 servings: This group is important because it provides essential protein, B vitamins, zinc, and iron. Still, it constitutes just a small portion of total calories. All in all, you should only consume a total of 5 to 7 ounces from this group on a daily basis.

Best choices: Choose lean meats, fish, and poultry. Trim away all fat and remove skin from poultry. Try to include at least one or two vegetarian meals in the diet per week.

What counts as a serving:

- 2–3 ounces of cooked lean meat, fish, or poultry
- 1 egg (1 ounce)
- ½ cup cooked dry beans
- 2 tablespoons of peanut butter

How we measure up

To find out how Americans are doing when it comes to following the Food Guide Pyramid, the USDA sent out a nationwide food consumption survey to nearly four thousand people. What they found was that although Americans are choosing a wide variety of foods, they are still not eating enough from the fruit, dairy, and meat groups. Even for the two groups that did meet the suggested number of servings, the amounts were on the low side—for example, people ate only a little over 6 servings from the grain group, just making the recommendations of 6 to 11 servings.

So what are we eating? Too much fat and sugar from the tip of the Pyramid. When the Pyramid was created, it was ideally based on lower-fat food choices like skim milk instead of whole, and whole-grain bread instead of a Danish. But in reality, many people are instead choosing the higher-fat options from each group.

Furthermore, the amount of discretionary fat used in cooking—oils, margarines, and butter—is also high. The Pyramid assumes about 15 percent of calories should come from discretionary fat. Actual numbers hover around 25 percent.

Sugar is another calorie culprit. Americans consumed an average of 19 teaspoons of sugar daily. That's well above the 12 teaspoons recommended for a 2,200-calorie diet. While cakes, cookies, pastries, and sweetened cereals are responsible for much of our sugar intake, it is our rapidly rising soda consumption that concerns most nutritionists. It's the number-one beverage consumed in this country, ousting milk and fruit juice as the most popular drink.

Food Group	USDA Food Guide Pyramid RECOMMENDATIONS Servings	1994 Average American Diet INTAKES Servings
Grain	6–11	6⅔
Fruit	2–4	1⅔
Vegetable	3–5	3⅓
Dairy	2–3	1½
Meat	5–7 ounces	4¾ ounces

Some other notable findings:
- Almost half of all Americans surveyed (48 percent) failed to consume even one fruit a day.
- Less than one-quarter met recommendations for the dairy group. Teenage girls and women (who have higher calcium needs than others) were especially low.
- More than twice as many men ate the suggested intake for the meat group as women.

The cost of poor nutrition

From a health perspective, we still have far to go. The high levels of fat, sugar, and calories in our diet, along with a general lack of exercise, has led to a nation of overweight adults. Since it is now believed that fruits and vegetables can help prevent serious, life-threatening conditions such as cancer and stroke, it stands to reason that low consumption rates increase our risk for these diseases. Fiber in the diet is also lacking (legume intake is very low), resulting in a number of digestive disorders and making us more susceptible to heart disease and cancer. Still, we are headed in the right direction. Now Americans are much more aware of the right foods to eat.

blood glucose

Glucose is the fuel your body uses to run your organs, muscles, brain, and nervous system. It is a simple sugar, or monosaccharide, and is often referred to as blood sugar or dextrose. All the carbohydrates we eat (both starches and sugars) are broken down by the body into glucose. Whatever we don't burn up as fuel is first stored as glycogen in muscle and the liver. Any excess carbohydrates are then converted into fat. But storing carbohydrates as fat is not the body's primary function (see also **Carbohydrates,** page 283). Under normal conditions (if someone has a reasonably healthy diet), relatively few carbohydrates are turned into fat—most are burned as energy. For information on glucose and exercise, see **Glucose,** page 189.

The role of insulin

Since glucose is so important to running your body, maintaining a constant supply is crucial. Your body maintains its glucose level through a series of checks and balances regulated by hormones. Insulin is one of the hormones secreted by the pancreas in response to high circulating blood-glucose levels.

Basically, insulin allows the cells to absorb and utilize glucose. In addition, it stimulates glucose uptake by the liver and muscle (as glycogen) and converts any excess into fat for storage.

Insulin is directly responsive to the meals we eat. After you eat, carbohydrates are broken down into glucose in the bloodstream. These high glucose levels signal the pancreas to release insulin and effectively lower blood glucose to normal levels.

Unfortunately, some 25 million adult Americans are thought to be insulin-resistant. In these people the cells do not respond to insulin's call to take up sugar. This, in turn, causes more insulin to be secreted, the net effect being an overproduction of the hormone. High insulin levels are undesirable because they are associated with an increased risk of heart disease, and they predispose people to develop diabetes. How can you reduce high insulin levels?

1. Lose weight. Most overweight people are insulin-resistant. Studies show, though, that if weight is lost, insulin's effectiveness improves.

2. Exercise. Not only does exercise burn more calories, it also helps the cells get glucose faster by lowering the amount of insulin needed to do its job. This is particularly helpful for people with diabetes.

diabetes

Over 16 million Americans are afflicted with diabetes, and nearly 800,000 new cases are diagnosed each year. Currently, it is the seventh leading cause of death in the United States, but actual mortality rates may be even higher due to the high number of complications associated with diabetes.

People with diabetes are two to four times more likely to die of heart disease or suffer a stroke than others. Their risk of high blood pressure, kidney disease, and blindness is also greater, as is nerve damage and lower limb amputations. The reason the complications are so serious is that diabetes has the potential to affect nearly every system in the body. Still, it is possible to live a long, productive life with the disease as long as it is managed properly.

Diabetes, technically known as diabetes mellitus, or DM, is a metabolic disorder whereby the body cannot regulate or utilize blood glucose. It does this by effectively blocking the body's use of insulin. There are two types of diabetes, Type I and Type II.

Type I Diabetes

Type I diabetes, insulin-dependent diabetes (IDDM), is particularly common in children and young adults. In some cases, the pancreas stops producing insulin altogether. Scientists are not sure what causes the pancreas to malfunction, but they have speculated on a number of theories, ranging from a virus to a genetic defect.

Undiagnosed Type I diabetes is very serious. Since the body produces no insulin and is unable to utilize any glucose, it begins breaking down fat and protein. Fat breakdown results in a buildup of ketone bodies, a toxic substance, in the blood. Too many ketones in the blood leads to coma and eventually death.

The symptoms are also quite pronounced as people with Type I diabetes will display a voracious appetite yet continuously lose weight.

Warning signs for Type I diabetes

- Frequent urination
- Abnormal thirst
- Excessive hunger
- Rapid weight loss
- Irritability

Type II Diabetes

Type II is an adult-onset disease, with the majority of cases occurring after age forty. Most people with diabetes (90 to 95 percent) have Type II, or noninsulin-dependent diabetes (NIDDM). They produce too little insulin or insulin that is not effective. Either way, the result is the same: abnormally high blood-glucose levels, also called hyperglycemia.

When it comes to symptoms and outcomes, Type II diabetes manifests itself in a manner completely different from Type I. Since insulin is still being produced and some glucose is being used, symptoms are mild and some people can live for years without ever being diagnosed. Unlike people with Type I diabetes who lose weight and grow thin, people with Type II tend to be obese. Since the cells are unable to get enough fuel to satisfy them, they signal the brain to keep eating. Overeating causes these people to gain weight and put on fat. Excess fat cells, in turn, increase insulin resistance, which leads to a vicious cycle.

Warning signs for Type II diabetes

- Drowsiness
- Itching
- Blurred vision
- Excessive weight gain
- Tingling and numbness of feet

Nutrition therapy

For most people with Type II diabetes, nutrition therapy or diet management alone can control blood-sugar levels. (Even for those who need insulin therapy, diet still forms the backbone of diabetes management.) Balancing meals throughout the day to produce a steady supply of glucose is crucial because people with diabetes are unable to handle the normal ups and downs that accompany skipping a meal or overeating. But aside from this restriction, they can eat a fairly flexible range of foods.

In 1994 the American Diabetes Association abandoned the standard "diabetic" diet for a more individualized approach. At the same time, it also liberalized some of its more stringent rules regarding sugar, weight loss, the proportions of fat and carbohydrate allowed, and the amount of fiber eaten.

The new ADA guidelines allow more choice and flexibility. Some of the changes include:

- Sugar and sugary foods are no longer off limits.
- There is no set standard "diabetic diet" with specific numbers for protein, fat, and carbohydrate.
- Weight loss should be viewed as a way to maintain optimal blood sugar and lipid levels rather than to achieve a specific weight goal.
- Follow the high-fiber diet recommended for the general public (20 to 35 grams of fiber daily). Previously it was thought that people with diabetes should have more.
- Drink alcohol in moderation.

Getting Tested

The American Diabetes Association recently lowered the threshold for diagnosing diabetes in individuals—from 140 milligrams of sugar per deciliter of blood to 126. By so doing, the ADA hopes to reduce a lot of the damage that has already occurred at the 140 rate, lowering the risk of complications long term. They recommend that everyone forty-five years old and older get tested every three years.

Hypoglycemia

Hypoglycemia is low blood sugar. Ironically, many people with diabetes suffer from the effects of hypoglycemia, particularly if they miss a meal or take too much insulin. In the general population, however, hypoglycemia is far less prevalent. In fact, although it is blamed for a number of malaises, from fatigue and weakness to panic attacks, experts estimate it affects far less than one percent of the population.

In the general population, hypoglycemia falls into two categories: reacting and fasting. Reactive hypoglycemia occurs within two to five hours after eating a meal. One theory is that insulin takes too much blood sugar out of the bloodstream, creating dangerously low levels. Another theory says glucagon, the hormone responsible for pulling sugar out of storage, is not doing its job.

Fasting hypoglycemia, on the other hand, occurs in response to not eating for eight hours or more. This type of hypoglycemia is usually associated with other more serious conditions, such as diabetes or cancer.

Many of the symptoms for hypoglycemia are so general that it's difficult to pinpoint them to a specific condition. Furthermore, testing can be difficult since not all people who have what's classified as low blood-sugar levels exhibit symptoms. Others suffer hypoglycemic symptoms even in the normal blood sugar range.

Warning signs for hypoglycemia

REACTIVE HYPOGLYCEMIA SYMPTOMS	FASTING HYPOGLYCEMIA SYMPTOMS
Fatigue and weakness	Headache
Shakiness and irritability	Loss of mental acuity
Symptoms of a panic attack: sweats, rapid heartbeat, trembling	Confusion or anger
	Seizures and unconsciousness

The treatment

For a person with diabetes, the first thing to do when they feel a hypoglycemic attack coming on is to eat or drink something as quickly as possible. Something as simple as a glass of orange juice or a handful of raisins can do the trick. While this approach is also appropriate for other hypoglycemics, a better choice is to prevent the attacks altogether. To do this nutritionists recommend:

1. Eating five or six small meals, well spaced throughout the day. It's important that these meals contain a mixture of protein, fat, and carbohydrates.

2. Restrict or eliminate coffee.

3. Avoid alcohol.

breakfast

Nutritionists often cite breakfast as *the* most important meal of the day—and with good reason. Refueling your body after eight or nine hours of sleep helps you feel better, perform better, and prevent many of the adverse effects of fasting such as irritability and fatigue. It also helps improve strength and endurance later in the morning.

Physical stamina, however, is not the only benefit of eating breakfast. Recent scientific studies have shown that by raising blood glucose levels, breakfast can also improve mental performance. This is because sustained mental work requires the brain to use large amounts of glucose.

Research conducted at the University of California at Davis found eating breakfast has a positive affect on both simple and complex cognitive processes. This means kids who eat breakfast were found to perform better in school—scoring higher on tests for memory, recall, verbal skills, and creativity—than kids who don't eat breakfast. For adults, breakfast, particularly in the form of carbohydrates, can improve short-term memory and concentration.

Nutritionally, eating in the morning is essential because it supplies important nutrients—carbohydrates, protein, and fat—to the body. Studies show that energy as well as vitamins and minerals missed at breakfast are not made up by other meals eaten during the day.

Getting off to a nutritionally good start first thing in the morning can pay off throughout the day, too. Because they are not overhungry, people who eat breakfast tend to make better food choices during the course of the day. Case in point: A recent report by the American Health Foundation found children who skip breakfast tend to be more overweight than those who eat breakfast.

Quick, healthy breakfast ideas

A healthful breakfast should be low in fat, high in fiber, and include about one-fourth to one-third of the day's total protein, carbohydrates, cholesterol, and sodium. Vitamin-fortified cereal, milk, and fruit are about your best bets among typical breakfast fare and provide generous amounts of vitamins and minerals like calcium, riboflavin, folate, and vitamin B_6. But any food can be considered good breakfast fare—a slice of pizza, a taco, a banana-nut muffin, yogurt, a granola bar, and a box of juice or milk—as long as it's balanced and the food is quick, easy, and available. What's most important is eating *something* in the morning to get your body going.

For those people who don't have time for a sit-down morning meal, think about nutritious grab-and-go breakfasts like a peanut butter and jelly sandwich or a muffin. With a little planning, these can be prepared the night before and offer a quick, convenient meal at the office, school, or home.

caffeine

More than 80 percent of all adult Americans consume caffeine-containing foods and beverages every day. The average intake—280 milligrams a day—is about the amount found in three cups of coffee, six cups of tea, or eight cans of soda. Despite its widespread use, however, caffeine's physiological and behavioral effects are still controversial.

Caffeine stimulates the central nervous system, and taken in large amounts can increase heart rate and blood pressure. At lower doses, 100 to 300 milligrams, caffeine has the ability to increase alertness, boost energy levels, and improve mood. Doses above 400 milligrams tend to produce negative effects like anxiety and nervousness, though there have been some cases where people have reacted this way to doses as low as 200 milligrams.

Feeling a caffeine boost doesn't take long either. Usually it happens within 30 to 60 minutes after ingestion, when concentration peaks in the bloodstream. In addition, clearance time is slow. It typically takes four to six hours for caffeine's effects to wear off. That's why many people find it difficult to fall asleep after having an evening cup of coffee.

Caffeine buzz

Keep in mind there is a difference between being alert and being sober. Contrary to popular belief, coffee or caffeine does not reduce the effects of alcohol or sober someone who is drunk. At best, it will only keep a drunk person wide awake.

Caffeine Health Alert: Pregnancy and Infertility

Although the FDA recommends that pregnant women either avoid caffeine or reduce their consumption of it, many of the studies on which this recommendation was based are inconclusive or contradictory. Nevertheless, always prudent, the FDA still officially stands by its 1980 caution.

When it comes to fertility or getting pregnant, however, mounting evidence shows caffeine may have a negative effect. These studies are controversial and still under intense scrutiny by the scientific community, but if you are having trouble getting pregnant, it couldn't hurt to cut back on caffeine.

Caffeine as a mood-altering drug

Caffeine is a drug. In some people it can be very positive, making you feel alert and full of energy; in others it creates tension and anxiety, sometimes known as the coffee jitters. And like almost all drugs, caffeine is addictive.

Going cold turkey can lead to headache, fatigue, lethargy, muscle pain, and an overall bad mood. In some cases, headaches can be so severe they disrupt normal activity. If you want to cut caffeine out of your diet, cut back slowly to avoid these uncomfortable side effects. If you feel a caffeine headache coming on, take a few sips of coffee or cola to relieve the pain. Also be aware that caffeine is found not only in coffee, tea, chocolate, and cola, but in some over-the-counter pain relievers, cold preparations, and sleep suppressants.

Part of the problem behind determining caffeine's potency is that no one knows just how much or what kind of effect caffeine will have. Sensitivity to caffeine varies greatly from individual to individual. Age (older people are more sensitive to caffeine than younger ones), medical condition, regularity of use, and physical state during consumption all influence caffeine's effects.

People can also develop a tolerance for caffeine, so while two cups of coffee wouldn't effect a four- or five-cup-a-day coffee drinker, it could make a nondrinker bounce off the walls.

Can caffeine improve athletic performance?

Not only can caffeine rev up the body and increase alertness, it can also speed up reaction time for certain tasks. For well-trained athletes, these beneficial side effects can improve athletic performance. For this reason, caffeine is listed as a restricted substance by the International Olympic Committee. Though the extent of its benefits are controversial, caffeine is believed to enhance performance of endurance athletes (runners or cyclists) by sparing muscle glycogen, the kind of energy stored in muscle. Another theory is that caffeine releases endorphins that modify the perception of pain. It has no affect on short-term, high-intensity exercise.

What's in a cup?

Although coffee is the most concentrated source of caffeine in the American diet, it is also found naturally in tea and cocoa. As a food additive, it is added to some soft drinks, over-the-counter and prescription drugs, and diet aids.

Common Foods and Beverages Containing Caffeine

Item	Caffeine (mg)
Coffee (6 oz)	
Drip brewed	100
Instant	70
Tea (6 oz)	50
Cola soft drinks (12 oz)	36
Solid milk chocolate (1 oz)	6
Solid dark chocolate (1 oz)	20

The Truth About Tea

Current science touts the benefits of traditional green, black, and oolong tea as reducing the risk of developing heart disease, hypertension, some infectious diseases, and dental caries. Although 80 percent of the tea consumed worldwide is black, green tea is the better choice according to recent research. Green tea contains catechins, compounds that may protect us against stomach, intestinal, lung, skin, and esophageal cancers, while black tea has very few of these beneficial compounds.

Green, black, and oolong tea all come from the leaves of a green, bushy shrub called *Camellia sinensis,* known as the "tea plant." The difference between the teas has to do with processing: Green teas are simply dried tea leaves, black teas are fermented (resulting in their black-brown color), and oolong teas are semifermented.

calories

A calorie is the unit we use to measure the energy value of food. Technically, it is the amount of heat needed to raise the temperature of one kilogram (2.2 pounds) of water one degree Celsius. In layman's terms, kilocalorie, kcalorie, and calorie are all used interchangeably. When evaluating calories or any other nutrient found in food, scientists use gram weights. There are 28.35 grams (this number is often rounded up to 30) in one ounce. One hundred grams equal 3½ ounces.

Although we attach specific caloric numbers to food ingredients and recipes, in actuality, the energy value of any food—even within the same food type—varies depending on how much carbohydrates, protein, and fat it contains. For example, an apple grown in Washington state and an apple grown in New York may differ by 10, 20, 30, or more calories, depending on the size, variety, soil, and climate the apple was grown in.

Nevertheless, calories are the best way we have to monitor our energy intake, which is an important thing to do in the pursuit of a healthy, fit lifestyle. Too much energy (no matter the source) will be stored as fat; too little energy will lead to fatigue, anemia, and the loss of valuable muscle protein.

For Americans, excess calories are more of a problem than caloric deficits. The average male consumes about 2,500 calories a day, while the average female takes in about 1,600 calories per day.

All it takes, however, is an extra 500 calories a day to put on the pounds. At that rate, in one week, your body would have an extra 3,500 calories, which is exactly what it needs to store one pound of body fat. Excess fat accumulates almost imperceptibly at first and, as every dieter knows, is harder to take off than put on.

Counting Calories
- One gram of carbohydrates = 4 calories
- One gram of protein = 4 calories
- One gram of fat = 9 calories
- One gram of alcohol = 7 calories*

Alcohol contributes food energy or calories but nothing else. Since it does not support growth, maintenance, or cell repair, it is classified as a toxin rather than a nutrient.

All calories are not equal

Keep in mind that the amount of calories is not the only thing that influences fat storage. It's easier for your body to store fat than to store carbohydrates or protein because both carbohydrates and protein must be converted to fat—using up energy—before they can be stored. For example, to store 100 excess carbohydrate calories, your body needs to burn about 25 calories, so only 75 of the original 100 calories are converted to fat and stored. But to store 100 fat calories, the body expends only 3 calories, storing 97 fat calories. That's why fat calories are considered more fattening than carbohydrate or protein calories.

Calories and exercise

The amount of calories consumed during exercise is based on how much oxygen passes through the body. For instance, when you walk briskly, about 1 quart of oxygen is consumed each minute; therefore, your body uses about 5 calories. When you jog, oxygen consumption jumps to 2 quarts a minute, and calorie usage in that time goes up to 10. More oxygen equals more calories. (But remember: Working harder aerobically means you can get out of breath—experience an oxygen deficit—and thus be more apt to burn *sugar,* not fat.) To receive the same training benefits from walking as from jogging, you'd need to walk for *twice* the time you run.

Do you consume or save calories?

Caloric needs and usages are individual, all dependent on levels of activity, lifestyle, and, most important, body composition. Muscles are calorie consumers, feeding on calories even while at rest. Fat is essentially what results when calories are stored.

People who are *calorie consumers*

- have a higher ratio of muscle to fat (they're leaner)
- exercise regularly
- have a more active lifestyle in general
- eat what their bodies need at one time and not much more

People who are *calorie savers*

- have a higher ratio of fat to muscle
- don't exercise
- have a sedentary lifestyle
- eat more food than their bodies can store at one time—and thus convert excess calories to fat

But each individual also experiences a large variance in caloric requirements, since daily activities and circumstances change.

- On an average day, with 45 minutes of exercise, you might need 1,800 calories.
- On a highly active day, say one in which you take a 2-hour hike, you may need up to 2,200 calories.
- On a rest day, you may take no exercise and sit all day working—and therefore need only 1,600 calories.

Factors that can increase your body's caloric needs include more activity and exercise, menstruation, pregnancy, and stress.

Burning calories

People are concerned with the number of calories used during different types of exercise—and yes, the body uses more than its normal share during exercise. But exercise typically lasts only 30 to 60 minutes. The more important number is how many calories are used the rest of the day (i.e., how rapidly the metabolism works). The number of calories used in exercise, however, can boost the number of calories used for the rest of the day.

The body also uses about three-quarters of its calories in the daylight (from about 6 A.M. to 6 P.M.) and the other one-quarter at night (from 6 P.M. to 6 A.M.). If we keep this in mind, we should be eating three-quarters of our calories when the body is most active and making our last meal the smallest one—feeding the body calories when it is most apt to use them for fuel. (See also **Calories and Exercise,** page 163.)

carbohydrates

Carbohydrates—starches, fiber, and sugars—are the primary source of energy for the body. Chemically, they are composed of carbon, hydrogen, and oxygen molecules.

In food

Complex carbohydrates: Complex carbohydrates include the obvious breads, cereals, pastas, and grains as well as starchy vegetables like potatoes, corn, peas, and legumes and starchy fruits like bananas and apples. As these fruits ripen, the starches in them break down into sugars and give the fruit its characteristic sweet flavor.

Fiber: Fiber, a type of indigestible polysaccharide, is found in fruits, vegetables, and whole grains. It aids the body in digestion and elimination without supplying any energy or calories.

Simple sugars: Simple carbohydrates are monosaccharide or dissaccharide sugars. Glucose and fructose are the most common naturally occurring monosaccharide sugars. (All carbohydrate-rich foods contain glucose.)

Although the majority of carbohydrates, both simple and complex, come from the plant kingdom, there are some sugars contained in milk (lactose) and in some shellfish.

In the body

In the body, all carbohydrates are eventually broken down into glucose. Starches are the preferred source of glucose while fruits and some vegetables tend to supply fructose and sucrose.

Since they do not have to be broken down through digestion, simple sugars like fructose are readily absorbed by the bloodstream. After circulating in the blood, other simple sugars are usually converted to glucose by the liver.

Fruit juices are a concentrated source of fructose, as is candy, table sugar, and honey. Whole fruits, on the other hand, although still high in this sugar, are diluted with water (water content for fruit is very high as are vitamins and minerals). For this reason, fruit does not have the same dramatic effect on blood glucose as eating candy or even drinking fruit juice.

Carbohydrates that have to be broken down, like starches, go through the digestive system, where enzymes break the units into smaller pieces in the small intestine.

Once in the bloodstream, glucose can either be taken up by the cells and used for fuel (its primary purpose), stored in the liver or muscle as glycogen, or converted to fat for later use. Levels are regulated by a complex system of hormones.

Since only a small amount of glucose is stored as glycogen, it must be replenished on a daily basis by eating. If levels are low, your body will turn to fats for fuel, but some glucose is required in order to burn fats efficiently. Without glucose, the body can still burn fats, but a dangerous condition called ketosis could result.

Unlike the other organs in the body, which can use fat to run, the brain and nervous system depend exclusively on glucose for their energy needs. If no glucose is available, the body will break down valuable protein and convert it to glucose to be used by the brain and nervous system. For all of these reasons, reputable health experts advise against a low-carbohydrate diet. At the very least, most nutritionists will recommend consuming 100 to 150 grams of carbohydrates daily.

Recommended intakes

Most of the foods you consume—55 to 65 percent of your total calories—should be in the form of complex carbohydrates, such as whole grains, legumes, fruits, and vegetables. How does this translate into everyday eating? If you looked at a plate of food, about two-thirds of it would consist of starch and vegetables, the other third would be the meat or cheese portion of a meal.

carcinogens

A carcinogen is any substance that causes cancer. There are environmental carcinogens like cigarette smoke or toxic fumes, chemical carcinogens that show up in our food supply as pesticide or chemical residues, and natural carcinogens like aflatoxins that are produced by fungi and found on cereal grains and peanuts.

In the 1950s, Congress included a special clause (the Delaney Clause) in the Food Additives Amendment to eliminate even trace amounts of carcinogens from processed foods.

At the time, it was relatively easy to enforce: Chemicals were detected at one part per million and anything less was considered zero. Today, however, technology has advanced more than anyone in the 1950s could have possibly imagined. So now, carcinogens can be measured at parts per trillion (and soon it may even be parts per quadrillion), enabling scientists to detect infinitely minute levels of carcinogens in foods that were previously considered zero. Such small amounts of carcinogens do not necessarily pose any harmful risk to us—the presence of a carcinogen does not always translate into an increased cancer risk. Risk must also be assessed according to

- potency of the carcinogen
- number of exposures
- amount of carcinogen present

In 1996, President Clinton signed a bill that effectively abolished the outdated Delaney Clause. Instead, a "reasonable certainty of no harm" standard now applies to both processed and fresh foods. This will most likely classify foods with a one-in-a-million cancer risk as safe.

Reducing your risk of cancer through dietary changes

Despite all the media attention surrounding pesticide residues, our risk of developing cancer from these substances is far less than the hazards posed by not cooking or handling foods properly (contracting a food-borne illness). Cancer risk, however, is greatly affected by the *kind* of food we eat.

According to leading health authorities, at least one-third of all cancer-related deaths are attributed to diet. Most of these are linked to obesity as a result of excess fat and calories along with a sedentary lifestyle. The good news is that you can greatly reduce your chances of contracting cancer—or any illness for that matter—by following a healthy lifestyle and getting plenty of regular exercise.

Here are some of the ways nutritionists recommend:

Cut the fat

There is strong evidence that a high-fat diet can increase the risk for certain cancers like prostate and colon cancer. For this reason, groups like the American Cancer Society recommend going easy on high-fat foods and meat (which also tends to be high in fat). Type of fat, however, does make a difference. Monounsaturated fatty acids and omega-3 fatty acids (from fish) do not promote cancer and may even have a protective effect; while hydrogenated vegetable fats and saturated fats have the opposite effect.

Watch your weight

Obesity is a major risk factor for developing prostate, colon, breast, gallbladder, uterus, and ovarian cancer. When and where the weight is gained also makes a difference.

Some scientists think even just a small weight gain can increase some people's chance of getting certain cancers. For example, several studies show women who gain as little as 10 to 15 pounds in their adult years can significantly raise their risk of breast cancer compared to women who do not gain weight.

High-calorie diets: Some scientists think the more calories you consume, the more likely your chances may be of getting cancer. That's because animal studies show that high-calorie diets raise cancer rates and restricting calories makes cancer rates fall. Furthermore, it doesn't matter what type of calories are eaten—any type of high-energy intake tends to be associated with a rapid rate of growth, large body mass, and low physical activity, which have all been shown to increase cancer risk. So far there is no experimental evidence of this in humans, but researchers think this phenomenon can be observed in some populations.

Eat high-fiber foods

High-fiber foods like dried beans, whole grains, fruits, and vegetables offer a wealth of benefits and are particularly useful for protecting against colon cancer. The National Cancer Institute recommends that we eat somewhere between 20 to 30 grams of fiber each day. Unfortunately, the majority of Americans do not reach this goal.

Eat a varied diet

Consuming a wide variety of foods, along with plenty of fruits and vegetables, is the best insurance for lowering your risk of cancer. Plant foods especially contain valuable vitamins, minerals, and phytochemicals, non-nutritive substances that fight precancerous cells and protect against the disease. For this reason and others, most health groups recommend getting the majority of your calories from plant sources.

Avoid smoked, cured, and salted foods

High consumption of these foods has been linked with higher rates of specific cancers. For example, in Japan, where the practice of eating salted fish is commonplace, stomach cancer is high. Consequently, nutritionists recommend eating foods like hot dogs, bologna, or bacon only occasionally.

Limit alcohol intake

Heavy alcohol consumption has been associated with head and neck cancers, breast cancer, and a much higher risk of liver cancer. Many heavy drinkers also have low intakes of yellow and green fruits and vegetables, missing out on powerful vitamins and other substances that can fight against cancer. Limited alcohol consumption of two drinks a day for men and one drink a day for women is considered acceptable and may even offer some health benefits.

On the Grill

Grilling is one of the easiest and tastiest low-fat cooking methods around, but if it's not done properly it can increase your risk of cancer. Why? When meat, poultry, or fish is cooked over charcoal, it is exposed to high temperatures—like those of a flame—that increase your exposure to two kinds of cancer-causing compounds: heterocyclic amines (known as HCAs) and polycyclic aromatic hydrocarbons (or PAHs). HCAs form in the proteins of meat, fish, and poultry cooked on the grill, and are highest in charred or blackened pieces. PAHs are carcinogenic compounds in the smoke that coat these grilled foods. They're formed when fat drips on the hot coals, flames, or heating element. Because of these substances, high intakes of grilled foods have been linked to colon, stomach, liver, and rectal cancers.

For those who enjoy an occasional summer barbecue, the actual risk of getting cancer from grilled foods is low. But it does become higher for people who grill meat, chicken, or fish more than several times a week. How can you reduce exposure to these potentially dangerous compounds?

• Precook foods in the microwave first. The reason: The longer food stays on the grill, the more HCAs and PAHs are formed. Precooked meats reduce grill time and help prevent foods from charring (charred, burned, and overcooked foods are loaded with HCAs).

• Choose lean meats. Trim all visible excess fat off meat and remove the skin from the chicken. Fat causes flames to flare up. This can burn food and form PAHs, which can then fall back onto the food.

• Use low-fat marinades with flavorings like wine, vinegar, soy sauce, or lemon juice. One study found marinating meat substantially reduced one type of HCA.

• Cook foods over moderate heat—not high—at a minimum of six inches above burning coals or lava rocks.

• Don't use meat juices from the cooked meat to make gravies or sauces.

• Defrost meat before grilling. This prevents foods from cooking too fast on the outside (which increases the chance of charring) while still raw or undercooked on the inside.

• Whenever possible, wrap foods in foil to lessen smoke exposure.

cholesterol

Cholesterol is a soft, waxy, fatlike substance found in every cell in the body. It is necessary to build cell structure, some hormones, and bile acids. In food, it is found in all animal meats and animal products. Like other important nutrients, the body doesn't rely solely on diet for its cholesterol quota. To ensure a constant supply, the liver also produces it.

Dietary cholesterol is the term we use to refer to any cholesterol we eat. Blood cholesterol is the cholesterol circulating in the bloodstream. Trouble occurs when too much cholesterol is circulating in the blood. As a result, two things happen: First, the blood becomes thick and viscous, slowing down circulation and making the heart work harder. Second, excess cholesterol, along with other substances, stick to the sides of the arteries, clogging up passages and increasing blood pressure. If cholesterol builds up too much it can effectively block oxygen-rich blood from getting to the heart altogether, causing part of the heart muscle to die. This is what happens when you have a heart attack. Consequently, reducing blood cholesterol levels effectively reduces your chances of having a heart attack.

In the bloodstream, fats are transported by special carriers called lipoproteins (part protein and part fat or lipid), and they come in two kinds: low-density lipoproteins (LDLs) and high-density lipoproteins (HDLs).

LDLs: Low-density lipoproteins are often referred to as the "bad" cholesterol, because they are the ones most responsible for the build-up of plaque, the hard fatty deposits that narrow cell walls and clog arteries. They carry cholesterol from the liver to the artery walls where they deposit it.

LDLs must be oxidized, or chemically changed by oxygen, in order to do their damage. For this reason, some scientists believe antioxidants may help protect against heart disease. About two-thirds of your cholesterol is carried by LDLs.

HDLs: High-density lipoproteins are considered the "good" cholesterol. This is because they carry cholesterol away from the arteries and back to the liver. A high HDL count has a protective effect against heart disease and a low HDL count is associated with an increased risk for coronary heart disease. About one-third to one-fourth of blood cholesterol is carried by HDLs.

Heart disease

High blood-cholesterol levels are considered a major risk factor for coronary heart disease, the number-one killer in the United States. The American Heart Association estimates that over 50 percent of the population has cholesterol levels over 200 milligrams per deciliter and over 20 percent fall into the over 240 milligrams per deciliter category. Consequently, lowering blood cholesterol levels is a top priority for the nation's public health. Diet is perhaps the easiest way to start lowering cholesterol, particularly since there's so much room for improvement, but it certainly is not the only method for combating high cholesterol levels. Here are a few ways to keep cholesterol levels in check.

Reduce saturated fat in the diet: Research shows saturated fats have much more of an impact on blood cholesterol levels than dietary cholesterol. In the past, heart-healthy diets emphasized the consumption of fewer high-cholesterol foods, but this is actually the least of your worries. Foods high in saturated fat—fatty meats, cheese, butter—are much more dangerous than, say, shellfish or even eggs, which can be included in a low-cholesterol diet. Still, you shouldn't go overboard. Recommendations say you should take in no more than 300 milligrams per day. Saturated fat, on the other hand, should be watched carefully. It should make up less than 10 percent of your total calories.

Reduce total fat: Too much fat, of any kind, will raise blood cholesterol levels. Trans fatty acids, the kind in hydrogenated vegetable products like margarine and processed cakes and cookies, are especially bad. Recent findings indicate they may be even worse than saturated fat when it comes to raising blood cholesterol levels. Although there are no recommendations yet for trans fatty acid levels, keeping total fat intake low (below 30 percent of total calories) will probably do the trick.

Lose weight: Losing weight will automatically decrease LDLs and total blood cholesterol levels, particularly if you are very overweight.

Slow down and relax: High-stress lifestyles are associated with high blood cholesterol levels.

Exercise regularly: Physical activity not only lowers LDLs, but it also has the added perk of raising beneficial HDLs. This is one of the best ways to get your cholesterol level under control.

Follow a healthy diet that is high in fiber: Many studies have shown fiber can lower cholesterol and reduce the risk of heart disease as well as prevent other chronic diseases such as cancer. So stock up on fruits, vegetables, and legumes. The benefits will really pay off.

Try soy

Soy protein may be another boon for people trying to lower their cholesterol. A number of studies have shown that regularly including soy protein in the diet can reduce LDL cholesterol and other fats in the bloodstream. In fact, the higher the cholesterol level, the bigger the drop in cholesterol when soy is eaten regularly.

How can you get more soy in your diet? Try substituting tofu for ground beef in chili, lasagna, and casserole-type dishes, or prepare it by itself in soups or stir-fried dishes. Other soy products include soy milk, soy flour, miso (usually prepared in Japanese soup), and tempeh (another Japanese bean cake).

It's in the genes

Even if you diligently watch your diet, get regular exercise, and don't smoke, there are no guarantees that your cholesterol level will be in the safe range. That's because there are factors we can't control that also influence cholesterol:

- Gender (males have higher cholesterol levels than females)
- Age
- Genetics (the liver may normally produce high amounts of cholesterol)

Getting started

Some people who need to change their diet because of a heart attack or other health problem often feel overwhelmed at the thought of a bland existence, never enjoying their favorite foods again. But it doesn't have to be that way. In fact, changing your diet isn't as painful as people think as long as you keep one thing in mind: Don't try to do too much too fast. For example, try switching from whole milk to 2 percent, then eventually 1 percent or even skim milk. Or add one meatless meal to your dinner schedule. Here are a few suggestions to get you started:

1. Choose lean meats and always take the skin off poultry.

2. Select low-fat dairy foods.

3. Opt for steaming, stir-frying, or sautéing (in only a little olive oil) rather than deep-frying foods.

4. Increase your intake of fruits and vegetables.

5. Try to include legumes in your diet at least once a week.

What's Safe?

In order to determine your risk of heart disease, doctors measure blood cholesterol levels—in addition to other factors, such as weight, gender, and age.

Total Cholesterol Levels

Less than 200 mg/dL	Desirable
200 to 239 mg/dL	Borderline high
Equal to or over 240 mg/dL	High

HDL Cholesterol Levels

Less than 35 mg/dL	Low (considered a risk factor)
Greater than 60 mg/dl	Desirable (high HDL confers a protective effect)

LDL Cholesterol Levels

Less than 130 mg/dL	Desirable
130 to 159 mg/dL	Borderline high
Equal to or greater than 160 mg/dL	High risk

Based on the "Second Report of the Expert Panel on Detection, Evaluation, and Treatment of High Blood Cholesterol" by the NHLBI's National Cholesterol Education Program.

dairy foods

Despite the fact that milk and cheese are notoriously high in fat, dairy products should not be excluded from the diet. They supply many valuable nutrients—protein, vitamin A, calcium, phosphorus, magnesium—important for a balanced diet. Their nutritional profile also classifies them as "nutrient dense," which means they deliver a large amount of nutrients in a relatively small amount of calories.

As far as fat goes, today there are dozens of top-quality low-fat and fat-free dairy alternatives available on the market. Some products, like skim milk and nonfat yogurt, have the same exact nutrient composition as their whole-milk counterparts—minus the fat. So skim milk actually has more calcium, vitamin D, and protein per ounce than whole milk. Taste-wise, many people prefer these lower-fat dairy foods because they are lighter and less filling than their full-fat counterparts.

What do dairy foods offer?

Protein: Milk supplies nearly 20 percent of the protein available in the U.S. food supply. It is a high-quality protein, providing all eight essential amino acids. One cup of milk contains about 6 grams of protein, which equals 9 percent of the recommended USDA for men and 12 percent of the recommended USDA for women.

Calcium: Milk and dairy products are the primary sources of calcium in the American diet.

In fact, about 75 percent of the calcium in our food supply comes from dairy products. Just three servings from the milk group (i.e., one cup of milk, 1 ounce of cheese, 1 cup of yogurt) is enough to meet the new adult calcium recommendations of 1,000 milligrams per day.

Riboflavin, vitamin A, and vitamin D: Riboflavin (also known as vitamin B_2) is found naturally in high amounts in milk and milk products. Dairy foods, in fact, are the only foods that provide such a large amount of this vitamin. Over half of our riboflavin intake is derived from milk and milk products.

Vitamin A is a fat-soluble vitamin naturally present in the fat portion of the milk. However, when fat is removed—as in the case of skim or low-fat milk—so is the vitamin. Consequently, skim and low-fat milks are fortified with vitamin A.

Nearly all milk sold in the United States is also fortified with 400 international units of vitamin D per quart of fluid. Since most foods are naturally low in this vitamin, fortifying ensures that our chances of developing a vitamin deficiency are low. This is particularly helpful for children and the elderly, two nutritionally high-risk groups.

Keep the light out: Both vitamin A and riboflavin are light sensitive, meaning light can destroy them. Studies have shown that milk in a translucent jug sitting in the dairy case of a supermarket can lose up to 70 percent of its vitamin

A content and 20 percent of its riboflavin content after just three days. Furthermore, these lights can also impart an off-taste to the milk.

What's the bottom line? Buy milk in paper cardboard containers instead of jugs. If you can't do this, make sure the jug is opaque enough so you can't see the milk through it.

Milk Has a "New" Name

The Food and Drug Administration recently approved new labeling regulations for milk. The changes, which went into effect January 1, 1998, were designed to help clear up confusion regarding low-fat milk choices. Here's what they did:

Old Name	New Name
Skim milk	Fat-free milk, nonfat milk, or skim milk
1% milk	Low-fat milk
1½% milk	Light milk
2% milk	Reduced-fat milk

The benefits of dairy

Like other food groups, dairy foods have their own set of unique health benefits. Lower fat versions especially are nutritious, wholesome, and healthy. Furthermore, as part of a balanced diet, scientists believe dairy foods can help stave off such chronic illnesses as osteoporosis and hypertension. Some preliminary evidence has even linked dairy foods with anticancer abilities.

Osteoporosis

Osteoporosis is a brittle-bone disease that afflicts over 25 million Americans, mostly women. Low calcium and vitamin D levels are considered major risk factors for developing the disease (physical inactivity, smoking, and excessive alcohol intake are others). Since dairy foods provide most of the calcium in our diet, adequate intakes can significantly decrease, though not abolish, your chance of getting osteoporosis. Why?

Calcium is critical for building strong, healthy, dense bones. It's also important for optimal bone growth in children and teenagers. Developing healthy bones from an early age mitigates bone loss that naturally occurs as we get older.

Unfortunately, most people aren't getting the calcium they need. Some figures report close to 70 percent of Americans—two out of every three people—are shortchanging themselves on this nutrient, and according to USDA food consumption figures, we eat only about half of what's recommended by the Food Guide Pyramid for the milk group each day (one and a half servings).

Young adolescents and children are perhaps the most important audience to target because not only does a calcium-rich diet prevent bone loss later on in life, it also helps build healthy bone structure from the start (half of our bone mass is formed during these years). Currently only 12 to 14 percent of teenage girls meet calcium requirements. (See **Osteoporosis**, page 34.)

Hypertension

High blood pressure, or hypertension, affects one out of every four Americans. Sodium is most often associated with the disease, but not everyone is salt-sensitive, so reducing the amount of salt in the diet does not always lead to a drop in blood pressure.

Several recent studies, however, suggest calcium may help prevent or control high blood pressure. A recent landmark study called DASH (Dietary Approaches to Stop Hypertension), funded by the National Heart, Lung and Blood Institute in Bethesda, Maryland, found that following a diet low in total and saturated fat and rich in fruits, vegetables, *and low-fat dairy foods* could significantly lower blood pressure—just as much as taking high blood pressure medication.

Cancer

The newest frontier in cancer research involves a compound called conjugated linoleic acid, or CLA. In animal studies, CLA has proven to be a potent anticancer agent and immune enhancer. Researchers think it also may protect against coronary heart disease. Dairy products like milk, butter, yogurt, and cheese are the primary source of CLA, which is only found in animal fats (that means it's in beef and lamb, too).

Good for your teeth, too

Eating cheese helps build strong teeth and bones, because it's high in calcium and phosphorus, two minerals that are necessary for keeping tooth enamel healthy. But did you also know that eating cheese could have a protective effect on tooth decay?

Studies have found that aged cheese (cheddar, Swiss, blue, Monterey Jack, Brie, and Gouda) and processed American cheese can actually help prevent dental decay. Though the mechanisms are not completely understood, scientists think cheese's beneficial effects can be explained in two ways. First, it stimulates saliva production, which helps clear sugar and plaque from the teeth. Second, the fatty acids in cheese may have an antibacterial effect on teeth. Bacteria produce acid that eats away at teeth.

So the European practice of eating cheese immediately after a meal or as a between meal snack may be more practical than you think, particularly for your teeth.

More Cheese, Please

Over the years, Americans have developed quite a passion for cheese. Since the 1970s our consumption has more than doubled, increasing our total intake to nearly 28 pounds per capita. Much of this growth can be attributed to the fact that many consumers use cheese as a substitute for red meat in the diet. Thus, the last two decades saw a decline in red meat consumption, while cheese intake rose.

Lately, however, cheese has become more than simply a replacement for meat protein. The key to including cheese in a healthy diet is choosing the right kinds and keeping the quantities small. Sharp, flavorful cheeses like Parmesan, Gorgonzola, and feta are your best bet because you only need a small amount to satisfy your taste buds. Cheeses naturally low in fat are another option. All of these cheeses contain only 6 grams of fat per one-ounce serving:

- American processed cheese
- Goat cheese
- Feta
- Mozzarella

dieting

Dieting is one of our favorite national pastimes. That's not surprising since statistics show that one out of every three Americans is overweight. What is surprising is how much money we spend trying to trim down. Every year more than $33 billion is sunk into weight-reduction products, like diet food, diet pills, and diet drinks.

Unfortunately, most people are looking for quick fixes—easy ways to lose weight fast without changing dietary or lifestyle habits. Hence the popularity of fad diets like the cabbage soup diet, the grapefruit diet, and the recent flurry of high-protein diets. With all of these diets you will run into trouble sooner or later. Sometimes the ill effects on health can be so serious that they can be life-threatening. Fortunately, most people don't stay on these diets long enough to find out.

Fad diets

Recognizing what a fad diet is will help you avoid wasting time, money, and potentially risking your health. How can you decipher a good weight-loss plan from a bad one? The four signs that the diet in question is a bad one are:

- It excludes whole food categories, like meat, protein, or dairy products.
- It overemphasizes the importance of certain foods (i.e., cabbage or rice), often at the expense of other foods in the diet. Or if it promotes eating foods in a certain way, such as eat soft foods like peaches only in the afternoon.
- It does not encourage physical activity or other lifestyle changes.
- It promises the world. Remember: If it sounds too good to be true, it probably is.

Although the authors of weight-loss books or programs claim to be nutrition experts, the science they base their theories on is often either flawed or unfounded. Weight loss, if it does occur, is usually a result of a lower caloric intake (which comes from watching your diet) or water loss (as is the case for many high-protein diets).

Can pasta make you fat?

In the early 1990s, sensationalized news stories claimed that complex carbohydrates like pasta and bread cause weight gain, and promoted these foods as "fattening." The stories were based on a number of popular weight-loss books that capitalized on the insulin-resistance theory and advocated a high-protein, low-carbohydrate diet. They theorized that the overproduction of insulin, caused by a high-carbohydrate diet, results in more glucose being stored as fat—eventually leading to weight gain.

Although it is true that carbohydrates do cause a rise in insulin, and insulin does stimulate fat storage of glucose, the basic premise is flawed. Insulin does not cause weight gain; consuming too many calories does. In fact, too much of anything—fat, carbohydrates, or protein—will result in more fat being stored.

Studies have consistently shown that a high-carbohydrate, low-fat diet is the best way to lose weight. Replacing fat with complex carbohydrates is not only healthier because of the extra nutrients and fiber content it provides, but it is also significantly lower in calories (one gram of fat equals 9 calories while the same amount of carbohydrates yields 4).

The right way to eat

The best way to lose weight is slowly, by reducing your caloric intake by about 500 calories a day (there are 3,500 calories in one pound of fat) to promote a weight loss of 1 to 2 pounds per week. Couple this with regular physical activity and you could lose even more. But in reality, getting rid of unwanted pounds is more than just calories in versus calories out. Food is tied to our psychological, emotional, and social well-being, so there are many other factors involved in dieting. Keeping the weight off has its own set of issues. It often requires a new attitude about food in addition to lifestyle changes.

Making it work

1. Make a commitment. Having the right attitude is more than half the battle when it comes to losing weight. You have to be willing to go the distance, to really want to lose weight. Most diets or weight-loss programs fail not because there is something wrong with the diet but because the person was not ready to lose weight.

2. Set realistic goals. Choosing an unrealistic weight goal or time frame to achieve your weight loss is only setting yourself up for failure. Your ideal weight should be a healthy one where you feel your best. This may not conform to society's view of thin or even average, but it is what works for you. (See **Weight**, page 388, for more details.)

3. Don't deprive yourself. Some people feel they have to cut out all their favorite foods like ice cream, doughnuts, and chocolate. But doing this will only sabotage your weight-loss plans and cause you to crave the forbidden items even more. Instead, plan an occasional or weekly food fix and have the desired food in small amounts. This should satisfy your cravings without going overboard.

4. Learn to enjoy healthy foods. Dieting doesn't mean you have to eat like a bird. Fatty foods should be replaced by lots of healthy fruits, vegetables, legumes, and whole grains. Most people who are trying to switch to a healthier way of eating need to revamp their meal repertoire. If you try experimenting with different recipes, cooking methods, and foods, you won't even miss the fats.

It's All in Your Head

Dieters are often preoccupied with food, but can this cloud your thinking? Maybe. According to a British study at the Institute of Food Research in Reading, England, people on diets consistently performed worse on memory and attention tests than people who were not on diets.

The mechanics of weight loss

1. Limit fat intake. Fat has the highest concentration of calories (9 calories per gram) compared to other nutrients. It is also more likely to be stored as fat in the body than are carbohydrates and protein. High fat intakes have been associated with many health risks, including cancer and heart disease, so lowering it for any reason is a good idea. Figuring out how many fat grams you should be eating in a day is helpful, particularly when reading labels and calculating a day's intake. In general, however, the best way to cut back on fats is by avoiding high-fat meats and dairy products (choose low-fat or fat-free options instead) and go easy on the butter, margarine, and oil.

2. Watch the calories. Lowering fat intake usually lowers calories as well, but not always. If you're not careful you may find yourself downing large amounts of high-calorie, fat-free foods. Although not high in fat, the extra calories will undermine the best-laid weight-loss plan.

3. Get moving. Regular exercise will not only burn more calories, it will help suppress appetite so you won't be so hungry. It's also the best way to keep the weight off long term. Studies show that without regular physical activity people who lose weight are more likely to gain it back.

Lose the low-calorie diets

Though cutting calories is important, low-calorie diets, under 1,200 for women and 1,400 for men, are not the way to go. At such low levels it's difficult to get adequate amounts of such nutrients as folic acid, magnesium, and zinc. Furthermore, eating so little food puts your body in a perpetual state of starvation. Metabolism slows and the body works to conserve as much energy as possible; when normal eating is resumed, weight gain usually follows.

Research shows that over time, chronic dieters may lose the ability to read internal cues that signal hunger (a growling stomach, for example). This means they are more apt to eat as a result of an external cue (a television ad, for example) than as a result of hunger. Some preliminary evidence even suggests that taste perception may change as well, which can lead to overeating.

What You Need to Know

Calculating how much fat, carbohydrates, and protein you need in a day is easy once you know what to do. Based on a 2,000 calorie diet containing 30 percent fat, 15 percent protein, and 55 percent carbohydrates, here's what you do:

FAT

Multiply 2,000 × .30 = 600—the number of total fat calories

Divide 600 by 9 (9 calories in 1 gram of fat) = 67 total fat grams allowed

PROTEIN

Multiply 2,000 × .15 = 300—the number of total protein calories

Divide 300 by 4 (4 calories in 1 gram of protein) = 75 total protein grams allowed

CARBOHYDRATES

Multiply 2,000 × .55 = 1,100—the number of total carbohydrate calories

Divide 1,100 by 4 (4 calories in 1 gram of carbohydrate) = 275 total carbohydrate grams allowed

digestion

Digestion is the process by which the body breaks down food so it can be absorbed and utilized. It begins at the moment food enters your mouth and doesn't end until it leaves the body. Food can take anywhere from a few hours to a few days to be digested completely.

Everything we eat must be digested in order to be used. Like most systems in the body, however, digestion is not as simple as it looks: It involves a number of hormones, enzymes, muscles, and other organs. Here's a beginner's guide to the process.

The mouth

This is the starting point of digestion. Food is mechanically or physically broken down by the teeth and jaws and, as you start chewing, saliva is released, lubricating the food so you are better able to crush it. Sometimes just the smell or sight of food can initiate saliva production. Once the food is sufficiently chewed, it gets swallowed, traveling down the esophagus and into the stomach.

Although saliva's primary function is to moisten food, it also begins the chemical breakdown of food by releasing some digestive enzymes. (Enzymes are protein compounds that act as catalysts to cause a chemical reaction to occur without getting involved or altered in the process.) The enzymes in saliva are specific to carbohydrates, meaning they break down sugars and starches only. Proteins and fats, although chewed into smaller bits, leave the mouth in their same chemical form.

Mom always said . . .

Chew your food! Many a parent has admonished an impatient child in just this way. But heeding Mom's wise advice has more merit than you may think. In addition to speeding up the digestive process and preventing people from choking on their food, chewing has a more self-serving value: It enhances our ability to taste food. Research from the University of Connecticut shows that the length of time you spend chewing your food has a direct effect on how well you taste and ultimately enjoy your meal. How?

When food is chewed, the food molecules break down and release volatile or odiferous gaslike substances. These volatiles then travel through the nasal cavity up to the olfactory center of the brain where the specific flavors of the food are identified. So the longer you chew, the more volatiles you will release and the more flavor you will perceive.

There are other benefits, too. The longer you chew, the slower you eat, giving your body more time to digest, so it is less likely that you will overeat. It takes approximately 20 minutes for the brain to recognize satiety in the stomach. During this time, people who wolf down their food without chewing can stack up quite a bit of extra calories.

The stomach

Think of the stomach as a holding tank for the food you just swallowed. Since it is made of muscle it can extend or contract, depending on how much food it contains. That's why people who don't eat for a long period of time feel as though their stomach has shrunk, while overeating can cause you to feel bloated and stretched out. Like the mouth, the stomach works in two ways:

- Mechanically, by mixing and grinding the food, and
- Chemically, by breaking down food molecules with enzymes.

These enzymes are found in the gastric juice that is released when food first enters the stomach. Highly acidic gastric juices break down primarily protein and fat molecules. Although the juices are carefully controlled by the stomach, occasionally gastric acid will back up into the esophagus, producing heartburn. People who produce large amounts of gastric acid may also develop ulcers. In an ulcer, gastric acid actually eats away at the lining of the stomach or small intestine, causing pain and discomfort.

The small intestine

After leaving the stomach, the food mixture enters the small intestine for the final round in the digestion process. It is here, with the help of enzymes from the pancreas and bile from the liver, that protein is broken down into amino acids; fats are changed into fatty acids and monoglycerides (very small fat molecules); and carbohydrates become single-molecule saccharides, or sugars.

Once nutrients are in these basic forms, they are absorbed into the bloodsteam through tiny villi, fingerlike projections on the surface of the small intestine. Nearly 95 percent of all nutrient absorption takes place in the first half of the small intestine.

The large intestine

Little absorption takes place in the large intestine or colon—only some minerals and fluid pass through. The main job of the colon is to gather up undigested compounds like fiber, fluid, and other waste products and pass them out of the body through excretion.

Taste vs. Flavor

What's the difference between taste and flavor? Taste buds are located on the tongue while flavors are deciphered in the brain. While taste can tell us we are eating a sweet or tart fruit, it is flavor that differentiates between an orange and a grapefruit or an apple and a pear.

eating for fitness

Eating the right foods can rev up your energy, increase endurance, and help you perform at your peak during an athletic workout. Choose the wrong foods and your daily exercise routine is likely to be filled with fatigue and disappointment.

So, what are the right foods? The best diets stock up on plenty of carbohydrates (about 55 to 60 percent of your total calories), moderate amounts of protein (10 to 15 percent of calories), and low amounts of fat (20 to 30 percent of their total). Furthermore, it doesn't matter whether you are a lean, endurance marathon runner or a bulky, heavyweight bodybuilder, the same principles apply.

People who are physically active need more calories to replace the calories they burn while exercising. How much more depends on body size, type of activity, and frequency it is performed. Professional athletes can pack away 4,000 or 5,000 calories and still stay trim. Average exercisers, however, who work out two or three times a week, may need only a few hundred extra calories (if any extra at all) to maintain their weight. But no matter how much food you take in, the dietary pattern is still the same.

Maximizing your workout

Nutrients provide the necessary equipment for your body to run. Below are the major nutrients and why they are important for active people.

Carbohydrates

Carbohydrates are the fuel that feed your muscles. Eat too little and your muscles will be chronically fatigued, resulting in a poor performance and lower endurance. Why? During intense exercise, carbohydrates are broken down quickly, providing your body with a fast and easy way to get lots of energy. If there's not enough glucose to perform the work, your muscles will quickly build up lactic acid and burn and cramp. Too little carbohydrate can also cause a drop in the amount of blood glucose going to the brain, resulting in mental fatigue and a lack of concentration.

Thus, glucose is the primary source of fuel for endurance-type activities (90 minutes or more) like biking or marathon running, and for short intense exercises such as sprinting or weight lifting. Even when you are burning primarily fat—in low-level or moderate activities like low-impact aerobics—carbohydrates are essential. (Some glucose is required in order to burn fats efficiently.)

Normally, a small amount of glucose is stored in muscle as glycogen. This is what gives athletes their quick burst of energy for a race and the ability to withstand long hours of exercise. The liver also contains some glycogen, which it uses to regulate blood glucose levels.

Some serious athletes can increase their muscle glycogen uptake through a process called carbo-loading. During carbo-loading, carbohydrate intake is increased to about 70 percent of calories. This may be helpful for endurance athletes like runners or bikers who need a continuous supply of energy for long periods of time.

Just eating a diet high in carbohydrates alone, however, won't improve sports performance. It must be accompanied by a training regimen that allows muscles to become saturated with glycogen. Most times this can be accomplished the week before the event takes place.

For most athletes, eating a diet high in carbohydrates is the best way to get the most out of your workout.

Protein

Despite what you may have heard at your local gym, protein *does not* build muscle, exercise does. Bodybuilders and other athletes who load up on the hamburgers, chicken, and fish in the hopes of enhancing their sports performance are not helping their body, and in fact may actually be harming it instead. Three reasons why pumping up the protein may not be a good idea are the following:

1. Excess protein is converted to fat, not muscle, and the by-product of broken-down protein—urea—must be excreted in the urine. Hence too much protein can lead to increased urination and possibly dehydration.
2. Taking in all that protein also leaves little room left for carbohydrates. Consequently, high-protein diets tend to be low in carbohydrates, the fuel your body really needs for a workout.
3. Most of the foods of choice on this regime—hamburgers, cheese, and eggs—also tend to be high in fat, increasing the chance of long-term health problems like heart disease and cancer.

So, how much protein should a conscientious physically active adult consume? That depends. Athletes require more protein than their sedentary counterparts, but just how much is open for debate. Most nutritionists and sports scientists feel that protein needs are only slightly higher than what the average inactive adult needs. This extra protein is needed to repair the wear and tear well-trained muscles undergo during a workout and compensate for a larger muscle mass.

Since the average American eats more than enough protein to begin with, meeting these extra protein needs is usually not a concern—if you follow a healthy, balanced diet. Even if your protein requirements are high, this usually has more to do with a pattern of high calorie consumption than with actual protein intake.

If you look at numbers, the average sedentary person requires about .8 grams of protein per kilogram (the RDA for protein) or .4 grams per pound. For a 120-pound woman, this translates into about 50 grams of protein daily. Add in regular intense physical activity and, at most, protein needs jump to about 72 grams per day (Nancy Clark, M.S., R.D., *Nancy Clark's Sports Nutrition Guidebook,* 2nd ed. [Champagne, Ill.: Human Kinetics Publishers, 1997]). Though this extra 22 grams may sound like a lot, considering that most people eat well above the RDA anyway, this quantity is minimal. Food-wise it amounts to only an extra 2 ounces of meat plus ½ cup of beans and ½ cup of cooked vegetables.

Protein promises don't deliver: Many athletes mistakenly believe protein powders or amino acid supplements will give them an extra edge during competition or help them build bigger muscles. Unfortunately, this is just not true. Muscles grow by being used or trained—resistance exercise like weight training does it. Protein does not increase muscle mass, nor does it strengthen muscles.

Fill up on too much protein, which is easy to do when taking protein supplements, and the excess will be converted to fat, not muscle. Amino acid supplements or enzyme pills are no better. They are broken down in the digestive tract and absorbed similarly to protein. Since amino acids compete for carriers to be absorbed into the blood, overdoing one type of amino acid can lead to problems long term by causing a deficiency in the absorption of other amino acids.

All this means that protein supplements and the like are an unnecessary and costly expense, especially in light of the fact that many times the protein or amino acid in question can be acquired much more cheaply and efficiently in food sources.

Getting out of a Slump

Although carbohydrates should be the focus of your meal, they shouldn't be the only thing on your plate. Overdoing the pasta and vegetables during a workday lunch could make you feel sluggish and drowsy, making it hard for you to concentrate. Researchers think the carbohydrate itself is responsible. That's because high carbohydrate intakes, as in an all-carb meal such as a rice and vegetable stir-fry, leads to the release of serotonin, a brain chemical that makes you feel sleepy and less alert.

The good news is that there is a simple way to remedy this effect: eat protein. By adding some ham, turkey, or cheese to your salad or pasta you can offset this serotonin reaction, increasing alertness and satiety. So the next time you get a carbohydrate craving, keep energy levels high by balancing your meal with small amounts of protein and fat.

Fat

Like the rest of the population, athletes should keep fat intakes low, around 25 to 30 percent of calories. Eating high-fat foods can increase the risk of a number of serious illnesses, like heart disease and cancer. It can also affect your exercise workout by making you feel fatigued and sluggish. Since high-fat foods are digested slower than other foods, they can sit heavily in your stomach, making you feel uncomfortable. That's why it's not a good idea to work out after a fatty, high-calorie meal.

Too little fat, on the other hand, will have negative effects. Since fat is an essential nutrient, it is required for the brain, nervous system, and other organs to function. It also protects the internal organs and insulates the body against temperature changes.

For the average American, typical body-fat levels fall somewhere around 25 percent for women and 20 percent for men. The body-fat levels of well-trained athletes are usually lower, but beware of cutting out fat altogether. Men who drop below 5 percent body fat and women who go below 13 percent are in danger of depleting essential body fat that is needed for the body to run properly. Women whose body-fat levels drop too low often suffer amenorrhea (no menstrual period), a problem common among women athletes.

Fluids

Many people who religiously watch their diet often neglect to think about fluids. That's not good, since dehydration can be a serious problem with dire consequences. Too little fluid can lead to fatigue, headaches, and muscle cramps and increase your chances of injury.

Much of this water loss comes from sweat, your body's way of keeping cool. During an hour of intense exercise like running, you can lose more than 2 quarts of sweat. How much you sweat depends on the temperature, humidity, intensity of exercise, fitness level, gender (men sweat more than women), and a few other factors.

If you lose a lot of sweat, replenishing the water loss is difficult. According to the American College of Sports Medicine, even when fluids are readily available most people only replace one-half to two-thirds of their sweat losses.

Since thirst is not a reliable indicator of water loss—you've already lost a considerable amount of fluid before the thirst mechanism kicks in—you should not wait until you're thirsty to drink. Always drink, even before you feel thirsty, and once your thirst is quenched try to drink several more gulps.

General health recommendations advise everyone to drink about 64 ounces or more of juice or water a day, but people who regularly work out need much more than that. Experts advise exercisers to drink as much as they comfortably can, before (at least 16 ounces), during (5 to 10 ounces every 15 to 20 minutes), and after (at least 24 ounces) a workout.

How do you know you're drinking enough? The best way to ensure adequate fluid intake is to monitor the color and frequency of your urine. It should be pale in color and you should urinate often throughout the day. Another way to determine fluid loss and compensate accordingly is to weigh yourself before and after a workout. The weight you lose is pure water. For every pound you drop, you should drink 16 ounces of water or fluid.

eggs

When most people think of eggs, the first thing that comes to mind is cholesterol. But the egg is actually one of Mother Nature's most perfect foods: naturally high in protein, low in sodium, and rich with nutrients. Plus, they're extremely versatile, easy to prepare, and very inexpensive.

Eggs are such an important part of the American diet because of their nutritional makeup.

Protein

One whole, large egg provides a little over 6 grams of protein. This makes up about 12 percent of the total egg—quite a substantial amount considering that eggs are 75 percent water.

The quality of protein, however, is what makes eggs so beneficial. Not only do they supply all of the essential amino acids, but a large proportion of the amino acids closely match those the body needs. For this reason, eggs are often used as the standard by which all protein is measured.

In the egg, protein is distributed rather evenly, unlike other nutrients, which tend to be concentrated in the yolk. A little more than half the protein is found in the albumen, or white part, of the egg while the rest is in the yolk.

Vitamins and minerals

Eggs contain thirteen different kinds of vitamins and at least twelve different kinds of minerals. They are an important source of riboflavin, folate, B_6, B_{12}, vitamin A, vitamin E, iron, phosphorus, and zinc. They're also one of the few foods that naturally contain vitamin D. Except for riboflavin (half of which is found in the egg white), most of these nutrients are in the yellow yolk. Fat-soluble vitamins (A, D, E, and K) in particular are only found in the yolk, as are most of the minerals: choline, phosphorus, iron, and calcium.

Fat

One whole, large egg furnishes about 5 grams of total fat, only about a third of which—or 1.5 grams—is saturated. Throwing out the yolk will bring your fat quotient down to 0 (the whites do not have any fat) and also drop your calories—three-quarters of the 75 calories found in an egg are in the yolk—but you will also lose valuable vitamins and minerals. Because the yolk is so nutrient dense, people watching their fat intake might be better off reducing rather than eliminating the yolks in their diet. Many nutritionists recommend using one egg yolk for every two or three whites.

Eggs and cholesterol

As far as cholesterol goes, eggs may have gotten a bad break over the years. First, because of errors in calculations, scientists overestimated the cholesterol content of eggs. One large egg actually averages about 215 milligrams of cholesterol—22 percent less than the 274 milligrams they were originally thought to contain.

Moreover, dietary cholesterol is not as bad for you as once thought. Saturated fat has a much more harmful effect on blood cholesterol levels and heart disease risk than dietary cholesterol. In fact, a recent review of research concluded that restricting dietary cholesterol resulted in only a minimal reduction in blood cholesterol levels.

Studies done specifically with eggs have come to similar conclusions. At Columbia University in New York City, subjects who ate two eggs a day for three months showed only slight increases in total cholesterol levels.

How many eggs do we eat?

Ever since the early seventies, when the American Heart Association recommended that consumers watch their egg intake, consumption rates for eggs have steadily fallen. Today we eat about 241 eggs per capita annually, about 25 percent less than the 311 eggs we averaged in 1970.

The way we're eating eggs has changed, too. It used to be scrambled, fried, or over easy. Now we take the majority of our eggs in the form of cakes, cookies, and pastries. In fact, the amount of processed eggs we consume (in baked goods and frozen entrées) has more than doubled since 1960. How many eggs can we eat? The American Heart Association limits intake to three to four egg yolks a week and limits dietary cholesterol intake to 300 milligrams per day. If you are in good health and have no family history of heart disease or high cholesterol, experts say you can enjoy eggs on a regular basis in moderation.

Egg safety in numbers

Food safety has always been a concern when it comes to handling eggs. In the past, most of this was related to contaminated, dirty, or mishandled eggs. But recently, a new strain of bacteria called *Salmonella enteritis* has appeared. This bacteria, which is believed to be passed from the ovaries of infected hens directly inside the egg, can infect the inside of perfect-looking eggs that have been properly handled.

Symptoms of salmonella include diarrhea, chills, fever, upset stomach, and headache. Though it's not as dangerous as some other kinds of food poisoning, it can be life-threatening for vulnerable groups—the very young, the elderly, pregnant women. For most healthy people, however, the risk of getting sick from salmonella-infected eggs is pretty small. The Centers for Disease Control in Atlanta estimates that in the Northeast, only about one in 10,000 eggs are internally contaminated. In other parts of the country this number is even lower.

Still, it was because of the risk of salmonella that many restaurants stopped preparing classic Caesar salad or Hollandaise sauce, both of which contain raw eggs.

How to protect yourself from salmonella

- Avoid eating raw or undercooked eggs (including those in raw cookie dough or homemade mayonnaise).
- Cook eggs until well-done.
- Always keep eggs refrigerated.
- Discard cracked or dirty eggs.
- Promptly refrigerate unused or leftover foods containing cooked eggs.

Egg Substitutes

There are dozens of egg substitutes on the market today. Some are fat-free, made primarily from pure egg whites, while others have vegetable fat like corn oil added to the whites—giving them nearly the same fat content and taste as regular eggs without the cholesterol. Still other egg substitutes are vegetarian and contain no egg products at all. Choose an egg substitute based on how you will use it. For instance, if you are going to make an omelette, opt for an egg substitute with some color added and some fat to make it more palatable and visually appealing. On the other hand, if you are using eggs for baking, often you can skip the color and the fat without detracting much from the final product.

fats

In olden days, fat was a luxury to be savored and enjoyed. Today, we get more than our share of the nutrient in almost everything, from cakes and cookies to pizza and vegetable sauces. It is so prevalent in our food supply (about 34 percent of our calories come from fat) that it has become public enemy number one, responsible not only for our increasing weight gain but for a number of serious illnesses as well—heart disease, cancer, stroke.

Still, fat does have some redeeming virtues. In fact, we could not survive without it. Fat is required for us to absorb vitamins A, D, E, and K. It is also essential in the production of several hormones and other compounds (vitamin D and bile acids) needed by the body. Aside from providing us with a way to store extra energy for later use, fat insulates the body, thereby helping to regulate temperature, and cushions and protects our vital organs.

Fat facts

Fats can be divided into three categories: phospholipids, sterols, and triglycerides.

Phospholipids: Also known as lecithin, phospholipids are found in foods in relatively small amounts. Eggs are the best source of phospholipids, but liver, soybeans, wheat germ, and peanuts also supply some. Since one side of the molecule is water soluble and the other is fat soluble, phospholipids are considered emulsifying agents and are used in a number of processed products like mayonnaise and salad dressings. In the body, they are important constituents of the cell wall.

Sterols: Of all the sterols, cholesterol, which is only found in animal products—milk fat, meat fat, and butter—is the most important and most well known. An essential part of the cell structure, it is also involved in the synthesis of sex hormones, vitamin D, and bile acids. (See **Cholesterol,** page 289, for more details.) Nevertheless, too much cholesterol circulating in the blood can create blockages in arteries causing heart attacks or strokes.

Plant oils also contain some sterols. Most of these are believed to be beneficial, but research is still ongoing to find out exactly what they do and how they work.

Triglycerides: These are by far the most common type of fat. Ninety-five percent of the fats we eat are in this form. Chemically, a triglyceride is a glycerol molecule attached to three chains of fatty acids. Once inside the body, these fats circulate in the bloodstream by way of a lipid (the technical term for fat) carrier, called a chylomicron.

Other nutrients, aside from fat consumption, can also affect triglyceride levels. The liver converts excess carbohydrates (especially the simple ones like sugar, honey, and syrups) and alcohol into triglycerides, too. These other triglycerides are then carried through the bloodstream via very low density lipoproteins (VLDLs). So if you overdo the carbs, you can increase the amount of triglycerides circulating in your blood, thereby adding to your body's store of fat.

Tapping into Your Triglyceride Number

Both the American Heart Association and the National Heart, Lung and Blood Institute's National Cholesterol Education Program use these numbers as guidelines for triglyceride levels.

Blood Triglyceride Levels
milligrams per deciliter (mg/dl)

200 or less	Normal
200 to 400	Borderline high
over 400*	High

For those people who lack the enzyme to break down triglycerides, this number can reach 1,000 or more. Surprisingly, though, these people have a lower risk of heart disease than people in the 200–700 range. Researchers think it's because the higher levels of triglycerides build bigger compounds that can't penetrate the blood vessel walls, so they don't even have the opportunity to stick to arteries. However, kidney disease, alcoholism, and diabetes may be associated with such high triglyceride levels.

Triglycerides and your health

In the past, doctors paid little attention to triglyceride levels, focusing on blood cholesterol instead. Today, however, new research shows that elevated triglyceride levels may be more harmful than once thought. In fact, it may be an independent risk factor for coronary heart disease.

A study out of the University of Maryland Medical Center in Baltimore looked at over four hundred middle-aged and older adults who were already at risk for heart disease. Those with trigylceride levels above 100 had more than twice the risk of suffering and/or dying from a heart attack as those with levels below 100.

What makes triglycerides so dangerous? Scientists believe triglyceride levels of 190 or more increase "blood viscosity," thickening the blood and making it harder to transport oxygen and vital nutrients to the muscles. Often high triglycerides are coupled with low levels of high-density lipoproteins (HDLs—the "good" cholesterol responsible for removing fat from the arteries) and small, dense low-density lipoproteins. LDLs carry cholesterol to the arteries, and on their way they attach to cell walls, blocking blood flow and narrowing passageways. LDLs are more likely to be oxidized and stick to the artery walls, making you more prone to heart disease and high blood pressure.

What you can do

Since triglyceride levels are quickly elevated by what you've just eaten, it's required that you fast for twelve hours before testing. If, after several tests, triglyceride numbers still come out high, then perhaps you should consider reevaluating your diet and lifestyle. Here are a few measures you can take to drop triglyceride levels.

Lose weight if you are overweight: Obese people generally have high triglyceride levels that can be lowered simply by cutting back on fats and getting regular exercise.

Restrict or limit simple carbohydrates: This means cutting out all the sugar, corn syrup, honey, and molasses prevalent in products like cookies, candy, cakes, and ice cream. Simple carbohydrate sugars are readily converted to triglycerides by the liver. Some nutritionists even believe the proliferation of fat-free, high-sugar foods is partly responsible for many of the elevated triglyceride levels we are seeing today.

Avoid alcohol: Alcohol stimulates triglyceride production.

Eat more fatty fish: Omega-3 fatty acids found in fatty fish like tuna and salmon have been know to stabilize and even cut triglyceride levels.

The skinny on fatty acids

The three fatty-acid chains attached to the triglyceride molecule give the fat its characteristics, determining whether it's solid or liquid at room temperature. These fatty acids can be saturated, monounsaturated, or polyunsaturated and long, short, or medium in length.

If every carbon molecule is bonded to a hydrogen molecule, the fat is said to be saturated. If a carbon molecule does not have a hydrogen molecule attached, it is said to be monounsaturated. A fatty-acid chain with two or more points of unsaturation (or a carbon molecule bonded to a neighboring carbon molecule rather than a hydrogen molecule) is said to be polyunsaturated.

Virtually all triglycerides are mixed, meaning they contain more than one type of fatty acid (both saturated and unsaturated). The dominant fatty acid present, however, is what determines the fat's properties. It is also the basis for how we classify fats. So, we would refer to a fat as saturated even if it has polyunsaturated and monounsaturated components—provided the majority of its fatty acids were saturated.

In the body, broken-down triglycerides release fatty acids into the bloodstream. These free fatty acids can be taken up by the liver and used to form cholesterol and other compounds or they can be stored as fat. That's why too much of certain fatty acids can significantly increase cholesterol levels and have detrimental effects on your health.

Saturated fats

Fats that contain a large portion of saturated fatty acids are called saturated fats. Saturated fats are always solid at room temperature. The degree of saturation determines the texture: The harder the fat, the more saturated it is and the longer it will take to melt at high temperatures.

Sources of saturated fat

Saturated fats are prevalent in animal fats—meat, poultry, fish, and dairy. Two vegetable oils are saturated: coconut and palm; both resemble lard in their pure form, but few Americans ever see this because most of the coconut and palm oils we consume are in processed foods. Typically high in saturated fat are cream cheese, bacon, butter, whole milk, chicken skin, shortening, coconut products, and sour cream.

When it comes to degree of saturation, meat, poultry, and fish tend to be more saturated fats (and have longer chains) than dairy products.

The bad news about saturated fats

From a health standpoint, saturated fats are about the worst kind of fat you can eat. High intakes correlate with high rates of coronary heart disease because saturated fats clog arteries by raising blood cholesterol levels. In fact, of all fats, saturated fats raise blood cholesterol levels the most—even more than cholesterol itself.

There are other risks, too. Scientists have linked diets with high levels of saturated fat to an increased risk for colon, prostate, and possibly breast cancer. Furthermore, high intakes are usually associated with obesity, which itself is a risk factor in a number of chronic illnesses (see **Obesity and Weight Gain,** page 355).

Stearic acid

Researchers have been studying stearic acid, a saturated fat found in chocolate and beef, for over thirty years. What they found is that unlike any other saturated fat, stearic acid has little effect on blood cholesterol levels. Although this is good news, it does not give license to indulge in these foods; both chocolate and beef still contain other saturated fatty acids that raise cholesterol levels in the body.

Recommended intakes

Since saturated fats have such a negative impact on health, recommended intakes are low. Less than 10 percent of your total calories should come from saturated fats. To achieve this ratio, most Americans should:

- limit meat consumption to 2 or 3 ounces per meal
- eat some vegetarian meals on a regular basis

- opt for low-fat dairy products like skim milk and low-fat cheese
- pass up the butter for oil

Monounsaturated fats

Monounsaturated fats have one double-carbon bond (not attached to a hydrogen molecule). The carbon chains tend to be shorter than in saturated fats and most are a liquid or oil at room temperature.

Where they're found

Monounsaturated fats are found in a diverse array of plant foods, like avocados, olives, and nuts. Almonds, peanuts, hazelnuts, and sesame seeds are especially rich. There are also a number of monounsaturated oils available. Peanut, olive, and canola are the most popular.

The good news about monounsaturated fats

Among the fats, monounsaturated are the healthiest. Since they are neutral when it comes to raising blood cholesterol levels, they can effectively lower total and LDL (bad) cholesterol when used as a replacement for saturated fats. Monounsaturated fats also appear to raise HDLs, or good cholesterol, thereby protecting against heart disease. Some studies have shown that even high intakes of monounsaturated fats (over 25 percent of daily calories) can still reduce total cholesterol and the risk of heart disease.

On another front, monounsaturated fats may help diabetics better manage blood sugar levels. For this reason, a moderate increase in monounsaturated fat intake is recommended for certain types of diabetics.

Recommended intakes

Because of their purported health benefits, monounsaturated fats have the most lenient recommendations: 10 to 15 percent of total calories.

Polyunsaturated fats

Polyunsaturated fats have two or more points of unsaturation, or double-carbon bonds. These chains tend to be short or medium in length and, like monounsaturates, are liquid or oil at room temperature.

Two polyunsaturated fats are essential for the body and must be supplied by the diet, since they cannot be synthesized by the body like other fatty acids. Named for the position of their double-carbon bond, they are called omega-6 and omega-3 fatty acids. Sometimes you will also see them referred to by their technical names, linoleic acid and linolenic acid, respectively.

Where they're found

Walnuts, sunflower seeds, sesame seeds, safflower seeds, and corn oil are all considered high in polyunsaturated fats. The best sources of omega-3 fatty acids are fatty fish—tuna and salmon—or soybean oil and flaxseed oil. Some linolenic acid can also be found in canola oil. Omega-6 fatty acids are found in sunflower, safflower, and sesame seed oils.

How polyunsaturated fats help or hurt us

We can't live without the essential fatty acids—linoleic and linolenic acid. Some of the things they're vital for are brain function, vision, reducing inflammation, regulating blood pressure, and maintaining cell membrane structure. Luckily, we need only small amounts to per-

form these functions, so deficiencies are extremely rare.

When it comes to chronic illness, essential fatty acids also confer some health benefits. Studies show omega-3's found in fish oil have a protective effect against heart disease (see **Fish**, page 318, for more details) and scientists think omega-6's may do the same. Polyunsaturates, in general, reduce total cholesterol and LDLs (bad cholesterol) without affecting HDLs (good cholesterol).

Their role in cancer development, however, is still controversial. In the past, high levels of linoleic (omega-6 fatty acids) were shown to promote cancer in rats. Recently, however, preliminary evidence has found that omega-3's, or fish oils, actually prevent the formation of certain cancers.

Recommended intakes

Because of the cancer connection and because there are few long-term studies on the effects of high levels of polyunsaturates in the diet, the recommended intakes have stayed relatively stable. Nutritionists advise that no more than 10 percent of total caloric intake should come from this type of fat.

The truth about trans fatty acids

Hoping to stave off heart disease, many people switched from saturated fats like butter and lard to unsaturated fats like margarine and vegetable shortening. Little did they know that these foods can be just as dangerous as saturated fats thanks to trans fatty acids, man-made compounds not naturally found in any foods.

What are trans fatty acids? Basically, they are polyunsaturated oils bombarded with hydrogens. The hydrogens bond to the free carbon molecules, causing them to become saturated. The result is a solid or partially solid "hydrogenated" vegetable oil or shortening, such as margarine. Food companies use trans fatty acids to make fried foods crisp and cakes, cookies, and pastries stay fresher longer.

Although trans fatty acids have been around for decades, it wasn't until the 1980s that researchers began to suspect their connection to heart disease. By the early 1990s, several well-controlled studies had shown that trans fatty acids act like saturated fat when it comes to raising cholesterol levels, making them a major risk factor for coronary heart disease. Recent research from the Nurses' Health Study, a fourteen-year study from the Harvard School of Public Health and Brigham and Women's Hospital, found trans fatty acids may be even more harmful than saturated fats when it comes to raising your risk of heart disease. The study showed reducing trans fatty acids can potentially cut your risk of developing coronary heart disease by over 50 percent. On another front, scientists think high trans fatty acid intake may also be linked to an increased risk for breast cancer.

The problem is that trans fats are difficult to spot. Current nutrition labeling regulations do not require this fat to be listed on the label, and few companies voluntarily do it. The only way to tell how much trans fatty acid is in a food is to add up all the fatty acids (saturated fats, monounsaturated fats, and polyunsaturated fats) and then subtract the sum from the total number. The remaining fatty acid yield is trans fatty acid.

Luckily, the amount of trans fatty acids we consume is still small—only 5 to 10 percent of our total dietary fat. In fact, we consume far more saturated fat than trans fatty acids. For this reason, public health experts still emphasize reducing total fat and saturated fat, rather than concentrating on trans fatty acids.

What you can do to cut fat

So, does this mean you should switch from margarine back to butter? No way! Even though margarine has more trans fatty acids, butter is still much higher in artery-clogging saturated fat. But stay away from hard stick margarine; softer formulations in a tub or squeeze bottle have less trans. To help clear up the controversy surrounding butter and margarine, the American Heart Association has released new guidelines recommending soft margarines over stick. Another option is to avoid margarine altogether and use olive oil instead.

If you are in doubt as to whether a food is high in trans fatty acids, just remember to always choose the food with *less fat,* whether saturated or trans. Here are a few other tips to get you started.

- Beware of foods labeled "cholesterol-free," "low cholesterol," "low in saturated fats," or "made with vegetable oil." They may still contain trans fatty acids.
- Stay away from foods that list "partially hydrogenated fats" in their ingredients.
- Avoid deep-fried foods.
- Limit processed foods like chips, cookies, cake, and pastries.

Hidden Fats

Pure fats like oil and butter are easy to spot, especially for people consciously watching their fat intake. Hidden fats, on the other hand, are not so easy to recognize. Most of the hidden fat we eat comes from processed foods like cookies, cakes, doughnuts, and pastries, but meats (hot dogs, deli meats, sausage, etc.), cheese, and dairy foods also contain their share.

The biggest problem arises when fat is found lurking in foods not typically associated with being high in fat.

Some often forgotten foods containing hidden fats include:
• Vegetable butter sauces and creamy pasta sauces
• Pesto sauce
• Frozen dinners
• Muffins
• Crackers
• Granola-type cereals
• Deli meats

Reading labels is the best way to find out if a food contains hidden fats. Most times these fats are listed on the label as an ingredient, such as hydrogenated shortening or vegetable oil.

fat substitutes

Ever since fat has been ousted from the American table, food manufacturers have been cooking up ways for people to have the taste and feel of fat without the calories. Fat replacers reduce the fat and calorie levels of a food while still maintaining a desirable taste and consistency. They're most popular in salad dressings, condiments, and sauces, but they also have a big following in margarines, cheese, and frozen desserts.

Because of better technology, these reduced-fat or fat-free products have greatly improved in quality over the years, particularly in the dairy and frozen-food sections in foods like ice cream, sour cream, and butter. Today, they offer consumers a way to enjoy a healthful diet without giving up their favorite foods.

Fat replacement ingredients

Fat replacers can be made from carbohydrates, protein, or synthetic (fatlike) substances:

Carbohydrate-based fat substitutes
These have actually been around since the 1960s. Originally used as emulsifiers, stabilizers, and thickeners, starches and gums like carrageenan, polydextrose, and modified food starch are now used to reduce the fat in a variety of foods. They provide anywhere from 0 to 4 calories per gram and are used in salad dressings, dairy products, processed meats, baked goods, and frozen desserts.

Protein-based substitutes
Protein-based fat replacers are made from whey protein, milk, or egg white. When broken down into tiny particles, these molecules give a creamy feel to food. Known by the brand names Simplesse and Trailblazer, these fat substitutes are best used in frozen dessert–type products but can also be found in reduced-fat versions of butter, cheese, soups, mayonnaise, salad dressings, sour cream, yogurt, margarine, and sauces. They provide 1 to 4 calories per gram depending on their water content. Although both protein- and carbohydrate-based fat replacers can be heated, they cannot withstand the high heat of deep-frying.

Fat-based fat substitutes
Fat-based substitutes mimic the molecular shape of fat but provide fewer calories—anywhere from 0 to 5 calories per gram. Olestra is probably the most popular fat-based substitute. It is a man-made compound that is not absorbed by the body, so it provides zero calories—yet it looks, feels, and tastes like a cooking oil. And like oil, Olestra can be exposed to high temperatures, so it can be used for frying. Other fat-based ingredients are being used in chocolate, cocoa butter, margarine, spreads, sour cream, and cheese.

Although the FDA has approved Olestra for use, there has been some concern over its safety. Studies show Olestra inhibits the absorption of some vitamins and nutrients, including some of the fat-soluble vitamins. And in some people it can cause gastrointestinal problems. Still, many people feel these are minor drawbacks compared to the benefits of enjoying traditionally high-fat foods without the fat.

Do fat substitutes reduce weight?

No one really knows whether products like Olestra will help overweight people lose weight or make positive dietary changes. Some studies show people who eat reduced-fat or fat-free foods compensate for the loss of fat calories by eating more—thereby negating any positive effects of the low-fat food. Yet other studies point to the fact that reduced-fat or fat-free foods improve palatability of and compliance with low-fat diets. As with any food, reduced-fat or fat-free foods containing fat replacers should be used prudently—eaten in moderation and as part of a healthy, well-balanced diet.

fiber

Fiber is what gives plants their sturdy structure. Tough, woody, and chewy, fiber is a type of carbohydrate, a polysaccharide that humans cannot digest. Thus, it passes through the body relatively unchanged (a little is broken down by bacteria in the lower intestine) and supplies no calories. Yet fiber provides a number of benefits essential to our well-being. Primarily, fiber aids in digestion and absorption of nutrients, and in doing so, can prevent or treat a variety of common ailments from cancer to gastrointestinal distress.

Forms of fiber

There are basically two types of fiber. Soluble fiber, which includes pectin and gums, forms a gel-like substance in water. The highest concentrations of soluble fiber are found in fruit, oats, oat bran, barley, and legumes.

Insoluble fiber includes cellulose, hemicellulose, and lignins and is predominately found in vegetables, seeds, whole-grain breads, and cereals. It does not dissolve in water.

In the past, soluble fiber has received the most attention as a panacea for health, but lately insoluble fiber has also been showing promise. The goal is to eat more fiber, overall—no matter the type.

What fiber can do for you

Since it's found in fruits, vegetables, and legumes—foods that provide a wealth of other worthwhile components—fiber has many positive attributes. What we don't know is how much of a beneficial effect it has on certain diseases like cancer. To be sure, fiber is not a cure-all and too much can cause bloating, gas pain, and other problems, but these symptoms are minor compared to fiber's potential advantages.

Keeps the gastrointestinal track healthy: Eating high-fiber foods is the best way to prevent and treat constipation, and it reduces your chances of developing hemorrhoids. How does it do this? Fiber, especially the insoluble kind, absorbs fluid like a sponge (up to fifteen times its weight). This softens stools and increases their bulk so they pass more easily.

By relieving pressure on the colon wall, fiber can also reduce your chances of developing diverticulosis, a condition where small pouches form in the wall. For those who already have diverticulosis (a common problem among the elderly) fiber is also the recommended treatment.

Reduces your risk of heart disease: *Soluble fiber* lowers cholesterol levels, reducing your chances of having a heart attack. These findings are backed by years of scientific evidence. Fiber increases the excretion of bile acids (a type of digestive acid made from cholesterol), altering cholesterol metabolism. To make more bile acids, the body pulls cholesterol from the bloodstream, ultimately lowering blood cholesterol concentrations. Keep in mind, however, that fiber only causes a modest drop in cholesterol levels. Furthermore, it seems to be most effective on elevated cholesterol levels. Basically this means the higher the cholesterol, the bigger the potential drop from fiber intake.

Insoluble fiber was thought to be neutral in all of this, but new data shows that this type of fiber can also have a protective effect against heart disease. Although scientists are still unsure why this is so, they do believe the effect is separate from lowering cholesterol.

Overall, including more high-fiber foods in the diet is a good idea for anyone concerned about heart disease and cholesterol levels, since high-fiber diets are lower in fat and calories (two important factors that automatically reduce your chances of having a heart attack).

Lowers incidence of cancer: Several studies suggest high-fiber diets may have a protective effect against certain cancers, such as colon and breast cancer. But the relationship is not clear because scientists don't know if it's really fiber or the other anticancer substances like phytochemicals and antioxidants also present in plants that do the job.

Of the two kinds of cancers, the evidence connecting colon cancer and fiber is the strongest. Experts believe fiber can decrease the risk for this disease three ways: by diluting carcinogenic (cancer-causing compounds) concentrations in the colon, by binding with carcinogens so they can be removed from the body, and by reducing the amount of time the colon is exposed to these compounds.

Fiber's role in preventing breast cancer is more controversial, but health organizations like the American Cancer Society continue to advocate eating a high-fiber diet to combat the disease.

Helps control diabetes: Because soluble fiber slows down nutrient digestion, it prevents blood glucose from being absorbed too fast after a meal, and therefore makes blood sugar levels in diabetics easier to control. In addition, high-fiber foods tend to be low in calories and low in fat, two advantages that are particularly important for this group.

Aids in losing weight: High-fiber foods are a fundamental part of any weight-loss plan. Not only do they replace high-calorie, high-fat, sugary foods, but high-fiber foods also fill you up faster.

Are we eating enough fiber?

Unfortunately, many Americans fall short when it comes to eating their fiber. Actual intakes hover around 10 to 15 grams per day, well below the 20 to 35 grams health organizations like the National Cancer Institute recommend for optimum health. But experts are cautious about advising people to suddenly increase their fiber intake. Too much too soon can cause gas problems and bloating. Furthermore, if adequate fluids are not taken, fiber, especially the insoluble kind, can clog up your intestines, resulting in constipation. To avoid this complication, most people need only add two or three 8-ounce glasses of water or juice a day. (Remember, your overall goal is about 64 ounces or eight cups of fluid daily.)

How to increase fiber in your diet

The best way to increase your fiber intake is to start eating more fruits, vegetables, legumes, and whole grains. Here are a few hints to get you started:

- Switch to whole-grain bread—whole wheat, rye, oat bran
- Try to eat beans or legumes at least once a week or more. One cup of cooked beans supplies anywhere from 8 to 14 grams of fiber.
- Choose fresh or dried fruit as an afternoon snack.
- Start your day with a whole-grain cereal that contains at least 5 grams of fiber per serving.
- Eat dark-green, leafy, and deep-yellow or orange vegetables like spinach, kale, or carrots at least once a week.
- Eat microwaved or steamed vegetables crisp to preserve as much fiber and nutrients as possible.

fish

Although consumption rates have held steady at around 15 pounds per capita for the last ten years, America's taste for seafood has changed. Today, there are over three hundred commercially available species of fish and seafood on the market and many of them—tilapia, skate, catfish, carp—have only recently gone mainstream. Still, canned tuna is America's favorite fish. Shrimp is the top pick when it comes to fresh or frozen seafood, followed by Alaskan pollock (what surimi is made from) and salmon.

Nutritionally, the media has been touting the benefits of seafood for over a decade, and with good reason. No other protein food offers such a wealth of health-promoting substances as seafood does. Here's why fish is such a good catch:

High in protein

Seafood is a high-quality protein containing all eight essential amino acids (the building blocks of protein). And, unlike animal protein, fish protein is easily digested. This is because genetically, fish has very little hard-to-digest connective tissue (connective tissue decreases tenderness and gives meat that "chewy" quality). Without connective tissue, fish has a delicate, tender structure that flakes easily with a fork when cooked.

Low in calories

Generally low in calories, some species of fish—shrimp, lobster, cod, flounder, sole—contain less than 100 calories per 3-ounce cooked portion. Even fattier fish—salmon, mackerel, herring—rack up only about 200 calories or less per 3-ounce serving.

Low in fat

Fish is considered a low-fat food because the majority of both fish and shellfish have less than 5 grams of total fat per $3\frac{1}{2}$-ounce serving. Even the so-called fatty fish—salmon, tuna, trout—contain less than 10 fat grams per serving. Only two kinds of fish, king salmon and Atlantic mackerel, have more than 10 grams of fat per 3-ounce serving. And even they aren't terribly high, reaching no more than 15 grams of fat. For this reason the American Heart Association recommends eating fish instead of high-fat, protein-rich foods like meat.

As a rule, shellfish tends to be leaner than finfish and color is a good indicator of fat content, particularly among finfish. Dark-colored fish like tuna and salmon are fattier than light- or white-colored fish like sole and cod.

Type of fat is also important, and fish scores high marks in this area, too. Low in saturated fat, the predominant fat found in fish is polyunsaturated. This particular kind of polyunsaturated fat is called omega-3 fatty acid.

The shellfish cholesterol myth

Although shellfish has a reputation for being high in cholesterol, it isn't. In fact, most shellfish contains less than 100 milligrams of cholesterol per 3-ounce serving, an amount comparable to (and sometimes less than) many cuts of red meat. Three ounces of Alaskan king crab contains just 45 milligrams of cholesterol, and 3 ounces of lobster only 61 milligrams. Even shrimp weighs in at only 166 milligrams of cholesterol for a 3-ounce portion, allowing it to be occasionally included on low-cholesterol diets.

Low in sodium

Fish is naturally low in sodium, with most 3-ounce servings coming in under 100 milligrams of sodium. Saltwater finfish tend to be higher in sodium than freshwater varieties, but the numbers for both are still relatively low. Watch out for shellfish, though. It has higher sodium levels than many finfish and some species like lobster and blue crab can have over 300 milligrams of sodium per serving. The most sodium is found in processed products like surimi or fish frozen in brine. Alaskan king crab legs, notorious for their salty flavor, contain over 900 milligrams of sodium per serving.

Vitamins and minerals

Like other protein food, fish supplies a reasonable amount of B vitamins. Some fatty fish like mackerel and herring are also a good source of vitamin D, and if you eat the soft bones found in canned salmon or sardines you'll get a good dose of calcium. Clams and oysters are considered iron rich, providing up to 60 percent of the required daily value for iron. They also provide trace minerals like zinc, chromium, magnesium, iodine, and copper.

The omega-3 advantage

More and more research shows that omega-3 fatty acids reduce your risk of heart attack (even in people who have already had one), stroke, high blood pressure, and certain types of cancer. It can also mitigate the effects of rheumatoid arthritis, bronchial asthma, migraine headaches, psoriasis, and possibly depression. Here are specific examples of how omega-3 fatty acids can keep you healthy:

Heart disease: There are two types of omega-3 fatty acids that have potentially powerful health-protecting properties: eicosapentaenoic acid (EPA) and docosahexaenoic acid (DHA). Both are found in fish but play very different roles in the body.

EPA thins the blood, making it less likely to form clots that can stick to plaque and lead to heart attacks or strokes. DHA helps stabilize the heart muscle, preventing irregular heart rhythms, or arrhythmias. Several studies have shown that people who eat fish on a regular basis tend to have lower rates of heart disease. The Chicago Western Electric Study found men who ate about 8 ounces of fish a week cut their risk of dying from a heart attack in half. Other studies show a steady supply of omega-3's can keep arteries clear after a heart attack and subsequent angioplasty.

Strokes: Large doses of omega-3's in the form of fish-oil supplements slow blood clotting and lower blood pressure, reducing the risk for certain kinds of strokes. But supplements can put some people at risk for bleeding-type strokes, especially if combined with other substances that thin the blood—aspirin or vitamin E.

For this reason, experts advise seeking a doctor's advice before taking any fish-oil supplements.

Rheumatoid arthritis: In more than a dozen studies, omega-3 fatty acids have been shown to lessen morning stiffness and the discomfort of tender and swollen joints. Scientists think omega-3's somehow work to suppress or block the immune system from attacking the joints (a symptom of arthritis).

Fishing for omega-3's

The richest source for omega-3 is fish, particularly fatty fish, like salmon, tuna, mackerel, and rainbow trout. Yet even lean fish, when eaten regularly, offers a wealth of benefits.

Some omega-3's are in plant foods—green, leafy vegetables, nuts, and some oils like canola and soybean oil—but their availability is limited. In these foods, the body must convert another omega-3 fatty acid to DHA and EPA, a process that's not very efficient. Consequently, nutritionists recommend eating several 3-ounce portions of fish a week.

There has been some concern about toxins such as mercury, PCB's, and other pollutants contaminating fish. If they are present, these toxins are usually concentrated in the fatty part of the fish. But careful monitoring of commercial fishing by the seafood industry, along with an increase in farm-raised fish, has significantly reduced the risk of getting exposed to toxins in fish.

Check the Label, or Sorry, Charlie!

Most people assume water-packed tuna is always better than oil-packed tuna, but this is not necessarily so. Sometimes tuna packed in water can have more fat calories than tuna packed in oil. How can this be? It all depends on the tuna. Normally, most companies will use low-fat white tuna for both water-packed and oil-packed cans. But when demand exceeds supply, some manufacturers may resort to high-fat tuna (which lives at a lower depth and temperature than low-fat tuna). Since high-fat tuna packed in water can contain more fat than its oil-packed counterpart, it's important to read the label before buying.

food additives

In the broadest sense of the word, a food additive is any substance added to a food either directly or indirectly as a result of production, packaging, processing, and treatment. Over 150 pounds of additives are consumed by Americans each year and over 90 percent of these are in the form of salt, sugar, corn syrup, and dextrose.

The Food and Drug Administration is responsible for safeguarding the additives put in our food and about a hundred new petitions for food and color additives are submitted for approval each year. Only after a thorough evaluation and extensive safety testing (sometimes taking years) does an additive receive the green light. Sometimes a substance, because of its prior use or background, is classified as "generally recognized as safe" (GRAS). Items listed as GRAS include salt, sugar, and spices.

What additives do

Despite their negative perception, food additives do more good than harm, enabling us to enjoy a variety of safe, wholesome, palatable foods all year round. Food additives perform the following functions:

- Maintain product consistency. Usually in the form of stabilizers, emulsifiers, and thickening agents, these additives ensure a consistent, uniform, high-quality product.

- Improve or maintain nutritional value. Vitamins and minerals are considered additives when they are used to enrich or fortify foods such as cereal, flour, milk, and margarine.
- Maintain palatability and wholesomeness. Many food additives act as preservatives, retarding spoilage and rancidity.
- Provide leavening or control acidity and alkalinity. Leavening agents help cakes, cookies, breads, and other goods rise during baking.
- Enhance flavor and color. Spices and other natural and synthetic flavors and colors give foods the look and taste we expect them to have.

Common and controversial additives

Not all food additives are necessary nor are all of them completely harmless. Below are some common and some controversial additives, followed by information on what they do, where they're found, and whether they pose any risk to our health.

Acetic acid, ascorbic acid, and citric acid

These three additives add tartness and flavor as well as maintain quality during storage by acting as preservatives. They are all considered safe.

Acetic acid: Most familiar to us as the main ingredient in vinegar, acetic acid is found in ketchup, mayonnaise, pickles, and mustard.

Ascorbic acid: The technical name for vitamin C, it is added to food not only to improve nutritional value but because its antioxidant properties preserve and increase shelf life. Sodium ascorbate is another form of the vitamin (vitamin C with the addition of salt) and is often used along with BHT and BHA in processed meats.

Citric acid: This is produced by the fermentation of sugar and is naturally found in such citrus fruits as lemons and limes. In addition to acting as a preservative, citric acid prevents discoloration in fresh and frozen fruits.

BHA and BHT

Butylated hydroxyanisole (BHA) and butylated hydroxytoluene (BHT) are two synthetic substances that are used to prevent rancidity and protect flavors in high-fat foods and oils.

In the early eighties, the safety of BHA was questioned when research linked high levels to tumors in rats. After an in-depth investigation, however, the FDA cleared BHA of any charges, finding that at the levels it is consumed, it posed no risk of cancer to humans. In fact, other, later findings suggest BHA and BHT may even prevent cancer.

Nevertheless, over the years, manufacturers have slowly decreased the amount of BHA and BHT added to foods. Some activist groups still recommend these two substances be avoided altogether. BHA and BHT remain on the GRAS list.

Gums

Thirteen types of gums are commonly used in food processing. While guar gum, pectin, xanthan, gum arabic, and carrageenan come from plants, many others are synthetic. Generally, gums function to improve consistency and texture by acting as a thickener, but lately, many gums have been used as fat substitutes in fat-free or low-fat foods. In either case, they are considered safe, and as a fat replacer they may even help people struggling on a low-fat or low-cholesterol diet.

Monoglycerides and diglycerides

Derived from fats, these two compounds often act as emulsifiers. In baked goods they add texture while in processed foods—peanut butter, ice cream, margarine—they keep ingredients from separating. They are also often added to hydrogenated shortenings. Since they are used in such small amounts, they provide a negligible amount of fat calories and are considered safe.

Monosodium glutamate (MSG)

MSG is a flavor enhancer that has been used in Asian cooking for thousands of years. Originally made from seaweed, it is now produced by fermenting sugar, sugar beets, sugar cane, or molasses. Similar in appearance to salt or sugar, MSG alone has no distinct taste, but combined with meat or poultry it greatly increases their meatlike flavor.

Although MSG is a GRAS substance, the FDA has been reviewing it for the past thirty years mostly because a small segment of the population is thought to be "MSG sensitive." In these people, ingesting MSG can result in a variety of symptoms from nausea and headache to tingling sensations in the neck and forearms to chest pain. Because MSG is found in soy foods and tends to be used heavily in Chinese food, this collective effect was initially referred to as "Chinese restaurant syndrome."

Today, the FDA requires all foods that contain MSG to list the additive on the label. (In addition to its pure form, MSG can also be found in hydrolyzed vegetable protein, or HVP.) Restaurant foods, however, are not covered by this regulation, though many have decreased usage and some voluntarily provide MSG information on request. Although MSG-sensitive individuals should avoid this food additive, overall, the FDA considers MSG safe for the general population.

Sodium nitrite and sodium nitrate

Both of these salts have been used for centuries to preserve and cure meats. Today, they're likely to be used in such foods as hot dogs, bologna, and ham. In general, they keep meat a pink color, contribute a tangy flavor, and inhibit the growth of the harmful bacteria that causes botulism.

Nitrites can be converted to cancer-causing nitrosamines, especially in foods cooked at high temperatures, such as bacon. Nitrates are potentially risky because they are easily converted to nitrites by the body and by the bacteria found in foods. Vitamin C prevents nitrosamines from forming and is frequently added to nitrite-containing foods by manufacturers. The USDA has set safe limits on the amount of nitrites permitted in foods.

Sulfites

Sulfur-based preservatives, or sulfites, stop light-colored fruits and vegetables—apples or potatoes—from turning brown, prevent bacterial growth and fermentation of foods like wine or dough, and are used to protect the quality of fresh shrimp and lobster. In sulfite-sensitive people, a food containing this additive produces an allergic-type response. For asthmatics, the effects can be severe.

The FDA estimates that one out of every hundred people are sulfite-sensitive, but pinpointing a number is difficult since many cases go unreported and undiagnosed. Currently, sulfites are banned on all fresh fruits and vegetables that are to be eaten raw. They are still found in a number of cooked or processed foods like precut or peeled "fresh" potatoes, dried fruit, maraschino cherries, condiments, baked goods, shrimp, beer, wine, jam, and gravy. But sulfites must be listed on the labels of all packaged and processed foods that contain them.

A World of Color

Color additives can be either natural or man-made. Natural colors are derived from vegetables, minerals, and animals. For instance, annatto, the pigment that gives American or cheddar cheese its orange color, is from a plant, while caramel color is produced by heating sugars and other carbohydrates. Man-made colors or synthetic dyes are commonly used in our food supply.

For years scientists have suspected synthetic colors of causing cancer. Over the years, some additives, like Red No. 3, have been banned and many others are still being investigated.

Currently, Yellow No. 5 is being studied. It is the second most popular food dye (behind Red No. 40) and is used to color beverages, candy, ice cream, custards, and other foods. In some people it has been known to cause hives, headaches, and itching. All certified or man-made colors must be listed on the ingredient label.

fruit

Nutritionally, you just can't go wrong with fruit. It's packed with vitamins and minerals, low in calories, and high in fiber, plus it's naturally sweet and juicy. Fruit is high in a type of sugar called fructose, and also contains lots of water—on average about 85 percent.

As fruit ripens, starches are converted to sugars, acid decreases, and volatile compounds form. These are the things that give fruit its distinctive color, flavor, and aroma. Vitamin content also increases as fruit ripens.

Nutritional powerhouses

While each fruit tends to have its own nutritional identity—like oranges and vitamin C or bananas and potassium—there are still some common denominators among all fruits. In general, fruit is our chief source of vitamin A or beta-carotene, vitamin C, fiber, and potassium. Some fruits also supply minerals like iron, calcium, folic acid, and magnesium.

The fattiest fruit

Almost all fruits are low in calories and virtually fat-free—except for the avocado, which can derive anywhere from 70 to 90 percent of its calories from fat. Rich in vitamins A, B_6, and C, and potassium, avocados are also high in calories—ranging from 100 to 150 per 3-ounce serving. If you're watching your weight, choose a Florida-variety avocado rather than one grown in California. Despite their larger size, Florida avocados are lower in fat.

A banana a day?

Unfortunately, most Americans are not taking advantage of fruit's natural goodness. USDA food consumption surveys show fruit consumption rates are painfully low. On average, people eat only $1\frac{2}{3}$ servings of the 2 to 4 daily servings recommended on the Food Guide Pyramid. Furthermore, almost half of the survey respondents failed to consume even one fruit a day. Despite an increased awareness of the importance of fruits and vegetables, statistics show that over the last twenty years, consumption rates for these foods has been steadily dropping.

Why are so many people passing up fresh fruit? There are many reasons, but most people cite cost, preparation time, and spoilage. Buying fresh fruit is just too inconvenient.

To make eating fresh fruit easier, many supermarkets now offer fruit already cut and cleaned, though it may be more expensive. Other options for people who can't be bothered with fresh fruit are canned, frozen, and dried varieties. And there's always fruit juice. Of course, fresh fruit is better than fruit juice, but if the choices are fruit juice or no fruit at all, choose the juice. And don't be worried about losing out on any nutrients if you eat processed fruits instead of fresh. Some canned varieties have an even better nutritional profile than their fresh counterparts.

The best of the bunch

When it comes to type of fruit, our top picks at the grocery store are bananas, apples, oranges, melon, and grapes. Despite the many fruits available in the marketplace, most people tend to stick with the same four or five. Consequently, variety is what we should strive for. The Food Guide Pyramid recommends we eat citrus fruits, melons, and berries regularly. The National Cancer Institute is more specific. They suggest we eat at least one vitamin A–rich fruit or vegetable a day, one vitamin C–rich fruit or vegetable a day, and one high-fiber fruit or vegetable a day.

Apples: Although apples are not a nutritional standout compared to other fruits, they do provide a respectable amount of fiber, both soluble and insoluble. Consequently, they're a good choice for people having some gastrointestinal problems like constipation or diarrhea. Nutritionally, they provide some vitamin C, beta-carotene, and potassium. Because they're crisp and juicy, but don't stick to the teeth, they also help keep dental cavities at bay.

Bananas: Besides being a favorite among children, bananas are the number-one fruit for adults as well—and with good reason. They're a sweet, starchy fruit with a low water content and a high concentration of carbohydrates. Athletes like them because they provide energy (calories) and substantial amounts of potassium, a nutrient usually lost during heavy physical activity. In fact, bananas have more potassium than almost any other fruit.

Berries: Small and juicy, berries have a high sugar content despite their relatively low calorie level (berries range from 50 to 70 calories a cup). A good source of vitamin C, potassium, and fiber, they may also help fight against cancer. Research shows cranberries, raspberries, strawberries, and loganberries contain ellagic (a phytochemical that may help prevent certain cancers from developing).

Strawberries are by far the most popular berry around. They also provide the most vitamin C: one half cup of strawberries provides 70 percent of the RDA.

Citrus: Citrus fruits—oranges, grapefruits, lemons, limes—are well known for their vitamin C content. But they also contain fiber, potassium, and folic acid. The American Heart Association recently awarded Florida grapefruits and grapefruit juice the Heart Check certification to help promote it as a good food to include on a heart-healthy diet.

Melon: Watermelon and cantaloupe are the top fruits in this category. Both are high in vitamin A and cantaloupe also provides a good deal of potassium. Because of their high water content, melons are usually thought of as a refreshing summer fruit.

Exotic fruits: Available tropical or exotic fruits run the gamut from papayas and mangos to star fruit and kiwi. Over the last few years, consumption of this foreign produce has risen rapidly and in tandem with the growth in exotic fruit choices.

Like other fruits, tropical fruits are also a good source of vitamins A and C, fiber, and potassium. In fact, kiwi is the most nutrient-dense of all fruits with substantial amounts of vitamin C, fiber, potassium, and vitamin E, among other nutrients.

Dried vs. Fresh Fruit

For people on the go, dried fruits are a life-saver. They're quick, easy, convenient, and loaded with nutrients. Because they're so concentrated, a little goes a long way. A 4-ounce serving of dried apricots contains twice as much potassium and vitamin A and six times as much fiber and iron as the same size portion of fresh apricots.

Dried fruit are also higher in calories—dried apricots have six times more calories than fresh. Most dried fruits tend to be four or five times higher in calories. So keep an eye on portion size.

grains

Grains—rice, pasta, and cereals—should make up the bulk of our diets. Unfortunately, many Americans still don't reach the six to eleven daily servings recommended by nutritionists. And most of the grains we do eat are refined or processed in the form of bread or bread products. Refined grains lose much of their nutritious ingredients during processing.

What we really need is to increase our consumption of whole grains that are unrefined and minimally processed. Whole grains such as barley, bulgur, quinoa, rye, and amaranth are becoming more popular and can now be found in many health food and specialty stores as well as on many restaurant menus. These grains add a dose of vitamins, minerals, and much-needed fiber to the diet.

Grainology

True grains—wheat, rice, rye, oats, millet, corn, triticale, barley—are the small fruits or seeds of grass. Other grains—amaranth and quinoa—are botanically different but the kernels or seeds are still similar in composition. A kernel or single grain is composed of three parts.

The endosperm: This is the large, starchy part of the kernel. It accounts for over 80 percent of the grain's weight and contains most of the protein and carbohydrates as well as several B vitamins and some minerals.

The bran: This is the outer coating of the kernel, normally removed during processing. Almost all of a grain's entire dietary fiber is found in the bran, as well as a large portion of the grain's B vitamins like niacin and riboflavin. Bran is what gives whole-wheat flour its brown color.

The germ: This is the smallest part of the kernel (only 2 percent by weight). It is primarily made up of polyunsaturated fat that's rich in vitamin E, but it still contains a few B vitamins. Because it can go rancid, many manufacturers will remove the germ to increase the keeping quality of the flour.

Refined flour

Refined flours, such as white all-purpose flour, do not contain bran and germ. These are generally removed—along with most of the vitamins and minerals and all of the fiber—during the milling process. To offset nutrient losses, some companies enrich bread products with B vitamins (riboflavin, niacin, thiamin, and folic acid) and fortify them with iron, but this does not replace all the nutrients lost.

Health benefits of grains

Considered a complex carbohydrate, grain foods are virtually fat free and contain few calories. Since they are filling without being high in calories, they are often used as the cornerstone of weight-loss diets (see **Dieting,** page 299) and are an effective way to maintain and control weight. Whole grains have the extra benefit of being a high-fiber food.

Grains to go for

Rice is a staple for more than half of the world's population and wheat, often called the "staff of life," is next in line (it's been the main grain in the Western Hemisphere for thousands of years). Recently, however, Americans are discovering other grains, like couscous, quinoa, and bulgur. Although less familiar than wheat, corn, and rice, they have been dietary staples in other cultures for centuries. Here's a rundown of a few varieties.

Amaranth

A staple in the diet of the ancient Aztecs, amaranth dates back to 4,000 B.C. Technically, it is the fruit of a plant and not a true grain, but the tiny brown granules, similar in size to poppyseed, are treated and eaten as a grain food.

A nutritional powerhouse among this group, amaranth is an excellent source of high-quality protein, with more methionine and lysine (two amino acids) than other grains. Most notable is its high calcium and iron content. In addition, it contains substantial amounts of folacin, fiber, magnesium, and some A and E vitamins. Unlike other grains it also has some vitamin C.

Cooked, amaranth has a very distinct, earthy flavor. Since it contains no gluten (the protein that gives bread its structure), it must be combined with other grains to make baked products. Boiled, it has a porridgelike consistency that can be used in puddings or casseroles. Otherwise, it can be toasted and sprinkled over soups or salads as a garnish. One cup raw yields about 2⅔ cups cooked.

Barley

Most often used as a malt for beer, barley can also be eaten cooked as a grain. Like oats, it is an excellent source of soluble fiber and has been shown to have a cholesterol-lowering effect. Barley also supplies a generous amount of protein (one-half cup can provide about 10 grams).

Pearled barley is ivory-colored barley that has undergone a certain process to remove the outer husk and nutrient-dense bran layer. Though it is still a very good source of fiber, it is not as nutritious as hulled barley. Hulled barley has only the inedible husk removed, while the bran layer stays intact. Hulled barley also has more thiamin, iron, and trace minerals than pearl.

The flavor of barley is nutty and the texture is chewy. In cooking, it is commonly used to thicken soups. Hulled barley has a more pronounced taste and chewy texture and it takes longer to cook than pearled barley. One cup raw yields four cups cooked.

Bulgur

Made from wheat that has been steamed, dried, and cracked, bulgur is a popular food in the Middle East. Most people are familiar with it in the dish tabbouleh, but bulgur is also found in stews, soups, pilafs, and salads. It is available in three different grinds: coarse, medium, and fine.

Nutritionally, bulgur is fairly low in calories, high in fiber, and an excellent source of potassium. It has a nutty flavor and soft texture that makes it a good stand-in for rice. One cup raw yields four cups cooked.

Couscous

Traditionally found in North African cuisine, couscous is a cooked, dried pasta made from semolina (a type of hard durum wheat) that is formed into tiny granules that cooks up into a light, fluffy starch. Like pasta, couscous's primary nutritional advantage is as a low-calorie, fat-free, complex carbohydrate. It is not enriched and so contains fewer B vitamins and iron than some macaroni products. However, unrefined, whole-wheat couscous, which is higher in fiber, is now easy to come by in many markets.

Culinarily, couscous is extremely adaptable. It has a bland flavor, similar to pasta, that can go with just about any food, and it is not uncommon to see couscous as a breakfast cereal, sweet dessert, savory side dish, or robust main entrée. Today, there are a number of quick-cooking varieties on the market that only need to be rehydrated, but even regular couscous does not take long to prepare. One cup raw yields three cups cooked.

Quinoa

Cultivated in the Andes mountains of South America, quinoa was a major food source for the ancient Incas. It is sometimes called a super-grain because it is packed with protein and other vitamins and minerals. What makes it so unusual is that unlike other grains, quinoa contains all eight essential amino acids, making it an excellent source of protein. It also offers more in the way of iron, potassium, magnesium, and zinc and is a good source of several B vitamins.

Flavor-wise, quinoa cooks up light and fluffy with a delicate, nutty taste. Its tiny beadlike granules cook up in half the time it takes to cook rice. One cup raw yields four cups cooked.

Triticale

A result of hybridization, triticale is a cross between wheat and rye and so has the benefits of both. It is high in protein and a good source of the B vitamins, vitamin E, copper, iron, zinc, magnesium, and selenium.

Triticale has a nutty flavor richer than wheat but not as strong as rye. To reduce cooking time, the whole berries should be soaked overnight. One cup raw yields $2\frac{1}{2}$ cups cooked.

Cholesterol-Catching Rye

It's a well-known fact that large amounts of oat bran can reduce cholesterol, but now researchers have found another grain that can do the trick: rye. A recent study by scientists at the Harvard School of Public Health, the National Cancer Institute, and Finland's National Public Health Institute found regular servings of rye bread has a protective effect against heart disease.

Most of this effect is believed to be due to rye's high fiber content. Three slices of traditional rye bread supplies about 10 grams of fiber, about a third of the fiber recommendations put out by the National Cancer Institute. What's interesting is that most of the fiber found in rye is the insoluble kind. It was previously thought that only soluble fiber played a role in cholesterol metabolism. This study shows that all fiber—soluble and insoluble—can guard against heart disease.

herbs

Leaves, roots, seeds, and bark—made into teas, tinctures, or poultices—have been alleviating illness since the beginning of time. Early in this century, and only in Western culture, modern pharmaceuticals supplanted most of the herbal remedies of the past with synthetic drugs and isolated compounds, ultimately resulting in generations of Americans who prefer powdery pills over plants when it comes to treating sickness.

Lately, however, questions about drug safety and concern over potent side effects have driven many consumers back to their herbal origins and ancient natural remedies. In the last decade, this trend has helped to build a healthy $3.24 billion herbal industry.

But natural doesn't necessarily mean safe. Despite the fact that herbal remedies are thought to be milder than mainstream drugs, they can still be potent—in fact, some can be extremely toxic. Nonetheless, many are good medicine for minor ailments like upset stomach, insomnia, colds, and flu, even mild depression. In countries like Germany and China, where herbal remedies are part of the medical culture, herbs are also used to treat serious conditions like cancer and heart disease. But here in the United States, few medical practitioners are trained in their use, and we don't have tight manufacturing controls, so herbs should probably not be used to treat serious ailments.

A few facts about herbs

If you are interested in herbal remedies or would like to take herbal supplements there are some things you should know before starting:

- No industrywide standardization. Unlike the U.S. pharmacology industry, which requires drugs to undergo rigorous testing for safety, efficacy, and consistency, herbal remedies require no such regulations. Herbs do not have to prove safety or effectiveness.

- Plant variations affect herb potency. Herb potency varies not only by how a plant is processed or prepared but also by the plant itself. Differences in soil, growing, and harvesting conditions, as well as how long the herb sits on the shelf can affect the consistency of the dosage. This means that even though two supplements may look alike, one can be more potent than the other.

- Herbs are considered a dietary supplement. Under the 1994 Dietary Supplement Health and Education Act, manufacturers selling herbs can make limited claims about the structure or function of the herb as long as it does not imply the preparation prevents, alleviates, or cures a specific disease. Thus, an herbal claim cannot say it "protects against stroke," but it can claim it "improves circulation." These statements are purposely vague to avoid legal problems.

- Herbs can interact with other drugs. Since herbs contain potent ingredients, they can interact with over-the-counter or prescription drugs. Even something as innocent as aspirin can cause problems if taken with certain herbal supplements like garlic (which also thins the blood). For this reason, it is important to consult with your doctor before taking an herbal remedy.
- Many herbs should not be taken by pregnant or nursing women, or children. Herbs can be extremely potent, especially in smaller bodies.

The most popular herbs— and what they can do for you

Chamomile: A member of the daisy family, the chamomile flower contains an oil that may aid in digestion. It is also thought to have anti-inflammatory properties. Usually taken in tea form, it is not recommended for people with ragweed allergies or allergies to flowers in the daisy family.

Echinacea: Reported to boost immunity, particularly against upper-respiratory infections. Sold in an extract form, it is used to protect against colds and flu.

Feverfew: Used since biblical times, this herb is believed to diminish the frequency and the severity of migraine headaches. It is sold in commercial tablet form, and potency varies widely.

Garlic: Most likely the world's most popular herb, garlic can help lower cholesterol and thin the blood, thereby reducing risk of cardiovascular disease and stroke. It also appears to have anticarcinogenic and antibacterial properties. Pills should be coated to prevent breakdown in the stomach or you can eat about four or five cloves of raw garlic a day. But beware: It can cause heartburn and flatulence.

Ginger: This healing root is thought to aid in digestion and is effective against motion sickness. Ginger also helps the prevention and relief of nausea.

Ginkgo: An extract made from the leaves of the ginkgo tree, this herb appears to improve blood circulation by thinning out the blood. Because it increases blood flow to the brain, it appears to improve short-term memory and concentration problems in some people. It also acts as a powerful antioxidant.

Ginseng: Gensenosides are the active ingredient found in ginseng root. This herb is believed to enhance immunity and promote overall well-being. Some people also think it increases stamina and physical endurance as well as helping the body combat stress.

Milk Thistle: Native to Mediterranean Europe, the extract, made from the seeds of the milk thistle plant, is purported to help prevent liver disease, especially hepatitis and cirrhosis. It may also be used to treat jaundice.

Saw Palmetto: Saw palmetto is the fruit of a small palm that grows in Florida. It is believed to help men with benign prostate enlargement by improving urinary flow. Not effective as a tea.

Valerian: Widely used in Europe, valerian is a popular sleep aid that calms the nerves and acts as a mild tranquilizer. It is not habit forming, nor is it related to the drug Valium.

On the herbal horizon

Several herbs you may expect to see more of in the future:

St.-John's wort: Known as nature's Prozac, sales figures for St.-John's wort are booming. Extracts from the yellow flower of this plant are believed to relieve mild to moderately severe depression. At the same time, it has demonstrated none of the side effects experienced with common antidepressant drugs. Currently, researchers are testing the herb in clinical trials.

Bilberry: An antioxidant herb that strengthens capillaries and improves vision, especially night vision, bilberry is typically sold in highly concentrated, powdered extract capsules.

Hawthorne: Called a cardiovascular herb, hawthorne dilates blood vessels, decreases blood pressure, and helps heart function. Because of its action on the heart, it is best not to take it without a doctor's approval.

Grape-seed oil: Thought to be a strong antioxidant, it also helps circulation and has been used to minimize the appearance of varicose veins. One study has even shown grape-seed oil can raise HDL levels.

Herbal Teas

Ironically, herbal teas can come from any plant other than the tea plant. They can be brewed from the roots, flowers, berries, bark, peels, and/or seeds of the plant.

Although herbs are diluted in teas, herbal teas do have medicinal value. They also contain thousands of biologically active compounds, increasing the chances that at least one of these compounds can help or prevent a certain condition. Some herbs like echinacea, ginkgo leaf, saw palmetto, and milk thistle are worthless as teas, because their active constituents are not water soluble. With other herbs, the concentration needed for a purported beneficial effect is so high it can only be derived from an extract, pill, or capsule, not from a tea.

lactose

Often called milk sugar because it is naturally found only in milk, lactose is a disaccharide, or two-sugar chain, composed of glucose and galactose. Compared to other sugars, it ranks lowest on the scale of sweetness and so milk is most often characterized as bland rather than sweet-tasting.

Misconceptions about milk digestion

All of us are born with the ability to produce an enzyme called lactase. Lactase breaks down lactose and allows us to digest milk sugar in the small intestine. As some people age, they stop producing lactase, resulting in a condition mistakenly known as "lactose intolerance." Lactose intolerance is actually the inability to digest milk sugar and can lead to a variety of symptoms, including gas, bloating, diarrhea, and stomach cramps.

Incidence of lactose intolerance is highest in Asian and African-American populations. Some manufacturers of lactose-related products suggest that nearly 50 million Americans suffer from this problem and cannot drink milk or eat any dairy products. The real number is merely a fraction of this estimate.

A recent study in the *American Journal of Clinical Nutrition* showed that one in three people who think they are lactose intolerant actually aren't. And even the people who are considered lactose intolerant may be able to handle two cups of milk a day without any ill effects.

Intolerance or maldigestion?

What most people call lactose intolerance, researchers in the field call maldigestion. What's the difference? A true intolerance means a person would suffer stomach problems *every* time he or she would consume milk or milk products like ice cream. These gastrointestinal symptoms are not always present for lactose maldigesters. In fact, the majority can handle one cup of milk and many can even drink two if they're spread out through the course of the day or imbibed with meals. How can this be? There are several reasons:

1. Many maldigesters can still produce the lactase enzyme, just in reduced amounts. This means some dairy products can still be digested.

2. Other bacteria in the gut can digest some lactose, even without lactase present.

3. There appears to be a "use it or lose it" aspect to lactose digestion—if you eat dairy foods in small amounts you will be able to digest them better than if you avoided these foods altogether.

4. If you believe that you can digest milk, perhaps you can. Although this may seem like the weakest argument for drinking milk, the power of the mind is a strong motivator. It can also work the opposite way. In one

blind study a group of people were given both regular and low-lactose milk; some subjects reported unpleasant symptoms no matter which beverage was consumed.

Learning to live with lactose intolerance

If you suspect you have a lactose-intolerance condition, it is important not to avoid milk and milk products altogether. Not only will you be missing out on many important nutrients (in particular calcium) but most lactose intolerance is not an all-or-nothing condition; rather, it's a matter of degree. Finally, some lactose intolerance may be temporary, brought on by a bout of illness.

What can you do?

- Start small. Drink small amounts of milk at a time. Then, if you can handle it, gradually begin to increase consumption so you can get your body accustomed to drinking milk.

- Have milk and other dairy foods with meals. Eating these foods with meals slows their digestion and allows the gut more time to process them. Furthermore, diluted with food, milk can be more easily absorbed.

- Eat aged or hard cheeses. Most of the lactose in cheese is removed during processing. Aged cheeses like Colby, Swiss, and Parmesan are particularly low in lactose.

- Buy special products. There are a number of lactose-free and reduced-lactose products on the market. There are even enzyme droplets you can add to food and lactase pills you can take. However, these aids should be used as a last resort, since they can be unnecessarily expensive and taste, particularly for reduced-lactose milk (it's sweeter than normal), is affected.

legumes

Legumes are technically edible seeds enclosed in pods, such as dried beans, peas, and lentils.

Types of legumes

The difference between one bean, pea, or lentil and another is not so much their nutrient content as their size, shape, and color. Dried beans tend to be kidney shaped or oval, peas are round, and lentils are flat disks. There are over a hundred species of beans and more than fifty kinds of dried peas and lentils cultivated around the world. Unfortunately, Americans remain unfamiliar with most of them. But heirloom or specialty beans and peas are starting to pop up in gourmet stores and catalog companies, so legumes like red lentils, black baby chick peas, and pink beans are now available.

Nutritionally, legumes are considered the super foods of the plant kingdom. They're high in fiber, complex carbohydrates, protein, and a number of vitamins and minerals. (It's best to eat legumes with vitamin C–rich foods like tomatoes, green peppers, broccoli, or citrus fruit, in order to increase iron absorption.) In addition, they're extremely low in fat—with the exception of peanuts and soybeans—low in sodium, and cholesterol-free. Calorie-wise, a $\frac{1}{2}$ cup serving supplies between 110 and 145 calories. And beans are cheap—the most inexpensive protein source in our food supply, costing only about 20 cents per serving.

What are legumes?

Protein: Beans are 21 to 25 percent plant protein—or about 7 or 8 grams of protein per $\frac{1}{2}$-cup serving. With the exception of soybeans (which contain all eight essential amino acids), all bean protein is incomplete, meaning it's missing one or two compounds of amino acids. To make up for this deficiency, legumes are traditionally paired with cereal grains, which tend to be high in the amino acids beans are lacking. Dishes like corn tortillas and refried beans, red beans and rice, and pasta e fagioli (pasta and bean soup) not only taste good but also create complete proteins.

Complex carbohydrates: Over 60 percent of legumes are composed of starch. On average, that's about 25 grams of carbohydrates per serving. A small amount of these carbohydrates are simple sugars and some are oligosaccharides (the compound that causes gas), but the majority are polysaccharides—long, complex chains of simple sugars. These sugars combine to produce starch.

Fiber: Legumes are loaded with both soluble and insoluble fiber, with lentils and split peas boasting the highest fiber count. One-half cup of legumes provides 9 grams of dietary fiber. By comparison, vegetables average 5 grams of fiber and grains average 3.

Vitamins: Beans are a good source of the water-soluble B vitamins, especially thiamin, riboflavin, niacin, and folate. Legumes, in fact, are the richest source of folate there is.

Minerals: Eating legumes will boost your mineral intake considerably. A one-cup serving supplies substantial amounts of iron, phosphorus, magnesium, manganese, potassium, copper, calcium, and zinc.

Health benefits of legumes

Legumes exhibit both protective and therapeutic effects for a number of chronic diseases.

Legumes and coronary heart disease: Study after study has shown beans to be a formidable enemy against heart disease. Why? Because they're loaded with beneficial soluble fiber, which we know significantly lowers blood cholesterol levels. They also lower other serum lipids circulating in the blood.

Homocysteine and heart attacks: Aside from improving cholesterol profiles, researchers think beans can also protect against heart disease by reducing levels of homocysteine in the body.

Recent evidence from several studies, including the Framingham Heart Study, Tufts University, and the Harvard School of Public Health, found elevated homocysteine levels to be an increased risk factor for heart disease. Although homocysteine is an amino acid normally present in the body, high levels can damage blood vessels, making it easier for cholesterol to build up on artery walls. Some scientists think homocysteine may be the reason why people with little or no risk factors for heart disease can still suffer a heart attack.

Although researchers still don't know how much homocysteine is considered a risk, they do know that levels are strongly influenced by diet. Intake of vitamins B_6 and B_{12} and folate has been proven to break down homocysteine, lowering concentrations. Folate, especially, has been directly related to homocysteine in the blood—low blood folic-acid levels are associated with high homocysteine concentrations.

So early evidence indicates that legumes, because they are an excellent source of folate, may help fight heart disease by reducing homocysteine levels.

Diabetes and beans: The high fiber content of beans is an important health benefit for people with diabetes since it has been shown to help control blood glucose levels. Beans are generally digested slowly, producing a very low glucose and insulin response, particularly when compared to simple carbohydrates like white bread or potatoes. This slow digestion results in better metabolic control of blood glucose levels and provides beneficial long-term effects on diabetes.

Beans for weight management: Beans are a boon for people trying to lose weight. Because they are digested slowly, they provide a number of positive effects, including a slow, sustained release of glucose and increased insulin sensitivity. Fiber also fills you up.

The legume-cancer connection: Like all high-fiber foods, legumes reduce the risk of certain cancers like colon and breast cancer. Since they are also low in fat, beans are often promoted by groups like the National Cancer Institute as an ideal way to get valuable nutrients in the diet.

Despite these touted health benefits, the American population still hasn't jumped on the bean wagon. Our annual consumption of dried beans, peas, and legumes is very low, less than 8 pounds per capita. Most of this can probably be attributed to the fact that many people just don't know how to prepare dried beans.

Although canned beans are a quick and easy alternative, you need to look out for sky-high sodium levels. Be sure to rinse canned beans well to remove some of the salt. Dried beans are a healthier choice, but any which way, don't miss out on your legumes.

Bean rundown

Beans, peas, and lentils cover a wide range of textures, colors, and flavors, and they're used in cuisines all over the world. America's craving for ethnic foods has done much for the bean cause. Here is a rundown of some of the most common beans and what they're used for.

Black beans: Also known as turtle beans, Spanish black beans, or Mexican black beans, lately these legumes have taken off, particularly in restaurants, where they're often served as a side dish. Many of these dishes have a Latin-American influence, such as Cuban black beans or Mexican burritos, but they also can be used in salads, soups, and stews. Black beans are small with a black skin and a sweet, earthy taste with mushroom overtones.

Black-eyed peas: Known for their black "eye" and creamy white skin, these beans are a favorite down South, where they appear in dishes like Hoppin' John (a mixture of black-eyed peas, ham, and rice) and are often eaten on New Year's Eve for good luck. Because they have a thin skin, they don't need presoaking. Their flavor is subtle, savory, and light.

Chickpeas: Also known by their Italian name, garbanzo beans, these legumes cook up into a medium to large size with a yellow color. They have a nutlike flavor with a firm texture, so they do take longer to cook than other beans. Chickpeas are used in a number of dishes from Middle Eastern falafel or humus to African chickpea stew.

Great northern beans: These beans look like large, white ovals and have a mild taste with a powdery texture. A versatile bean, they can be used in just about any soup, stew, or casserole.

Red kidney beans: A large kidney-shaped, deep reddish brown or light red bean, they have a robust, full-bodied taste and soft texture. They used to be the most popular bean used in chili and southern red beans and rice, but lately they have been replaced by small pink or red beans.

Lentils: Lentils come in an amazing number of colors and sizes, from small, bright orange flattened disks to round black ovals. They have a full, earthy flavor that lends itself to a number of seasonings. They require no presoaking and cook quickly. Lentils are a mainstay in many cuisines from Indian dal to French lentil soup and offer a wealth of culinary possibilities.

Lima beans: Large, flat-shaped, smooth white or light-green in color with a creamy, sweet flavor, lima beans are low in popularity among the younger set (the older generation still has a fondness for them). An American Indian staple, lima beans can be found in succotash, a dish prepared with squash and tomatoes.

Navy beans: Small, white, oval beans with a mild flavor, navy beans are the matured white seeds of the green bean. They're probably the most widely used bean and are most well known as the main ingredient in traditional Boston Baked Beans.

Pinto beans: A medium-sized bean, mottled beige, brown, or pink in color, pinto beans have risen to become the most popular bean in America. They have an earthy, full-bodied flavor and are most often used in Mexican and South American cuisine.

Split peas: Split peas are dried green or yellow peas that have been split, or physically broken. They have a mild creamy taste and, like lentils, don't require soaking. Because they don't hold their shape well after cooking they are best in soups or stews. Split pea and ham soup is the way most people have come to know this legume, but there are many other versions available, such as curried or vegetarian split pea soup.

They May Be Good for Your Heart, but . . .

Beans are notorious for one thing: gas. But that shouldn't stop you from eating them, particularly since you can easily lessen their effect.

Beans contain a type of carbohydrate called oligosaccharides, which are bigger than a disaccharide but smaller than a polysaccharide. Since we have no digestive enzymes to break down this compound, oligosaccharides pass whole into the lower intestine. Fortunately, friendly bacteria there do the work, breaking them down for us, and the by-product of this reaction is gas. The only way to reduce the flatulence is to reduce the amount of oligosaccharides in the beans. Cooking the beans naturally removes some oligosaccharides, but there are also other ways:

- Change the water after soaking beans.
- Use the hot soak method: Cover beans with water and boil for 2 minutes. Turn the heat off, put a lid on the pot, and soak for one to four hours before cooking.
- Add acidic ingredients—tomatoes or vinegar—after the beans have cooked.
- Gradually increase consumption; the more you eat, the more likely your body will adapt.

macrobiotic diets

Based on the Eastern philosophy of balance and harmony, macrobiotic diets were first introduced to Americans in the 1960s by George Oshawa, a Japanese educator. The diet is basically vegetarian in nature, although some fish and shellfish are allowed on occasion.

Advocating a simple, wholesome way of life, the principal dietary tenets emphasize the use of whole grains, beans, and locally grown vegetables. No processed, canned, or frozen foods are allowed nor are refined and simple sugars, refined flour, or polished grain products.

The macrobiotic guidelines also specifies eating only certain vegetables and excluding others. Fruits are allowed only occasionally, two or three times per week, and beverages are basically limited to certain kinds of tea and water.

Nutritional needs are determined by physiology, activity level, and climate or geographic location. Accordingly, foods are divided into groups—either yin (cool foods) or yang (hot foods)—and obtaining a balance between the two is thought to lead to health and happiness.

Due to its restrictive nature, a macrobiotic diet is not recommended by reputable nutritionists. Studies have shown that adults and children following this diet fall well below RDA intakes for vitamins D, B_6, B_{12}, riboflavin, niacin, and folic acid. Calcium, iron, and magnesium levels can also be compromised. Generally, few people find a macrobiotic diet palatable for long.

Daily Dietary Recommendations for a Macrobiotic Diet

50 to 60 percent whole cereal grains (examples: organically grown brown rice, barley, millet, oats, corn, rye, wheat, and buckwheat)

5 to 10 percent soup (examples: soup made from vegetables, beans, and grains)

20 to 30 percent vegetables (examples: organically or locally grown cabbage, kale, broccoli, cauliflower, pumpkin, collards, mustard greens, onions, turnips, burdock, carrots, winter squash, and radish)

5 to 10 percent beans and sea vegetables (examples: azuki, chickpeas, and lentils, tofu, tempeh, nori, wakame, kombu, and agar-agar)

What's off-limits on a macrobiotic diet

- Red meat, poultry, animal fat, eggs, and all dairy products
- All refined and simple sugars, refined and polished grains and flour products (no chocolate, molasses, honey, or vanilla)
- Tropical and semitropical fruit including bananas, oranges, lemons, limes, figs, mangoes, and avocados and fruit juices
- Any hot or strong foods or spices like black pepper and curry powder
- All artificially colored, preserved, sprayed, or chemically treated foods
- Certain vegetables including potatoes, green peppers, eggplant, tomatoes, zucchini, spinach, and asparagus

The list for foods consumed only occasionally (about two to three times per week) is even longer and includes such healthy foods as peas, mushrooms, grapes, peaches, raisins, olive oil, clams, shrimp, bulgur, couscous, and black beans.

Treating Cancer Macrobiotically

In the past, people have sought out macrobiotic diets as a way to treat cancer and other serious illnesses. However, there is no scientific evidence to support this, and it could be dangerous for people in a weakened state. In addition to providing only very low levels of important vitamins and minerals, the diet is relatively short on calories and high-quality protein—two things cancer patients especially need more of.

meat

Meat includes cuts of beef, lamb, pork, and veal, as well as cuts from game such as venison. In recent years, red meat has earned a bad reputation, mostly because of its high saturated-fat and cholesterol content. In truth, the same amount of lean red meat may actually be lower in fat than certain kinds of chicken or seafood. That's because the meat industry has worked hard to breed leaner and lighter animals and they're trimming more external fat in the processing plant than they used to. In fact, beef is 27 percent leaner and pork is (on average) 31 percent lower in fat than in the past. Lamb meat is naturally low in fat since it has little internal fat or marbling, and most of the fat is located on the outside of the meat.

Nutritionally, red meat is an excellent source of protein, iron (which women are often short on), zinc, and B vitamins (which help convert food into energy). The USDA and most leading health organizations recommend two to three 3-ounce servings of meat per day. This portion size amounts to about one small hamburger, one average-size chicken breast, or three slices of roast beef—a quantity that's visually comparable in size and thickness to a deck of cards or the palm of your hand.

Less is best

Nevertheless, it would be a good idea to watch red meat intake, since consumption of red meat, regardless of fat, has been linked to cancer. To a lesser degree, researchers have also raised concerns about chemical residues, antibiotics, and hormones like bovine somatotropin (BST) or bovine growth hormone (BGH). Approved by the Food and Drug Administration and the Department of Agriculture for use and safety a few years back, BST is a genetically engineered hormone injected into cows to increase milk production. Critics say cows treated with BST have a greater chance of becoming ill and, therefore, of being treated with antibiotics. If not monitored carefully, these antibiotics can leave residues in milk.

Lately, Americans have become concerned about mad cow disease, or bovine spongiform encephalopathy (BSE). In cows, BSE is a fatal brain disease that affects the central nervous system, but it is believed that a form of the disease may be transmitted to humans who eat the meat of infected cows. Currently the only country to report cases of this disorder in cows or people is Great Britain.

To prepare healthier meat-based meals:

- Before cooking, be sure to trim off all excess fat.
- Always check the meat label for the freshness date. All USDA beef is inspected and most are graded: prime (highest quality), choice (less expensive, but still good quality), or select (leanest cuts with least amount of marbling).

- Stir-fry, broil, or grill with minimal oil or butter.
- Combine in mixed dishes with pasta, vegetables, or grains as extenders, or eat small portions of meat, filling up on vegetables and whole-grain breads instead.

The Healthiest Cuts

For beef, key cuts: loin and round		
CUT	TOTAL FAT	SATURATED FAT
fat grams per 3-ounce cooked portion		
BEEF TOP ROUND	4 grams	2 grams
FLANK STEAK	9 grams	4 grams
SHORT LOIN OF BEEF	7 grams	3 grams
For pork, veal, and lamb, key cuts: loin and round		
CUT	TOTAL FAT	SATURATED FAT
fat grams per 3-ounce cooked portion		
PORK TENDER-LOIN	4 grams	1 gram
PORK LOIN, CENTER CHOP	7 grams	3 grams
VEAL SHOULDER, ROAST OR STEAK	6 grams	2 grams
VEAL CUTLETS	3 grams	1 gram
LAMB SHANK	5 grams	2 grams
LAMB LEG	7 grams	2 grams

metabolism

Your metabolism or metabolic rate determines how fast you burn calories. The resting metabolic rate (RMR), also known as the basal metabolic rate (BMR) or the resting energy expenditure (REE), is the amount of energy or calories you expend to run all the involuntary activities needed to sustain life (such as breathing, the beating of your heart, blood circulation). Basically, it is the amount of energy you need in order to live. All other activities—from getting up out of bed to running a six-mile race—require additional energy. When people refer to their metabolic rate they usually include both the RMR and the energy needed to perform their usual everyday activities.

For most people, the lion's share of the energy expended goes toward the RMR. Only professional athletes or endurance athletes spend more energy on outside activities than on their internal functions. The rest of us generally increase our RMR by 30 to 60 percent depending on how active we are.

Although our metabolic rates are genetically programmed at birth, there are many other factors that influence it:

- Size: The taller and bigger you are, the more energy you produce.
- Body composition: Fat is basically a storage unit, thus it burns little fuel for maintenance. Muscle, or lean body mass, on the other hand, is metabolically active, meaning it burns calories even at rest. Consequently the more lean body mass or muscle you have, the higher and faster your RMR.
- Gender: Men tend to have a higher RMR than women, even when they're the same size, as men naturally have more muscle than women.
- Age: As we age we lose lean body mass and gain more fat, lowering our RMR and causing us to burn fewer calories. This can be offset by regular exercise.
- Food intake: Energy is required to digest and absorb food. That's why after a big meal your RMR goes up. To maximize your RMR and use up more calories, try to eat most of your food early in the day and less at night when your body is slowing down. Food eaten late at night is more likely to be stored as fat, rather than used as energy.
- Illness: In an effort to fight off the stress that is making your body weak, your energy needs increase when you're sick, raising the RMR during this time.
- Activity level: Active people tend to have a higher RMR. Not only do metabolism rates increase during exercise, but the effects can last hours after a workout. Aerobic exercise is about the best way to rev up metabolism and burn calories. Anaerobic exercise or strength training, because it builds muscle, also raises your RMR.

- Very low calorie diets or malnutrition: When food is scarce, the body becomes more efficient at conserving and storing energy. In an effort to "do more with less" it slows down its metabolism or RMR. While this system is very efficient during times of fasting it actually hinders people who may be trying to lose weight through "starvation diets." Rather than shaving off pounds, they slow down their metabolism. So when normal eating patterns are resumed the body is still operating on "low gear" and more energy winds up stored as fat. In these cases dieters gain weight even without overeating.

ACTIVITY LEVEL	RMR INCREASE
Sedentary (sitting, standing, watching TV)	20–30 percent
Light activity (housecleaning, golfing, garage work)	50–60 percent
Moderate activity (skiing, bicycling, dancing)	60–70 percent
Heavy activity (football, soccer, basketball, jogging)	90–100 percent

How many calories do you burn in a day?

It's important to know your metabolic rate so you can balance the energy in (the food you eat) with the energy out (how active you are). Because of different activity levels, each person's metabolic rate is different. Follow these steps to calculate the amount of calories you burn in a day. Remember, if you eat more than the calculated amount of calories, those extra calories eventually get stored as fat.

1. Convert your weight from pounds to kilograms by dividing by 2.2 (2.2 pounds = 1 kilogram). So, a 130-pound woman would weigh 59 kilograms.

2. Women: Multiply the results of Step 1 by .9 (59 × .9 = 53). Men: Skip this step and go directly to Step 3.

3. Multiply the results of Step 2 (or Step 1 if you are a man) by 24. This gives you the minimal number of calories you need to survive, or your RMR (53 × 24 = 1272 calories).

4. To calculate the extra calories you need in order to perform your normal activities, you must calculate a certain percentage of the RMR. Then add it to the RMR for that day's calorie needs. For example, a relatively sedentary day—say, a lazy Sunday spent watching TV or laying around—would require only a 20 percent increase in calorie expenditure (1,272 × .20 = 254 extra calories). So, 254 added to 1,272 equals 1,526 calories.

Activity levels vary depending on how vigorous an activity it is and how long you're active. At left is a general rule of thumb based on nutritionists' recommendations for energy.

minerals

Minerals are essential for normal body function because they regulate chemical reactions, provide structure, and maintain the acid-base balance in fluids. Scientists have recently discovered that minerals may also prevent or treat illness. They are currently studying the relationship between certain minerals and chronic conditions such as diabetes, hypertension, cancer, heart disease, and osteoporosis. Most of these studies have looked at the negative impact of suboptimal mineral levels on disease, but some are also investigating the effects of boosting intakes.

The majors and the minors

Basically, there are two categories of minerals—the major minerals and the trace, or minor minerals. Major minerals are those present in the body in amounts greater than 5 grams (one teaspoon). Calcium, phosphorus, potassium, sulfur, sodium, chloride, and magnesium are considered the major minerals. They tend to form salts that dissolve into our body fluids and then help regulate water levels.

Trace minerals, on the other hand, are needed in only minute quantities, but they are no less important than the major minerals. Iron, zinc, iodine, selenium, chromium, fluoride, copper, and molybdenum are trace minerals. The National Academy of Sciences has recently reviewed recommended intakes for calcium, phosphorus, magnesium, vitamin D, and fluoride with the intent of optimizing health and reducing the risk of disease. Ultimately they decreased phosphorus and magnesium intakes, increased calcium recommendations, and left vitamin D (for adults) and fluoride alone. Revised recommendations for other nutrients are currently in the works.

Here's the latest information on the complex roles some of the most studied minerals play in our body.

Calcium: Calcium is primarily responsible for bone health. Adequate intakes are essential not only for building strong teeth and bones but also to prevent losses from occurring later in life, reducing the risk of the debilitating disease osteoporosis. For this reason, the government recently raised its recommended intake for calcium to 1,000 milligrams per day.

Potassium: Since potassium, like sodium, is involved in fluid regulation in the body, it is believed to help control high blood pressure. Although findings are considered controversial, more and more experts believe that eating potassium-rich foods like fruits and vegetables can lower blood pressure.

Potassium supplements may also be helpful, but it's important to ingest calcium and magnesium along with potassium in order to maximize the benefit of this mineral.

Mineral	What It Does	Getting Too Little Can Lead To	Getting Too Much Can Lead To	Food Sources	RDA
CALCIUM	• Important for bone and teeth health • Essential for muscle and nerve function • Maintains normal blood pressure	Osteoporosis	Kidney stones; may interfere with absorption of other minerals	Dairy products (milk and cheese), green leafy vegetables, dried beans, broccoli, and calcium-fortified products	1,000 mg
MAGNESIUM	• Critical to enzyme reactions • Synthesizes protein • Important for bone health	Heart problems; increased risk of high blood pressure, diabetes, and osteoporosis	Diarrhea; toxic in large quantities	Nuts, legumes, whole grains, and green vegetables, seafood	Men: 420 mg Women: 320 mg
PHOSPHORUS	• Important for bone and soft tissue growth and nerve function	Anemia; muscle weakness; bone pain and rickets	Low blood-calcium levels	Meat, poultry, fish, eggs, dairy, dried beans	700 mg
POTASSIUM	• Essential for nerve function, muscle contractions, and to maintain normal blood pressure	Not known	Toxic: can cause cardiac arrest and death	Fruit (bananas, canteloupe, raisins), vegetables (potatoes, lima beans), seafood, milk	Estimated minimum requirement: 2,000 mg per day
SODIUM	• Maintains body's acid-base balance • Regulates body fluids	Not known	Possibly hypertension	Table salt, some vegetables, most processed foods	2,400 mg

Mineral	What It Does	Getting Too Little Can Lead To	Getting Too Much Can Lead To	Food Sources	RDA
CHROMIUM	• Required for insulin to process carbohydrates	Diabetes-like condition	Not known	Whole grains, nuts, cheese, brewers yeast, meat	Estimated safe and adequate intake: 50–200 micrograms
FLUORIDE	• Important for teeth and bone health	Tooth decay	Chronic toxicity can discolor tooth enamel and affect bone health	Drinking water	Men: 3.8 mg Women: 3.1 mg
IRON	• Responsible for making red blood cells to carry oxygen	Anemia	Hemochromatosis (iron overload) can lead to chronic illness (diabetes and arthritis); can cause death in large quantities, especially in children	Red meat, poultry, eggs, legumes, whole or enriched grains, dark green leafy vegetables	Men: 10 mg Women: 15 mg
SELENIUM	• Antioxidant	Heart problems	Toxic: hair loss, diarrhea, nerve abnormalities	Widely distributed in meats, shellfish, vegetables	Men: 70 micrograms Women: 55 micrograms
ZINC	• Involved in: growth, reproductive organs, taste perception, wound healing	Stunted growth, skin changes, loss of appetite, impaired immunity	Toxic: inhibits iron absorption; can cause death.	Meat, shellfish (oysters), eggs, liver, legumes, and whole grains	Men: 15 mg Women: 12 mg

Chromium: In the last few years, much attention has been paid to chromium because of popular claims that this nutrient can "melt away" fat, build muscle mass, increase energy and stamina, reduce cholesterol, and control diabetes. Unfortunately, there is no conclusive scientific evidence that any of these claims are true. The only thing we know for sure is that chromium is an essential nutrient required to process carbohydrates.

Selenium: Selenium is known for its antioxidant powers. Researchers think it may help prevent cancer and cardiovascular disease but it's still too early to tell.

Zinc: Zinc became a popular nutrient when a 1996 study from the Cleveland Clinic showed that a certain type of zinc lozenge reduced the severity and shortened the duration of cold symptoms. But proceed with caution: Researchers still don't know how and why zinc works. Furthermore, high doses of zinc, like those found in supplements, have been found to *suppress* immune function, interfere with other mineral absorption, and lower HDLs (good cholesterol). Megadoses can even be toxic.

How do we get the minerals we need?

As far as availability goes, minerals are all around us—in the water we drink as well as the vegetables, fruits, and animal foods we eat. Still, many of us don't get all the minerals we need, mostly because of a general lack of fresh fruits and vegetables in the diet. Our heavy reliance on processed foods (which tend to be devoid of minerals) doesn't help either.

For people looking for an easy answer, supplementation is not it. Taking doses too high in many of these minerals can lead to toxicity. Even in moderate amounts, supplements may upset the body's delicate balance for absorbing minerals. Since minerals compete for absorption, taking too much of one can actually cause a deficiency in another. For instance, high calcium intakes can interfere with zinc absorption. So, unless your doctor recommends mineral supplements, your best bet is to eat a balanced diet with plenty of fruits and vegetables.

nutrients

Nutrients are substances your body needs to live, breathe, and move each day. There are six classes of nutrients that are required for life: Water, Carbohydrates, Protein, Fat, Vitamins, and Minerals. Together they provide energy, build structure, and support the body's growth, maintenance, and repair. Four of the nutrients—carbohydrates, protein, fat, and vitamins—are organic, meaning they are made from living organisms. Organic compounds contain the element carbon and are more fragile than inorganic substances, and they can easily be destroyed by heat, sunlight, or acid. So it is important to handle foods containing organic compounds with care during preparation.

Essential nutrients

Essential nutrients are compounds the body cannot produce by itself or cannot produce in sufficient quantities to meet physiological demands. Thus, they must be acquired from an outside food source. Vitamins, minerals, and water are essential nutrients.

Lipids, carbohydrates, and proteins include both essential and nonessential compounds. Nonessential compounds are produced by the body and therefore are not needed from food. For example, cholesterol is a nonessential fat, since it is produced by the body, but linoleic and linolenic fatty acids cannot be produced by the body, and so must be obtained from food.

Water

The most abundant of all the nutrients, water makes up about 60 percent of your body weight.

What does it do? As a transport medium carrying substances throughout the body, water is involved in almost every function your body performs. Water also cleanses the bloodstream, lubricates joints, cushions organs, and acts as the body's coolant. (See **Water,** page 386, for more details about this nutrient.)

How much do we need? Not surprisingly, the body's need for water far surpasses that of any other nutrient. Nutritionists recommend drinking at least 48 to 64 ounces of water a day.

Carbohydrates and fats

Known as macronutrients because of their size and because of the large quantities the body requires, carbohydrates and fats are energy-yielding.

What do they do? The macronutrients produce energy when they're broken down. It's this energy that keeps your organs (the heart, the lungs) working and allows you to perform everyday activities like eating, walking, or sleeping.

The body's primary source of energy is glucose, normally derived from carbohydrates. When broken down, glucose yields energy in the form of a compound called ATP (adenosine triphosphate) plus the by-product carbon dioxide. Fatty acids can also produce energy, but glucose is normally required during the process. If glucose is not present (as is the case for people on very low carbohydrate diets) energy can still be produced, but so will ketones, a potentially dangerous by-product. (See **Blood Glucose,** page 274, for more information on ketones.)

Much like the way wood fuels a fire, macronutrients, which keep the body running and are vital to everyday life, must be constantly replenished.

How much do we need? How much energy we need depends on body size, weight, and activity level. Typically, we supply our body with this needed source of energy three times a day at breakfast, lunch, and dinner.

Protein

Protein is another macronutrient.

What does it do? Although it is able to provide energy if necessary, protein rarely performs this function. Instead, its main duty is to build the body's structure (bones, teeth, muscle) and maintain cell growth and repair.

How much do we need? Government recommendations are 50 grams of protein a day for women. Most Americans, however, eat well over that amount. In fact, it's not unusual for some people to consume more than twice the RDA for protein.

Some heavy-duty athletes may have an increased need for protein. But considering the large intakes normally consumed, any extra protein should be easily obtained from a healthy, well-balanced diet.

Vitamins

Vitamins are organic compounds that are much smaller in size than macronutrients. They are also consumed in much smaller amounts. Still, their presence is just as important.

What do they do? Although they do not provide energy, vitamins are necessary for the energy-yielding nutrients to do their job. Without their help the body would not be able to digest, absorb, metabolize, or excrete nutrients and other compounds. Every action in the body requires the assistance of vitamins.

How much do we need? There are thirteen vitamins known to man. Most are water-soluble, but some—vitamins A, D, E, and K—are fat-soluble (meaning they are only found in the fatty or oily parts of foods). In the past, vitamin deficiencies were our biggest problem. But with many foods now vitamin-fortified, deficiencies have been more or less eradicated in this country. Instead, because of the number of supplements available, and the marketing hype associated with them, toxicity or vitamin overload has become more of a concern. Eating a diet high in fruits, vegetables, legumes, and whole grains will help you avoid either of these problems (see also **Vitamins,** page 381).

Minerals

Like vitamins, minerals are also "helper" nutrients. The difference between them is that minerals are inert, inorganic compounds that are virtually indestructible.

What do they do? Like vitamins, minerals are regulators and assist the body in all processes. In addition, they provide structure, making up teeth and bones, and are essential in maintaining fluid and electrolyte (electrically charged ions) balance in the body.

How much do we need? Recommended intake varies according to the mineral. In general, the body requires large amounts of major minerals like calcium, sodium, and phosphorus, while only minute quantities may be necessary from the minor or trace minerals like selenium, copper, or iodine. Some sixteen minerals are known to be essential to human nutrition (see also **Minerals,** page 345).

nuts

Since nuts are naturally high in fat, many Americans forgo this food in favor of lower-fat choices. But it's time to rethink nuts. In addition to containing lots of plant protein, nuts are rich in vitamins, minerals, and other compounds most Americans could use more of. In fact, even the fat in nuts is the kind we should be eating more of—unsaturated.

Nutrition in a nutshell

Almonds, walnuts, peanuts, Brazil nuts, pecans, cashews, chestnuts, and macadamia nuts are a few of the foods we classify as nuts. Although botanically diverse—almonds are actually a seed, while peanuts are technically legumes—all tree nuts and peanuts have similar nutritional composition.

Protein: Nuts are known for their high protein content—they fall into the meat, eggs, poultry, and fish group in the USDA Food Guide Pyramid. Some nuts, like almonds and peanuts, can have as much as 6 or 7 grams of protein in one ounce; walnuts and hazelnuts hover around 4 grams per ounce. One-third cup of nuts has the same amount of protein as a one-ounce serving of meat.

Fat: No doubt about it: Nuts are high in fat. An ounce of peanuts supplies anywhere from 165 to 200 calories and 14 to 21 grams of fat—about 80 percent of the calories found in nuts come from fat. Most of this fat, however, is unsaturated. And there's more good news: Nuts are naturally cholesterol-free.

There are two exceptions to the general rules about nuts and fat: Chestnuts are the only true low-fat nut; one ounce contains less than one gram of fat. And though coconuts are lower in fat than other nuts (one ounce supplies about 10 grams of fat), almost all of it is saturated fat.

Vitamins and minerals: Nuts are rich in many vitamins and minerals including: vitamin E, folate, vitamin B_6, niacin, copper, iron, calcium, zinc, magnesium, manganese, boron, potassium, and phosphorus.

Phytochemicals: Some of the beneficial phytochemicals already identified in nuts are flavonoids, carotenoids, indoles, and phenolic compounds.

Nuts against disease

As a disease-fighter, nuts offer a number of potential health advantages.

Cardiovascular disease

Several studies from Loma Linda University in California suggest that a high nut intake does not increase risk for heart disease and may actually have a protective effect against the illness. Based on a careful review of the dietary records of more than 30,000 Seventh-Day Adventists (a group of people who are vegetarian and do not smoke or drink), researchers found that those who ate two ounces of nuts (primarily almonds, walnuts, and peanuts) five times a week cut their risk for heart attack in half.

What's the explanation? Perhaps it has to do with the fatty acid profile of nuts. Studies looking at diets high in unsaturated fats and supplemented with either almonds or walnuts showed decreases in both total cholesterol and the "bad" LDL cholesterol, while HDL, the "good" cholesterol, was unchanged.

In addition, many nuts are high in vitamin E, a powerful antioxidant. Vitamin E can prevent LDLs from being oxidized (oxidized LDLs are the ones that cause the most damage to your arteries), possibly reducing the risk of heart disease. Nuts also contain a respectable amount of folic acid, which is known to have an inverse relationship with homocysteine levels in the blood (high homocysteine levels are believed to increase the risk of heart disease). Finally, nuts are an important source of copper and magnesium, two minerals that protect heart health.

Cancer

Since nuts are a good source of fiber, they can decrease the development of certain cancers like colon or rectal cancer. Vitamin E, another component in nuts, has also been linked to cancer prevention. Finally, the number of phytochemicals present in nuts may also have a protective effect against cancer.

The best nuts

Almonds: The majority of fat in almonds is monounsaturated, like that found in olive oil. Because of this, almonds lower levels of LDL, while still maintaining HDL.

These nuts are also one of the best sources of vitamin E in our diet, supplying more than 35 percent of the RDA for this nutrient. Other vitamins and minerals almonds are noted for include: calcium (almonds contain more calcium than any other nut), magnesium, iron, zinc, phosphorus, and folic acid. Almonds are also rich in phytochemicals, particularly flavonoids and plant sterols.

Brazil nuts: These are fairly rich in calcium, phosphorus, and thiamine, but they are most well known for their antioxidant properties from the mineral selenium. One average Brazil nut supplies as much as 100 micrograms of selenium—that's well over 100 percent of the 70 micrograms advised by the government in their Recommended Daily Allowance tables.

Peanuts: Peanuts are 25 percent protein, a larger percentage than in any other nut. That's not surprising since peanuts are actually a legume. A more complete protein than other nuts, peanuts are particularly high in arginine, an amino acid involved in healing wounds and immunity.

Walnuts: Walnuts are the number-one ingredient nut in America. Unlike other nuts, which are primarily monounsaturated, most of the fat in walnuts (about 70 percent) is polyunsaturated. And this polyunsaturated fat is a good source of linolenic acid, an essential fatty acid your body uses to make omega-3 fatty acids. For people who eschew fish, walnuts may offer the same heart-healthy benefits as seafood.

Not surprisingly, several studies concluded that eating walnuts on a regular basis significantly lowers total cholesterol and LDL.

Dry Roasted vs. Oil Roasted

There are two types of processed nuts—dry roasted and oil roasted. Dry roasted nuts are cooked in ovens with hot forced air. Oil roasted are basically deep-fried in hot oil. Nevertheless, the nutritional differences between the two processes are minimal. Oil roasting adds about 10 calories per ounce of nuts (or 1 gram of fat). Salting nuts, however, can make a big difference: Naturally low in sodium, one peanut yields about 5 milligrams of sodium; make it a salted nut and that number jumps to over 400 milligrams. Your best bet: salt-free, dry-roasted nuts.

obesity and weight gain

Despite an almost obsessive interest in health and nutrition, Americans are getting fatter. Studies from the National Center for Health Statistics show that one out of every three Americans is considered obese—technically, having a body weight 20 percent above the ideal or healthy range for height.

What's even more shocking is that in 1980, only one in four Americans was clinically obese. Experts blame part of the shift on our increasingly sedentary lifestyle, but that's not all. People are doing less *and* eating more. Average caloric intake rose from 2,000 calories per day in the late seventies to 2,200 calories in 1990. So even though the percent of total fat in the diet has dropped (from 36 to 34 percent), actual fat grams have gone up a few points.

Most of this can be attributed to our cravings for high-calorie, low-fat processed foods like fat-free cakes, cookies, and muffins, and to an overall trend toward bigger portions, particularly at restaurants.

Body composition

Just because you weigh more than what's on the chart doesn't mean you're fat. In a healthy adult, acceptable body-fat levels are 18 to 23 percent for men and 25 to 30 percent for women. Most people, however, have no way of knowing their body composition.

To get more accurate readings, more and more researchers are using Body Mass Index, or BMI, to monitor obesity. BMI is a formula that measures weight relative to height. A healthy BMI falls into the 19 to 25 range.

The National Center for Health Statistics uses a BMI of 27 or above to track overweight people, but most nutrition textbooks consider anyone with a BMI of 30 or more to be obese.

Apples and pears

Where you put away the fat also makes a difference. People who gain weight around the middle—known as having an apple shape—are more susceptible to chronic illness than people who typically gain weight in the lower body—hips, thighs, and buttocks (pears).

Excess fat around the abdomen has been linked to higher rates of coronary artery disease, cancer, diabetes, and high blood pressure. Pears, on the other hand, have none of these extra risk factors. Scientists still don't know why there's a significant difference, but they think it's because the type of fat that settles around the stomach is more likely to be broken down and enter the bloodstream. The good news is that regular exercise along with a diet high in vegetables rather than meat may help reduce the chances of fat accumulating on your belly, particularly in your older years.

What are the health risks of obesity?

Being overweight has numerous negative effects on your health. Overall, it has been shown to increase the risk for

- high blood pressure
- high blood cholesterol
- coronary heart disease (scientists think it may be an independent risk factor)
- diabetes
- cancer (especially breast and endometrial)
- arthritis and joint problems
- depression
- sleep problems

Getting older, getting fatter

It used to be that weight gain was an acceptable part of growing older, something that normally happened over the years. Recent scientific evidence, however, shows that this is just not true. Weight gain later in life is not inevitable, but it can be harmful. Putting on pounds in adulthood has more of a negative impact on health than gaining the weight early in life (and keeping it on).

But keeping the weight off in later years can be hard, considering that after age thirty-five your metabolism slows and the body's fat-burning ability decreases. Eating large amounts of food at one sitting only exacerbates the problem. Exercise, on the other hand, wards off pounds and reverses the effects of aging on metabolism.

The good news is that your weight loss doesn't have to be dramatic to have a serious impact on your health. Studies have shown that losing as little as five or ten pounds can have a positive effect on blood lipid and blood glucose levels.

Calculating Body Mass Index (BMI)

To determine your BMI, find your height (in inches) in the far-left column. Move across the row to your weight. The number on top of that column is your BMI.

Body Mass Index

Height (in.)	19	20	21	22	23	24	25	26	27	28	29	30	35	40
						Body Weight (lbs.)								
58	91	96	100	105	110	115	119	124	120	134	138	143	167	191
58	91	96	100	105	110	115	119	124	129	134	138	143	167	191
59	94	99	104	109	114	119	124	128	133	138	143	148	173	198
60	97	102	107	112	118	123	128	133	138	143	148	153	179	204
61	100	106	111	116	122	127	132	137	143	148	153	158	185	211
62	104	109	115	120	126	131	136	142	147	153	158	164	191	218
63	107	113	118	124	130	135	141	146	152	158	163	169	197	225
64	110	116	122	128	134	140	145	151	157	163	169	174	204	232
65	114	120	126	132	138	144	150	156	162	168	174	180	210	240
66	118	124	130	136	142	148	155	161	167	173	179	186	216	247
67	121	127	134	140	146	153	159	166	172	178	185	191	223	255
68	125	131	138	144	151	158	164	171	177	184	190	197	230	262
69	128	135	142	149	155	162	169	176	182	189	196	203	236	270
70	132	139	146	153	160	167	174	181	188	195	202	207	243	278
71	136	143	150	157	165	172	179	186	193	200	208	215	250	286
72	140	147	154	162	169	177	184	191	199	206	213	221	258	294
73	144	151	159	166	174	182	189	197	204	212	219	227	265	302
74	148	155	163	171	179	186	194	202	210	218	225	233	272	311
75	152	160	168	176	184	192	200	208	216	224	232	240	279	319
76	156	164	172	180	189	197	205	213	221	230	238	246	287	328

oils

Despite their "good" or "bad" reputation, all oils are created equal when it comes to how much fat they contain. One tablespoon of oil, no matter the kind, has about 120 calories and 14 grams of fat. Oil is 100 percent pure fat. That's why it's important not to overdo it when pouring on the olive oil. Oil, like other fats, can quickly rack up calories.

What's in a name?

So, what's the difference between one oil and another? Basically it comes down to the source of the fat—canola, olive, corn, etc.—and its composition. The source determines taste or flavor characteristics and color of the oil. Composition is related to health benefits and cooking performance (some oils are more stable at high cooking temperatures than others).

All fats (solid or liquid) contain three fatty acids:

- Monounsaturated fatty acids
- Polyunsaturated fatty acids
- Saturated fatty acids

Although fats are composed of all three types of fatty acids, they are classified by the predominant fat or fatty acid they contain. Thus, olive oil is considered a monounsaturated fat even though it still has some polyunsaturated and saturated fats. Because of their liquid nature, oils can only be polyunsaturated or monounsaturated. Saturated fats are solid at room temperature, so there are no oils high in this type of fatty acid (even coconut oil and palm oil look more like lard or shortening at room temperature than an oil).

When choosing oils it's best to stick with monounsaturated types (polyunsaturated oils are your second-best bet). Olive oil is probably the most popular, but it has a strong taste some people don't care for and may be too expensive for an all-purpose oil. Another option is canola oil, a bland-flavored oil, good for almost any cooking application. Made from the seeds of the rape plant, it contains linolenic acid—an omega-3 fatty acid. This fatty acid is also found in tuna and salmon and is believed to lower cholesterol and triglyceride levels.

Sorting Out Your Poly's and Mono's

Poly-unsaturated	Mono-unsaturated	Saturated (All Solid)
Corn	Almond	Animal shortening
Cottonseed	Avocado	Beef fat
Safflower	Canola	Butter
Sesame seed	Grape seed	Coconut oil
Soybean	Hazelnut	Palm oil
Sunflower	Mustard	Lard
Vegetable oil	Olive	
Walnut	Peanut	

organic

Organic foods have gone mainstream. And thanks to the success of natural foods supermarkets like Fresh Fields, Bread & Circus, and Whole Foods stores, sales are booming. In 1996, Americans spent about $3.5 billion on organic products, almost double what they spent just three years earlier. In fact, since the early nineties, the industry has been growing steadily at a rate of 20 percent each year. But do people really know what they're buying?

What is organic?

Recently the United States Department of Agriculture proposed national standards for the term *organic* (currently only a few states have a definition for it). According to these new USDA guidelines, 100 percent organic raw products means no man-made pesticides, fertilizers, or chemicals can be used on the product (natural ones like compost or manure are allowed). Processed organic products must contain at least 95 percent organic ingredients and products carrying a "made with certain organic ingredients" label must have at least 50 percent organic components.

Although these new rules mark a step in the right direction, many groups are not happy with the new proposal. Because the definitions are less stringent than those created by the National Organic Standards Board (an advisory organization founded under the 1990 Farm Bill), experts say these new rules don't go far enough—particularly when it comes to farm-management techniques (like crop rotation and certain soil and water-management practices), land-usage practices (such as the kind of soil the organic crops can be grown on), and how to raise organic livestock.

But clearly, the most controversial part of the new rules has to do with what they do not say. They have yet to take a stand on genetic engineering, food irradiation, and the use of sludge as fertilizer, leaving the door open for use of these on organic products in the future.

Still, these proposals are only preliminary. The USDA is expected to address these issues in the next few years and release final standards—with revisions—by the year 2000.

Is organic more nutritious?

Most people choose organic foods because they think they are healthier and better for them than conventionally grown and raised products. Indeed, many natural food stores make claims of organics' nutritional superiority. But in truth, no one really knows if organic foods are more nutritious than their conventionally grown counterparts, particularly produce.

Research on the subject is difficult since there are so many confounding factors to control like soil type and climate. Furthermore, any studies that have been completed offer conflicting results. So until there is stronger proof to substantiate it, most scientists feel there is little or no nutritional distinction between organic and conventionally grown produce.

Keep in mind, however, that other factors—handling, storage, length of transportation time, and maturity of the produce when picked—can influence the nutrient content of produce. Since the organic food industry is still young, it does not have a well-developed distribution system, so produce may take longer to get to market (losing precious nutrients and quality along the way). Conventional produce, on the other hand, moves from farm to market fast and efficiently, in some cases making it more nutritious than organic.

Pesticide-free

Although many consumers are concerned about pesticide residues in produce, all this worrying may be needless. Why? Because no evidence has ever shown that food treated with such chemicals can harm us. In fact, both government and many health agencies have assured us repeatedly that the pesticide residues in our foods pose no appreciable risk when it comes to cancer.

So why spend the extra money? Organic produce can cost you anywhere from 20 to 50 percent more than regular produce. Many proponents swear by the superior flavor of organic food, but given both choices, the average consumer, most likely, could not tell the difference. There may be more compelling social reasons for going organic.

Helping the earth

Buying organic produce protects the environment, the earth, and, indirectly, society at large. Because no pesticide and chemical fertilizers are used, there is no chance of contaminating soil and water supplies with residue

runoff, no expensive clean-up projects, and no loss of wildlife. Crop rotation actually replenishes the soil with nutrients, and natural pest-management techniques reduce the risk of developing insects resistant to many of our chemicals. For all these reasons and more, the federal government plans on moving more toward an organic approach to farming in the coming years.

Getting Over Appearance

New technology and farming techniques have really improved the way most organic produce looks. But it is still a long way away from the polished, perfectly shaped conventionally grown fruits and vegetables sold in the average supermarket. Unfortunately, most consumers still expect 'physical perfection' from their produce. So if the organic food industry is going to survive and thrive, people must get used to the normal imperfections and blemishes that come with raising food organically. It's only natural.

How to spot organics

Today, natural food stores are not the only places to buy organic products. Many of the larger mainstream supermarkets now have organic sections, displaying processed, canned, or frozen items. In the produce department organics are identified with a sign.

Some states even label their organic produce with the words *certified organic*. Certified means a third-party (public or private) verified that the food met certain organic standards. But not all states have this requirement.

Another good place to find organic produce is your local farmers' market, which provides the added advantage of being locally grown.

Organic meat and poultry products are not as easy to come by because the USDA does not allow the term *organic* to appear on the label of any meat or poultry product (it can only appear on point-of-sale material, articles, or advertisements related to the product).

Home on the Free Range

Many people mistakenly confuse the terms *free-range* and *organic,* especially when it comes to poultry. Free-range, by definition, means the birds are allowed access to the outdoors. This freedom does not guarantee humane treatment, nor does it mean the birds are any more nutritious or disease-free than conventionally reared poultry. A true free-range bird may get the run of the pasture, but others may just have their pens put outside. Unfortunately, most people just don't know if their chicken was true "free-roaming" or not. Still, many people are prepared to pay the premium price that free-range poultry costs in order to get what they hope will be a better tasting and more "environmentally correct" bird.

Although there are no national standards for organic, some states do sell "organic" poultry, with the exact definition depending on the area. Keep in mind, however, that hormones are not permitted in raising any poultry. And nearly all poultry (free-range or otherwise) is considered "natural," meaning it contains no artificial ingredients or added color and is only minimally processed.

phytochemicals

Healthy eating used to be a simple matter of vitamins and minerals. Today, however, good nutrition is a lot more complicated. In addition to worrying about good and bad fat and cholesterol, there's now a whole new world of compounds we need to keep us healthy.

What are phytochemicals?

Phytochemicals are biologically active, non-nutritive substances that naturally occur in plant foods ("phyto" means plant). So fruits, vegetables, grains, legumes, seeds, and nuts are loaded with them. As a class, phytochemicals are more diverse and prolific than any other group of compounds we know of—the thousands that have been discovered to date represent only the tip of the iceberg. Because of their nutritional potency, certain phytochemicals—flavonoids, carotenoids, phenolic acids, and indoles—have already made headlines. Others are only just beginning to break scientific ground.

What, exactly, do phytochemicals do?

In plants, these substances regulate growth, protect against disease and predators, and give the plant its natural color. In our bodies, their impact is just as far-reaching: They protect the body against illnesses ranging from osteoporosis to cancer.

Since phytochemicals are most potent when they are working in tandem with other plant compounds, they're difficult to study. What we do know is that you need to eat whole foods like fruits and vegetables to benefit from phytochemicals; supplements just don't have the same effect.

A guide to phytochemicals

There are many phytochemicals, and many of their properties are still unknown. Here is a review of those that have undergone rigorous scrutiny by scientists; their benefits are better understood:

Lycopene is the substance that gives tomatoes their ruby red color. One of more than six hundred colorful pigments found in nature, it belongs to a family of compounds known as "carotenoids." In addition to vine-ripened tomatoes, it can be found in pink grapefruit and watermelon. Lycopene is most concentrated in tomato products like ketchup, tomato juice, and tomato sauce.

As a disease-fighter, lycopene holds much promise in the war against cancer. In human studies, it reduced the risk of digestive system cancers, such as esophageal, stomach, colon, and rectal, and prostate cancer. In the prostate cancer study, tomato sauce (followed by pizza with tomato sauce) had the greatest impact on reducing risk. It seems that lycopene needs some fat—provided by the olive oil in tomato sauce and cheese in pizza—to be fully absorbed. Just drinking tomato juice did not have as dramatic an effect.

Allyl sulfides are actually a group of sulfur-containing phytochemicals called organosulfur compounds. Found in the lily family of plants (which includes onions, garlic, leeks, and chives) they are what gives these plants their characteristic pungency and odor.

Garlic is by far the most medicinally active of the allyl sulfides. For thousands of years this potent herb has been used to treat almost any medical condition. The major phytochemical in garlic is allicin, which can account for up to 90 percent of the dry weight of some cloves. Undisturbed, a clove of garlic has only a few active ingredients; chopping, crushing, or even chewing a clove, however, can lead to the formation of over a hundred biologically active sulfur-containing compounds. When a clove of garlic is ruptured in this manner, allin converts to allicin.

Though we don't know which active compound is responsible for which health benefit, we do know that allyl sulfides in general can:

- have a positive effect on blood lipid levels—meaning they may lower total blood cholesterol, LDLs, and triglycerides
- thin out the blood
- lower blood pressure
- reduce the risk of certain cancers, especially colon and possibly breast cancer
- have natural antibiotic properties
- act as an antioxidant in the body
- boost immunity

Sulforaphane, just one of many phytochemicals found in cruciferous vegetables, was first identified in 1992 by scientists at Johns Hopkins University. It is classified in the group of substances called isothiocyanates and in tests on rats has proven to be a highly effective anticarcinogenic agent. Sulforaphane is believed to block cancer by stimulating the liver to produce enzymes that destroy cancer-causing compounds.

In foods, the highest concentrations of sulforaphane are in broccoli sprouts (the immature buds of mature broccoli). This uncommon food, which looks and tastes similar to alfalfa sprouts, can contain up to fifty times more sulforaphane than regular broccoli. Smaller amounts of this compound are also present in cabbage, cauliflower, brussels sprouts, and turnips.

Genistein is one of the two major isoflavones in soybeans. Isoflavones are part of a group of phytochemicals called phytoestrogens—plant compounds that, in the body, have estrogen-like activity. Because of its disease-fighting ability, genistein has become one of the biggest and brightest stars in the phytochemical universe.

Current research is focused on whether genistein alone can confer the same advantages as soy. Taken in the form of soy, genistein may

- reduce the risk of heart disease by lowering total cholesterol and LDLs and raising HDLs
- keep blood vessels healthy
- reduce the risk for breast and prostate cancer
- reduce the risk for osteoporosis
- offer relief from menopausal symptoms

Nutritionists believe we can reap these health benefits simply by adding two ounces of soy protein to our daily diets. Tofu, tempeh, miso, soy milk, soy flour, and TSP (textured soy protein, sometimes called textured vegetable protein) are all suitable forms. Many of these products are now widely available in vegetarian entrées or side dishes as well as organically minded markets.

Quercetin is just one of over four thousand phenolic phytochemical compounds, all part of the flavonoid group, a chemically similar class of substances that is even further subdivided into a number of smaller groups. Quercetin falls into the flavonol group of flavonoids and is one of the most prevalent flavonoids in nature, found in a variety of plant foods, including onion, lettuce, broccoli, tomato, apple skin, tea, red wine, cranberries, olive oil, and oranges.

In studies, it has shown be an effective antioxidant and may be protective against coronary heart disease, cancer, and stroke.

Beta-carotene Backfires

A few years back, beta-carotene (an orange-colored pigment) was the newest star of the carotenoid group. As an antioxidant, it was thought to protect against cancer. But when supplements of this substance were given in a large controlled study of smokers, lung cancer rates actually increased *rather than decreased. Still, researchers haven't given up on beta-carotene. Many believe the carotenoid is still important for protecting against disease, but only for certain people and* only *in its natural, whole-food state.*

poultry

Poultry consumption has nearly doubled since the 1970s, now reaching about 64 pounds per capita annually, while red meat intake has been declining steadily.

Why are so many people turning to chicken or turkey in place of beef? One reason is versatility. Poultry, especially chicken, can be found in almost every cuisine around the world. It can be paired with any spice or flavor from soy sauce and chilies to garlic and tomatoes, so its culinary possibilities are endless. Furthermore, chicken is cheap, costing much less than the same amount of red meat. But perhaps poultry's biggest advantage is its health benefits. Low in fat and calories, chicken and turkey have become the protein source of choice for people watching their diets.

Why poultry is naturally nutritious

Like red meat, poultry is an excellent source of protein. It also provides iron, as well as some B vitamins, phosphorus, zinc, and potassium. Still, like most protein foods, it can be high in fat and cholesterol. Fortunately, most of this fat is found under the skin and in pockets throughout the bird, which makes it easy to remove. In fact, just by taking off the skin of a chicken breast you can cut your fat grams nearly in half.

To skin or not to skin

Many people think that in order to eat a lean chicken breast it must be devoid of all fat and skin before cooking. But research shows it doesn't really matter whether the chicken is cooked with the skin on or off. That's because fat from the skin is *not* absorbed by the chicken meat, as was once thought. What's more important is removing the skin before you eat the meat.

That's good news, because chicken cooked with the skin on is generally juicier and more tender than chicken cooked without the skin.

A poultry primer

Despite popular belief, not all poultry is low in fat. A skinless chicken thigh can supply more fat than a 4-ounce sirloin steak. And one 4-ounce serving of chicken wings can have up to 22 grams of fat. But if you know how to choose wisely, poultry is still deserving of its lean reputation. Chicken breast, the most popular poultry pick, is still leaner than most red meat, and skinless turkey breast, another sought-after bird, is the lowest in fat of the bunch (weighing in at only 1 gram of fat per 3-ounce serving). Here are a few tips to keep your birds as lean as possible:

- Stick to white meat. Dark meat is higher in fat, calories, and cholesterol than white meat in both chicken and turkey.
- Watch out for the wing. Since they are attached to the breast, wings are usually considered part of the white meat of poultry. Yet it's probably the fattiest part of the bird with little meat, just skin and fat.

- Read the labels on ground turkey and chicken. Ground turkey can be an excellent alternative to ground beef as long as it doesn't contain a lot of fat and skin. So read the labels carefully. Labels marked just "turkey" or "chicken" usually grind up fat and skin along with the meat. Look instead for ground products called "lean" or those that list "turkey breast" on the ingredient label.

- Try game meats. Because they are raised in the wild and not artificially fattened up, game birds such as pheasant and quail are often leaner than domestically raised poultry. Thus, they are lower in both fat and calories. But there is a price to pay: The meat in game birds is usually tougher, less tender than domestic cuts, often with a strong gamey flavor.

Don't forget duck

Recently, the USDA released new data on the composition of white Peking duck. The new nutritional data showed boneless, skinless duckling breast to contain only 2.5 grams of fat, almost half of the total fat in skinless chicken breast. The change in numbers is a result of hard work by domestic duckling growers, who over the years have successfully bred a leaner duck with less fat and more lean meat than in the past. In addition, most of the fat on duck is located between the skin and the meat, making it extremely easy to remove.

Because of its genetic makeup, all duck meat, including the breast, is dark in color. In fact, when cooked, the texture and taste of duck resembles red meat more than it does chicken. As far as taste goes, domestic birds have become milder and the flavor more refined than ten years ago. Today, duck has a sweet, rich taste that's very distinctive.

The Best of the Breasts

Per cooked 3-ounce serving (100 grams)*

Poultry	Calories	Total Fat	Saturated Fat	Cholesterol
Turkey breast, no skin	135	1 gram	0 grams	83 mg
Duckling breast, no skin	140	2.5 grams	1 gram	143 mg
Chicken breast, no skin	165	4 grams	1 gram	85 mg

*Based on USDA data from Nutritionist IV software and information from The Duckling Council.

protein

Protein is vital for all functions of your body, providing cell structure and the working material needed for all cells, including muscles, to do their job. Of all the nutrients, protein is probably the most versatile, involved in nearly everything the body does:

- Growth and maintenance of all cells. (Throughout the life cycle, cells are constantly being broken down and regenerated. Protein is necessary for growth, repair, and replacement of cells.)
- Enzyme function. (Enzymes make chemical reactions [digestion, for example] happen in the body.)
- Proper hormone function. (Hormones regulate a number of body processes.)
- Production of antibodies. (These are the body's foot soldiers: They are called to battle whenever any foreign substance such as a cold virus or toxin is introduced into the body.)
- Maintain fluid and mineral balance in the body.
- Regulate acid-base balance in blood and other body fluids.
- Provide energy. (Protein can provide fuel for the body when carbohydrates and fats are in short supply.)
- Transportation. (Proteins transport important substances such as oxygen or lipids to and from tissues all over the body.)
- Blood clotting.
- Body structure. (Bones, skin, tendons, ligaments, organs, and other structures are all composed of protein.)

The building blocks of life

Like carbohydrates and fats, proteins are composed of carbon, hydrogen, and oxygen, but with an extra element added in—nitrogen. Together, these four substances form a compound called an amino acid, and amino acids are the building blocks of proteins. Of the twenty amino acids found in nature, more than half can be synthesized by the body. The remaining nine are essential—that is, they must be obtained from food.

High-quality proteins like meat, milk, and eggs supply all of the essential amino acids and then some. These are complete proteins. As a rule, all animal proteins are complete. Plant proteins, on the other hand, are usually missing one or two essential amino acids, so they are considered "incomplete" proteins. To get complete protein from plant sources, it's necessary to eat "complementary" plant foods, such as beans and rice or peanut butter on whole-wheat bread.

Nutritionists don't feel it's necessary to consume complementary proteins in the same meal, even for vegetarians. Rather, they advise eating a wide variety of foods including protein from many plant sources over the course of a few days. This less stringent approach ensures that you'll get the right amount of protein without restricting the kinds of foods eaten at each meal.

Protein in the body

In the body, proteins are broken down into amino acids, which are then used to build the different proteins (and other substances) needed for various functions in the body. Excess protein, like excess carbohydrates, gets stored as fat, so if you eat too much protein, you will put on weight.

How much is enough?

Despite its many uses in the body, we really don't need that much protein, particularly compared to other nutrients. Health authorities advise that protein should constitute no more than 15 percent of your total caloric intake. Recommended Dietary Allowances for protein set by the National Research Council in 1989 vary by age, but in general, adult women should be getting about 50 grams of protein a day; adult men, about 63 grams. *Note:* This number is based on the accepted rate of .8 grams of protein per kilogram (2.2 pounds) of body weight per day.

According to the USDA Food Guide Pyramid, Americans can easily meet these needs by eating two or three servings from the milk group, two or three servings from the meat group, three to five servings from the vegetable group, two to four servings from the fruit group, and six to eleven servings from the bread group.

The Protein Power of Plants

The following chart shows examples of the three major sources of vegetable proteins: grains, legumes, and seeds and nuts. Although other plant foods—broccoli and leafy greens—also contain protein, the quantity and quality aren't as great. In order to make a complete protein, you must choose foods from at least two of these groups.

Grains	Legumes	Seeds and Nuts
Barley	Dried beans (black beans)	Cashews
Bulgur	Dried lentils	Walnuts
Cornmeal	Dried peas (split peas)	Nut butters
Oats	Peanuts*	Other nuts
Pasta	Soy products (tofu)	Pumpkin seeds
Rice		Sesame seeds
Whole-grain breads		Sunflower seeds

*Peanuts' nutritional profile makes them part of the legume family.

salt

Many people think salt and sodium are one and the same. They're not. Sodium is a basic chemical element, an electrolyte that we need to live. The body relies on sodium to regulate blood volume, to maintain the acid-base balance, and to transmit nerve impulses and muscle contractions.

Salt, on the other hand, is sodium chloride, a simple compound composed of 40 percent sodium and 60 percent chloride (chloride, like sodium, is essential to life and important for maintaining the acid-base balance in the blood). Although sodium can also be found in things like baking soda (sodium bicarbonate) and mineral water, in our diets, sodium chloride—pure, white table salt—is by far the dominant form consumed.

Currently, the average adult in the United States consumes 4,000 to 6,000 milligrams of sodium daily. Even at the low end, 4,000 milligrams of sodium comes out to about 10 grams of salt, or nearly 2 teaspoons, every day. Considering that the government sets a minimum of 500 milligrams for adequacy and the Daily Values in the U.S. Dietary Guidelines recommends moderate sodium intakes of 2,400 milligrams daily—found in about 6 grams of salt—we eat much more salt than we need to. Whether high salt intakes are actually bad for us is another issue and one that is surrounded by controversy.

Throughout the centuries, salt has been a valuable commodity. It's used as a preservative and processing agent in such foods as breads, meats, and pickled vegetables. Some foods, like cheese, cannot be formed without salt. Today, its main purpose is as a flavor enhancer, heightening and intensifying natural flavors, at the same time adding its own characteristic flavor—a taste many people crave.

According to the Food and Drug Administration, about 75 percent of the sodium we consume is in the form of processed foods—canned, frozen, and convenience items. The rest of our sodium comes naturally from food (about 15 percent) and as salt (about 10 percent) in its pure form, added during cooking or straight from the shaker once the meal is served.

Hidden salts

Part of the reason people have so much trouble lowering their salt intake is that many times they just don't know they're eating it. Food doesn't have to taste salty to be high in sodium. These hidden sources of salt are our worse enemies. Take for example the difference between potato chips and corn flakes. Most people assume the potato chips are higher in salt. But a one-ounce serving of potato chips contains about 150 milligrams of sodium; the same size serving of corn flakes has nearly twice that amount. Following are some other surprisingly high sodium foods:

FOOD	SODIUM CONTENT (IN MG)*
Canned corn, ½ cup	285
Instant vanilla pudding, ½ cup (from box mix)	410
Canned tuna fish, 2 ounces (light chunk, packed in water)	300
Pizza, frozen, ¼ pie (4.5 ounces)	770
Cheese, American, processed, 1 ounce	410
English muffin, 1	365
Ketchup, tomato, 2 tablespoons	360
Turkey hot dog	485

*Figures are based on Jean A. T. Pennington's Food Values of Portions Commonly Consumed, 16th ed. (Philadelphia, Penn.: J. B. Lippincott Company, 1994).

Salt and hypertension

Despite its illustrious past, over the last few decades salt has fallen out of favor with the American public because too much salt is said to trigger hypertension, or high blood pressure, in some individuals. Hypertension, defined as a blood pressure reading of 140/90 or above, afflicts nearly 50 million Americans and is believed to play a role in 700,000 deaths a year, primarily from heart disease, stroke, and kidney disease.

Results from a massive 1988 research project called Intersalt found that the more sodium a person excretes in the urine, the higher their blood pressure. Since, in general, urinary sodium levels are directly related to the amount of salt a person consumes, the research concluded that people who eat more salt have higher blood pressure than people who eat less. The study also showed that high salt intakes increases the rise in blood pressure that naturally occurs with age.

But some scientists do not believe everyone needs to reduce salt consumption. Research from Toronto, Canada, found that older adults who already have hypertension could only mildly lower their blood pressure levels by restricting salt in their diet. Moreover, there was no benefit associated with a low-salt diet for younger people with normal blood pressure.

The problem is that not everyone's blood pressure will respond to changes in salt intake, and there is no way of knowing who is salt-sensitive and who is not. In any case, the medical community does agree that salt is only part of the picture.

The most promising findings for controlling hypertension come from DASH (Dietary Approaches to Stop Hypertension), a recent landmark study that looked at total diet and high blood pressure. Through careful clinical trials, DASH researchers concluded that a diet low in fat, and rich in fruits and vegetables and low-fat dairy foods lowered blood pressure levels just as effectively as many antihypertensive drugs.

Researchers think the result is a combination of several factors: the high mineral content found in fruits and vegetables, the calcium in dairy foods, the low fat intake, and the reduced salt intake (participants were given a constant 3,000 milligrams of sodium per day).

Other health risks associated with salt

Eating a diet high in salt exacerbates calcium losses, ultimately leading to a loss in bone density. At a sodium level of 2,400 milligrams a day, taking in the recommended RDA of 1,200 milligrams of dietary calcium will sufficiently protect your bones; consuming more salt requires an increase in calcium. Since few Americans meet the calcium RDA as it is, women, especially, should keep salt intake in check.

In addition to osteoporosis, scientists think taking in large amounts of sodium over a long period of time may be related to asthma, kidney stones, and stomach cancer.

How to reduce your salt intake

Even if you don't have hypertension or other health problems, cutting back on salt may still be a wise decision. The easiest way to do this is to pinpoint the source of most of your salt intake. Since convenience foods contain the largest amounts of sodium in the average diet, steering clear of these products or choosing low-sodium brands is your first step. Here are a few others:

- Read food labels to see if a product is high in sodium. Try to choose foods with fewer than 480 milligrams of sodium per serving.

- Stay away from salty foods like pretzels (buy unsalted), potato chips, olives, and pickles.

- In cooking, replace the salt with extra herbs and spices to pump up the flavor in soups, sauces, and entrées. Some good choices are garlic, lemon, basil, mint, oregano, thyme, and parsley.

- If you do use salt, add it in at the end of cooking or use the salt shaker at the table instead. Cooking mutes salt's flavor, so adding it in later means you'll need less salt in the long run.

- Watch out for processed meats, frozen foods, and canned items. They are usually loaded with sodium. Choose low-sodium or sodium-free varieties if available.

sugar

Sugars are simple carbohydrates, and like all carbohydrates, they contain only 4 calories per gram. In the body, there's no difference between the carbohydrate in a slice of bread or in a chocolate bar; they all eventually break down into glucose.

Single sugars like fructose can bypass the digestive system and be readily absorbed into the bloodstream. Starches and disaccharides, however, must be digested—they must be broken down before they can be used.

Simple sugars

Sugars fall into two categories: monosaccharides and disaccharides. Monosaccharides are single sugar units; disaccharides are two-sugar units.

Monosaccharides (simple-sugar units): glucose: blood sugar, found in all carbohydrates; fructose: fruit sugar, the sweetest tasting of all the sugars, $1\frac{1}{2}$ times sweeter than sucrose—used to sweeten beverages and desserts; galactose: needed in order to make milk sugar.

Disaccharides (two-sugar units): sucrose: sometimes called refined sugar, common white table sugar, and found naturally in sugar cane or sugar beets; lactose: milk sugar—least sweet of all the sugars; maltose: malt sugar, formed during the fermentation of alcohol.

Dissolving some sugar myths

From a health perspective, sugar has been blamed for everything from obesity to hyperactivity in children. Furthermore, most people think sugar is off-limits on a healthful diet. Yet this doesn't have to be the case. In fact, sugar has been wrongfully accused of many ailments.

Obesity: Although many people are quick to point a finger at sugar when it comes to weight gain, it is an intake high in fat and calories that is the biggest culprit. While high sugar intakes can contribute to obesity (sugar consumption rises as the incidence of obesity increases), no scientific studies have actually linked sugar with being overweight. In fact, some studies have shown that lean people eat more sugary foods than people who are overweight.

Diabetes: Eating too much sugar does not cause diabetes, as some people used to think, but it may increase your chances of getting the disease. According to a study from the Harvard School of Public Health, women who ate diets high in refined carbohydrates and low in fiber were two and a half times more likely to develop Type II diabetes than women who followed a high-fiber, refined low-carbohydrate diet.

Hyperactivity in children: Although many parents believe sugar can cause their kids to go bouncing off the walls, there is no scientific evidence to support this notion. Researchers have never proven any link between diet—and specifically sugar—and hyperactivity in children.

Cavities: Contrary to popular belief, eating too much sugar is not detrimental to the health of your teeth, nor does it lead to dental cavities. We know that carbohydrates in the mouth cause bacteria to produce acid, which can eat away at tooth enamel. But not all carbohydrates are the same when it comes to your teeth. The longer the carbohydrate stays on your teeth, the more likely it is to form a cavity. Sticky, starchy foods like raisins, bananas, bread, and pasta are not as readily cleared by saliva as sugar is. So a slice of bread can actually pose more of a tooth decay risk than a piece of candy.

Don't overindulge

So if sugar is so innocent, why has it gotten such a bad reputation? Maybe it's because sugary foods tend to be empty calories devoid of vitamins, minerals, and fiber. Or maybe it's because so much of it is used in our food supply. Over two-thirds of the sugar we eat is added to our food, much of it hidden in processed foods like ketchup, yogurt, cereal, soups, and sauces.

Eating lots of concentrated sweets not only raises calories, it often takes the place of more nutritious foods in the diet. Aside from calories, sugar provides no significant nutrients, so even though it may not be as bad as was once thought, it's still a good idea to watch the sweets.

A taste for sweets

Sweetness is the only taste we have an innate preference for—we are all born with a sweet tooth. All other tastes are acquired or learned. Scientists speculate that it was a matter of survival. Back when man still foraged for food, sweet things tended to be good for you, while bitter- or bad-tasting foods could be potentially dangerous.

Most of the sugary foods we eat today are paired with fat, which would explain why so many of us have a learned preference for fats. This fat-sugar mixture is even more preferred than sugar alone.

Is one sugar better than another?

If you think honey is nutritionally better than white table sugar, think again. In the body there is no difference between natural and refined sugars. Chemically, honey and table sugar are exactly alike. And brown sugar is simply white sugar sprayed with molasses for flavor and color.

What differs is the amount of sweetness each of these sugars provide. Honey, since it is more concentrated, is sweeter than sugar—so you don't have to use as much. It also contains more calories ounce for ounce than white granulated sugar. Except for the caramel flavor, brown sugar and white sugar can be used interchangeably.

How Do You Spell S-U-G-A-R?

In food, sugar can appear in a number of ways. And it has just as many names. If any of these words appear in the list of ingredients it means your food has been sweetened:

Beet sugar

Brown sugar

Concentrated fruit juice sweetener

Corn sweeteners

Corn syrup

Crystallized cane juice

Dextrose

Fructose

High-fructose corn syrup

Honey

Invert sugar

Lactose

Maltodextrin or dextrin

Maltose

Maple syrup or sugar

Molasses

Raw sugar

Sucrose

Turbinado sugar

vegetables

Vegetables are the cornerstones of a healthy diet. High in complex carbohydrates and fiber, they supply an abundant amount of vitamins and minerals. At the same time, they're low in calories (averaging about 25 calories per serving) and virtually fat-free.

Of all the food groups, vegetables are the most diverse, with literally hundreds of varieties to choose from in all sizes, shapes, flavors, colors, and textures. Each has its own nutritional benefits, but, overall, vegetables provide vitamin A, vitamin C, folate, iron, magnesium, and fiber. They're also full of phytochemicals, non-nutritive plant compounds we're only just beginning to understand. Some of these phytochemicals—isoflavonoids, carotenes, and indoles, for example—are known to fight cancer, heart disease, and many other illnesses.

How they stack up

Categorizing vegetables is hard since there are so many different kinds, but these are the basic groups they fall into:

Leafy greens: These are dark-green leafy vegetables—spinach, arugala, collard greens, kale, Swiss chard, watercress, romaine lettuce, and other salad greens. Many of them are eaten raw, but because of their high water content they can also be cooked (though they shrink quite a bit when cooked). Nutritionally, greens are an important source of beta-carotene (a precursor of vitamin A), vitamin C, folic acid, iron, and calcium.

Color is the key factor for choosing the best of these vegetables for freshness, quality, and nutrient content. Basically, the darker the green color, the better it is for you. Darker greens provide more vitamin A and more valuable phytochemicals than lighter ones.

Flowers, buds, stems, and shoots: These are vegetables like asparagus, broccoli, cauliflower, celery, and artichokes. They tend to be rich in vitamin C, beta-carotene, calcium, potassium, iron, riboflavin, and fiber.

Some of the so-called cruciferous vegetables (named because the flower they bear looks like a cross) also fall into this category. They include broccoli, cauliflower, cabbage, radishes (a root vegetable), brussels sprouts, mustard greens (brussels sprouts, cabbage, and mustard greens are also in the leafy-green category). They contain a wealth of phytochemicals and carotenoids, some of which are known to have a strong protective effect against certain cancers.

Seeds and pods: This is the legume family—dried beans, peas, and lentils. Corn is also part of this group. These are starchy vegetables high in complex carbohydrates and calories (particularly when compared to leafy greens and the flower vegetables). Protein is their best nutritional attribute—they're also packed with B vitamins, zinc, potassium, magnesium, calcium, iron, and lots of fiber.

Fruit vegetables: These are peppers, eggplant, tomato, squash, pumpkin, cucumber, and okra. They come in a myriad of sizes, shapes, and flavors. Generally, they have a high water content and relatively few carbohydrates. Because they are not as sweet as fruits, they can be used to season a number of dishes. Nutritionally, they're a good source of vitamins A and C, depending on the type of vegetable.

Roots, tubers, and bulbs: These are vegetables that grow below ground. Carrots, potatoes, parsnips, turnips, beets, garlic, onions, fennel, and leeks are a few examples. Most tend to be winter produce, but some, like carrots, onions, and garlic are available year-round. Like legumes, these dense vegetables are high in carbohydrates, and so higher in calories. Nutritionally, they are rich in vitamins, minerals, and fiber, again depending on the vegetable. For example, white potatoes are an excellent source of vitamin C and potassium. Orange or yellow vegetables like sweet potatoes and carrots, on the other hand, are high in vitamin A. All provide plenty of fiber, too, particularly if the skin is left on.

Eat your vegetables

According to USDA consumption figures, we eat $3\frac{1}{3}$ servings of vegetables a day, just barely making the minimum of 3 to 5 daily servings as recommended by the Food Guide Pyramid. But if you take into consideration how many calories we consume, nearly 60 percent of us aren't eating as many vegetables as we should.

We also need to rethink the kinds of vegetables we're choosing. Potatoes make up about a third of our vegetable consumption, but legumes are only about 6 percent, and dark-green leafy vegetables are even less, about 3 percent of our total vegetable intake.

To encourage more variety in the diet, the Food Guide Pyramid recommends choosing vegetables from every group, including dark leafy greens, yellow-orange vegetables, starchy vegetables, legumes, and others like green beans, lettuce, tomatoes, and peppers. Because they're so important, the Pyramid specifically advises dark-green leafy vegetables and legumes be eaten several times a week.

Cooking tips

Many of the vitamins and minerals found in vegetables can be lost if the vegetables aren't cooked properly. In particular, vitamin C and the B vitamins, since they are water-soluble, can leach out if vegetables are overcooked and boiled in lots of water. High heat also causes some vitamin losses.

Color is the best indicator of nutrient retention. If vegetables change from a bright, vibrant green to a drab olive color, it means you've probably lost a good bit of the nutrients. To avoid this problem, cook vegetables quickly and at lower temperatures. Also, be sure not to overcook.

A few more cooking tips:

- Microwave whenever possible. Microwaving is the best cooking method because it is the quickest and requires very little water.
- If you don't have a microwave, use the second-best method for preserving nutrients and flavor: steaming.

- Rather than covering vegetables with water, use only a small amount or just what's necessary to cook vegetables without burning them.
- Cook vegetables whole or in large pieces, then cut them up. (Cooking this way decreases the amount of surface area exposed to heat, lessening vitamin losses.)
- Bake or roast root vegetables in their skin rather than boiling them.

It's all in the can

If you think canned fruits and vegetables are nutritionally inferior to fresh or frozen varieties, it's time you changed your attitude. A recent study from the University of Illinois found thirty-three canned fruits and vegetables—among them, carrots, peaches, pineapple, spinach, and tomatoes—to be nutritionally equivalent to fresh.

In fact, in some cases, canned vegetables turned out to be even better than fresh. That's because canned produce is processed at the peak of freshness, and, once processed, the amount of nutrients it contains are stabilized. Fresh produce, on the other hand, suffers nutrient losses throughout the distribution chain. Precious vitamins and minerals are lost if vegetables spend too much time in storage, in transit, or even just sitting in your refrigerator.

Some more surprising facts about canned vegetables:

- Canned pumpkin provides significantly more vitamin A than fresh-cooked.
- The vitamin C content in some canned asparagus can be even higher than fresh-cooked.
- Canned tomatoes are loaded with lycopene, a carotenoid compound (and another phytochemical best known for fighting prostate cancer). In fact, the lycopene in cooked tomatoes was found to be even more effective than that found in fresh.
- Fiber content in canned beans, peas, carrots, and other foods is the same as those in fresh. Cooking does not break down the fiber, but it may make it more soluble, and therefore more useful to the body.

There is one difference between canned and fresh produce though—salt. Canned foods contain much higher levels of sodium. If you're concerned about salt intake, look for low-sodium brands, and rinse all vegetables before you eat them.

vegetarianism

Over 12 million Americans consider themselves vegetarians, meaning they abstain from some or all animal products. Most of this vegetarian phenomenon can be attributed to the recent movement toward meatless meals and a more vegetarian-style of eating among mainstream consumers. Although classified as vegetarians, many consumers have not entirely eliminated meat and meat products from their diet but, rather, reduced the amounts eaten. Without these "almost vegetarians," true vegetarian or vegan numbers are much smaller, probably in the range of 1.5 to 2 million.

Still, growth in vegetarianism is evident in almost all areas of the food supply. Most supermarkets and retail food stores now carry a well-stocked supply of vegetarian items, particularly in the frozen food aisles, and produce departments have become prime draws, including an average of over four hundred items to choose from. In restaurants, vegetarian meals are also making inroads. Over three-quarters (on average) of all restaurants surveyed by the National Restaurant Association offer vegetarian menu options and about one-third or more adult Americans are likely to enjoy meatless items when dining out.

Why are so many people turning away from meat and meat products? Although vegetarians will cite any number of reasons for turning green—environmental, ethical, and religious—health benefits are the most likely motivators.

In general, vegetarians tend to have lower rates of heart disease, hypertension, diabetes, and some types of cancer than nonvegetarians. They're also usually leaner than meat-eaters with weights closer to desirable levels. Some studies have even shown that vegetarians as a group live longer than meat-eaters.

Not all vegetarian diets are healthy. Like nonvegetarian diets, meatless meals can be loaded with fat, calories, and sodium, particularly if dishes are heavily laden with eggs and cheese. But because most animal meats are high in fat, the majority of vegetarian diets are lower in fat, saturated fat, and cholesterol than meat-based diets. Healthful vegetarian entrées rely on vegetables, fruits, grains, and nuts rather than dairy foods, and include a wide variety of foods that add texture, color, and flavor.

How do vegetarians get nutrients?

Protein: Although it's a tough fact for some carnivores to digest, protein is not a problem for most vegetarians. It is an abundant nutrient in grain and grain products, legumes, seeds, nuts, and some vegetables. In fact, most vegetarians meet or exceed their Recommended Dietary Allowance for protein.

In the past, nutritionists recommended that certain plant foods be combined in the same meal in order to create complete complementary proteins, and many of the most popular vegetarian foods historically make up complete proteins: red beans and rice, minestrone soup, lentils and rice, and peanut butter on whole-wheat bread. Today, rather than worrying about the protein makeup of each meal, vegetarians are counseled to include a wide variety of protein-rich foods in their diet throughout the day.

Still, there are some nutrients that vegetarians and particularly vegans need to pay special attention to. These are:

Calcium: Vegetarians who consume dairy products have no trouble consuming enough calcium, but strict vegans sometimes do. For them calcium can be obtained by eating dark-green leafy vegetables like collards, turnip greens, spinach, Swiss chard, sorrel, and parsley. Dried beans and peas are also good sources. In addition, there are many calcium-fortified products on the market—soy milk, orange juice, and tofu. Children, teens, and women of childbearing years should pay particular attention to these foods since their needs are high.

Iron: Like calcium, iron is widely distributed in plant foods and contained in dried beans, dark-green leafy vegetables, watermelon, dried fruits, and many nuts and seeds such as almonds, cashews, sesame seeds, and sunflower seeds. Iron-enriched or -fortified breads, cereals, and grains are also available. To enhance iron absorption, these foods can be combined with vitamin C–rich fruits and vegetables like broccoli, tomatoes, green peppers, and citrus fruits or fruit juices.

Vitamin B_{12}: This particular B vitamin is found in all animal products. Vegans can get this vitamin through a supplement or specially fortified cereals, milk, yeast, and some meat analogs. Since only small amounts of B_{12} are needed, any vegetarian who eats milk, cheese, eggs, or other dairy products, even on occasion, will still get plenty of the vitamin.

Zinc: Most people, vegetarian or not, have a hard time getting enough zinc. It can be found in whole grains, legumes, wheat germ, nuts (especially peanut butter), and seeds.

Vitamin D: In the United States, milk and milk products are fortified with vitamin D. In addition, the body manufactures this vitamin when the skin is exposed to sunlight even for just ten to fifteen minutes twice a week (depending on where you're located). Only those vegans who do not consume dairy products and are not in the sun on a regular basis should consider taking a vitamin D supplement.

The vegetarian continuum

Even within categories, vegetarian eating patterns vary tremendously. Many people today are "almost vegetarians," who eat fish and/or poultry, eggs, and dairy but avoid red meat. Although they may not consider themselves strictly vegetarian, they are consuming more meatless meals and are at the start of the vegetarian continuum. On the other end of the spectrum are strict vegans, who consume no animal foods at all. With so many kinds of vegetarians, it is difficult to describe them, but they can be described by what they have in common rather than what sets them apart.

Following are some general classifications of vegetarians:

Pescovegetarians: eat fish, eggs, and dairy but not animal flesh

Lacto-ovovegetarians: eat dairy products and eggs but not fish, poultry, or red meat. (The largest number of vegetarians are lacto-ovo.)

Lactovegetarians: consume milk and milk products but not eggs or animal flesh.

Vegans: rely exclusively on plant foods and eat no animal products or animal flesh. Many vegans also do not eat honey because it is produced by bees (another living creature). They comprise about 4 percent of all vegetarians.

vitamins

Vitamins are organic compounds that act like metabolic catalysts in the body, regulating or driving virtually all biochemical reactions. There are thirteen vitamins and they fall into two categories: water soluble and fat soluble. Although we need only very small quantities of them, they are essential to life. Except for vitamin D, which the body can synthesize with the help of the sun, all vitamins must be obtained through diet.

The water-soluble vitamins

Water-soluble vitamins include the B vitamins and vitamin C. They are usually absorbed directly into the bloodstream and for the most part are not stored. Excessive amounts are excreted in the urine, so a toxicity or overdose from these vitamins is unlikely. However, adverse reactions have been reported with vitamin B_6, vitamin C, and niacin when large dose concentrations from supplements were taken.

In food, preserving the water-soluble vitamins requires careful handling. They can easily leach out in cooking and washing water and are often destroyed by direct exposure to light.

The fat-soluble vitamins

Vitamins A, D, E, and K are fat soluble. They occur in the fatty or oily portion of foods and are absorbed and transported in the bloodstream in a manner similar to fat. Unlike the water-soluble vitamins, these vitamins can be stored, primarily in fat tissue and the liver, so they have the potential to build up in toxic concentrations.

Since these vitamins need fat to be absorbed, a very low fat diet over a long period of time can result in a vitamin deficiency. Fat malabsorption diseases like Crohn's disease or ulcerative colitis can also bring about a deficiency.

In food, the fat-soluble vitamins are adversely affected by careless handling (like temperature abuse) and long storage times.

What the body needs

Vitamin needs vary depending on age, gender, and outside factors that affect the body, such as smoking. In any case, we can get all the vitamins and minerals we need through food, by eating a well-balanced, healthy diet. As a rule, vitamin supplements are generally not necessary. Only people who consistently eat an unhealthy, imbalanced diet need to worry about supplements. A couple of bad eating days won't create a nutritional deficiency or drain the body's vitamin stores.

Physically active people may need slightly more B vitamins and a few minerals like zinc, but this is easily acquired in the diet. Since serious athletes generally consume large quantities of food, vitamin supplements are again a moot point. However, for people who work out more than 90 minutes a session, several times a week, and do not compensate by eating healthy, hefty meals, taking a multivitamin may be a good investment for protecting vitamin stores. A multivitamin might also be recommended if you're following a low-calorie or restricted diet.

The most current recommendations

Ever since 1941, the National Academy of Sciences' Food and Nutrition Board has been preparing Recommended Dietary Allowances (RDAs) of essential nutrients. Since these recommendations are meant to meet the needs of almost all healthy individuals, they add in a safety factor so that recommended amounts actually exceed the nutrient requirements for most people.

Throughout the years, the RDAs have been updated and revised to coincide with new research findings in the field of nutrition, with the last revision completed in 1989. At this time, the Food and Nutrition Board is again in the process of reevaluating the RDAs.

In the past, the RDAs were mainly concerned with preventing deficiencies—ensuring that people got enough nutrients. Today, the atmosphere is one of overnutrition rather than undernutrition. In response, the new RDAs are targeted to optimize health, and to reduce the risk of chronic disease.

Nutritionary

The following guide to nutritional terms will help you to understand charts and food labels.

Dietary Reference Intakes (DRI): Umbrella term for RDAs, AIs, EARs, and ULs (see below).

Recommended Dietary Allowances (RDA): The adequate nutrient intake required for decreasing the risk of chronic disease in almost all healthy individuals in a specific age and gender group.

Adequate Intakes (AI): These are similar to RDAs; the intakes advised when there is not enough scientific data to set RDA.

Estimated Average Requirements (EAR): Optimal nutrient needs for half of the individuals in a specific group.

Tolerable Upper Intake Levels (UL): Maximum amount unlikely to pose an adverse health risk in almost all healthy adults. You should not exceed this amount. ULs are not a recommendation.

A summary of new findings

B vitamins and folic acid: Research shows B_6, B_{12}, and folic acid can keep in check blood levels of homocysteine (an amino acid broken down from protein). This is important because elevated homocysteine levels are thought to be the newest risk factor for heart disease.

Furthermore, there is strong evidence that folic acid protects against spina bifida, a birth defect affecting the spinal cord. For this reason, ever since January 1, 1998, all enriched grain products are fortified with folic acid.

Vitamin C: Although new vitamin C recommendations have not come out yet, a new study out of the National Institutes of Health found 200 milligrams of vitamin C daily to be the optimum level for absorption for healthy young men.

Vitamin E: There is now mounting evidence that high doses of vitamin E (taken in supplement form) can fight heart disease.

Vitamin D: The right amount of vitamin D is vital for maintaining healthy bones, but take too much and it can have the opposite effect, causing bone loss.

Vitamin K: Recent research has found that vitamin K, known for its blood-clotting properties, is also important for bone health. One study found that high levels of vitamin K can significantly increase bone-building protein. Fortunately, eating this much vitamin K is easy to do through diet since plenty of the vitamin is found in green leafy vegetables like Swiss chard and spinach.

Nutrients and What They Do

Nutrient	What It Does	What Can Happen If You Take Too Much	What Can Happen If You Take Too Little	Food Sources	RDA
VITAMIN A	• Important for eye health • Helps immune function • Maintains body linings: skin, nose, mouth, and digestive tract	Hair loss, stunted growth, bone pain, birth defects	Night blindness, skin problems, impaired immunity, reproductive abnormalities	Yellow-orange vegetables (i.e., sweet potatoes, carrots), dark green leafy vegetables, fortified milk, cheese, cream, butter, eggs, fruit	Women: 800 IU Men: 1,000 IU (5,000 retinol equiv.)
VITAMIN D	• Essential for bone and teeth health • Regulates calcium and phosphorous metabolism	Bone loss, hypercalcemia, reduced renal function	Rickets or abnormal bone growth	Fortified milk, fortified butter and margarine, eggs, fatty fish, and liver.	All adults: 5 micrograms or 200 IU
VITAMIN E	• Antioxidant • Protects and maintains cell membranes	Large doses may interact with anticoagulant medication	Anemia	Plant oils, nuts, seeds, wheat germ, fortified cereals, poultry, fish, and eggs	Women: 8 mg Men: 10 mg
VITAMIN K	• Essential for blood clotting and bone health	Red blood cell breakdown and, in rare cases, brain damage	Hemorrhages	Dark leafy greens, spinach, cabbage, broccoli, scallion; also, synthesized in intestine	Women: 65 micrograms Men: 80 micrograms
VITAMIN C (ASCORBIC ACID)	• Antioxidant • Promotes healing • Keeps connective tissue, bones, teeth, collagen healthy	Diarrhea, nausea, and cramps	Scurvy	Citrus fruits, cruciferous vegetables (broccoli, cabbage, and brussels sprouts); potatoes, peppers; fruits (cantaloupe, strawberries, papaya, and mangoes)	All adults: 60 milligrams
VITAMIN B1 (THIAMIN)	• Involved in energy metabolism	No known toxicity	Beriberi: loss of sensation in hands and feet; muscle weakness	Pork, ham, leafy green vegetables, yeast, whole-grain cereals, legumes	Women: 1.1 mg Men: 1.5 mg

Nutrients and What They Do (cont'd)

Nutrient	What It Does	What Can Happen If You Take Too Much	What Can Happen If You Take Too Little	Food Sources	RDA
VITAMIN B2 (RIBOFLAVIN)	• Involved in body's energy releasing mechanisms	No known toxicity	Deficiency affects skin, eyes, and mouth	Dairy products, liver, yeast, spinach, mushrooms, whole-grain breads	Women: 1.3 mg Men: 1.7 mg
VITAMIN B3 (NIACIN)	• Helps convert carbohydrates into energy	A flush or tingling sensation on skin	Pellagra, characterized by diarrhea, dermatitis, and dementia	Meat, poultry, fish, enriched breads and cereals, milk, eggs, fruits, and vegetables	Women: 15 mg Men: 19 mg
VITAMIN B6	• Protein metabolism • Helps regulate blood glucose	Nerve damage in high doses	Weakness, irritability, anemia, and decreased immune function	Meat, poultry, milk, shellfish, fish, legumes, green and leafy vegetables	Women: 1.6 mg Men: 2 mg
VITAMIN B12	• Along with folate makes red blood cells • Protects and maintains nerve fibers	No known toxicity	Anemia, birth defects	Meat, poultry, fish, eggs, and dairy	All adults: 2 micrograms
FOLATE	• Helps synthesize DNA needed for new cells	No known toxicity	Anemia, birth defects	Widely available in foods: leafy green vegetables, fruits, liver, yeast, green peppers	Women: 180 micrograms Men: 200 micrograms
BIOTIN	• Involved in energy metabolism	No known toxicity	Very rare	Widespread in foods	No RDA; estimated safe and adequate intake per day: 30 to 100 micrograms
PANTOTHENIC ACID	• Involved in energy metabolism	No known toxicity	Very rare	Widespread in foods, especially meat, fish, poultry, whole-grain cereals and legumes	No RDA; estimated safe and adequate intake per day: 4 to 7 mg

water

Water is often called the forgotten nutrient since many people take it for granted, but water is essential to life. We can live with less than enough food for weeks, months, even years, but take away our water and we last just a few days.

Water makes up about 60 percent of the average adult's weight. It is the medium the human body uses for nearly every activity it performs and has many functions, including:

- Carrying nutrients in the body
- Cleansing the body's waste products
- Acting as a solvent, dissolving minerals, proteins, carbohydrates, vitamins, and other substances
- Being involved in many chemical reactions in the body
- Lubricating joints
- Acting as a shock absorber for many organs
- Helping to regulate body temperature

Since water is so important, its balance is delicately monitored by a number of mechanisms. Our brain signals us to drink when the sodium concentrations in the blood become too high or when blood volume drops too low. Unfortunately, by the time this thirst mechanism kicks in, we are already in the beginning stages of water deficit. That's why nutritionists recommend drinking *before* you are thirsty.

This is particularly important for the elderly population because as we age we become less sensitive to our thirst mechanism. At the same time, our percentage of body fluid drops, so it's easier to become dehydrated faster.

Young children are also at a higher risk for dehydration, but for another reason: Their thirst mechanism is not yet fully developed, nor are they always able to recognize when they are thirsty.

Water needs vary with each individual, but in general, nutritionists still abide by the old rule of eight glasses—64 ounces—or more of fluid a day. Water is your best bet, but it is certainly not the only way to get fluids. Fruit juice, seltzer, milk, lemonade, and soft drinks can also quench thirst. Alcohol and caffeinated beverages like tea and coffee do not count because they are actually diuretics, meaning they cause you to lose fluid rather than retain it. Foods like soup, cucumbers, watermelon, lettuce, tomatoes, and oranges are high in water and a good way to supplement your liquid intake.

The Truth About Bottled Water

Store-bought bottled water is not always superior to tap. It all depends on the source of the water and how it's treated.

Most bottled water comes from protected underground springs, but some brands are simply municipal water (tap water) that has undergone several purifying processes. Some health authorities say up to 25 percent of bottled water comes from the same source as tap water. How do you know where your water is coming from? Read the label: Products using municipal water supplies must say so on the label.

weight

It used to be that everyone wanted to be model thin, striving for an elusive number on a chart, known only as the "ideal" body weight. Developed by life insurance companies, these "ideal" body weights became the yardstick by which everyone was measured.

Today, both scientists and health professionals have discarded the notion of "ideal" body weight for the more appropriate "healthy" weight range. Healthy weights are higher than the old ideal weights, and they offer a range instead of one hard and fast number.

Your perfect weight

Recently, many nutritionists have encouraged patients to set healthy weight goals even if these weights are higher than what the charts recommend. This is particularly important for people who have struggled for years to maintain or achieve a certain weight. For them, achieving a low or socially acceptable body weight is like fighting Mother Nature.

Finding your own healthy weight is not always easy, particularly if you have yo-yoed up and down for several years. A reasonable or healthy weight is the one you are comfortable with, a weight that is not too demanding to maintain, and that poses no serious health problems. Here are a few ways to help you find your healthy weight:

- Look at your family background—weight gain is genetic. If no one in your family has been or is thin, chances are that you won't be thin either. However, you can lower your body weight to a healthy level.
- Take into consideration bone structure and body shape—someone with large bones will never be as thin as someone who is small and petite.
- Choose a weight you feel most comfortable and happy with—this is extremely important because body image and weight are often closely tied to personal happiness.

Eating Disorders

A negative body image will not only cause you to gain weight or try crash dieting, it can also lead to serious eating disorders like anorexia nervosa (self-starvation) or bulimia (binge eating followed by purging). In fact, many people who develop these disorders start out being overweight.

Although cases of anorexia nervosa were recorded in the mid-1800s, the disease has since come to be known as a late-twentieth-century illness that is a result of society's overemphasis on external appearance. Primary candidates for anorexia nervosa are young females, ages twelve through twenty-five, who tend to be over-achievers.

Physically, anorexia nervosa is classified as a 25 percent or greater loss of original body weight. The symptoms include fear of being fat, distorted body image, denial, and the refusal to maintain a normal body weight. Treatment involves both behavioral and psychological counseling in addition to a refeeding program.

Bulimia is another psychological eating disorder. Unlike anorexics, bulimics can keep their binge-eating patterns hidden for years because they don't lose weight.

wellness

Minding the Body and the Mind

Building your muscles and bones, pumping your heart with aerobic exercise, and eating a varied, nutrition-packed diet are all integral parts of health and longevity. Unfortunately, though, fit living isn't always enough. There are external factors, things that are beyond our control: personal and professional stresses, environmental toxins, and genetic predispositions that threaten to upset the internal well-being we work so hard to engender and maintain. Sometimes we need to do something more.

This section, *Wellness,* explores a broad range of alternative healing techniques—both as forms of treatment and prevention. Because the body and mind are so inextricably linked, you'll discover that the relaxation response triggered by meditation, for example, can lower your heart rate and increase your mental alertness. Similarly, the meridians of energy flow discussed in the chapters "Acupressure," "Acupuncture," "Chinese Medicine," and "Tai Chi" correspond to physical symptoms and emotions. In the pages that follow, you can educate yourself about the philosophies behind an amazing variety of nontraditional healing arts and systems and learn dozens of specific self-care methods that will enhance and extend your quality of life.

acupressure
and shiatsu

According to practitioners of Oriental medicine, people do not get sick, they get out of balance—and this creates an environment for physical, mental, or spiritual dis-ease. Eastern medical practices center around promoting the normal, healthy flow of chi or ki—vital life energy. Although traditional Western medicine doesn't recognize this concept, in the East, generating its normal flow is thought to be as critical as breathing.

Acupressure and shiatsu aim to rebalance energy by massaging certain sensitive points all over the body in the same way (and in the same locations) that acupuncture does with needles. But acupressure (which is Chinese) and shiatsu (which is Japanese) evolved from folk medicine, and are both older—from two thousand to five thousand years old—and easier healing arts for laymen to practice.

These pressure-point treatments stimulate organs, glands (the endocrine system, which governs hormones), muscles, joints, skin, and also the release of endorphins (brain chemicals that block pain, relieve stress, and promote well-being). Acupressure and shiatsu treatments are good for

- preventing illness
- treating some medical conditions
- treating overuse injuries (especially among athletes, dancers, and exercise enthusiasts)
- enhancing appearance (the flow of formerly blocked energy flushes cheeks and adds vitality)
- balancing extreme hormonal shifts, especially in women with PMS or who are going through menopause
- easing emotional disturbances and worry
- treating people who don't have diagnosable conditions—that is, people who don't feel well but have no changes in blood chemistry.

Meridians, points, and the great waterway

Eastern medicine looks at the energy that flows between body, spirit, and mind as a great waterway system with rivers, streams, and lakes. The idea is to avoid floods or drought and to keep a constant steady flow of clean, running water.

The energy flows down fourteen intricately documented "channels," "meridians," or "tsubos"—twelve are on the right and left sides of the body (mirror images of one another) and two run through the central axis of the body (one toward the front of the face, one to the back of the head). Unlike nerves or blood vessels, these meridians don't have a physical manifestation in the body, but practitioners and followers of Eastern medicine believe they are just as real.

Each meridian corresponds to a specific organ as well as an emotional state generally categorized as yang (warm) or yin (cold). Organs and meridians are also related to specific emotions so that a blockage in energy along one or more of the meridians would affect not only physical health but emotional well-being. In turn, acupressure can ease physical ills and restore emotional balance. The meridians are thought to travel part of the way through the body and partly on the skin, ending on the hands and feet. For this reason, it's possible to work on the outside of the body and affect a specific internal organ as well as the skin, muscles, joints, emotions, and thoughts.

There are 365 points along the meridians. Blockages of energy usually occur in and around these points. So acupressure or shiatsu massage therapists will put their thumbs (also palms, elbows, knees) into these areas to release the blockage. Shiatsu massage addresses other areas of sensitivity beside these points.

Because the points are located along these energy pathways, someone can press on your foot and you'll feel a tingling or release of energy somewhere else.

What causes imbalance?

Perhaps the question ought to be: What doesn't cause imbalance? Excesses and shortages (floods and droughts) of emotions and outside influences are the main culprits.

Both acupressure and shiatsu, as well as other forms of "complementary" medicine, work best in conjunction with "right living" (exercise, healthy nutritional habits, rest, and a positive attitude) and shouldn't be used as substitutes for medical treatment, especially with serious illness.

Precautions

If you have a serious illness be sure to see a professional, because if massage is not done correctly, it can actually worsen symptoms.

Avoid pressure-point massage if you
- have just eaten a big meal
- are recovering from a serious cut or wound
- are pregnant (can induce labor)
- are extremely tense (calm yourself first)
- have had a serious operation or have given birth within the last six weeks

General Tips for Giving a Pressure-Point Massage

- Use fingertips or, better yet, thumbs (practitioners do thumb push-ups for strength).
- Start with a light touch and gently increase pressure.
- Go to the point where pleasure meets pain; if there is sharp pain, stop.
- Hold for 3 to 5 seconds to stimulate the area.
- Stay on the area for 1 to 3 minutes to produce calm.

Six Easy Self-Massages

• To relieve tension, rub your belly 60 times in a circle.

• To relieve neck tension, rub four fingers up along one side of the neck for a minute. Switch sides. Then with the thumb, press in and up in the small indent where the head and neck connect.

• To energize face (and the stomach and small intestine meridian) rub hands together to warm them. Rub palms up and down cheeks for one minute. Then with forefingers, massage up and down both sides of nose (this is the stomach and bladder meridian).

• To clear a foggy mind, take fingertips and "knock" on the scalp (from the top of the head to the ears (stimulates gallbladder, bladder, and sends heat through the body) for one minute.

• To prevent a double chin, hook thumbs under the jawbone and gently massage at random points along the jaw for one minute.

• To enhance spiritual awareness, place the index or middle finger at the very top of the head (at the crown chakra) and the thumb or forefinger of the other hand slightly above and between the brows (the "third eye"). Hold for one minute.

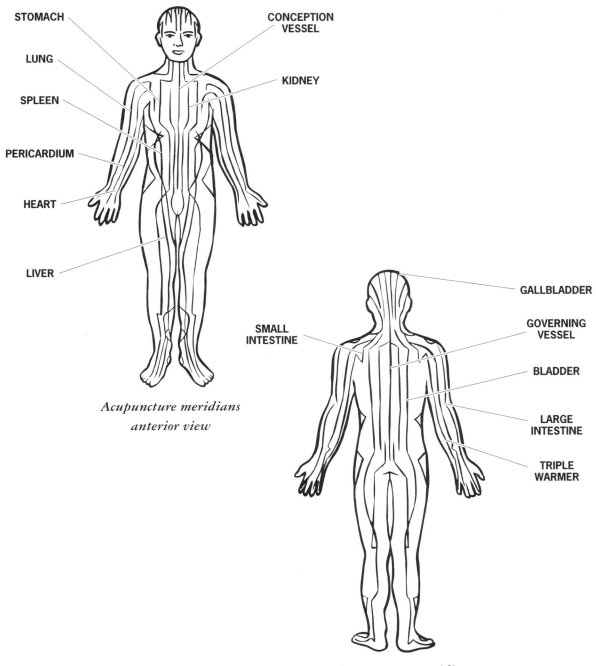

STOMACH

LUNG

SPLEEN

PERICARDIUM

HEART

LIVER

CONCEPTION
VESSEL

KIDNEY

*Acupuncture meridians
anterior view*

SMALL
INTESTINE

GALLBLADDER

GOVERNING
VESSEL

BLADDER

LARGE
INTESTINE

TRIPLE
WARMER

*Acupuncture meridians
posterior view*

acupuncture

Acupuncture is the artful science of rebalancing the flow of energy through the body, spirit, and mind by stimulating with needles (and also electrostimulation and lasers) specific points, or "gateways," where energy is believed to be blocked or weak. These points are located on the fourteen energy channels, pathways, or meridians that have been extensively mapped throughout the body (see **Acupressure and Shiatsu,** page 392) over the thousands of years that Asian medicine has evolved. Each meridian corresponds to a specific organ and each organ corresponds to certain emotions. The meridians run both inside the body and along the surface of the skin, which is why it's possible to stimulate the outer body and affect an organ, emotion, and corresponding mental state deep within (see illustrations, page 395).

Acupuncture can be used to prevent, diagnose, and treat a whole host of ailments, from the very minor to the severe. Its purpose is to remove any obstacles that hinder the body's natural ability to heal itself. The desired outcome is a steady, even flow of *chi* (vital life energy), *xue* (blood and other essential fluids), and other substances too numerous to mention that nourish organs, tissues, and bones. The needles dissipate excess energy (which pools and stagnates like water behind a dam) and revitalize areas where the flow has fallen to a trickle.

While Western doctors tend to isolate specific ailments with specific drugs and treatments (often with unpleasant side effects), Eastern doctors treat the whole person—body, mind, and spirit—not just the current condition. They factor in the patient's

- emotional life (anxiety, depression, anger, etc., are considered precursors to other conditions)
- work and lifestyle habits
- age and sex
- personality type (based on the five elements—wood, metal, fire, water, and earth; see **Chinese Medicine,** page 424)
- the climate
- the season
- plus their complete medical history

Any side effects from acupuncture treatments (tingling, relaxation, or fatigue, for example) are intentional. Acupuncture works best when treatments are combined with balanced eating habits, rest, moderate exercise, and meditation. Patients should not rely on treatments alone to get well.

Acupuncture may not always heal a disease, especially a terminal illness, but it can definitely improve the quality of life. Many terminally ill patients have reported that acupuncture treatments (especially in conjunction with other healing methods) help them feel "whole" and "healed" before dying.

Ailments that respond to acupuncture

Although many U.S. insurance companies still don't cover acupuncture treatments, the World Health Organization has created a list of ailments they believe can be treated successfully with acupuncture. These include (but are not limited to):

- Anxiety
- Arthritis
- Back pain
- Bronchitis
- Bursitis
- Cerebral palsy
- Common cold
- Depression
- Digestive disorders
- Flu
- Infections of the eyes, ears, nose, and throat
- Insomnia
- PMS
- Sciatica
- Skin disorders
- Symptoms related to menopause

If you go for treatment

A visit to the acupuncturist is more than getting needles stuck in your skin. In addition to taking an extensive history, asking personal questions about your habits (elimination, menstrual, sexual, dietary, sleeping, etc.) and emotional and mental states, the doctor will read your tongue for signs of organ imbalance and take your pulse—not to determine heartbeats per minute but to discover if the pulse is faint, erratic, or any of twenty-eight different qualities! A trained acupuncturist can actually sense if there is an energy blockage anywhere in your body by feeling the pulse on your wrist. Your voice and speech patterns, color and shape of face, posture, smell, and sensitivity to touch may also be evaluated.

You'll lie down for treatment, which involves inserting sterilized needles into various points all over your body—especially hands and feet where the meridians originate. Unless you have a lot of broken blood vessels near the skin surface, the needles won't make you bleed.

Many acupuncturists will stick needles inside your ear, since it contains many critical points helpful to both the overall health of internal organs and overcoming addictions. Some acupuncturists only work in the ear, using it as a map of the entire body. Points on the ear correspond to internal organs (in the way that reflexology uses the foot as a body map), so stimulating these points can release energy blockages elsewhere.

You may feel a tingling sensation, a rush of warmth, or deep relaxation after the needles are inserted. The needles will penetrate the skin from a fraction of an inch to several inches, depending on your body type and constitution. After all needles are in place, you may be left in the room by yourself for up to forty-five minutes and may fall asleep—or notice that you feel certain emotions.

Your doctor may decide to give you electro-stimulation or laser treatment instead of needles and/or do something called moxibustion, which is the burning of the herb mugwort on specific acupuncture points. Moxibustion is especially useful for dispelling conditions that arise from cold and damp. It doesn't hurt; doctors simply put a slice of ginger between the skin and the burning cone of herbs.

Many acupuncturists also prescribe herbal remedies plus meditation and Chi Kung (Chinese exercise; see **Tai Chi and Chi Kung,** page 458) to help you get your *chi* flowing again. If your conditions are mild, you can expect to feel better after a few treatments. If severe, you may need many sessions before symptoms improve.

aging

People used to think that declining health was inevitable with aging, that eventually our bodies would just deteriorate and we'd die. But lately there's been a big shift in the Western view of aging prompted, no doubt, by the fact that the bulk of the population will soon be over fifty. With our shifting attitudes and the new light being shed on aging, never before has age looked so good.

What is aging? One of the most popular theories is based on oxidation. Age happens when we're subject to various elements inside and outside our bodies, the same way a car is subject to rust. Our bodies contain oxygen atoms, which 99 percent of the time battle toxins and disease. But every so often they take a good thing too far and end up destroying the host by changing the structure of cells, proteins, fat, and DNA. These errant oxygen atoms, commonly known as free radicals, are released into the system when we eat and gravitate to body fat. Since every cell in the human body has a fat membrane, this makes the whole body vulnerable to damage—and a high-fat diet inspires even more free-radical devastation.

Americans have been popping antioxidant vitamins (C, E, A) to stop the proliferation of free radicals and therefore slow aging (see **Antioxidants,** page 267). Vitamin supplements, however, can't slow the aging process unless they're combined with lifestyle changes, including regular exercise, low-fat diets, lower

stress, and increased happiness (since negativity causes free radicals as much as high-fat diets). Aging well, therefore, needs to occur on all levels—physical, mental, emotional, and spiritual—and can be a well-orchestrated conscious act.

Changing our attitudes about aging

Medical findings have begun to reveal that aging isn't the inevitable breakdown of the machinery we once thought it was. Experts believe that 99 percent of the body's functions are completely unaffected by age! Even well into our golden years, our cells completely replace themselves at such a fast pace that we get new skin cells every month, liver cells every six weeks, and skeletons every three months.

After age thirty, however, the precision and function of our cells may start to deteriorate by about 1 percent a year. But even at that rate, we have seventy more good years before our organs and bones diminish to the point where they should give out. So why do we get "old" so much faster than this?

Part of it has to do with what we think and part of it with what we *do.* Positive attitudes and actions can slow the aging process. However, another factor is society. In the United States and other Western cultures, youth is often worshiped while age is devalued. Older people are often stripped of purpose, not honored for their wisdom and contributions, and often die because they see no reason to live. But as the baby-boom generation tries "conscious aging," we may witness an entire generation aiming to change the face, body, and spirit of aging.

We don't have the power to stop time. But we do have the power to alter our biological and psychological ages. In their book *Biomarkers: The 10 Keys to Prolonging Vitality* (New York: Fireside, 1992), Tufts University researchers William Evans and Irwin Rosenburg (with Jacqueline Thompson) have outlined ten biological markers that can all be changed with regular exercise and balanced eating habits! They are:

- Lean muscle mass
- Strength
- Basal metabolic rate (BMR)
- Percentage of body fat
- Aerobic capacity
- Blood pressure
- Blood sugar tolerance
- Ratio of good (HDL) cholesterol to bad (LDL) (Research has shown that this ratio is as important as cholesterol levels. For more information, see also **Cholesterol**, page 293.)
- Bone density
- Body temperature or blood circulation

Optimal aging

Aging well involves more than a devotion to exercise and sensible eating. We wear our attitudes and beliefs not only on our faces but also on the interior walls of our bodies.

Common traits that seem to slow the aging process are:

- Sleeping eight hours a night
- A regular exercise routine
- A regular work routine
- Not overeating
- Maintaining a steady, healthy weight
- Moderate drinking
- Eating breakfast every day
- Feeling connected to others
- Having a sense of purpose
- Having a relationship with a higher power
- Feeling free from excess worry
- Willing to learn new things
- Being creative
- Adapting to change
- Simply wanting to be alive

How Old Are You Really?

Gerontologists (people who study aging) have divided age into three categories:

Chronological age is determined by the actual number of birthday candles. This has less bearing on health than people realize.

Biological age is the current state of cells, organs, bones, and other tissues as compared to other people of the same chronological age. Lifestyle choices greatly affect biological age.

Psychological age is the most nebulous of the three, since it reflects attitude, belief, and self-image. Some people find this the easiest to change, others the hardest.

Becoming ageless

The secrets of optimal aging aren't so secret or complicated. They're age-old practices that many people don't know about or simply don't make time for. In the book *Long Life Now* (Berkeley, Calif.: Celestial Arts, 1996), author Lee Hitchcox, D.C. (Doctor of Chiropractic), explores some of the common threads that link three of the world's most famous longevity cultures: the Hunzas (of the Hunza Valley in the Himalayas, northwest of Pakistan), the Vilcabambas (of the Vilcabamba Valley in the Andes Mountains in southern Ecuador), and the Georgians (of the Republic of Georgia in the Caucasus Mountains in eastern Europe).

In all three places, people live active, healthy lives until their nineties, hundreds, or slightly higher, but their biological ages were between sixty-five and seventy-five. Each of these peoples had a number of lifestyle aspects in common:

- They ate low-fat, low-protein, high-carb diets (between 1,200 and 2,000 calories a day, 12 to 15 percent fat and 10 to 18 percent protein—with more fat and protein in the colder climates).
- They ate carbs in the form of grains (not processed starches).
- They ate fresh fruits and vegetables (both cooked and raw).
- They ate small amounts of animal protein and weren't strict vegetarians.
- They had active lifestyles with daily exercise—hiking, horseback riding, working in the fields.
- They never retired, always contributed.

- They did not depend on the government or medical care systems to take care of them.
- They valued the wisdom of age and imparted their knowledge to younger people.
- They often lied about their age to sound older.
- They suffered a decrease in health as more outside influences affected their diets—usually higher intakes of fat, protein, and alcohol.

alexander technique

The Alexander technique seeks to retrain unconscious postural habits to promote better physical and mental health. It was created by F. M. Alexander, an Australian man born in the late nineteenth century. He started his exploration of the "right use of the body" when, as an actor, he kept losing his voice. In setting out to correct the problem, he noticed that he carried a lot of neck tension, and in the process of retraining himself, he opened the door to the mostly unexplored (at least in the West) world of kinesthetic awareness.

He discovered that some ways of moving the body are better than others. But his work doesn't simply cover big, full-body moves, as in exercise, but also subtle motions, as when we sit, stand, talk, brush our teeth, eat, and so on. Alexander believed that most everyone learns bad body use at an early age, usually by patterning our movements after our parents, who also practice bad and unconscious body placement. Then, as we get older, we accelerate the breakdown of our health by sitting too much, walking too little, and, when we do walk, by shuffling and limping along. The remarkable thing, he noted, is that we adapt to these postural defects and think they're normal. Unless these problems are corrected, he believed, time and rigorous exercise make the problems worse.

The Alexander technique is not a science, a massage (Alexander himself didn't believe in manipulation), or a relaxation technique. It's the close observation and retraining of bad habitual movement. Some (but not all) Alexander technique practitioners are certified, but certification isn't always a sign of competency. To find a qualified teacher in your area, call the North American Society of Alexander Teachers at 800-473-0620 or visit their website: nastat@ix.netcom.com.

What to expect if you go for treatment

You will be closely observed, asked to lie down, sit, stand up, and perhaps even asked to go about normal routines: how you brush your teeth, comb your hair, pick things off the floor, and so on. You may be gently remanipulated into proper alignment, but mostly you'll be schooled on how to make these changes yourself.

The work begins in the head and neck. Alexander observed that the gross majority of people throw their heads back and jut their chins forward when they stand. But the neck should be long (not rigid) and slightly forward of the spine. And since head placement affects the entire body, this is perhaps the most critical area of concern.

Once neck and head placement are addressed, then it's time for shoulders and chest. Alexander observed that many people slide their chests over to one side (creating scoliosis) or round forward (kyphosis). Many people also let their shoulder blades stick out in the back. So the treatment involves centering the chest and broadening the shoulders so the "wing bones" reach out rather than back.

Next the pelvis, legs, and feet are addressed. Many people either have an exaggerated sway back or a flattened lower back. Both cause lower back problems. In the Alexander technique, proper placement of the pelvis is somewhere between these two extremes. The pelvis should be tipped slightly forward so the genitals point more forward than down to the floor—and knees should never be locked.

The challenge with the Alexander technique is not making the adjustments in treatments but implementing them throughout otherwise unconscious parts of your life.

These three seated postures employ more "right use" of the body than twisting, slumping, or crossing legs:

1. The deep squat: If you have to sit on the floor for a while and deep squatting doesn't bother your knees, it's actually a safe way to sit. It also helps elimination.

2. Cross-legged position: Keep an upright but not rigid torso. Remember to incline slightly forward at the pelvis. Ankles can be crossed or soles of the feet brought together.

3. Sitting in a chair: Although some women may find this "unladylike," it promotes "right use." Sit up straight, with hands resting on legs (or desk, computer keyboard, etc.), feet flat on the floor, legs hip-distance apart or slightly wider.

Ailments that retraining can improve

Alexander did much of his work with dancers, actors, and musicians—people whose subtle changes in posture can affect their performances and, therefore, their livelihoods. But he also claimed that retraining could positively affect all kinds of illnesses and disturbances, from arthritis and asthma to intestinal disorders and migraines. By helping us conserve energy and allowing the body to function smoothly, Alexander therapy can improve overall health.

Easy Ways to Implement the Alexander Technique

• Sit with your pelvis to the back of the chair. Don't cross your legs (a big no-no)—this pulls on the lower back. If you must cross something, cross the ankles. Incline your torso slightly forward from the pelvis, not the lower or upper back, so that pelvis and spine are one.

• Avoid slumping as you sit. It's better to lie down and support your back with pillows than to sit hunched forward or twisted.

• As you eat, bring the food to your mouth, not your mouth to the food.

• As you breathe, breathe into your back, not your chest. Lifting chest and lungs to force breathing can throw off alignment. Breathing into your back also widens the shoulders.

a woman's body passages

Within one year, 98 percent of all the atoms in our bodies are completely replaced: Every five weeks, we create all new skin cells; every three weeks, our fat cells dump out the old fat and take in the new; every six weeks, our liver cells regenerate themselves; and every three months, our bone cells are completely rebuilt.

So, if our bodies regenerate themselves at this pace, then it raises some questions: What is aging? And if we have the power to constantly renew ourselves, why do we get old and die?

Twenties

In your twenties, your muscle tone is naturally firm and your metabolism is still relatively high. Your bones reach peak mass and strength between the ages of fourteen and twenty-four and arrive at full maturity around age thirty. The amount of bone mass you achieve before age thirty-five can affect the rest of your active life.

During this decade, exercise and eating habits are usually inconsistent. You may still have a few leftover adolescent bad habits: eating sugary, fatty foods; partying; drinking and eating too much then dieting; taking too much exercise or not enough. Extreme behaviors like excessive dieting and too much or no exercise at all can contribute to bone *loss* even in your twenties. (Some doctors estimate that 50 percent of all bone loss happens *before* menopause.) But if you get in shape now, you'll conquer many of your immediate demons and lay the groundwork for lifelong health.

What to do in your twenties

• Be physically active. It doesn't matter what you choose, but do something physical at least three times a week. Play a sport, take dance or fitness classes, go for hikes—just move!

• Start a weight-training program to build a strong base of support for your whole body. Put your primary focus on torso—back, chest, abs, and upper legs.

• Avoid becoming a yoga or dance Gumby without also building stronger muscles. Hyper-flexibility without the muscle strength to support the joints could set you up for arthritis and risk of injury to tendons and ligaments later in life.

• If you have a baby, try not to hold on to the majority of your postpartum fat for more than six months after delivery. Your body will hold on to an extra 5 or 10 pounds as long as you're nursing. Once you stop, you'll lose it more easily. A sensible program combining strength and cardiovascular exercise will get you closer to your prebaby shape—and offers a psychological boost, giving you at least the illusion of having control over your life!

Thirties

In this decade, the big differences start to show between those who stay physically active and those who don't. If you *don't* stay active, your metabolism slows down. Your waistline starts to thicken. Fat clings to hips and thighs more readily now, and after age thirty-five your bones start to lose density—about 1 percent a year. Regular exercise, of course, can change all this.

What to do in your thirties

• Learn to love strength training. Hit the weights once or twice a week to stay lean, strong, maintain bone strength, keep good posture, and create a new you.

• Pick aerobic workouts that make you feel great and train at least three days a week.

• Stretch to stay limber in body and mind (stretch after your workouts or add separate yoga/stretching classes).

• If you don't have the time, make the time. Surely you can fit in four thirty-minute weekly workouts. That's only two hours of exercise.

Forties

This is the decade of big body changes. If you stayed inactive throughout your thirties, now the piper demands payment (your bill adds up to 5 to 10 percent of your muscle mass, and 10 percent of your bone mass!). Even if you exercise regularly, you feel the shift. Hips widen. Old injuries demand special care. Your knees tell you not to run on concrete. You discover your need for balance.

For many women, this is the time of perimenopause—the beginning of "the change," marked by irregular periods, hot flashes, increases in bad cholesterol, sleep changes, and mood swings more extreme than PMS. Menopause officially begins a year after the end of the last period. But perimenopause, a nebulous time with no clear beginning, can last for years. The good news is that symptoms such as hot flashes and night sweats are about half as likely to happen when you maintain regular exercise. Exercise also provides you with the best prevention against bone loss and heart disease, helps you avoid excess weight gain and depression, and maintain function, posture, strength, and agility in body and mind.

What to do in your forties

• Become a weight-lifting warrior if you haven't already. Hire a trainer or teach yourself by reading good books on the subject. Twice a week is all you need.

• Pay extra attention to muscles in the upper back, lower back, and abdominals to keep good torso strength and posture—particularly if you sit all day.

• Switch from running to brisk walking to protect your knees.

• Take mini-workouts wherever you can. Take the stairs instead of the elevator. Walk to town instead of driving. Park in the farthest parking space, even when it's raining.

• Take up yoga, Tai Chi, or Aikido (for energy and mental clarity).

• Take up something fun because you've always wanted to: ballroom dancing, rock climbing, scuba diving.

Fifties

If you haven't stayed active, your bones will lose 2 to 5 percent more of their former mass in the two to five years after menopause. Then bone loss will stabilize back to 1 percent per year. But there are ways around this. A Tufts University study on postmenopausal women showed a 1 percent *gain* in bone density in leg and back bones after one year of strength training, compared to a 2.5 percent loss in the non-training group! But remember to get enough calcium. You need 1,500 milligrams of calcium a day, 1,000 if you're on hormone replacements—yet most women only get 25 percent of the RDA. Take supplements if you need to (see **Bones,** page 31, for suggested bone-healthy eating habits). Neither exercise nor calcium alone will prevent bone loss. They work as a team.

What to do in your fifties

• If you suffer from joint pain, try softer forms of exercise like water aerobics or brisk walking instead of jogging.

• Stick with or start weight training to prevent osteoporosis.

• Stay flexible in your body and mind with yoga or Tai Chi.

• Work in your garden. Walk around your neighborhood. Keep moving.

Sixties and Beyond

Although there's a big difference between sixty and ninety, many of the same suggestions apply throughout these years. As you age, your brain continues to make new neural pathways. In other words, you can learn new things up until you die. But if you lack stimulation of any kind (mental, physical, spiritual, sexual) your interests and abilities atrophy. Once you stop learning, creating, loving, or contributing, your vitality diminishes and depression sets in. Perhaps one of the biggest problems with age, at least in American society, is lack of connectedness.

If you take no other exercise, walk. Walk to town, walk in the mall, walk with friends, get out, get some fresh air, and stand up straight. If it's necessary, use a walker or cane. Simply being in a vertical position with gravity exerting weight on your bones is good for the muscles, bones, and spirit.

In addition, start lifting weights. Controlled, slow exercises are within the grasp of most people—and are not stressful. You're never too old to improve. A study of a hundred nursing home residents over age ninety showed an increase in strength of 110 percent after just ten weeks of training!

What to do in your sixties and beyond

• Walk for wellness.

• Continue with or begin strength training, studying yoga, Tai Chi, or other practices.

• Take a water-fitness class—especially in warmer pools to ease arthritis.

• Make connections with friends, family, children, and pets.

• Stay mentally keen. Read books and newspapers. Go to movies, plays, museums.

aromatherapy

Aromatherapy is a sensually pleasing holistic therapy based on the belief that odor informs us. We've all had the experience of catching a certain scent and remembering places, people, or whole scenes from our lives. Smells bypass logic and sink into the deep, primal part of the brain called the limbic region before our conscious minds can actually label what that smell is. When the odors are bad, we're turned off fast (people reject each other as lovers, friends, and business partners just because they don't "smell right"). But when the odors are pleasant, they arouse us, melt our defenses, enhance hunger, creativity, promote relaxation, motivation, and a host of other responses that are usually governed by the autonomic nervous system (the system that controls breathing and heartbeat). Pleasing odors inspire the secretion of various hormones:

- Endorphins—pain inhibitors that also stimulate sexual feelings, well-being, and euphoria
- Encephaline—similar to endorphins
- Serotonin—relaxing, calming hormones
- Noradrenaline—stimulating hormones that promote alertness
- Scientists have also shown that the so-called pheromones of "male armpit musk" inspire ovulation in women—at least in those attracted to the smell.

Aromatherapy, therefore, is a great mood enhancer, based on the notion that if you adjust the mental state, the body and spirit will follow, and the body will heal itself or reawaken a sense of vitality. Filling your room or car with an odor can therefore alter depression, sluggishness, poor concentration, sleep disorders, stress, and many other conditions.

This also works well in conjunction with toxic therapies like chemotherapy and, if nothing else, adds a sense of inner balance, sensuality, and pleasure. Some aromatherapies are also prescribed internally, but this can be dangerous without professional supervision.

A final word: Aromatherapies cancel out homeopathic remedies. Do one or the other.

Making scents

The essences found in aromatherapies are condensed from various flowers, leaves, seeds, resin, bark, woody pulp, and the skin of fruits. Plants actually have oil glands that produce these odors. The plants use them to attract or repel insects or other things. By themselves, these essences are watery and, if brushed on the skin, quickly evaporate in the air, leaving only their essence. But they mix well with fatty oils and soaps, as well as honey and alcohol, so they blend with lotions and body rubs. Store your scents in dark glass bottles; light causes the aromas to fade.

There are many ways you can scent your environment:

- Aroma lamp—usually a small ceramic bowl that sits over a flame. Heat a small amount of water and add a few drops of your favorite essence. You can also add aroma to a regular bowl of water and place it on a heater.
- Humidifier—add a few drops to the water
- In your car—a heater plugs into your car lighter (a good way to ease through a commute)
- On lightbulbs—you can hang a ceramic ring full of essence off a lightbulb to fill an entire room
- In the sauna or steam room—add a few drops to the heater
- In the bath—sprinkle a few drops in your bathwater
- Hot compress—warm a washcloth and lay it over the forehead (great during a massage)

Common Scents for Common Ailments

Although oils are typically mixed and matched to create the most potent treatments for hundreds of symptoms and conditions, the following general categories are a good place to start your exploration of aromatherapy.

STIMULATING OILS, used to treat low blood pressure or a general lack of energy, include basil, black pepper, cardamon, ginger, peppermint, rosemary, and thyme.

RELAXING OILS, for relieving emotional or physical tension, include chamomile, cypress, frankincense, jasmine, lavender, marjoram, rose, and sandalwood.

EXPECTORANT OILS, those used to treat colds, coughs, or congestion, include eucalyptus, peppermint, rosemary, and thyme.

ANTISEPTIC OILS can be used to treat any kind of virus or infection. The oils that fall into this category include basil, clove, eucalyptus, fennel, lavender, lemon, rosemary, tea tree, and thyme.

ayurveda

Ayurveda is more than a form of preventive medicine; it's a way of life that promotes balance in body, mind, and soul. This ancient practice began in India over 3,500 years ago and was founded on the belief that humans cannot discover their divine purpose unless they achieve health on a very basic physical level. This ancient system is still considered valid and can help people find balance in a stressful, modern world.

The Ayurvedic system is easy to understand. People are divided into certain types, or *"doshas,"* based on body type and constitution (this also takes into account sleeping habits, speech patterns, learning speed, memory, hair and skin quality, etc.).

Many Ayurvedic recommendations center around food, since it's believed that proper elimination prevents disease. But Ayurveda also includes various forms of detoxification, daily cleansing rituals, meditation, mantras, yoga, herbs, aromas, massage, and behavior adjustments as seasons change. It's also important in the Ayurvedic system to discipline emotions such as anger, greed, jealousy, and selfishness. Overcoming them is thought to remove years of aging.

Ayurveda is similar to Chinese medicine in many ways. Both aim to rebalance "life energy" (called *chi* in the Chinese system and *prana* in Indian culture). Both also share the belief in meridians where energy either flows or gets blocked, creating predisposition to disease.

What is your dosha?

Your *dosha* represents the body type and general programming you were born with. Although some people may resent being categorized, in fact, determining your type can give you greater self-understanding, a better handle on which foods and actions serve you and which don't, and greater insight into others. Although your type doesn't change as you go through life, your physiological and psychological habits may improve as you fine-tune your daily habits.

There are three *doshas,* and everybody exhibits characteristics of all three to some degree, although most people have one that is dominant or at most a combination of two. A few rare people are a balance of all three. Determine the one or two that most suit your body type and personality.

Vata

Vata represents movement, thought, energy, air, space, *prana*—and of all the *doshas* is the most misunderstood and easiest to get out of balance. Changeability is Vata's most noticeable feature.

Physical features may include:

- Slight build, thin frame, small shoulders and hips
- Quick speaking voice

- Large teeth
- Small mouth
- Dry, often rough skin
- Dark, cool eyes
- Light sleeping habits (and sleep on the left side)

Other characteristics (especially when out of balance) are:
- Fast learner but bad retention
- Frequent worries and depression
- Small appetite
- Irregular habits
- Constipation, intestinal upsets
- High blood pressure
- Loss of energy
- Menstrual cramps
- Aching joints
- Enthusiastic bursts of energy followed by exhaustion (starts things but doesn't finish)
- Restless thoughts (especially at night)

Behaviors that are in balance:
- Good-natured, agreeable
- Highly creative, active imagination
- Deep spiritual connections
- Appreciates beauty, culture, philosophy
- Well-suited to be a teacher, counselor
- Capable of blending sexuality and spirituality
- Does best when encouraged to find own path, rather than trying to conform to the lives of Pitta or Kapha

To rebalance Vata, you should:
- Do anything grounding, warm, and soothing
- Stick to a regular schedule (eat, go to bed, work, etc., at regular times)
- Get plenty of rest to avoid mental burnout
- Meditate
- Avoid drafts or getting cold
- Don't drink alcohol
- Keep surroundings warm and bright
- Avoid raw foods and cold drinks
- Don't exercise too much or with too much intensity, especially aerobics. Vata thrives on yoga and other types of relaxing exercise.
- Dress for warmth and to feel attractive and confident. Vatas may like the serious, tailored look, but softer, flowing clothes in natural fibers and pleasing jeweled earth tones minimize the lean and hungry look.

Vatas and food: Vatas can eat all they want and gain little weight; they need substantial meals. A lettuce and tomato salad for lunch leaves them unsatisfied and anxious, as do sour, pungent foods. Vatas don't do well on raw foods either. Feed Vatas comfort foods such as soups, stews, grains, and hot cereals; a breakfast that gives long-term, grounding energy; midmorning or mid-afternoon snacks such as tea and a bagel or a low-fat muffin. Sugar can make nervous Vatas more nervous. When eating sugar, take it with a milky beverage to neutralize the effects. It doesn't have to be cow's milk. Try rice, soy, and/or almond milk and sweeten with honey and cardamom or cinnamon. Spicy foods like chilies, curry, or ginger can stimulate Vata's otherwise erratic digestion. Sweet fruits such as ripe mangoes or bananas are soothing, but Vatas should avoid unripe or sour fruits.

Sesame and almonds are good choices for Vatas. Sprinkle ground-up sesame (Gomasio) over grains. Or eat five to ten almonds a day. (Soak overnight and remove skins. Chew slowly.)

Pitta

Pitta represents metabolism, fire, water, heat. Like Vata, Pitta is an intense *dosha*. But rather than raw energy, Pitta's is more directed, intellectual. Pittas are known for their overwhelming drive and ambition.

Physical features may include:

- Medium build
- Toned, muscular body
- Fair skin
- Fine, prematurely gray hair
- Small, yellowish teeth
- Penetrating eyes
- Sudden, sharp hunger pains (Pittas don't like to skip meals)
- Get easily overheated; don't like hot, humid summer weather
- Sleep six to eight hours—often on the back
- Have a precise speaking voice
- Sensitive to bright light

Other characteristics (especially when out of balance) are:

- Rashes, hot flashes, sunburn
- Heartburn
- Bad breath and pungent body odor
- Bloodshot, yellowish eyes
- Highly aggressive and demanding (often forget that other human beings share the planet)
- Workaholic
- Easily irritated, given to angry outbursts
- Highly critical and judgmental of others

- Impatient
- Jealous and resentful, especially when they don't get the respect or recognition they think they deserve (once they get it, they can move forward)
- Sexually promiscuous
- Sometimes chase only the spoils of the material world

Behaviors that are in balance:

- Pioneer thinkers who transform ideas into reality; good leaders, visionaries, humanitarians
- Joyful, caring people (especially as they temper their will and ego)
- Great capacity to serve others when energy moves through the heart
- Monogamous, intimate partners when sex is noble and caring
- Natural athletes; best at handling moderate amounts and all kinds of exercise, but should avoid outdoor exercise in noonday sun
- Manage time, energy, and money in moderation (except for indulgences on luxuries; Pittas love nice surroundings and beautiful clothes)

To rebalance Pitta, you should:

- Do things to calm down
- Take time to rest and meditate—also to appreciate accomplishments
- Be in nature, appreciate art and culture, family
- Be considerate, compassionate to others
- Practice patience
- Avoid rash, impulsive conflicts, heated arguments
- After 6 P.M., stop working

- Dress in an elegant but subdued style. Pittas already make an entrance and tend toward eccentric fashions and overstatements. Look best in fine natural fabrics and understated lines.

Pittas and food: Although Pittas can tolerate many foods, they should avoid spicy, sour foods (which throw them off balance) and too many sweets because sugar makes them eat too much. Feed Pittas cool foods like salads and cool drinks, especially in summer. (Pitta's energy is hot. Overheating is bad for the hot Pitta constitution. Cooling them down puts them back in balance.) Avoid sour foods like pickles, yogurt, sour cream, and vinegar (use lemon in salad dressings—causes less imbalance). Go for herb teas and sparkling water instead of coffee and alcohol. Stimulants put an extra edge on already sharp moods. Eat a vegetarian diet. Pittas do well on grains, vegetables, and milk and don't need meat, especially red meat. High carbs minimize Pitta's sudden sharp hunger pains and sustain energy. Avoid fats, oils, fried foods, spicy foods, and salt (all overheat the body). Dry salty snacks plus alcohol aggravates appetites and moods. At cocktail time, go for the carrot sticks and sparkling water instead of pretzels and wine.

Kapha

Kapha represents structure, the earth. Kapha energy is steady, dependable, slow, and nurturing.

Physical features may include:
- Large frame, full figure (in India, considered the most sensual body type)
- Oily skin
- Thick, wavy hair
- Large mouth with full lips
- Big, warm eyes
- Speak slowly, deliberately
- Slow, steady appetite, slow digestion.
- Need eight hours of sleep; often sleep on their stomachs
- Have the potential to have impressive physical strength and endurance
- Don't like the cold and damp

Other characteristics (especially when out of balance) are:
- Can become depressed, lethargic
- Tendency to be overweight
- Overcompensate (when cooking for two, make enough for eight)
- Hard for them to part with old possessions, clean closets, basement; things make them feel secure but stagnant energy becomes inertia
- Desire for love may make others feel stifled
- Procrastinates
- Digestive problems
- Prime candidates for adult-onset diabetes (unless lifestyle is healthy)
- Often have allergies, sinus and lung problems, asthma, hay fever, and such
- High cholesterol
- Water retention, heavy bloated feeling

Behaviors that are in balance include:
- Very warm, generous, forgiving people
- Intimate lovers/spouses, close friends, nurturing parents
- Possess and/or enjoy the earthly pleasures of art, poetry, music, dance
- Well-suited for all kinds of athletic activities—can work out intensely without imbalance, graceful movers

To rebalance Kapha, you should:

- Do things that warm you up or make you feel "lighter"
- Kaphas need stimulation—exercise regularly (for energy and weight control)
- Don't eat heavy, fatty, oily foods or overeat
- Seek stimulation from a variety of experiences: art, nature, pleasing environments
- Stay warm; avoid cold-induced inertia
- Clear away useless possessions
- Wear a variety of different styles—from simple and flowing to tailored and crisp. (This commanding body type looks best in clean, elegant styles.)

Kaphas and food: Kaphas love to eat and enjoy sweets and heavy foods. They have to beware of fat and sugar—and overeating. All make them overweight and create health problems. Too much salt also makes them hold water. Kaphas should eat to maintain a light, warm feeling. Feed Kaphas small, frequent meals: These boost Kapha's otherwise slow metabolism. Meals should consist of warm, lightly cooked foods (not fried) or salads, and raw fruits in the summer. (During the rest of the year, Kaphas do well on warm food.) Kaphas should avoid cheese, butter, ice cream, and cream. Dairy products produce too much mucus, which Kapha already has in excess. Wheat can also cause this problem. Kaphas should eat spicy, pungent foods to warm the system and speed metabolism. Ginger is an especially good spice. A cup of ginger tea before a meal can clean the palate without encouraging overeating—and it's good for easing congestion. Kaphas should eat a light breakfast every day to get going in the morning. Hot spiced tea and dry toast is a good Kapha meal. Lots of vegetables and fewer meats is the way to go with veggies steamed or fresh, in salads. Since Kaphas need warmth, they should avoid cold drinks. They should also go light on the sweets. If dessert is a must, hot apple pie is better than ice cream.

blood pressure

Blood pressure is created by a natural two-part rhythm that measures the pressure blood exerts against the walls of arteries and veins (see **Circulation,** page 165, for a full explanation).

Whenever we're in a crisis situation, the heart beats faster and more blood rushes into the brain (perhaps to help us figure out what to do next). But this leaves the body with less, so the heart has to pump even harder to do its job. In a temporary situation—steering clear of a big rig on a highway, for example—elevated pressure helps us escape from a perceived threat. But problems arise when people stay in a semi-permanent anxious state and end up with permanent high blood pressure. Blood traveling at high pressure can damage the inside of the arteries. To make matters worse, when plaque builds up inside the arteries (atherosclerosis), or hardening of the arteries occurs (arteriosclerosis), sooner or later the blood can't get through at all, resulting in a heart attack or stroke.

About one-third of all Americans have what's called borderline hypertension (a blood pressure reading of 140/95 or higher). Approximately half of all people who die each year in the U.S. have blood pressure in this range. Even a slight rise in blood pressure can be deadly.

What causes high blood pressure?

Many Western medical professionals say that blood pressure increases with age. But in other cultures, such as those in Asia and Africa, where low-fat, high-grain diets (also low in processed carbs and sugars) are the norm, blood pressure (and its cousin, high cholesterol) don't increase. Evidence points to the usual suspect components of the typical American lifestyle (especially when there are multiple risk factors):

- High-fat diet
- High level of body fat
- Stress
- Smoking
- No regular exercise

Blood pressure can also rise with different emotions or times of day. The blood pressure of stockbrokers, police officers, ambulance drivers—basically anyone who perceives work as stressful—can remain elevated for hours after the incident that caused the stress.

Still, doctors don't truly understand why blood pressure rises. The pressure is determined by the brain and is part of the autonomous nervous system (the same system that governs digestion), once thought to be out of our control. But a 1974 Harvard Medical School study showed that twenty-two hypertensive patients were able to lower their blood pressure by an average of ten points by practicing meditation. They brought their diastolic pressure into the acceptable range, although their systolic pressure remained somewhat high. Meditation also proved helpful in lowering high total cholesterol.

Best preventions

Luckily for the human body, the things that prevent high blood pressure also prevent high cholesterol, cancer, obesity, and countless other health problems:

- Low-fat eating habits, especially eating a variety of fruits and vegetables (it also helps to avoid heavily processed foods, refined sugars, and carbohydrates like white flour and chemical food additives)
- Regular exercise
- Relaxation
- Meditation
- Being calm and spending time in settings or with people who nourish heart and soul
- Avoiding stimulants like nicotine and caffeine
- Avoiding high intakes of sodium (processed fast foods are loaded with sodium and fat)
- Calcium supplements (1,000 milligrams at night, 500 in the morning)

High cholesterol: hypertension's first cousin?

As most people know, high amounts of bad cholesterol can clog the arteries with plaque, impede blood flow, raise blood pressure, and further increase the risk of heart attack and stroke. At the same time, a high ratio of good cholesterol helps scrub the arteries clean of such wastes. The same lifestyle prescriptions listed for lowering blood pressure also lower levels of bad cholesterol. Although there are medications for both high blood pressure and high cholesterol, many doctors prefer to prescribe these lifestyle changes instead; they're cheaper, and there's no risk of the side effects that can accompany medications.

Aside from healthy lifestyle habits, the following foods can also help lower cholesterol:

- Oat bran
- Onions and garlic
- Shiitake mushrooms
- Chili peppers
- Japanese green tea
- Omega-3 fatty acids (found in fish oils; salmon and sardines, rinsed of excess oil are good sources)

Estrogen: a natural protector

In premenopausal women, estrogen keeps blood pressure and bad cholesterol levels low and good cholesterol levels high. But after menopause, estrogen levels decrease and women's risks for hypertension, high cholesterol, cardiovascular disease, heart attack, and stroke rise dramatically.

Estrogen clearly protects the heart, although many women fear taking estrogen replacement therapy because of the reported increased risk for breast cancer. But eight times more women over age fifty-three die every year from cardiovascular disease than all cancers combined.

Reading Blood Pressure

Since the ebb and flow of blood pressure is, by nature, always shifting, you should take several readings within a few days and figure an average to get a more accurate picture.

Invest in a blood-pressure cuff so you can read it at home in a relaxed setting. Many people are nervous in a doctor's office, so pressure rises. Many cuffs have digital readouts, making it easy to learn the result.

Pay attention to the second number, not just the first. Although your resting (diastolic) pressure rises about half as quickly as your active (systolic) pressure, both set the stage for cardiovascular disease. If this second number is above 100, work with your doctor to monitor the pressure and adjust your lifestyle now to bring it down.

breathing

Every life-sustaining activity that takes place in our bodies depends on oxygen. Yet so many people forget to take full advantage of this substance that gives us energy, calms our nerves, and is available all around us.

Breathing is one thing everyone can do both consciously and unconsciously. It is the link between our voluntary and involuntary (autonomic) nervous systems. The breath informs the body how to feel and the body sets the tempo of the breath.

When we're stressed, we take shallow, rapid breaths that fill only a fraction of our lungs. This sends the message to our involuntary nervous system that something's wrong, so, physiologically, we prepare to run or do battle (the old fight-or-flight syndrome). Consequently, our heart rate increases, blood pressure rises, digestion is interrupted, and adrenaline and other ready-for-battle hormones are released into the bloodstream.

But when we take full, deep breaths our bodies get the message that it is time to relax. So our heart rate slows, blood pressure drops, digestion resumes, and endorphins and other feel-good hormones are released into the bloodstream.

When we stay in a perpetual state of anxiety (which is the case for many people with hypertension, ulcers, arrhythmia, etc.), the body stays prepped to fight-or-flee. This can create an environment for all kinds of diseases.

In *Dr. Dean Ornish's Program for Reversing Heart Disease Without Drugs and Surgery* (New York: Random House, 1990), deep breathing became a key part of the therapy. He found that heart patients have a much smaller breathing capacity than most people, yet they have a greater need for oxygen and oxygenated blood. Deep-breathing exercises help heart patients get the oxygen they need. Dr. Ornish points out that deep belly breathing presses down the diaphragm muscle, which creates a vacuum that sends more air into the lungs and increases the amount of oxygenated blood, which then returns to the heart.

Chi, prana, spirit

Mystics, martial artists, yogis, and philosophers from all over the globe have long credited breath as the carrier of a more subtle energy, which exists on a subatomic or quantum level. Although scientists have yet to determine exactly what this substance is, it has intrigued humans for thousands of years and has been at the center of many spiritual practices. In several languages, in fact, the names for breath and spirit are the same: *chi, prana, pneuma, spiritus*.

The primary purpose of yoga, Chi Kung, meditation, and other practices has been to generate, preserve, manipulate, and heal others with this essence, which, at least in part, rides on the breath. Practitioners believe that if we can do this, we may achieve health and longevity.

some common breathing techniques

Belly breathing. Sit or stand with your spine erect, back of the neck long. If standing, place feet hip-distance apart. Put hands over belly and exhale all your air. As you inhale, first fill the belly, then lungs. Inhale for 4 counts. Exhale for 8 counts, pressing the belly to empty the air.

Pranayama. This alternate nostril-breathing technique comes from the yogic tradition. This may sound a bit far-out to Western minds, but it's based on the fact that we already breathe primarily through one nostril for a few hours at a time, and switch back and forth. It's believed that the left nostril opens to the right hemisphere of the brain—the intuitive, spatial, creative side—while the right nostril opens to the left, logical side. Breathing this way aims to balance both hemispheres.

With your right hand, place your thumb over your right nostril. First exhale then inhale through the left. Place your finger over your left nostril. Exhale then inhale through the right. *Note:* Always start with an exhale as you change nostrils. Rest your arm against your body so it won't get tired.

Nervous system tranquilizer. Andrew Weil, M.D., gives a very basic but powerful exercise in his book *Natural Health, Natural Medicine* (Boston: Houghton Mifflin, 1995). Throughout this exercise, keep your tongue on the roof of your mouth (believed to be the intersection of positive and negative currents of energy or meridians that flow through the body).

1. Exhale completely with a "whoosh" sound.
2. Inhale through the nose for 4 counts.
3. Hold the breath for 7 counts.
4. Exhale through the mouth with a "whoosh" for 8 counts.
5. Repeat this 4:7:8 cycle for a total of four breaths. (Only do one cycle per breathing session for the first month. Then increase to eight total breaths. If you get dizzy at first, don't worry. Your body will adapt.)

Breathing lessons

There are as many different philosophies about breathing as there are people who teach them. Some say force the breath and count it; others say don't force or count anything, just let it flow. One might say it's a sad state of affairs when we have to relearn something we once did naturally as babies. But once we accept this, learning how to breathe again isn't that difficult and is one of the best tonics for health.

Although breathing coaches may disagree on technique, most agree on several points:

- Inhale through the nose, exhale through the mouth. Nose hairs filter out impurities and warm the air. Unlike the mouth, the nose has a direct link to the brain.

- Make your exhalations about twice as long as your inhalations and focus on pushing all the air out of the lungs with the diaphragm. This enables you to take deeper breaths. As you become more adept at this, allow natural pauses between breaths as well.

- Do these exercises in the morning, whenever you feel agitated, and before going to sleep.

- Keep eyes closed or soften focus and look at something pleasing (a candle, an ocean, a mandala, etc.).

- Practice for one to five minutes at a time. Gradually increase.

- Do before meditation or as meditation.

chakras

Chakras are often described as receivers of energy, like little satellite dishes, which, instead of pulling in television channels, tune in to the subtle essence of the universe. In Sanskrit, the word *chakra* means "wheel." These spiritual funnels supposedly spin and vibrate as they draw in energy, then deliver it throughout the body along the pathways of "subtle energy"—the meridians or nadis (see **Acupressure and Shiatsu** [page 392], and **Acupuncture** [page 396]). Jung called chakras the "gateways of consciousness."

Western science hasn't yet proved their existence, but chakras aren't attributed to the physical body, anyway. They're organs of the "subtle body," which in turn feed our organs and glands. In Hindu and Tibetan tradition, the chakras are thought to pass through the spinal cord. More modern interpretations place them in the front of the body. Various systems list the number of chakras as seven, nine, and twenty-one, though seven is the most common.

People who claim to see chakras (chakras have been described by clairvoyants for thousands of years, in different cultures and on distant continents) describe them as liquid flowers, resonating vibrations, emotions, colors, and sometimes the spirits of various deities. Chakras, on average, are thought to be about 2 inches wide, but they grow bigger and brighter as a person awakens spiritually.

Western believers connect chakras to the endocrine system, the manufacturing plant of various hormones, which sends all kinds of messages throughout the body. Although the chakras don't always align exactly with their associated glands, the essence of those glands and their corresponding chakras are similar. Just how all these systems work together remains a mystery.

Yogis, mystics, and other adepts have long believed that without guidance, consciousness tends to drift down and hold us captive to our "lower selves." But if we steer our consciousness up from the root to the higher chakras, we can improve our health, cultivate our full potential, and get a feel for the divine.

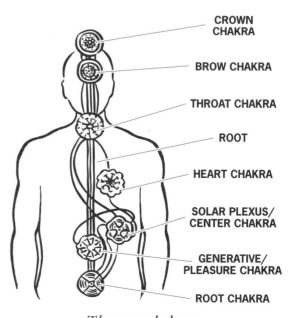

CROWN CHAKRA

BROW CHAKRA

THROAT CHAKRA

ROOT

HEART CHAKRA

SOLAR PLEXUS/ CENTER CHAKRA

GENERATIVE/ PLEASURE CHAKRA

ROOT CHAKRA

The seven chakras

To open your chakras, begin by meditating on your lowest chakra and gradually work your way up to the crown, sensing the essence of each one.

Where are my chakras?

1. Root chakra. This is the "grounding" chakra. It's associated with our basic will to live, survival instincts, and issues of security. It governs our desire for physical things, including exercise, good food, and touch. Although some people put down the first chakra as unevolved, putting your consciousness on this chakra can help make you more comfortable with your desires.

Color association: Red.

Physical manifestation: Base of the spine.

Endocrine connection: Adrenal glands. Hormones secreted here prepare the body to fight or flee, deal with stress, and regulate the balance of fluids.

Spiritual profile: The home of the coiled, sleeping kundalini energy. This raw energy is associated with powerful unconscious forces. Cultivated with an ethical, spiritual, meditative practice, the kundalini is thought to awaken and spiral upward in a union of earthly and celestial energies. However, many books warn that if the kundalini energy is aroused without a balanced spiritual practice, it could burn the delicate membranes around the chakras and result in illness or even death.

When blocked: A feeling of not being "in the body" and, thus, being unaware of one's own needs. Unrealized potential.

When clear: A solid sense of embodiment, a firm foundation for spirit.

2. The generative, or pleasure, chakra. Related to the genitals and procreative organs, it is often linked with the root chakra. It represents fertility and creativity (unrelated to sex). This chakra is often the first to open in people who are becoming more aware of their creative self.

Color association: Orange.

Physical manifestation: Four finger widths below the navel.

Endocrine connection: Hormones secreted here include estrogen, progesterone, and testosterone (men and women have all three).

Spiritual profile: Combining sex with spirit is at the foundation of Tantric yoga. The spirit energy that originates here is feminine (called Shakti) and earthy in nature, and its intended destination is a merging with the celestial spirit (Shiva) in the seventh chakra.

When blocked: Because of past experiences of rejection and fear, this chakra can become charged with compulsive behaviors, especially in relationships. People often get stuck in a cycle of pleasure and pain and often form addictions to people, substances, or stimuli.

When clear: Once someone is able to let go of old patterns of fear and disillusionment, especially in a relationship, the energy can flow, merging sex and spirit.

3. Solar plexus, or center, chakra. Situated in the very center of the digestive system, this chakra represents the transformation of raw physical material (food) into energy that sustains life. The "fire in the belly" is also identified with the fire of desire and unpredictable emotions. The third chakra is typically identified with the point in a person's life when they first create their own identity.

Color association: Yellow.

Physical manifestation: The pancreas (behind the navel).

Endocrine connection: The pancreas controls the level of glucose and insulin in the blood. (Insulin helps the body store fat.)

Spiritual profile: Sprouting out of the two lower chakras, the spirit energy here is often dominated by the ego wanting to prove its uniqueness to the world. Can be a vigorous, youthful energy or, in excess, the will can become so strong that it fails to consider the existence of other people.

When blocked: Can be arrogant, condescending, and controlling or, when conflict arises, depressed and lethargic. Lets energy dribble down.

When clear: Genuine warmth, caring, service-oriented work may result when someone has cleared away the blocks. Also highly intuitive, especially on a "gut" level. Sends energy up.

4. The heart chakra. This is the first of the "higher" chakras, signifying an awareness beyond the self, associated with both human and divine love. As the heart opens, the ego diminishes and a universal identity is born.

Color association: Green.

Physical manifestation: The thymus gland, a mysterious organ believed to govern growth and immunization.

Endocrine connection: Hormones secreted here assist the immune system.

Spiritual profile: This is regarded as the leaping-off point into spirit and unselfish love. When the heart opens, there's a surrendering. This leads to compassion and disciplining of the will, which eventually transforms the whole person.

When blocked: There is overall numbness, blocking out both pleasure and pain.

When clear: Although both pain and pleasure increase, there's a sense of oneness and a deep desire for others to feel similar joy.

5. Throat chakra. Represents communication, especially in the voice (a mouthpiece for the heart) and the eyes. Related also to higher forms of communication, not just with others but with one's own spirit. Also represents the qualities of the breath, movement, and sound.

Color association: Blue.

Physical manifestation: The thyroid gland (behind the throat).

Endocrine connection: Hormones secreted here regulate metabolism, brain, nerve, and muscle function. Also governs level of calcium in the blood, and responsible for bone remodeling.

Spiritual profile: At this stage of our development, we pass from consciousness into a larger, more reflective awareness. This chakra represents cleansing, as if we have triumphed over the downward pull of the lower chakras.

When blocked: Difficulty expressing oneself in speech, written words, or other forms of expression.

When clear: Ease in expression. Also a flood of creativity, especially harmonies, songs, stories, poems, and "voices" seemingly from out of nowhere.

6. Brow chakra. The lower of the two head chakras. This is where the seemingly separate parts of the self merge into pure consciousness. This is the center of perception and intellect, also the merging of positively and negatively charged meridians and the right and left hemispheres of the brain.

Color association: Indigo.

Physical manifestation: Some systems associate this chakra with the pineal gland and others with the pituitary.

Endocrine connection: The pituitary is the "master gland" for the whole endocrine system, especially the thyroid, adrenals, and sex glands. If it ceases to function these other glands whither and die.

Spiritual profile: The sixth chakra provides an opportunity to surrender to a greater consciousness. To dwell comfortably in its essence takes trust and surrender of old fearful behaviors. Surrender to the realm of the sixth chakra can bring tremendous relief.

When blocked: People get stuck "in their heads," try to impose their mental pictures on others, and easily get cut off from reality.

When clear: Intuition increases, often about very practical things (like what to eat for dinner). You're able to live in tune with natural rhythms. Yet unless there is a balance of rational thought, someone who stays here too long could seem "spaced out."

7. The crown chakra. This is the last stop, the stepping-off point into greater awareness. (People with near-death experiences often report leaving their bodies through a hole in the top of their heads.) The crown chakra is also called the thousand-petaled lotus and represents a pristine state of being, or Buddha consciousness.

Color association: Violet.

Physical manifestation: The pineal gland, a mysterious gland the size of a peanut, rests in the center of the head behind the eyebrows and the pituitary. Although Western science hasn't determined its functions, the pineal gland has been called the seat of the soul and the third eye. This gland is bigger in children than in adults, and bigger in women than in men. It ceases functioning around age seven.

Endocrine connection: The pineal gland secretes melatonin (which regulates sleep patterns) and saltlike phosphorus tears.

Spiritual profile: The crown chakra is host to our beliefs about God and our sense of the sacred. It's also thought to be the realm for communication with nature spirits, angels, guides, and other nonembodied entities. The "nectar" of the crown chakra is mostly revealed in meditation but can also be accessed in dreams. The consciousness here is highly spatial and aware and beyond the everyday worries of the rational mind.

When blocked: No consciousness of a higher power, no unification of the self.

When clear: Consciousness rises about the essence of all beings. There is a sense of unity, love, and at-oneness with all.

chinese medicine

Ancient Chinese doctors didn't charge their patients until they got well. They didn't think they deserved payment unless they'd successfully guided a person back into health, which they considered a natural state. Except for the billing practice, the philosophy of Chinese medicine hasn't changed much.

In Chinese medicine, balance is key. Excesses, deficiencies, and extremes are to be avoided, in food, emotions, behaviors, and even in the weather. All of these can upset the flow of vital energies, which would otherwise course evenly throughout the body, maintaining health. These energies are known as

- *chi* ("basic life force"—there's no equivalent word for this in Western medicine)
- *xue* (blood, which also carries spirit)
- *shen* (spirit, consciousness)
- *jing* (fluid that governs growth and development, as well as new life)
- *jin-ye* (sweat, urine, mucus, and all other fluids that aren't *xue*).

Chinese medicine can treat many ailments, from mild to serious. It's especially good for treating conditions (such as mild depression, lack of energy, etc.) that might cause Western doctors to say, "There's nothing wrong with you." Chinese medicine also works well in conjunction with Western medicine and other forms of complementary medicine such as Ayurveda and chiropractic. It's a good idea to address health problems from both conventional and complementary perspectives.

Although there are many aspects to Chinese medicine, it mostly draws its treatments from the "four pillars of well-being": balanced diet, herbs, exercise and meditation, and acupuncture (or acupressure). Since these last three are covered more extensively in other chapters, we'll focus here on food.

The Chinese way to eat right

Although you might not realize this from eating mu shu pork and deep-fried egg rolls, the Chinese approach to eating right is very simple.

Foods aren't grouped into carbs, fat, and protein. They're categorized as dry or moist, cool or warm, hot or cold, sweet or bitter, salty or sour. The foods that fall under these categories don't always match their descriptions. For instance, bananas are sweet and cool, but so is Swiss chard. Guidelines call for common sense and moderation:

- Eat fresh, organic foods; avoid pesticides, irradiated foods, and other chemicals.
- Make grains, beans, vegetables 75 percent of your food intake.
- Make 10 percent of your food intake fruit.
- Limit animal protein to about 10 percent (use it as a garnish, not a main dish).

- Limit oils and sweets to about 5 percent.
- Avoid raw foods, heavy protein, and fats. (All force your metabolism to "cook" the food inside your stomach and cause an energy imbalance.)
- Eat foods in season, when they're at their peak (and contain the most *chi*). This also naturally prepares the body for the coming season.
- Chew well.
- Don't overeat.
- Avoid drinking liquids with a meal. (Drink a glass of water *before* a meal to aid digestion.) If you must drink water while you eat, drink it at room temperature. Water that's too cold taxes the kidneys (although drinking cool water when you're hot and working out is fine).
- Eat slowly and in a relaxed atmosphere (wolfing down a Big Mac on the freeway doesn't cut it).
- Eat in good company if you can.
- Eat at regular times.

Self-care and Chinese medicine

Like all medical professionals, Chinese doctors possess no magic potions. The most successful patient participates in his or her own well-being. The best way to align yourself with the Chinese way of balance is to keep a journal, noting your habits and inner state. This gives you a clear picture of your inner state and helps you improve some habits that may impede your good health.

Start by writing down what you eat. What do you most favor: carbohydrates, protein, fat? Sweet, salty, spicy? How does the food make you feel? Tired, energized, bloated? How were your moods? Digestion? Elimination? How about PMS, better or worse this month? How much do you eat at one time? How many meals do you eat each day?

First change the most obvious habits that don't work for you anymore (like skipping breakfast or grabbing a sugary, high-fat muffin on the way to work). Find substitutes that make your body feel better (for example, try oatmeal or another grain for breakfast).

Gradually start to fine-tune your eating habits, one piece at a time. For instance, if milk makes you bloated, switch to nonfat rice, soy, or almond milk. If caffeine makes your PMS worse, try decaf Chai (an Indian spicy tea) with warm vanilla soy milk.

depression

Almost everyone gets the blues from time to time. But depression is a more serious matter and can take a toll on health, work, and relationships, especially when sustained for several weeks. The deeper the depression, the greater the toll.

Depression takes many forms. There's situational depression (a response to outside circumstances) and a deeper sort that grows from within. Working through problems with a counselor is the best way to handle situational depression, so you uncover the cause. But more serious depression requires additional treatment.

The most serious types of depression are

- clinical depression—a deep, dark, hopeless feeling. Can last for weeks or months
- bipolar, or manic depression—a crazed dance of extreme ups and downs
- dysthymia—a foggy, gray numbness that can last for years
- SAD, or Seasonal Affective Disorder— usually affects people who live in cold, gray, wintry climates and lasts through the season

Depression isn't a character flaw. It's a serious condition affecting over 17 million Americans each year. All types of depression are treatable. However, finding the right treatment for serious depression takes patience because treatments are highly individual.

What causes depression?

Buddhists believe that depression is a consequence of seeking stimulation. The high inevitably brings the low (manic depression is a perpetual cycle of highs and lows). Buddhist philosophy says it's better to tread the "middle path of the Buddha" than feel upset when the lows inevitably come.

Medical professionals think depression is a combination of brain chemistry and habit (that we get into a pattern of negatively responding to experiences). But what hasn't been fully addressed is how our negative responses impact our brain chemistry, how we set ourselves up for depression.

Any number of things can propel you into the abyss:

- A disruptive change in life (death of someone close, losing a job, a painful breakup, etc.)
- A family history of depression
- Serious illnesses such as cancer
- Giving birth (postpartum depression affects about 15 percent of new moms)
- PMS
- Infertility (depression may even contribute to infertility)
- New motherhood (increased stress, loss of control)
- Isolation
- Substance abuse

- Stress
- Hormonal shifts
- Poverty
- Having been victimized or abused
- Feelings of helplessness and low self-esteem
- Being elderly and alone

How serious is your depression?

So how do you know if you've got a clinical depression or just a bad case of the blues? The National Institute of Mental Health recommends that if you have five or more of the following symptoms for more than two weeks, your depression is serious and you should seek professional treatment:

- Persistent sadness
- Little interest in things you once enjoyed (including sex)
- Feeling irritable, vulnerable, crying a lot
- Feeling helpless, hopeless, desperate
- Sleeping too much or too little
- Eating too much or too little
- Feeling perpetually exhausted
- Entertaining serious thoughts of death or suicide, attempting suicide
- Difficulty concentrating, making decisions
- Chronic physical symptoms that don't respond to treatment, such as headaches, digestive problems, pain

Treatments for mild to moderate depression

The following treatments may ease depression:

- Aerobic exercise. Thirty minutes a day, three to five days a week can raise endorphin levels. Although you might not feel like working out, investing effort into your recovery could do wonders.
- Meditation. It's not a quick fix, but it can lower blood pressure, heart rate, and let you transcend your worried mind.
- Diet. A low-protein, high-carbohydrate, low-fat diet keeps metabolism on a steadier keel.
- Moderation. Avoid alcohol and recreational drugs—in the long haul these make depression worse. Also avoid caffeine—it creates unstable moods.
- St.-John's-wort, an herb, has been used in clinical trials in Germany to treat more moderate cases of depression, although it needs further study here.
- Full-spectrum light boards have been very effective in easing SAD.

For more serious depression

Early detection is important and can save a lot of grief. Fifteen percent of people hospitalized for depression eventually commit suicide. Perhaps some can avoid this fate with early intervention.

A combination of talking therapy and medications ease clinical depression, manic depression, and that foggy sustained depression (dysthymia). Talk therapies can be short term or long, individual or group. Drugs (like Prozac) can return people to "normal," although there are side effects, such as weight gain, constipation, and loss of libido. People on such drugs report that although they may ease suffering, many psychiatric drugs also diminish joy and shrink the spectrum of experience to a smaller bandwidth. These drugs also don't address environmental causes.

Electroconvulsive stimulation is a more radical therapy for manic depression. Its purpose is to change brain chemistry and is a kind of last resort when other treatments have failed.

Need Help?

For more information on depression, call the National Institute of Mental Health at 800-421-4211 or visit their website at http://www.nimh.nih.gov/newdart.

environmental
wellness

Although we may think our houses are clean and safe, we're exposed to more dangerous chemicals in the home than anywhere else. There are toxic substances in food, water, air, cleaning products, appliances, carpets—the list goes on and on. These sources of indoor pollution are almost impossible to avoid, and can cause health problems, such as flulike symptoms, headaches, depression, asthma, birth defects, liver damage, cancer, a weakened immune system, and even death!

Instead of living in a hermetically sealed box, one of the best ways to defend against toxic chemicals is to strengthen the immune system with exercise, rest, antioxidants, clean water, and food. Another smart move is to get rid of unnecessary chemicals, especially for the sake of children, the sick, and the elderly—who are most vulnerable.

Chemicals

Put all dangerous chemicals outside. Keep pesticides, paint thinners, removers, and such compounds in a well-ventilated room or outdoor work shed. If you must work with these, ventilate your work space, wear a mask, gloves, goggles, and drink lots of water afterward. Call your local refuse and recycling company for info on how to safely dispose of such chemicals (do not pour them down the drain!). If you live in an apartment or have no outdoor storage space, it's important to dispose of harmful chemicals as soon as you're through using them. Check with the sanitation department or the Environmental Protection Agency (EPA) to be sure you're disposing of chemicals safely.

Avoid "sick-building syndrome." Formaldehyde fumes from particle board (compressed wood used in new construction and kitchen cabinets), carbon monoxide from gas appliances, and chemicals from new acrylic carpets can make you sick, especially if your building is tightly sealed. If you can't change these things, at least keep windows open to keep fresh air circulating. Or consider using a HEPA air filter (High Efficiency Particulate Air), available in most drug, home, and department stores. They're also good if you live with a smoker, have allergies, or live in a smoggy city.

Ventilate gas appliances to the outdoors and make sure fumes can't get back in. (Electrical appliances don't cause this problem.) Install a carbon monoxide detector to alert you to high levels of these deadly, odorless fumes.

Consider replacing acrylic carpet with a cotton/wool carpet that hasn't been mothproofed, or install safer flooring (tiles, wood planking). If this isn't feasible, you can buy a vapor barrier sealant that will prevent some fumes from seeping upward.

Check for radon—a natural radioactive gas that filters up through the soil and into homes. It's odorless and colorless but it's deadly and is the second leading cause of lung cancer after smoking. To find out if you live in a radon area, call your local branch of the EPA (Environmental Protection Agency). If you do, have your house tested for radon by a contractor or buy a radon-testing kit at a hardware store. Make sure it says "meets EPA requirements" on the box. If you have high levels of radon, have cracks professionally sealed and improve ventilation so radon is piped up to the roofline, where it can dissipate.

Wait before you rip up asbestos. Houses built between the mid-forties and late seventies often have asbestos fibers imbedded in vinyl tiles, textured paints, and insulation sprayed as foam onto walls, ceilings, and around pipes and heaters. Asbestos fibers are carcinogenic, but they're only dangerous when airborne. So before you rip out the asbestos, call a specialist or leave it alone.

Kitchen safety

Water. Tap water is a major source of contaminants. Before you buy a filter system, call your water department to find out what impurities you have. This is very important since the system you choose may not get rid of your prob-

lem. Some common contaminants include chloride, chlorine, fluoride, asbestos, bacteria, arsenic, and lead (especially from old plumbing pipes). There are a number of products that can eliminate water contaminants:

Carbon filters are the most economical device. Good for removing chemicals but not lead or other metals, fluoride, or bacteria. These work only as well as the filter. Change frequently.

Reverse osmosis. A fairly expensive under-the-sink unit. Removes asbestos, lead, rust, other metals, and fluoride but not bacteria, chemicals, or chlorine.

Distiller. A bit more expensive than reverse osmosis but the most effective. Removes bacteria, asbestos, lead, rust, and fluoride. Choose a glass distiller over stainless steel since this contains aluminum (see below).

If you buy bottled water, check labels to be sure you're not buying imported tap water. (For more information on drinking water, see **Water,** page 247.)

Cookware. Throw out old aluminum cookware, heavily scratched nonstick pans, and stainless steel. High levels of aluminum have been linked to Alzheimer's, memory loss, and headaches, although the evidence is not conclusive. (Aluminum is also found in aspirin and antacids.) Acidic foods like tomatoes and applesauce absorb even more aluminum. Scouring stainless-steel pans can release toxic metals that seep into foods. Doing the same to nonstick pans exposes food to plastic. Choose cast iron, glass, enamel-coated cast iron, and stainless steel (but don't scour!).

Ingredients. Avoid pesticides and dyes in food. Buy organic produce as much as possible.

Apples, peaches, grapes, oranges, strawberries, potatoes, carrots, lettuce, green beans, peanuts, and wheat are the most heavily sprayed foods. If you can't buy organic, wash with a small amount of liquid soap (see below) and a vegetable brush. Peel skins if possible. Stay away from unnaturally colored foods (especially popular in kids' cereals). Food dyes can be carcinogenic.

Green Cleaning Alternatives

Keeping a clean house can be dangerous for your health if you choose toxic cleaning products that leave residues, which you, your family, or pets later touch and ingest. Buy nontoxic, Earth-friendly alternatives in health food stores or make your own safe and cheap cleaning solutions.

Start with raw ingredients: distilled white vinegar, lemon, Borax (in the soap aisle), liquid soap (not dish detergent—a famous brand is Dr. Bronner's), and nonchlorinated scouring powder. Add various strengths of liquid soap or Borax, depending on the nature of the job, to hot water. Add lemon or vinegar and pour into a spray bottle.

Around the home and office

Microwaves. Don't stand in front of the microwave while it's on. The jury is still out regarding the safety of microwaves and whether or not they damage the growth and repair of cells. They're mostly considered safe except when they leak due to poor seals on doors (you can have yours checked for leaks). But it's still not a good idea to stand right in front of the microwave when it's in operation. Use it for heating and defrosting only. Cooking meats for more than ten minutes can change the composition of proteins, which may be harmful.

Electromagnetic fields. There's still much debate about the danger of electromagnetic fields created by electrical wires and appliances. However, there have been several cases of "cancer clusters" among children who live near high-power electric lines. Minimize your risk by keeping your distance from EMF's. Unplug appliances when not in use. Don't sleep or sit right next to a clock radio. Keep your blow dryer about twelve inches from your head. Warm up your electric blanket or heating pad then turn them off before using them. Don't stand next to buzzing power lines. Don't sit too close to your TV.

If you work at a computer, sit as far from the screen as possible—30 inches is ideal. If feasible, buy a laptop with a liquid crystal display (LCD) screen. Or buy a grounded screen (which plugs in) to block out EMF's. Screens that limit glare don't block EMF's.

Lighting. Change the lighting. Fluorescent lightbulbs have been linked to several maladies including fatigue and changes in brain waves and hormone levels. Replace regular fluorescents with full-spectrum fluorescent bulbs.

fatigue

Being tired can feel good after a hard day's work and help you sleep. But being fatigued, especially when it's relentless or caused by some unknown source, doesn't feel so good.

Deep, excessive fatigue can be the first warning sign of depression or serious illness and shouldn't be ignored. Cancer, heart conditions, thyroid disease, problems of the immune system, and many other illnesses often first show up as persistent fatigue. It may not only be the symptom of illness but the cause, since it can weaken the immune system and create a friendly environment for the growth of viruses, bacteria, and errant cells. Masking fatigue with caffeine or other drugs may provide a quick fix, but in the long run, these things create more fatigue. The best form of preventive medicine is to change the behaviors that cause fatigue.

Two of the main causes are improper use of the body (sedentary lifestyle, poor nutrition) and mental and physical stress (worry, too much work).

A sedentary lifestyle wastes energy that would normally get spent throughout the day. In Chinese medicine, this is regarded as stagnant energy. Improper diet and overeating, especially excess fat and protein, makes the digestive system work overtime. An inordinate amount of energy gets funneled into this process, leaving less energy for you. Stress creates chronic tension. Energy goes into holding muscles rigid. This blocks the normal energy flow.

Chronic fatigue syndrome

Chronic fatigue syndrome (CFS) is a relatively new ailment that has gotten a lot of press. Doctors have been somewhat mystified as to its cause or if it really exists, since the virus hasn't been identified. It's also confused with the Epstein-Barr virus (a form of mononucleosis), but these two things aren't the same.

CFS primarily affects young, otherwise healthy people and can persist for several months or up to five years. It impairs memory, sleep, and often creates sore throats, fevers, and swollen glands. As many as 50 percent of chronic fatigue patients suffer from depression before the symptoms of CFS show up.

Western doctors mostly treat chronic fatigue with antidepressant drugs (often with little success). In addition, you can try the following:

- Some medications that doctors prescribe for CFS can do more harm than good. If you're not responding well to something your doctor has prescribed, discuss possible alternatives.
- Try Astralagus root or a product called Astra-8.
- Eat two cloves of garlic each day. You can swallow whole cloves like pills without devastating your breath.
- Take antioxidant vitamins like A, C, E, and selenium.
- Take B complex.

- Do moderate aerobic exercise for up to thirty minutes, five days a week, but don't push yourself to exhaustion.
- Have faith. The symptoms eventually subside.

How to have more energy

Energy is like love. The more you give it away, the more you have. But there's a stipulation: To get it back, you have to invest in healthy things. Don't hoard it or spend it all in one place.

- Take regular, moderate exercise. Overdoing it can zap your energy.
- Aerobic exercise prevents and benefits heart conditions, digestive problems, emotional upsets, and many other conditions that can grow from untreated fatigue.
- Stretching helps nutrients get into muscles, reduces chronic tension, benefits the nervous system, helps release energy blocks, and lifts moods.
- Strengthening exercises done with careful attention to form brings an intelligence and vitality into the muscles. Resistance shouldn't be too heavy (it causes excess tension, fatigue, and injury) or too light (it doesn't produce an adaptive response— i.e., you don't get stronger).
- Cultivate your *chi* and *prana*. (See **Tai Chi and Chi Kung** and **Yoga,** pages 458 and 461, for specific energy-enhancing exercises.)

- Breathe. Fill your belly, lungs, and brain with oxygen. (For specific breathing instructions, see **Breathing,** page 417.)
- Meditate. Learn to focus your attention, wash your brain of worry, and, in the process, lower your blood pressure and heart rate, increase the blood flow, and lower your biological age. (See **Meditation,** page 441, for more information.)
- Drink water. Fatigue is one of the first signs of dehydration.
- Get up and walk around at least once an hour if you have a sedentary job.
- Sit up straight. Slumping cramps your organs, puts your back at risk, and impedes blood flow. At your desk, keep your spine upright, without resting it on the seat behind you. Put both feet on the floor.
- Stimulate your mind. Learning new things, being with energetic people, and visiting beautiful places give you energy.
- Laugh away your stress. Taking life too seriously can bring you down.

homeopathy

Homeopathic medicine is a controversial, often misunderstood, but very effective way of treating a number of conditions. It's also very safe, and doesn't create side effects or weaken the immune system the way some traditional Western medicines can. Although it's only beginning to gain widespread popularity in the United States, homeopathic medicine has been a standard medical treatment around the world for decades.

Homeopathic remedies work on the principle of similars, that the very thing that causes an ailment can be used in small doses to cure it. Homeopathic remedies, therefore, contain heavily diluted herbs, metals, poisons, and diseases. Remedies are typically made up of the substance (1%) mixed with alcohol (99%), making some people think the remedies are placebos or magic potions. However, in double-blind studies against placebos, homeopathic remedies are shown to be highly effective and even work on babies and animals, who don't know about the placebo effect.

Much like Chinese medicine, remedies are thought to work on an energy level (or "vital force" as it's known in homeopathy) by assisting the body's self-healing mechanism. Both Chinese medicine and homeopathic doctors treat patients by taking a full assessment: mental state, emotions, quality of voice, language, skin, odors, and so on.

Although remedies are harmless, it's not a good idea to simply walk into a health food store and pull a remedy off the shelf, since one ailment can have many different remedies. It's best to take homeopathic remedies under the guidance of a professional or consult a good book on the subject.

Homeopathic Remedies Can Heal

Acne	Hemorrhoids
Anemia	Hay fever
Anxiety	Headaches
Arthritis	Heartburn
Asthma	Impotence
Bronchitis	Insomnia
Bruises	Menstrual
Burns	irregularity
Caffeine	Menopausal
addiction	symptoms
Cold sores	Motion sickness
Cold, flu, cough,	Nerve pain
sore throat	(neuralgia)
Colitis	Ovarian cysts
Conjunctivitis	PMS, cramps
Constipation	Psoriasis
Enlarged prostate	Rheumatism
Fatigue	Sciatica
Fibroids in	Skin problems
the uterus	Stress
Herpes	Toothache

How and how not to take your remedies

Remedies mostly come in tablets, tinctures, or oral sprays for children. If you take tablets, pour only the amount you need into your hand. Don't touch the medication if you're giving it to someone else—pour the pills into the bottle cap. If you touch a pill and don't use it or happen to drop it, throw it away—pills become easily contaminated.

If symptoms are severe, take a higher dosage more often. Take a half-hour before meals. Let tablets dissolve under your tongue. Don't drink anything and avoid brushing your teeth. As symptoms subside, cut dosage. You should notice a change after about six doses. If not, stop and seek advice. As symptoms disappear, stop taking the remedy—it could make you sick again. Be sure to store medicine in your refrigerator, away from perfume, cleaning solutions, your computer or microwave.

Strong smells, substances, and emotions can counteract effectiveness. Avoid the following for as long as you take remedies:

- Caffeine
- Menthol/eucalyptus (usually found in cough syrups and lozenges)
- Camphor (found in Tiger Balm, moth balls, deep-heating rubs)
- Peppermint toothpaste, mouthwash, tea (brush your teeth with baking soda and try a different herbal tea)
- Alcohol and recreational drugs

Bach flower remedies

These delicate flower essences are similar in spirit to homeopathic remedies. Dr. Edward Bach created them in the early twentieth century as a way to remedy people's emotional upsets, which he believed created illness. He isolated seven negative moods:

- Fear
- Uncertainty
- Insufficient interest in present circumstances
- Loneliness
- Oversensitivity to other people's influences and ideas
- Despondence, despair
- Overconcern for the welfare of others

Through a painstaking process, in which he assumed the physical, mental, and emotional ailments of his patients, Dr. Bach came up with thirty-nine remedies made from the dew that forms on nonpoisonous wildflowers.

Rescue Remedy is an all-purpose tincture for stress, upset, shock, anxiety, stage fright, and general negativity. It can also be used topically on burns, bites, and sprains. All Bach flower remedies are harmless, and are gentle enough for children and animals.

immunity

The immune system is made up of a combination of cells, organs, and other structures that essentially act as the body's armed forces. Their job is to "fight" unwelcome invaders such as bacteria, fungus, viruses, cancers, parasites, even "foreign" transplanted organs.

Unlike other systems in the body, there's no designated area where the immune system lives. It's comprised of seemingly unrelated parts, from the lymphatic system (the glands) to the blood. Doctors used to remove some of these parts—tonsils, adenoids, the appendix, the spleen, the thymus gland (the gland that regulates growth)—indiscriminately because they didn't understand their functions.

White blood cells and the bone marrow that creates them play a major role in strengthening immunity. Although white blood cells are outnumbered by red blood cells (the ones that carry oxygen) half a million to one, they're tough. There are several types of white blood cells. T-cells are probably the most well known.

When it works best, the immune system keeps the body free of all sorts of ailments. It runs into problems, however, when it becomes underactive or overactive. Underactivity makes the body more susceptible to infections and cancer. Overactivity makes the body more susceptible to allergies and autoimmune diseases. Allergic reactions occur when the body becomes too zealous at fighting its invader and responds in an extreme way to otherwise harmless threats, like cat hair and dust.

Autoimmune diseases occur when the body starts to attack its own tissues. These diseases affect all parts of the body, from skin to joints to glands, and include leukemia, lupus, rheumatoid arthritis, AIDS, psoriasis, Graves disease (a thyroid condition), and diabetes. Even multiple sclerosis is considered an autoimmune disease.

Boosting immunity

Use antibiotics wisely. The immune system grows stronger whenever it emerges victorious from a battle. If you take antibiotics at the tiniest sign of illness, you rob the immune system of its chance to get stronger. Your doctor should prescribe them only for serious conditions.

Don't ignore warning signs of illness such as little growths or discolorations, fatigue, and swollen glands. Fighting low-level infections for long periods of time severely taxes the immune system. It's like losing battle after battle.

Avoid consuming high levels of animal protein—meat, poultry, and dairy products (especially those that are high in fat). Despite the popularity of high-protein diets, low-protein, high-carb diets still make more sense for total health, especially for someone with allergies or who is prone to autoimmune diseases.

Don't drink alcohol excessively or smoke.

Take antioxidant vitamins—vitamins C, E, and beta-carotene (a form of vitamin A). These boost immunity by fighting free radicals. Free radicals are cells that oxidize and form dangerous chemicals, which then go on a rampage and cause other cells to become malignant.

Avoid exposure to radiation. Question a dentist's or doctor's need for X rays. Radiation gives the body a double whammy—it both causes cells to mutate (into malignancy) and weakens the immune system's ability to fight that malignancy. Don't sit out in the midday sun or go to a tanning parlor. The ultraviolet light in both bright sun and a tanning booth damages DNA in skin cells. Wear high SPF rating sunblock and a hat when you go outside.

Beware of chemicals in cleaning solvents, paints, and pesticides. If you must work with them, wear a mask.

Have safe sex, to protect yourself from the HIV virus and other diseases.

Don't worry, be happy. A positive attitude can do wonders for health (otherwise placebos wouldn't have such a high success rate!). Depression, anger, and general negativity can impair the nervous system, which impedes immunity. Putting on a false happy face is not good, either. Dealing with real emotions and working toward a positive outcome, however, can do wonders for health. (See **Endorphins**, page 173, for more on emotions and health.)

And of course, exercise.

How regular, moderate exercise strengthens the immune system

- fights off minor infections (colds, flu, etc.) (Excessive exercise, however, can weaken and stress the body, therefore impair immunity.)
- creates a short-lived increase in the blood levels of white blood cells
- increases body temperature; this short-term "fever" can build an unfriendly atmosphere for infections
- increases the processing of metabolic wastes (protects colon)
- protects women against cancer because it lowers the levels of estrogen circulating in the body. (A lifetime of circulating estrogens [uninterrupted by pregnancies] can stimulate the growth of cancer cells in the breasts, uterus, and ovaries.)
- counteracts depression, lowers stress, and creates a feeling of well-being that strengthens immunity

Should You Exercise When You're Sick?

If the illness is a minor head cold or sinus condition, then it's best to try a light workout at about half normal intensity. If it makes you feel better and clears sinuses, then it's OK.

If the illness is more severe, located in lungs, stomach, intestines, and is accompanied by fever and diarrhea, then don't exercise. Rest will help the body heal faster.

massage

Throughout history, virtually all cultures have used the power of touch to heal. By reducing stress, massage stimulates the body's ability to cure itself and, in the process, eases a number of conditions, including:

- Digestive problems
- Muscular aches and spasms
- Poor alignment
- Injuries
- Connective-tissue sprains
- Respiratory problems
- Blood circulation
- Malfunctioning organs
- Blocked energy
- Constipation
- Uncomfortable pregnancy
- Stress (and its attendant physical symptoms, high blood pressure, higher heart rate, higher adrenaline output)
- Anxiety
- Poor body image
- Grief

Massage used to be a regular part of a nurse's education and was once a common treatment in hospitals. But drugs helped push massage out of favor. Now it's beginning to make its way back into more open-minded medical centers. Typically, however, to get a good massage you need to go to a licensed massage therapist (LMT). To get the most out of a massage, prepare yourself mentally, don't eat right before, and drink a glass of clean water afterward.

Basic massage techniques

Swedish is the most popular and well-known form of massage. It combines long strokes (from light to deep) with circular moves, kneading, shaking, pounding, pressing, and a passive manipulation of limbs to increase range of motion.

Esalen-Swedish massage, created at Esalen Institute in Big Sur, California, primarily uses the longer, more relaxing strokes of Swedish massage to elicit a blissful calm. It's more of an overall balm for the body-mind-spirit than a specific treatment for injury or illness.

Sports massage is an essential part of training for many athletes, dancers, martial artists, and so on. It helps speed recovery from simple overuse injuries by loosening and lengthening muscle fibers, reducing swelling, and easing tension. Sports-massage therapists often focus on the most-used muscles and employ a variety of methods, as in Swedish massage.

Lymphatic massage is a highly specialized technique. Lymph is the fluid that contains white blood cells, which deliver waste products into the bloodstream to be eliminated. Lymph moves through the body when stimulated by muscle contractions, both the voluntary muscles and those that line the organs. Most massages usually stimulate the lymphatic system, but lymphatic massage speeds up the process and unblocks lymph as it collects in some of the eight hundred lymph nodes located near the spinal cord, and is often recommended after surgery or trauma. This can be a light or deep massage, depending on the therapist.

Trigger-point massage works on the belief that muscles are mapped with little bumps that are sore when touched. These are different in everyone and are thought to appear genetically or to be caused by years of disuse, accidents, stress, and such. Trigger points not only affect the area around them but radiate into distant parts as well. Trigger-point therapy has immediate and long-term benefits. Aside from relieving spasms, increasing blood flow, and eliminating pain with very specific treatments, it also aims to break the vicious cycle of pain and spasms caused by inefficient use of the body. It's often followed up with stretches and movements to lengthen and reeducate muscles.

Trager psychophysical integration, created by Milton Trager in the 1940s and 1950s, seeks to retrain the body to feel light, effortless, and free. Trager practitioners address muscles and joints with pleasurable motions (gentle jiggling, rubbing, rocking, and stretching) and never use force or pain. Trager work also includes "Mentastics" ("mental" plus "gymnastics"), which consists of light dance moves: effortless kicks, swings, and stretches. Both the hands-on and movement work aim to send positive messages to the central nervous system to ease stress and prevent disease.

Craniosacral therapy was created by Dr. William Sutherland, an osteopath (doctors who manipulate bones) in the early 1900s. He discovered that the skull is made up of twenty-two movable sections, attached by tissue. Craniosacral therapy not only works on the bones in the head but the spine, the sacrum (pelvis), and the membrane that connects them. This membrane surrounds the central nervous system and secretes a fluid (cerebrospinal fluid) to other membranes. It has a pulse of its own (called the craniosacral pulse, or CNS) that's separate from the heartbeat and beats at a rate of 6 to 12 bpms. Craniosacral therapists examine the pulse for irregularities, then manipulate skull bones and relax the membranes so the fluid flows in a regular fashion.

Rolfing (or structural integration) is the brainchild of Ida Rolf, a woman born in the late 1800s. This deep, often painful bodywork aims to create vertical alignment to promote optimal function, mechanics, and flow of energy. Rolfing manipulates the myofascia—a weblike substance that encases every muscle fiber, every group of fibers, bone, tendon, ligament, nerve, gland, organ, and blood vessel. It's like an intricate pair of support pantyhose that holds everything together. But when you get a snag (caused by muscle imbalances), the integrity of the whole system is affected. Rolfing sessions typically follow a set sequence and come in groups of ten, spaced a week apart. Rolfing is most effective when you consciously apply the new moving and alignment patterns.

Aston patterning is a movement-reeducation system, created by Judith Aston, a student of Ida Rolf's. It contains three parts: manipulation, a fitness program, and practical applications (how to sit, sleep, play sports more comfortably). The body work addresses the myofascia, muscles, and joints with spiral patterns. Aston fitness includes cardiovascular and muscle conditioning, joint flexibility, and light movements. Alignment in Aston patterning is on a slight forward lean. Sessions are highly individualized.

Hellerwork was created by yet another student of Ida Rolf's. Joseph Heller created a three-part system: a deep connective-tissue massage, a mindful movement methodology, plus a psychological component, which connects emotions to sensations, stored in the body. Eleven sessions guide you from infancy to adulthood and each has a different theme.

Pressure-point massage, see **Acupressure and Shiatsu,** page 401.

When Not to Get a Massage

Deep body work shouldn't be done directly on weak or broken bones; broken, tender skin; or a pregnant woman's belly.

meditation

Meditation is the ultimate form of brainwashing. It's a state of "relaxed alertness" that can greatly expand awareness. Unfortunately, people have projected all kinds of mystery and magic onto meditation. Intimidating mantras, levitating gurus, and religious cults have added to the "way out" image. But meditation is both the most easily available form of self-care and perhaps the most difficult.

Counting breaths, visualizing chakras, praying to deities, having a transcendental experience, or completely emptying the mind seem far beyond the reach of most people. Although meditation can be all of these things, it's easier to approach it as a time to clear away the thoughts that prevent you from experiencing increased awareness.

There are many benefits to meditation, though it's best not to enter into it to get something in return (improved health, more luck in business). In Hindu and Buddhist philosophy, desire is the source of all unhappiness. Don't expect instant enlightenment or radiant health. Anytime you start to worry that you're not reaching your goals, you're not meditating—such thoughts are counterproductive.

Surrendering to what is elicits an enormous relaxation response—a key factor in healing. Focusing the mind is the ultimate challenge (much harder than working on the body). And

practice helps. You don't need to be spiritual or religious to do it.

One final note: Some people meditate as their only form of preventive medicine. Like many other healthy habits, this works best in conjunction with eating well, exercise, and other healthy behaviors.

The physical benefits of meditation

Meditation may not be a cure-all, but as several studies have shown, it does have significant health benefits. Therefore, it's safe to say that meditation has been known to:

- Lower blood pressure, resting heart rate, and respiratory rate
- Increase blood flow
- Lower stress hormones (cortisol and adrenaline)
- Increase coping skills
- Lower biological age (meditation can improve the biomarkers that typically decline with age: hearing, blood pressure, and vision)
- Slow the decline of DHEA (a brain hormone associated with aging and such illnesses as osteoporosis, breast cancer, and coronary artery disease)
- Lessen symptoms of headaches

- Lower cholesterol by an average of 20 points (according to a study in Israel)
- Reduce the risk of getting cancer (by 50 percent), heart disease (by 80 percent)

Meditation 101

There are countless ways to meditate—from the sublimely simple Zen approach of counting breaths, to the intricate movement of energies in the Taoist system, to the Hindu meditations on various deities, to highly specific guided visualizations, to simple prayer. The choices are infinite and one is no better than another. Find an approach that suits you. (*Note:* To prepare yourself for meditation, you might want to try the breathing exercises on page 425 in **Breathing**.) Here are some standard meditative practices:

Count your breaths. Without forcing your breath, count a full exhalation and inhalation as 1. Group your breaths together in groups of twos so you don't have to worry about keeping track.

Use sound. Repeat any word, phrase, or sound. The vibrations of the voice can be very soothing. You can use simple vowel sounds like "ah" or "oh," or more traditional chanting sounds like "om." You can also use chants or prayers from any religious tradition, such as "Hail Mary full of grace."

Use visualization. Transport your mind to a serene setting—by a waterfall or on a warm beach with balmy ocean breezes.

Connect your energy and physical bodies. Recharge your organs, chakras, and meridians. Run energy in a steady current throughout your body and feel the power of it radiating several inches beyond your skin.

Become an objective observer of your life. Step away from your ego and personality and notice the things that you create (and destroy) in your life. Do this without judgment and with compassion.

Pray. There are really two types of prayers: those for help and those for thanks. Use the help prayers sparingly. Give thanks for the treasures in your life, including the things you take for granted, like the air you breathe.

Get the most out of meditation

The form of meditation you choose isn't as important as simply doing it on a regular basis. Many people try to meditate and give up in frustration. Learning techniques from a teacher can guide you in the right direction. So will diligent practice.

Practice is key. Try to meditate for 5 to 30 minutes every day. If you can't do it every day, then aim for 4 to 5 days a week. Consistency builds spiritual muscle.

Sit up straight. Keep your spine upright, without resting your lower back in a chair if you can handle this. Sit on a floor cushion or chair. Lie down if you must.

Choose a time that works for you. Many meditators say the best time to meditate is first thing in the morning and last thing at night. But any time and place will do.

When your mind wanders, bring it back to the breath. There's a word for this activity—it's called *dharana* in Sanskrit. Chasing the mind is not unlike chasing a curious puppy. Allow the chatter to continue without judging yourself for it. Simply disassociate yourself from it. These thoughts aren't you.

Don't go looking for the mystical experience. Meditation is a time to give up expectations (because what inevitably follows is disappointment).

menopause

With more women approaching menopause than at any other time in history, it's no surprise that we're looking at the subject in a new light. Menopause used to be regarded as a woman's official entry into old age. It heralded the end of mothering, youth, and sensuality (from which women drew their worth). But now, as women broaden their knowledge and attitudes about menopause, more see it as the advent of a new phase of life. In fact, women who hold this attitude tend to suffer fewer symptoms, to age less quickly, and to retain their vitality.

Every woman's menopause is different and, ideally, should be treated individually, especially regarding hormone-replacement therapy. As a general rule, women should consult with a physician or gynecologist before making any treatment decisions. There are, however, some guidelines that can improve every woman's passage.

The three phases of menopause

Perimenopause is a fancy name for premenopause. Like menarche (the beginning of the menstrual cycle), this phase is marked by sudden shifts in hormone levels and irregular periods. It typically lasts two to five years but can also last as long as ten years, and it can start as early as age thirty-five, although the average is forty-five. Smokers begin perimenopause younger than nonsmokers.

Menopause is the only condition that's defined by the date symptoms stop. Menopause officially begins a year after the end of the last period, average age fifty-one. With it comes a long list of changes. About 10 to 15 percent of American women experience no symptoms, while 10 to 15 percent experience symptoms that are serious and debilitating. The majority of women experience some symptoms to some manageable degree.

Postmenopause can be a time of liberation from PMS, child rearing, and social constraints, but it can also be a time of failing health. Postmenopausal women may still have to raise children or care for sick parents, but they are less likely to feel depressed and often have more time for self-reflection and clarity of mind than they had in youth.

Surgical menopause, brought on by removal of the ovaries, is an abrupt, unnatural type of menopause. Because of its sudden nature, symptoms can be much more severe.

Symptoms of menopause

Symptoms can be highly individual. The one constant women seem to experience is changeability. Some women have more energy, some much less. Some women become more interested in sex, others much less. Some women feel more control over their bodies, others relinquish control and let chaos reign.

Not all symptoms are bad. For instance, peri- and menopausal women often have increased intuition, greater mental clarity, and more assertiveness.

Other symptoms, however, are difficult and can be exacerbated by stress—divorce, illness, financial uncertainty, empty-nest syndrome, caring for sick family members, or simply a fearful, negative demeanor. Symptoms include:

- Hot flashes (see "Having a Heat Wave?" page 447)
- Depression (see **Depression,** page 426)
- Irregular sleep habits
- Headaches
- Extreme PMS symptoms
- Vaginal dryness

Those crazy hormones

Originally, menopause was thought to be an estrogen deficiency, and had been treated accordingly (with estrogen-replacement medications such as Premarin, which is made from the urine of pregnant mares). But doctors who first treated menopause with estrogen soon discovered that estrogen-replacement therapy (ERT) stimulated cell division (a cancer-friendly process) in the breast, uterus, and ovaries. This is why women who take ERT (and have a family history of cancer) increase their risk for cancer. Now menopause is treated with a combination of hormones.

Researchers suspect that menopausal problems may have more to do with an excess of estrogen and a deficiency of the hormone progesterone. Progesterone combats some of the symptoms that estrogen creates. For instance, while estrogen makes the body retain water, progesterone is a diuretic (as well as an antide-

pressant). The ratio between estrogen and progesterone (rather than the total amounts of these hormones) may be the real culprit.

Lack of progesterone may also cause bad PMS. Many menstrual cycles are anovulatory (the ovaries don't secrete an egg). Since progesterone is manufactured in the egg, such cycles have low progesterone levels. Those are the months when PMS symptoms are worse. One of the reasons PMS gets worse in perimenopause is that over time, women ovulate less.

Another key hormone is testosterone. Yes, the female body produces and needs this male hormone. It helps regulate sex drive and maintain bone and muscle mass. Testosterone levels can increase twenty times after menopause or dwindle. If there's an excess of testosterone, women's body types typically switch from "pear" to "apple" shaped. This also increases the risk of heart disease, hypertension, and raises levels of bad cholesterol. If there's a testosterone shortage, sex drive, energy, and well-being diminish.

Hormone imbalances can be treated with synthetic or natural hormone supplements. The important point is that one hormone supplement doesn't work for everyone. Talk to your doctor about hormone testing and see below.

Hormone-replacement therapy

Should you take it? The safest route is to make changes in diet and exercise habits first, then decide if your symptoms warrant HRT. This way you expose yourself to the least amount of harm from excess hormones. If you do opt for HRT, the hormones are used in lower doses than they used to be. You should also take estrogen with progesterone for at least part of your normal cycle. And examine your family history to see if you're genetically inclined toward specific diseases. Base your choice on all the evidence.

Women who take HRT have an increased risk of breast cancer, and the risk goes up with age (but there's also a 70 percent chance of conquering it with early detection).

HRT protects women against heart disease. After menopause, the risk of a woman getting heart disease equals that of a man, and women are twice as likely to die of a heart attack. Fifty-three percent of all women who die each year die of heart attack. Only 4 percent die of breast cancer.

Bone loss accelerates with menopause, predisposing women to osteoporosis. (See **Osteoporosis,** page 33, for information on this disease.) However, up to 50 percent of all bone loss may take place before menopause. HRT can prevent further loss but it won't build new bone.

More Pros and Cons of HRT

Pros	Cons
Relieves hot flashes	Causes PMS symptoms
May improve moods	May cause depression
Protects against colon cancer	Increases the risk of stroke
Improves balance	Causes weight gain, bloating
Improves concentration	Causes vaginal bleeding
Improves memory	Causes hair loss
Reduces bad cholesterol	Causes high blood pressure
Increases blood flow	Changes shape of the corneas, so interferes
Increases sex drive	with contact lenses

Natural menopause treatments

Women in other cultures suffer far fewer menopausal symptoms. Only 10 percent of Japanese women report menopausal difficulties—mostly, it's believed, because their diet is high in soy. Soy contains traces of natural protective estrogens called phytoestrogens. Consuming more soy products is just one way to deal with menopause the natural way.

Chinese medicine, homeopathy, and other complementary medicine practices offer treatments for menopause. Acupuncture has brought relief to many sufferers and herbs like ginseng root, *dong quai,* and sarsaparilla are also often recommended. Try natural hormones such as low-dose progesterone creams, available in health food stores. Or try patches (which are absorbed evenly into the skin), pills, capsules, injections. Be sure to consult with your doctor before trying even over-the-counter formulations. "Natural" progesterone creams differ from synthetics (Provera is a popular synthetic) and don't cause side effects. Pharmaceutical companies manufacture synthetic progesterone because "natural" can't be patented.

Having a heat wave?

What are hot flashes anyway? They've been called all kinds of things: power surges, thermal energy, and natural cleansing rituals thought to kill off cancer cells and viruses. About 80 percent of all American menopausal women have them, and they can occur over the course of a few months or years. They're harmless, but they get your attention. Some are brief, passing heat waves and others (like night sweats, which wake you up in a puddle) are more annoying.

Hot flashes occur when blood vessels dilate and send a rush of hot blood into the face, torso, and fingertips. Heart rate increases (although blood pressure stays constant). After the heat, a chill sets in.

Hot flashes can last a few seconds or up to three minutes, although some go on much longer.

Hot flashes consume B vitamins, potassium, magnesium, and vitamin C (so it's wise to supplement these nutrients). Women who exercise regularly have far fewer hot flashes. Certain things trigger hot flashes—among them alcohol, smoking, marijuana, sugar, hot drinks, hot weather, sauna, whirlpool, spicy food, and anger.

Natural Treatments

Do	Don't
Learn to love soy products like tofu and low-fat soy burgers, and try nonfat vanilla soy milk with Chai, a spicy Indian tea, available in decaf	Eat meat, poultry, and dairy, all of which contain estrogenlike hormones that increase the risk of cancer. (Excess protein also leaches calcium from bones.)
Eat yams, which contain phytoestrogens; eat beans instead of meat; and favor grains over processed starches	Consume too much sugar, which causes fatigue and hypoglycemia
Exercise, all kinds (aerobic, strength training, stretching, energy exercises like Tai Chi, Chi Kung, or yoga)	Drink caffeine, which increases blood pressure and causes cysts in the breasts or carbonated drinks (including carbonated mineral water), which contain phosphates that pull calcium from bones, increasing risk of osteoporosis
Meditation and deep-breathing exercises to lower stress (see **Breathing,** page 424)	Eat too much fat, which increases the risk of heart disease
Cultivate a positive attitude, especially about your changing body	

reflexology

Reflexology, like acupressure and shiatsu, is a trigger-point massage, usually performed on the soles of the feet but sometimes on the hands and ears. Specific points correspond with various body parts. Sensitive points indicate an energy block or some other kind of problem. Gentle or deep pressing on those sensitive points sends a healing rush of blood, oxygen, lymph, and energy to the body parts in question.

Reflexology is not just a foot massage or a medical treatment. It's energy medicine. In other words, it addresses the body on an energy level, just as acupuncture and acupressure do. In fact, many reflexology points correspond with the ends of the meridians or energy pathways (see also **Acupressure and Shiatsu** and **Acupuncture,** pages 392 and 396), which form the basis of Chinese medicine.

Like so many complementary therapies, reflexology draws from an ancient tradition. It's thought to date back to the time of the pharaohs in Egypt and also has roots in ancient Japan, India, Russia, and China. In the early nineteenth century, Dr. William Fitzgerald of Connecticut and his colleagues resurrected reflexology and modernized it.

Although reflexology isn't meant to cure illness, it can ease many conditions, most of them chronic but not serious. These include:

- Allergies
- Arthritis
- Asthma
- Back problems
- Colds
- Constipation
- Cramps
- Depression
- Fatigue
- Headache
- Heartburn
- Nausea
- Pregnancy
- Shoulder pains

The foot is thought to be a human body in miniature. The shape of the foot, when turned with toes up, mimics the curve of the spine. Also, if you put a footprint and a body side by side, they'd correspond as shown in the box below.

To make sure you address all body parts, draw invisible, parallel lines going from each toe to the heel. This divides the foot into five sections, with Zone 1 being under the big toe and Zone 5 being under the pinkie.

TO ADDRESS THE . . .	YOU'D WORK THE . . .
Head and neck	Toes
Chest, shoulders, lungs	Metatarsal
Internal organs	Under the arch
Pelvic area	The heel

Giving foot reflexology

Of course, it's best if someone does this for you. But you can give reflexology to yourself or someone else, even without much training. It's not that difficult and there are no harmful side effects.

First, take off socks (bare feet work best so you can use friction). Wash feet. If you're giving reflexology, make sure your hands are warm and clean. Have the person sit or lie down so the feet are in a toes-up position.

Before you begin the massage, touch both feet gently but firmly. Many people are ticklish, and this helps calm them and establishes trust. Hold both the tops and bottoms of the feet. Begin with a comforting massage. Use a small amount of massage lotion. Wait until it's mostly absorbed before applying pressure or feet will be too slippery.

Use your imagination to come up with various massage techniques: kneading, wringing, patting, knuckling, shaking, and slapping.

To give reflexology:

1. Start in Zone 5, at the heel. Press your thumb firmly but cautiously into the foot and run fingers upward. Too much pressure at first can be painful or ticklish. Read the person's body signs for stress or pain.
2. Work up the foot in a straight line.
3. When you get to the toes, gently bend them back, move on to Zone 4 and repeat.

If you hit a tender spot don't just dig into it (that puts attention on the pain). A good way to press the point without someone realizing it is to rotate the ankle joint so the foot revolves around the pressure point. If a person is still too sensitive for this, don't push it. Be sure to avoid pressing into cuts, bruises, and calluses. Before you change feet, hold one foot in both hands and slowly let go, so the person doesn't notice an abrupt change.

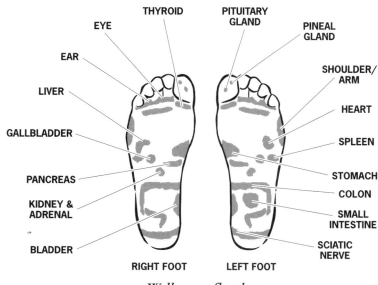

Wellness reflexology

sleep

Sleep is a time of body repair. When we're asleep, our heart rate, metabolism, and oxygen consumption decrease, giving our cells the chance to repair the damage we did while we were awake. Without sleep, we don't function well and we age faster.

Although most people need between seven and nine hours of sleep a night, we all have different sleep needs. Some people get along fine with five hours. Others still can't get started after nine. Certainly not everyone needs the standard eight hours.

You know you're getting enough sleep if you can get through the day without wanting a nap. If you must nap, sleeping for more than two hours can cause insomnia at night (although a fifteen-minute nap can do wonders). If you're sleepy all the time, see your doctor. Fatigue can be a symptom of more serious health problems (see **Fatigue,** page 432).

How to get a good night's sleep

The lists on page 452 offer general advice for making sure you get a good night's sleep every night.

Sleeping on the road

Any time you cross time zones, sleep is the first thing that suffers. Your biological clock doesn't know what time it is, since the body sets its circadian rhythm by the amounts of local darkness and light. You can do some simple things, however, to beat jet lag:

- Traveling east is harder than traveling west. Before your trip, start going to bed an hour earlier for each hour of time difference.
- Before a trip west, do the same in reverse, going to bed one hour later.
- Drink lots of water before, during, and after your arrival.
- Try to book a flight that gets you there in the evening.
- If you arrive in the day, stay outside in the daylight for as long as you can to reset your biological clock. If that doesn't work and you have to nap when you get there, don't sleep for more than two hours.
- Work out when you arrive. Exercise can calm you, ground you, and make you tired enough to sleep on local time.

Do	Don't
Stick to a regular schedule. Try to go to sleep and get up at the same hour every day. Staying up late and sleeping in on weekends can mess up your sleep cycles for the start of the workweek.	Drink or eat products containing caffeine. It can stay in your system for up to eight hours. And don't smoke. Nicotine is a stimulant.
Exercise regularly (not intermittently, that won't help you sleep). But if you exercise close to bedtime, an elevated heart rate and speedy metabolism could keep you awake.	Drink that nightcap. Although a little alcohol might help you fall asleep, it typically wakes you up in the middle of the night. Don't drink much of any liquid before bedtime, especially if you have trouble falling back to sleep once "nature calls."
Make your bedroom comfortable—not too hot or too cold. If you're bothered by street noise, wear earplugs or try a white-noise machine to mask the sounds. If your sleep partner's snoring keeps you awake, buy him or her BreathRight bandages, which fit over the bridge of the nose and minimize snoring. If light streams through your windows, cover them with thick drapes or buy a sleep mask.	Eat a big, spicy, high-fat meal right before bed. A full stomach makes your body work too hard just when it needs to rest. But don't go to bed starving either; that also raises your metabolism. If you need a bedtime snack, try some plain carbs (like crackers) and warm milk. Keep the sugar content low.
Assume the position. The position you wake up in is your natural sleep posture. If this isn't a comfortable position to start out with, find one that is. Try propping up bony knees, arms (and pregnant bellies) with pillows.	Avoid extended use of sleeping pills. They don't let you set your own biological sleep clock.
Take a hot bath before bedtime to relax.	

smoking

People are well aware of the health risks of smoking cigarettes. Nicotine is one of the most powerful known stimulants and is more addictive than heroin and crack; the carcinogens in cigarettes cause lung cancer. Yet 58 million Americans still smoke. Most would like to quit but can't. One of the reasons smoking is so addictive is that it brings instant gratification. One inhalation sends chemicals through the blood, into the heart, and then directly to the brain in a matter of seconds. Although people smoke to relax, twenty minutes after smoking, the body goes into a stress response:

- Blood vessels narrow, restricting blood flow to the brain
- Heart rate speeds up
- Blood pressure rises
- Digestive and urinary tracts get irritated.

The only way to counteract these reactions is by smoking another cigarette!

Addiction starts young. According to the American Cancer Society, 71 percent of all people who smoke are hooked by the age of eighteen. In fact, three thousand teenagers start smoking each day. Kids are starting earlier, too, often in eighth and ninth grade. Only half of all eighth-graders know that smoking is dangerous. Every year 400,000 people die from smoking-related diseases—that's one in five of all deaths. Half of all smokers who continue the habit eventually die of smoking-related problems.

How can smoking destroy lives?

Lung cancer. There are usually no warning signs for lung cancer. Once it shows up, it has usually spread beyond the point of treatment. Most lung cancer patients die of the disease. And lung cancer, not breast cancer, is the leading cause of cancer death in women.

Increased risk of heart disease and heart attack. Nicotine makes the heart work harder but constricts the arteries, so blood can't circulate and blood pressure rises.

Increased risk of stroke. Constricted arteries block blood flow to the brain.

Neurological problems. Nicotine depresses and halts the flow of information between nerve cells and causes hormonal imbalances.

Emphysema and other respiratory problems starve the body of oxygen and labor breathing.

Bladder cancer.

Cancer of the throat, mouth, and face.

Increases chronological age, brings on early menopause (even among women married to smokers), and typically makes skin look craggy and wrinkled.

Increases risk for osteoporosis.

Tobacco also worsens symptoms for anyone who is pregnant or has diabetes, heart or lung conditions, high blood pressure, or a family history of heart disease or cancer.

Avoid these dangerous combinations:

- Smoking and birth control pills significantly increase the risk of cardiovascular disease.
- Smoking and alcohol by themselves both increase the likelihood of cancer of the mouth, throat, stomach, or esophagus. Together they're even more dangerous.

What are you inhaling?

Nicotine isn't the only chemical going into your lungs. According to the American Cancer Society, there are over four thousand chemicals in cigarettes. Four hundred are toxic and forty-three are known carcinogens. Cigarettes may also contain radioactive particles.

What if you don't inhale?

Suppose you take up the fashionable habit of cigars. Or you want to look professorial and start smoking a pipe. Or you play baseball and chew tobacco. Are these safer? No. If you don't inhale, you won't get lung cancer, but you can get cancer of the mouth, throat, and face.

Quitting

Cold turkey is one of the most successful ways to quit. But nicotine substitutes also have a good track record, especially when combined with lifestyle modifications.

Nicotine replacement therapies include:

The nonprescription patch transports diminishing doses of nicotine through the skin. Presumably, after a few weeks, you're weaned.

Nicotine gum, also nonprescription, lets you administer the dosage and is good for people who have sensitive skin.

Nasal spray. Available by prescription, this spray delivers less nicotine to the brain than smoking does.

Zyban. This prescription drug affects brain chemicals that control nicotine cravings.

Here are a few other methods that work for some people. Perhaps success has something to do with how much each individuals wants them to work.

Acupuncture—needles are usually inserted around the ears and nose

Hypnosis—depends on individual susceptibility

Filters and low-nicotine, low-tar cigarettes—typically unsuccessful (smokers who use these tend to smoke more)

Replace nasty habits with good ones

Keep your mouth busy. Have healthy snacks on hand to satisfy the oral cravings (try carrot sticks, raisins, apple slices). Chew on a cinnamon stick or a straw if you need something in your mouth.

Keep your hands busy—try worry beads or Chinese metal exercise balls for your hands, or take up knitting or needlepoint.

Drink lots of water.

Take antioxidants to repair some of the damage to your cells.

Avoid drinks (alcohol and coffee) and situations that you associate with lighting up.

Exercise, especially aerobically, in short bouts if you can't sustain longer activity.

Do breathing exercises; meditate; calm your mind.

Tell a friend you're quitting and make yourself accountable to that person at the end of each day.

If you fall off the horse and smoke "just one," start quitting again the next day, and stick to it. **Give yourself rewards** for hanging in there. **Eat several small meals** throughout the day to keep your energy steady.

If you gain weight (the average is 5 pounds) don't be hard on yourself. In time, this will come off as you balance your oral fixation and learn to eat properly and exercise. The inconvenience of weight gain is minor compared to the health risks of smoking.

From the moment you stamp out your last cigarette, your health will start to improve. (The following statistics are from the American Cancer Society):

- After one day, your blood pressure, pulse, and levels of oxygen and carbon monoxide will all return to normal, and your chance of having a heart attack will decrease.
- After two weeks, your taste buds and sense of smell will be more sensitive. Your circulation will start to improve and your lungs will have regained 30 percent capacity.
- After several months, you'll be able to walk upstairs without wheezing. You'll lose your cough and feel more energetic.
- Within one year, you'll have cut your risk of heart disease in half.
- In five years, you'll have cut your risk of getting lung cancer in half and lowered your risk for stroke, throat, and mouth cancer.
- In ten years, your risk of getting lung cancer will equal that of nonsmokers and any precancerous cells will have been replaced with healthy ones.
- In fifteen years, your risk of coronary heart disease will be the same as a non-smoker.

Pregnancy and Smoking

Why isn't smoking during pregnancy illegal? Smoking increases the amount of carbon monoxide (like car exhaust) in the blood, and therefore decreases the amount of oxygen that goes to the growing baby. Nicotine pools in the placenta and is absorbed by the fetus. This can cause all kinds of health problems for the child, short term and long, or be fatal.

Smoking moms have more complications in pregnancy and delivery, more still-births, and more babies that die in the first month.

Babies born to smoking moms have a lower birth weight and a higher death rate. These babies are smaller at birth and, as they grow up, often remain shorter than average.

Children whose mothers smoked during pregnancy have more learning disabilities and behavioral problems.

Children whose mothers smoked ten or more cigarettes a day have double the normal risk for cancer.

stress

Stress is one of those words that is loosely thrown around. Almost anything seems to cause it. The question is: How can we handle stress so it doesn't make us sick?

One of the first steps is to realize that stress isn't the villain. We need some stress. Without it we'd fold into a little pile of flaccid muscle and die. When we exercise, for instance, we voluntarily put our bodies under stress. Adapting to it is what makes us healthier and stronger.

How we react to stress is the problem. We may not be able to control the situations that cause stress, but we can choose how to feel about them. Why is it, for instance, that some people can survive prison and torture and emerge from the experience still loving humanity while others rage when a shopkeeper doesn't wait on them fast enough? Attitudes, beliefs, habitual behaviors, and old resentments have a way of setting our stress levels, unless we make a conscious effort to handle stress differently.

External stresses are caused by threats—real or imagined. External stresses can be devastating but they're usually short-lived. Our bodies are wired, via the autonomic nervous system's fight-or-flight instinct, to survive dangerous confrontations. A series of bodily functions helps us run away or fight:

- The brain secretes adrenaline and cortisol, two stress hormones that interrupt the normal process of cell building and repair.
- Heart rate speeds up.
- Blood pressure rises.
- Muscles tighten.
- Breathing gets quick and shallow.
- Digestion stops.
- Hunger and sexual arousal disappear.

We often react to external stresses long after the threat—or perceived threat—has passed. This causes internal stress, which can go on indefinitely and therefore do more harm. Eventually, the body becomes catabolic. In other words, it starts to break down its own tissue for fuel. The nervous system no longer fires efficiently and the immune system gets weak. The body becomes susceptible to disease—and old before its time.

One way to overcome stress is to discipline the mind. We can't change the external stresses but we can change how we react to them and how we channel the pent-up fear, rage, and depression that come with stress.

Rechannel your stress

Four of the simplest, most profound stress relievers are:

1. Exercise (secretes feel-good endorphins instead of stress hormones)
2. Sex (more endorphins!)
3. Laughter (lowers blood pressure, increases the activity of immune system "killer cells" that fight disease)
4. Breathing (lowers blood pressure, slows heart rate, delivers oxygen throughout the body, aids digestion, secretes endorphins)

But there are many graceful ways to handle stress:

- Realize that outer circumstances need not color your internal world.
- Be creative—write down your thoughts and feelings and draw, sing, dance your inner state, even if (or, rather, especially if) you're not particularly talented in any of these areas.
- Give of yourself. Take your attention off your inner state and do something for someone who will benefit from your attention.
- Meditate. Return to a state of consciousness larger than your stress.
- Get a massage. Put yourself in someone else's hands for a while.
- Turn off the noise. Shut off the TV, the annoying radio. Play soothing or uplifting music.
- Call a friend, not just to talk but to listen.
- Play with children.
- Be with animals.
- Avoid spending time with negative people, if you can.
- Go out into nature.
- Look at beautiful things: art, flowers, etc.
- Count your blessings.

Tai Chi and Chi Kung

Every morning at sunrise, in parks all over China and the United States, millions of people of all ages practice Tai Chi and Chi Kung. Some do quick martial arts moves, while others do a slow dance as if being blown by the wind, and some stand completely still. What they're doing is manipulating the flow of chi (life energy), which, according to Chinese medicine, runs through the entire body along a system of invisible channels called meridians (see **Acupressure and Shiatsu, Acupuncture,** and **Chinese Medicine,** pages 392, 396, and 424). From these meridians, energy then flows into and rebalances organs, helping to prevent disease.

These energy exercises bear almost no resemblance to Western exercise. There are no push-ups or abdominal crunches, no strain to muscles, heart, or lungs. According to some Tai Chi and Chi Kung masters, Western exercise eats up too much energy, which suppresses the immune system. Tai Chi and Chi Kung don't force health, they allow it. This Eastern approach lets us reconnect with the energy we had in abundance as children but which dissipated as we aged.

Tai Chi and Chi Kung date back six thousand years and trace their roots to the Yellow Emperor, the father of Chinese medicine. These practices were traditionally passed down through families and shared in secret. Now, millions of people practice them as a way to maintain and improve health. Both Chi Kung and Tai Chi have been known to:

- Lower blood pressure
- Increase delivery of oxygen to the heart without raising the heart rate
- Improve the function of tissues, organs, glands
- Stimulate the central nervous system, and improve reflexes and mental clarity
- Increase immunity
- Decrease stress
- Ease back and knee pain
- Ease arthritis
- Improve balance (a recent study showed that Tai Chi prevents falls in the elderly up to 25 percent more than Western exercise)
- Heal others—external Chi Kung practitioners use their energy to treat patients in the same way acupuncturists use needles.

Both Tai Chi and Chi Kung are also practiced as martial arts. Though they may not look intimidating, masters have been known to throw attackers across the room without touching them, just by using energy.

The benefits of Tai Chi and Chi Kung may not become apparent until after several weeks or even years of steady practice. One final note: The Chinese prefer to practice outdoors in the fresh air, surrounded by trees. But if it's very cold or raining, practice in a well-ventilated room.

Tai Chi

Tai Chi is a choreographed series of movements called a form. This slow, graceful movement art is a study in constant flow between empty and full, hard and soft, yin and yang. The aim of Tai Chi is to stay in the middle state between two opposing forces, and to use only the appropriate amount of energy for each move.

Tai Chi takes some getting used to. You don't push your arms, kick your legs, or use your will. You learn to relax so the moves come through you. Tai Chi reflects the philosophy of the Tao, which is about constant change. The postures blend seamlessly from one to the next, without interruption. The weight shifts from one leg to the next, like water being poured between two pitchers. The muscles contract and relax, and the arms lift and lower. The torso twists and straightens. The steps move forward and back.

Although Tai Chi has a martial arts application (with "push hands" and weapons forms, sword and staff), it's mostly done solo. There are several variations—Wu, Chen, Yang, and Sun—all passed down from the early families. Chang Man Ch'ing is credited with populariz-ing Tai Chi in the West. His Yang short form with 18 to 37 moves (compared to the long form's 108) is still the form most widely prac-ticed.

Tai Chi not only keeps muscles, joints, and posture fluid and youthful, it also keeps the mind open and the spirit soft, all elixirs for a healthy and vibrant long life.

Chi Kung

Chi Kung exercises are so simple almost anyone can do them without difficulty. The moves may not look like much; their power comes from what goes on within. In fact, in many classes, the first basic exercise is simply standing like a tree. As you practice Chi Kung, you'll do some or all of the following:

- Breathe naturally
- Move slowly
- Visualize energy moving through the body
- Focus on what the Chinese call the *tantien,* the main reservoir of energy, found two fingerwidths below the navel and about a third of the way into the body toward the spine

Chi Kung takes a little getting used to. In the first few weeks, the exercises might cause tingling sensations, tremors, numbness, pain, or rushes of warmth. You'll probably become more aware of your asymmetries (one shoulder may feel tighter than the other, for example). With practice, the sensations change and improve.

*Two simple Chi Kung
exercises*

hold the ball

1. Stand with your feet hip-distance apart. Rock forward to your toes and back to your heels. Find the midpoint (under the arch) and soften the knees.
2. From the knees down, send your energy into the ground like the roots of a tree. Let the rest of your body spread upward like branches. Feel light and suspended.
3. Soften your focus and smile down with your eyes and spirit into your *tantien.*
4. Align your neck so the top center of your head is the highest point.
5. Align your feet, *tantien,* and head in a vertical line.
6. Hold an imaginary ball in front of your belly. Relax your wrists and fingers. Hold for 5 minutes.

support the sky

1. Stand in the above position. Imagine the ball is a helium balloon that lifts your arms over your head.
2. As your hands pass overhead, rotate the wrists so your palms face up.
3. Bend back your wrists and straighten your fingers. Inhale.
4. Straighten your arms overhead, pushing up with the heel of the hand, and press your feet into the ground. Exhale.
5. Inhale as you lower the arms. Repeat 8 times.

yoga

Perhaps the best way to describe yoga is to begin with what it is not. It's not simply a stretch workout. It's not a workout that melts away fat. It's not a religion or a cult. Yoga, which comes from the Sanskrit word for "union," offers other things: relaxation for tight muscles and nerves, rejuvenation for weary minds, and a sense of inner connection. Yoga addresses the development of both the body and spirit. Besides postures (or asanas), yoga also includes:

- Breathing (or *pranayama,* for breathing in both oxygen and spirit or energy)
- Relaxation (of both body and mind)
- Proper eating (usually a vegetarian diet)
- Meditation (redirecting thoughts to a higher consciousness)

Yoga can make the body both flexible and strong. But consistent practice is also thought to develop:

- Wisdom (as the intellect develops)
- Compassion (as the heart opens)
- Awareness of a higher power (as consciousness expands)
- Calm even in the midst of chaos (as body, mind, and spirit become one)

Statues dating from 3000 B.C. depict gods and goddesses performing yoga postures. Patanjali, author of the detailed text *Yoga Sutras* (written in 200 B.C.), is considered yoga's founding father. So many styles of yoga have developed (and continue to develop) since then that it may seem overwhelming just to choose a style (see "A Yoga Sampler," page 462). And with over 84,000 different asanas, mastering yoga may look like an impossible task. However, yoga can work its magic even in the simplest postures and styles. All forms of yoga essentially do the same things:

- Stretch and strengthen muscles, ligaments, and tendons
- Lower blood pressure
- Massage organs
- Decrease stress
- Increase energy
- Calm the central nervous system
- Improve circulation
- Ease back pain
- Relieve sleeping problems
- Relieve PMS and menopausal symptoms
- Help reverse heart disease

Since Dr. Dean Ornish included yoga and meditation in his landmark program for reversing heart disease, many other hospitals are doing the same.

Over 20 million Americans now practice yoga for all sorts of reasons—to relax, to improve athletic skill, to enhance mental performance. However, it's best to do yoga for its own reward, not to get something out of it. One of the philosophies of yoga is to maintain a practice but, at the same time, exercise nonattachment to results.

A yoga sampler

Following are a few of the many yoga styles out there today:

Hatha yoga

This is the most popular form of yoga. It consists of gentle stretches held for long periods of time and is a good beginner and all-level style. There are different types of Hatha yoga.

Iyengar yoga is named for B. K. S. Iyengar, who created an innovative yoga using such props as straps, wall straps, blocks, pillows, and blankets. Iyengar placed extreme importance on placement. This style often appeals to dancers and athletes.

Ashtanga yoga was created by K. Patabhi Jois. This style builds on a series of continuously flowing poses, some extremely difficult. This highly athletic, very sweaty form of yoga is sometimes called Power Yoga because of the way it promotes cardiovascular conditioning, strength, and flexibility all in one session. This form is also popular with athletes and dancers.

Kripalu yoga was created by Amrit Desai. This gentle yoga is less about holding asanas and more about connecting with one's inner state in each posture. It represents a more internal style than Iyengar or Ashtanga.

Integral yoga was created by Swami Satchidananda and, like Kripalu, emphasizes an internal approach over postures. This yoga is a way of life, and includes meditation, service to others, chanting, and prayer.

Sivananda yoga is similar to Integral yoga in that it encompasses a whole way of life. This methodology also includes vegetarianism and study of scriptures (from the *Bhagavad Gita*).

Kundalini yoga attempts to awaken and manipulate a powerful, sacred, and sexual energy called kundalini. Mastery of kundalini involves asanas, various breathing techniques, and meditation.

Bikram yoga was created by Bikram Choudhury. It consists of twenty-six specific postures and two breathing exercises, always repeated in the same order. In Bikram yoga, rooms are heated to about 100 degrees to assist stretches and rid the body of toxins. A very sweaty experience, it is not recommended for pregnant women, people with multiple sclerosis, or others sensitive to heat.

Yoga caveats

If you're shopping for a yoga class, be wise:

- Look for a style that suits you. Don't be frustrated if you can't do any or all of the postures. Yoga is meant to be noncompetitive. With practice, you'll improve.
- Don't be afraid to modify the postures to suit yourself or to find a knowledgable teacher who can help you adapt the poses. Yoga instructors in the United States don't need to pass certification the way trainers or aerobics instructors often do, so anything goes. If you don't know what to look for, at least find a helpful instructor. Avoid those who insist that you hold positions a certain way or, worse, force you into a stretch. You should surrender into postures, not get more stressed.

- Be careful not to overdo the stretches. Being super-flexible may look impressive, but if you stretch ligaments and tendons and not just muscles, these connective tissues can get injured and remain permanently loose, making you wobbly and vulnerable to future injuries. Many yoga "casualties" have had to hire personal trainers after discovering their connective tissue did all the stretching while muscles stayed weak.
- If anything hurts, don't do it.

Simple asanas (yoga postures)

You can do these in a series.

cat pose

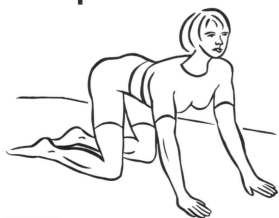 

1. Get down on all fours.
2. Inhale gently as you lift your tailbone and head to the ceiling. Be sure to keep abdominals supported.

3. Exhale and round the back.
4. Pull your abs up, chin to chest, and your tailbone toward the chin. Repeat 4 times slowly.

upward facing dog

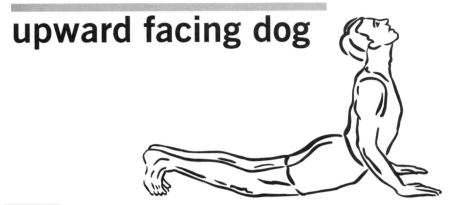

This pose opens up your breathing and stimulates the kidneys.

1. Lower the whole body, face down on the floor.
2. Press your palms on the floor just under the armpits.
3. Using abdominals to support your torso, inhale and raise your head up, keeping your forearms on the floor.
4. Lengthen the front of the body and look up to the ceiling (don't throw your neck back). Hold for 4 full breaths. If you want more stretch, straighten your arms but be careful not to overarch the lower back. You can raise your hips off the floor to protect the spine.

downward facing dog

1. Lying facedown on the floor, press up onto your hands and feet.
2. Exhale and lift hips up to the ceiling. Keep spine long and arms straight. Arch your lower back slightly to elongate the spine. If hamstrings are tight, bend knees slightly and lift heels off the floor.
3. As you relax, lower the heels (one or both at a time) to the floor and straighten legs. Hold for 4 breaths.

index